More praise for *King David*

"Engaging . . . Dramatic . . . Thought-provoking."
—*Columbus Dispatch*

"Excellent . . . This spotlights one of the most commanding figures of the Bible, one who was exalted as 'a man after God's own heart.'"
—*Oklahoman*

"Surviving accounts of ancient Israel's King David contain the stuff of epics and blockbuster novels. Kirsch takes advantage of this in [his] biography. . . . [King David has] enduring literary and psychological appeal."
—*Booklist*

"This book . . . welcomes a wide audience to a scandalous, violent, and surprisingly familiar ancient Israel, and both educates and entertains."
—*Publishers Weekly*

"There's no question that in Kirsch's hands, the Bible is more exciting than a Saturday night B-movie special."
—Beliefnet.com

Please turn the page for more reviews. . . .

Also by Jonathan Kirsch

MOSES:
A Life

THE HARLOT BY THE SIDE OF THE ROAD:
Forbidden Tales of the Bible

KING
DAVID

THE REAL LIFE OF THE
MAN WHO RULED ISRAEL

Jonathan Kirsch

BALLANTINE BOOKS • NEW YORK

146028962

Moses has the Ten Commandments, it's true, but I've got much better lines. I've got the poetry and passion, savage violence, and the plain raw civilizing grief of human heartbreak.
—KING DAVID IN *GOD KNOWS*, BY JOSEPH HELLER

And he said to Nathan,
As the Lord liveth, the man that hath done this thing shall
  surely die. . . .
And Nathan said to David,
Thou art the man.
—2 SAMUEL 12:5–7 (KJV)

Contents

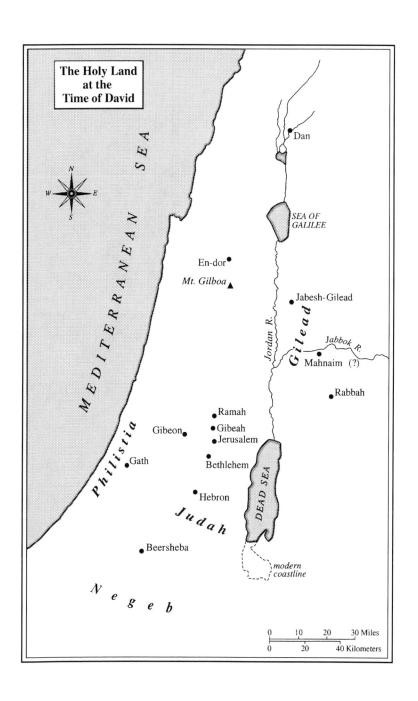

The Holy Land at the Time of David

N
W E
S

MEDITERRANEAN SEA

Dan

SEA OF GALILEE

En-dor

Mt. Gilboa ▲

Jabesh-Gilead

Gilead

Jordan R.

Jabbok R.

Mahnaim (?)

Rabbah

Ramah

Gibeon

Gibeah

Jerusalem

Bethlehem

Philistia

Gath

DEAD SEA

Hebron

Judah

modern coastline

Beersheba

N e g e b

0   10   20   30 Miles

0   20   40 Kilometers

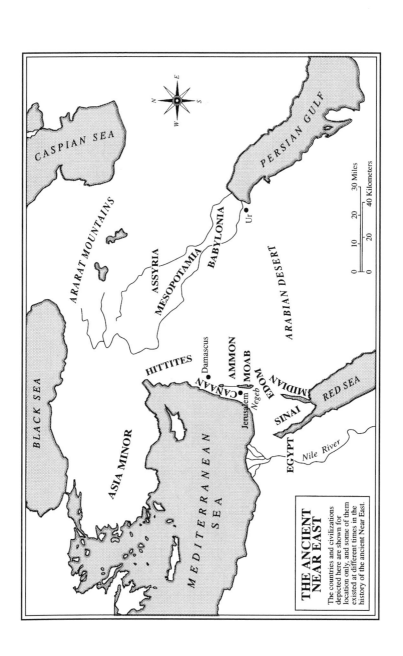

THE ANCIENT
NEAR EAST

The countries and civilizations
depicted here are shown for
location only, and some of them
existed at different times in the
history of the ancient Near East.

CASPIAN SEA

ARARAT MOUNTAINS

PERSIAN GULF

ASSYRIA

MESOPOTAMIA

BABYLONIA

Ur

ARABIAN DESERT

30 Miles
40 Kilometers
10   20
0   20

BLACK SEA

HITTITES

Damascus

AMMON

MOAB

CANAAN

Jerusalem

Negeb

EDOM

MIDIAN

RED SEA

SINAI

ASIA MINOR

MEDITERRANEAN
SEA

EGYPT

Nile River

KING
DAVID

Chapter One

CHARISMA

Like everyone else, from Samuel, Saul, and Jonathan
down to the present, Yahweh is charmed by David.

—HAROLD BLOOM, *THE BOOK OF J*

Something crucial in human history begins with the biblical figure of King David. He is the original alpha male, the kind of
man whose virile ambition always drives him to the head of the
pack. He is the first superstar, a figure so compelling that the Bible
may have originated as his royal biography. He is an authentic sex
symbol, a ruggedly handsome fellow who inspires passion in both
men and women, a passion expressed sometimes as hero worship
and sometimes as carnal longing. He is "the quintessential winner," as one Bible scholar puts it,[1] and the biblical life story of
David has always shaped what we expect of ourselves and, even
more so, of the men and women who lead us.

At the heart of the Book of Samuel, where the story of
David is first told, we find a work of genius that anticipates the
romantic lyricism and tragic grandeur of Shakespeare, the politi-
cal wile of Machiavelli, and the modern psychological insight of
Freud. And, just as much as Shakespeare or Machiavelli or
Freud, the frank depiction of David in the pages of the Bible has

defined what it means to be a human being: King David is "a symbol of the complexity and ambiguity of human experience itself."[2]

"He played exquisitely, he fought heroically, he loved titanically," observes historian Abram Leon Sachar. "Withal he was a profoundly simple being, cheerful, despondent, selfish, generous, sinning one moment, repenting the next, the most human character of the Bible."[3]

Above all, David illustrates the fundamental truth that the sacred and the profane may find full expression in a single human life, and his biography preserves the earliest evidence of the neurotic double bind that is hardwired into human nature and tugs each of us in different directions at once. Against every effort of Bible-waving moralizers who seek to make us better than we are—or to make us feel bad about the way we are—the biblical account of David is there to acknowledge and even to affirm what men and women really feel and really do.

Indeed, the single most surprising fact about David is the rawness with which he is depicted in the Bible. David is shown to be a liar and a trickster, as when, threatened by an enemy king, he feigns madness to save his own life. He is an outlaw and an extortionist, as when he uses the threat of violence to solicit a gift from a rich man with a beautiful wife and ends up with both the bounty and the woman. He is an exhibitionist, as when he performs a ritual dance in such spiritual frenzy that his tunic flies up and reveals his genitalia to the crowd. He is even a voyeur, a seducer, and a murderer, as when he peeps at the naked Bathsheba, recruits her for sexual service in the royal bedchamber, and then contrives to kill her husband when she is inconveniently impregnated with a bastard. David, whose very name means "beloved,"[4] attracts both men and women, inspiring sometimes a pristine love but more often a frankly carnal one. Some Bible critics, in fact, insist that David's famous declaration of love for his friend Jonathan—a love "passing the love of women"—ought to be understood as an expression of his bisexuality.

All of these episodes are reported in the Bible bluntly and honestly, and sometimes with a touch of titillation. If the writing of history and biography and literature in Western civilization originates with the biblical account of David, as some Bible scholars suggest, so does the stuff of bodice-rippers and tabloids—"the kind of details," cracks Bible scholar Peter Ackroyd, "for which, in our more sophisticated times, the Sunday newspapers of the slightly less reputable kind pay handsomely."[5] One of the overlooked secrets of the Bible is its earthiness and ribaldry, and nowhere are these qualities more extravagantly on display than in the biography of David.

THE FIG LEAF AT FOREST LAWN

At Forest Lawn, a cemetery in Southern California, mourners and tourists alike are invited to gaze upon a reproduction of Michelangelo's famous statue of David, faithful in every detail except one: David's genitalia are covered with a marble fig leaf. But the original statue itself is unfaithful to the truth as recorded in the Bible—Michelangelo, apparently paying more attention to his model than to the Bible, depicts the greatest king of Israel as uncircumcised!

Similarly, in strange and not-so-subtle ways, attempts have been made to conceal the flesh-and-blood David from us. Within the Bible itself, David's life story has been rewritten and "overwritten," as scholars put it, by generations of biblical authors and editors who were disturbed and confused by his taste for sex and violence. The Book of Chronicles, for example, is a bowdlerized version of David's biography as originally preserved in the Book of Samuel. If Chronicles alone had survived, and Samuel had been lost or suppressed in antiquity, we would know nothing of David's adulterous love affair with Bathsheba, or his passionate declaration of love for Jonathan, or the rape of David's daughter, Tamar, by his son Amnon, or the rebellion of his son Absalom, who very nearly succeeded in driving him from the throne.

"See what Chronicles has made out of David!" exclaimed Julius Wellhausen, the pioneering nineteenth-century Bible scholar who was among the first to discern the thoroughly human hands and minds that created the biblical text.[6]

Even after the composition of the Bible was completed and the canon was closed, Talmudic sages and Church Fathers alike tried to make David over into a plaster saint by concealing, denying, or explaining away the sins and scandals that the Bible discloses. Starting in antiquity, for example, the rabbis decreed that the most salacious stories of David were not to be translated out of biblical Hebrew or read aloud in the synagogue. The sages whose writings are collected in the vast anthologies known as the Talmud and the Midrash conjured up a kinder and gentler David—one stubborn apologist simply dismissed the abundant evidence of David's wrongdoing that is plainly recorded in the Bible and insisted that David couldn't have sinned with Bathsheba.[7] And the early Christian commentators preferred to focus on the messianic role of King David that can be teased out of the biblical text, where God is shown to vow an eternal kingship to David and his descendants.

The final emasculation of David is the work of the modern media. Today, David has been scaled down to the cartoonish figure of a little shepherd boy who slays the mighty warrior Goliath with a slingshot. To be sure, the theme of David and Goliath was no less favored by Michelangelo and Donatello, Titian and Rembrandt than it is by newspaper headline writers and Madison Avenue art directors. (Indeed, one example by Tanzio da Varallo appears on the cover of this book.) But there is something sad and sorry in the fact that the biblical figure of David, so potent and so full of passion, has been turned into a glyph for the ability of something very small to prevail against something very large.

The *real* David, as we shall discover, is not so small, not so simple, and not so child-safe.

KING OF THE JEWS

David is writ large in the pages of the Bible, where his name appears more than a thousand times and where an "undersong" of praise can be detected in passages where he is not mentioned at all.[8] The faith of ancient Israel, according to some scholars, was not Judaism or even Yahwehism but "Davidism."[9] David may start out as a lad who tends his father's sheep in a country backwater, but he ends up as the king of all Israel and the conqueror of an empire that stretches from the outskirts of Egypt to the far Euphrates.

According to the Bible, David rules by the grace of God—"The Lord has established him king over Israel, and exalted him king for his people Israel's sake" (2 Sam. 5:10)*—and every monarch in Western history who invoked the divine right of kings was relying on his example. That's why statues of King David and the other kings of Israel and Judah once decorated the medieval cathedral of Notre-Dame—and that's why the statuary was taken down and hidden away during the French Revolution lest the mob take David's head along with those of the reigning king and queen.

But the Bible exalts David above and beyond his long reign as King of the Jews. In life he is praised as the king whom God selected to reign on earth, and in death he is transfigured into a king who will reign on high: David becomes a shimmering theological symbol, the precursor and direct ancestor of the Messiah whom God will send to redeem a sinful and suffering humanity. "And there shall come forth a shoot out of the stock of Jesse, and a twig shall grow forth out of his roots" (Isa. 11:1) is the prophecy of Isaiah, a supercharged line of biblical text that identifies David by reference to his father and is generally understood to predict the coming of the Messiah. In fact, Judaism and Christianity, which contend with each other on so many other issues, share the thrilling idea that David's blood will flow in the veins of the Messiah.

---

*All biblical quotations are taken from *The Holy Scriptures According to the Masoretic Text* (Philadelphia: Jewish Publication Society, 1961) unless otherwise indicated by an abbreviation that identifies another translation. The Masoretic Text, which is regarded as the definitive version of the Hebrew Bible in Jewish usage, is the work of a school of rabbis and scribes who organized and standardized the biblical text over a period of several centuries starting around 500 C.E. See "A Note on Bibles and Biblical Usage" in the bibliography, page 347.

"If the Messiah-King comes from among the living, David will be his name," the Talmud teaches. "If he comes from among the dead, it will be David himself."[10] And Paul embraces the same credo from a Christian perspective when he attests that Jesus of Nazareth "was made of the seed of David according to the flesh, and declared to be the Son of God." (Rom. 1:3–4)

David is the very first man whom we can call "King of the Jews." He is crowned as king of Judah, the tribe from which the Jewish people are descended, before he achieves kingship over all twelve tribes of Israel.* A thousand years later, when the Magi follow a star to Bethlehem, they declare that they are searching for David's distant heir and successor, "he that is born King of the Jews." (Matt. 2:2) (KJV) Even today, the same yearning is expressed in a few poignant words from the Talmud that are sung aloud as a children's song at Jewish day camps and as a messianic anthem among settlers on the West Bank: "David, King of Israel, lives and endures."

Ironically, the glory that is heaped upon David tends to obscure the flesh-and-blood man. David is depicted in the oldest biblical passages as thoroughly mortal, which is to say that he is susceptible to all of the flaws and failings, all the sins and shortcomings, that afflict ordinary human beings. David is capable of embodying contradictory qualities at the same time—courage and cowardice, spiritual ecstasy and sexual frenzy, lofty statesmanship and low cunning and deceit—and the Bible confirms that he succumbs to his basest impulses as often as he answers to the angels of his higher nature.

Why then does the Bible preserve and exalt the memory of such a flawed man? How can David be, at the same time, "a man after God's own heart"[11] *and* a "bloodstained fiend of hell,"[12] as he is variously described in the Bible? The most pious of the biblical authors rely on a simple theological argument to explain away all of the unsettling contradictions in David's personality: David com-

---

*The terms "Jews" and "Judaism" derive from the Hebrew *Yehudah*, which was the name of the fourth son of the patriarch Jacob and the founder of the tribe of Judah.

plies with God's *will* even if he defies God's *law*, and that's all it takes to earn a divine pardon for his sins of the flesh. But it is possible to read the same sacred text and come to a very different conclusion—something deep in our nature prompts us to overlook the private sins and crimes of a powerful figure who captures our fancy and wins our confidence. For that reason, no matter how often or how scandalously David sins, the Bible reader, like God himself, is always ready to forgive and even to praise him.

CHARISMA

The very notion of charisma as a quality of leadership, a commonplace in the political vocabulary of our own era, can be traced back to King David. "Charisma" is given a technical definition in Bible scholarship: "the sudden appearance of a personal gift and power which was regarded in Israel simply as a charisma, the free gift of Yahweh to the individual, and which therefore swept the populace along with it."[13] But the word entered our modern vocabulary during the presidency of John F. Kennedy—and, in fact, the life of JFK may help us to understand how David was seen by the men and women of ancient Israel and the authors of the Bible. "Camelot," the Arthurian term that came to be applied to the Kennedy White House, applies with equal force to the court of King David.

Each man, the biblical David and the modern JFK, was regarded in his lifetime as a charming and compelling public figure. Each man was an authentic war hero who put his life at risk and distinguished himself in combat. Each was praised for his grace, wit, and eloquence—David was "the sweet singer of Israel" (2 Sam. 23:1) and Kennedy was honored with a Pulitzer Prize for *Profiles in Courage*. Each was admired for his vigor and rugged good looks by the men and women in his thrall. Each acted with ruthlessness to achieve power, each was a sexual adventurer, and each was forgiven for his ruthlessness *and* his sexual aggression. Indeed, the notion that a powerful ruler enjoys the right to take for himself "the fairest in the land" is not just a line out of a fairy tale; King David was presented by his courtiers with "a fair damsel" called Abishag after the whole of Israel had been canvassed for an appropriate consort, and Kennedy claimed the affections of Marilyn Monroe, the closest approximation to a goddess of love that the twentieth century produced.

Significantly, neither David nor JFK was toppled from the pedestal of public adoration by the disclosure of his dirty little secrets. David's squalid private life is luridly detailed in the pages of the Bible, and yet he never forfeits the favor of God *or* the biblical author. The same is true for John F. Kennedy, whose claim on the hearts and minds of his generation was not diminished when revisionist historians began to reveal the less savory aspects of his character and conduct. Even though the transgressions of both David and JFK provoke fear and loathing among the fussier citizenry, such revelations only excite the imagination and stoke the enthusiasm of their most ardent followers. Something deep in our nature prompts us to forgive a charismatic figure like David or JFK for excesses in the pursuit of power.

Although Bill Clinton is no Jack Kennedy, the same phenomenon was at work during the public frenzy that attended the disclosure of his sexual misadventures. Despite the best efforts of his political enemies to rouse public opinion against him, Clinton's adolescent gropings in the Oval Office did not truly surprise or shock anyone in America except the most puritanical of preachers and prosecutors. His performance as president received the highest public approval ratings at the very moment that the media were reporting the most scandalous details of his affair with Monica Lewinsky.

One man who knows the life story of David quite well was invited to the White House to minister to the President and the First Family in the aftermath of the messy affair. Indeed, the Reverend Jesse Jackson obliquely recalled the far messier affairs of King David by reciting the words of the Fifty-first Psalm, a bit of biblical poetry that is understood to represent David's plea for forgiveness after his fateful act of adultery with Bathsheba: "Wash me thoroughly from mine iniquity, and cleanse me from my sin," intoned the Reverend Jackson,[14] echoing the words traditionally (but wrongly) attributed to David (Psalm 51:4)—and, not incidentally, making the ironic point that Bill Clinton seems like a choirboy when compared to King David.

THE ULTIMATE MYSTERY

Strangely, but tellingly, the Bible depicts God himself as ready and willing to overlook the bloodiest deeds and nastiest sins of King David. The punishing deity who dictated so many stern laws of moral conduct to Moses does not appear to much care, for example, that David seduced and impregnated a married woman while her husband was serving as a soldier on the front lines and then conspired to murder the husband—thereby violating at least three of the Ten Commandments in one sorry episode.

"Yahweh," explains Harold Bloom in *The Book of J*, "is the God who fell in love with David."[15]

And here is where we glimpse a clue to one of the ultimate mysteries of the Bible. Why is God shown to be so much more enamored of David than of Moses or any other towering figure of the Hebrew Bible? Why is the life of David reported in such intimate, even titillating detail? Why were these sometimes troubling texts preserved with such care over the millennia? Why did the later biblical editors fail in their efforts to censor the life story of David? The answer to these questions may suggest the reason why the Bible was written, how it has endured for more than three thousand years, and why we still find ourselves so fascinated by it.

The authorship of the Bible remains a Gordian knot after some two thousand years of pious study and a century or so of modern scholarship. One theory proposes that the core of the Hebrew Bible originated as a formal biography of King David and the rest of the biblical text came to be attached to his life story in bits and pieces over the centuries. If this proposal is correct, we are confronted with the intriguing but unsettling notion that the

Bible as we know it today might not have come into existence at all but for an anonymous chronicler who set out to write a history of the king in whose court he served.

Let's entertain the idea, as many scholars do, that the biography of King David as we find it in the Book of Samuel was first composed during the reign of David himself (circa 1005–965 B.C.E.)* or perhaps during the Solomonic Enlightenment, as the reign of his son and successor, King Solomon, is sometimes called. And let's call the principal author of the royal biography "the Court Historian," even if we cannot know his (or her) name or the circumstances under which he (or she) lived and worked.

We know from what we find in the Bible that the Court Historian was an artful and watchful biographer of the royal household he served and celebrated. In stark contrast to what passed for history and biography elsewhere in the ancient Near East—king lists and battle lists, inventories of plunder and tribute, praise-songs and epic poetry—the biblical text shows that the Court Historian was as interested in the intimate private life of David and his highly dysfunctional family as in official dynastic history.

At roughly the same time, some scholars propose, another biblical author was at work on a companion volume to accompany the Court History, a "primal history" of ancient Israel that would explain how the Israelites had come to the land of Canaan. The author is known as the Yahwist (or "J")† because he (or she) preferred to call God by his personal name, Yahweh.‡ Drawing on the legend and lore that had been preserved in the rich oral traditions of the twelve tribes of Israel, and various texts that are now lost to history, the Yahwist wove a vast narrative tapestry, an

*See Chronology, page 315.

†The Yahwist is known in scholarly circles by the letter-code "J" because the pioneering scholars who first proposed his (or her) existence wrote in German and thus spelled "Yahweh" with a J. For a fuller discussion of this topic, including all strands of Bible authorship, see appendix, "The Biblical Biographers of David," page 307.

‡"Yahweh," sometimes rendered as "YHWH" or "YHVH," is an English transliteration of the four Hebrew consonants that spell out the personal name of God in the Hebrew Bible. See "A Note on Bibles and Biblical Usage," page 347.

epic that begins with the very moment of creation and explains in rich detail how a people who were descended from a single restless nomad ended up as the conquerors and rulers of the land of Canaan.

Threads of the biblical narrative that are conventionally attributed to J can readily be traced through the so-called Five Books of Moses,* especially Genesis, Exodus, and Numbers, and portions of Joshua and Judges. And the work of J can be seen as the "backstory" to the Court Historian's biography of David that begins in the Book of Samuel. When read as a continuous narrative—as the Bible invites us to read them—the two works both point to a single crucial and inevitable figure, King David. Indeed, Richard Elliott Friedman makes a convincing argument in *The Hidden Book in the Bible* that the Yahwist and the Court Historian were actually one and the same person,[16] and Harold Bloom in *The Book of J* imagines that the two sources were contemporaries and colleagues in the court of the Davidic monarchy in Jerusalem.

David is not mentioned in the Bible until the Book of Samuel, but we can begin to hear the strains of the "undersong" that Bible scholar Gerhard von Rad detected in the earliest passages of the Yahwist's primal history. In fact, the Five Books of Moses are seeded with clues that anticipate the coming of King David long before we actually encounter him. And these clues suggest that the Bible was first and always intended by its original authors to be a celebration of King David and the line of Davidic kings who sat on the throne of Israel and Judah during a reign that spanned five centuries, the longest-reigning dynasty in the ancient Near East and one of the longest-reigning in world history.

---

*The first five books of the Hebrew Bible (Genesis, Exodus, Leviticus, Numbers, and Deuteronomy) are variously known as the Five Books of Moses (because their authorship is traditionally attributed to Moses), the Pentateuch (Five Scrolls), or the Torah (Law or Instruction).

THE *REAL* BIBLE CODE

An intriguing and illuminating game can be played with the characters and stories that we find in the Bible. It is no mere parlor game, but rather a way to crack a kind of code that is deeply embedded in the Bible. Cracking the *real* Bible code is not a matter of teasing out prophesies and predictions of the far distant future by crunching randomly selected Hebrew letters into words and phrases. The original biblical authors salted the text with clues that were meant to stoke our anticipation for the coming of King David and our appreciation of his achievements as a man and a monarch; they seem to invite readers to search out the linkages between King David and the other figures and events in the earlier books of the Bible.

For example, the Bible opens with a famous scene of seduction, Adam lured by Eve into partaking of the forbidden fruit. Much later in the biblical narrative, there is another apparent seduction at the outset of the scandalous love affair between David and Bathsheba. Was the tale of Adam and Eve, as some scholars propose, meant by the biblical author to prepare us for the fateful sexual encounter between David and Bathsheba?

The same kind of foreshadowing can be detected in dozens of other biblical scenes. The rape of Dinah, daughter of the patriarch Jacob, by a prince called Shechem anticipates the rape of Tamar, daughter of King David, by her half brother, a prince called Amnon. The murder of Abel by his brother Cain anticipates the murder of Amnon by his half brother, Absalom, who sought to avenge the rape of Tamar. And when the Bible depicts the matriarch Rebekah conspiring with her son Jacob to steal the birthright of her firstborn son, Esau, by persuading the patriarch Isaac to give the blessing of the firstborn to the younger son, perhaps we are intended to see Bathsheba in conspiracy with Solomon to persuade the aging David to designate his younger son as king of Israel in place of Solomon's older brother.

Such linkages are not merely fanciful. Rather, they reflect the peculiar logic of biblical narrative, a dreamy and sometimes even phantasmagorical quality in which one scene may hark back or look forward to another scene at any given point in the text. Thus the Book of Genesis includes an odd and unexplained incident in which Reuben, firstborn son of the patriarch Jacob, crawls into bed with Jacob's concubine, Bilhah. The Bible does not pause to explain the cause or significance of the episode, but perhaps we are meant to think of Reuben when, much later, we come upon Absalom, son of King David, conducting a public orgy with David's concubines on the roof of the palace in Jerusalem.

At other moments, the encoded messages in the biblical text are straightforward and precise. The boundaries of the Promised Land, for example, are specified in several passages of the Bible, and in several different ways, but the very first description is found in the opening chapters of Genesis, where God is shown to promise the land of Canaan as a homeland to Abraham and his descendants. "Unto thy seed have I given this land," says God to Abraham, "from the river of Egypt* unto the great river, the river Euphrates." (Gen. 15:18) Not until the reign of David, however, does the Bible report that the kingdom of Israel actually approached these imperial dimensions—and the dynasty's sovereignty began to recede from that high-water mark on the death of his son Solomon. Some scholars see the passage in Genesis as the handiwork of a biblical source who has been characterized as "David's theologian,"[17] a royal apologist who sought to justify and celebrate the conquests of King David by backdating them to the earliest passages of the Bible

Thus, as the Bible is decoded, a stunning possibility emerges: perhaps the Bible exists today only because the Court Historian sat down to write the biography of King David in the royal palace at Jerusalem in the tenth century B.C.E. And perhaps another author of genius was inspired by the Court Historian's example to write a kind of prequel, collecting the myth and legend of tribal Israel and working the oldest traditions into a companion volume

---

*The "River of Egypt" is not the Nile but rather the Wadi el-Arish in the Sinai Peninsula.

to the Court History. Later generations of biblical authors and editors added to these core works, decorating them with fairy tales and folktales, putting a theological spin on even the earthiest incidents of David's life. David was slowly transformed in their hands: the ruthless bandit and the rude tribal chieftain was turned into a king, then an emperor, and finally a messiah.

The Bible, of course, bulked up over the centuries as new books were added to the ones that had crystalized around the life story of David. But even some of the later books were linked to David and the monarchy that he founded; the Book of Psalms, for example, is traditionally thought of as authored by David, and the Book of Proverbs by his son Solomon. That is why David can be regarded as the axial figure of the Bible—some of the biblical authors look back into primal history, some look forward to the end times, but all of them seem to be standing in the court of King David.

THE REAL LIFE OF DAVID

So David shines out across the centuries and millennia, and he still exerts a powerful allure for real men and women who struggle to make sense of their own stressful and messy lives. While it may come as a rude shock to the Bible-thumpers who rely on Holy Writ to condemn what they call humanism, the fact is that humanism begins with the biblical David and is still defined by his example. Indeed, the life story of David as we find it in the Book of Samuel offers the earliest and the longest-enduring definition of what it means to be a human being.

"How men and women imagine their lives today begins with the mature David," insists poet and Bible translator David Rosenberg. "To be able to hold in mind—side by side—laughter and tears, objectivity and fear, affords a fullness. And this quality, so original in David, allows us to be fulfilled when the ambiguous loyalties in others and in ourselves threaten to tear us in two."[18]

Nowadays the stresses and strains of human life—the hard tug between our best and worst impulses—are explored and explained in the language of psychology and genetics rather than the exalted words and phrases of the Bible. But the biographers of David seem to have penetrated the innermost secrets of the human heart and mind several thousand years ahead of Freud. For them—and for us—the figure of King David is both thrilling and unsettling, both comforting and troubling; it is larger than life and at the same time an enduring example of a life lived on a human scale. And perhaps that is why, as we shall come to see, David "lives and endures to this day."

Chapter Two

THE WRONG KING

Monarchy was a newcomer in Israel,
born out of season.
                    —GERHARD VON RAD,
                    OLD TESTAMENT THEOLOGY

An intriguing idea about David is offered by a few bold practitioners of modern Bible scholarship: King David was still alive on the day, some three thousand years ago, when the biblical author known as the Court Historian first picked up a goosequill pen and started setting down on parchment the earliest account of his remarkable life. If so, David's original biographer was writing about a flesh-and-blood figure who could be seen striding down the corridors of the royal palace, whose voice could be heard in the throne room or at the banquet table, and whose exploits, some heroic and some scandalous, were gossiped about in Jerusalem.

Not every Bible scholar is convinced that David still reigned when his life story was first recorded. Some suggest that the oldest passages of the Book of Samuel were composed during the reign of Solomon, shortly after David's death. Others argue that David had already passed from history into legend by the time the biblical author wrote what is now the core of Samuel. A few revisionists even insist that the biblical David *never* existed; they regard the man we encounter in the pages of the Bible as purely mythic. Of one thing, however, we can be absolutely sure. If David still lived and still reigned when the Court Historian set to work on his life story, the king did not resemble the iconic figure whom we find in illuminated Bibles of the Middle Ages, in the high art of the Renaissance, or in the TV advertisements of our own era. David was no longer—and may never have been—the boy who bested Goliath in single combat with only a slingshot. David was, instead, someone far more potent. David as the Court Historian may have known him is careworn and perhaps a bit thickset, but still charming, still handsome, still alluring to the men and women who seek his favor in the royal court at Jerusalem. At the same time, he still enjoys a reputation for ruthlessness in the pursuit of power. Those—including his own sons—who dare to conspire against him warn themselves against underestimating the old king who has shed so much blood in making his way from the sheepcote to the throne.

At this moment, David is not only the reigning king of all Israel but also the conqueror of an empire that stretches from Egypt to the Euphrates—no ruler of Israel who came before him enjoyed the same imperial reach, nor would any who came after. He reigns from a palace of fragrant cedarwood, a rarity and a luxury in the ancient world, and the palace stands on a fortified hilltop in Jerusalem, a place that David conquered by force of arms. His favorite wife is the charming Bathsheba, but a dozen or so other wives and concubines await his pleasure in the bustling harem. As if to emphasize that all of these glories are the result of his own ruthless will, he has named his royal capital after himself: it is called the City of David.

The Court Historian is of course familiar with the official biography of King David, the exploits of courage and derring-do, the victories and conquests, the reforms and innovations. He has heard the courtiers praise David's artistry at the lyre and in the dance, in the elegy and the psalm, and he has heard the priests celebrate David's piety and his observance of ritual, celebrating him as "a man after God's own heart." But the Court Historian knows other tales that are told only in hushed tones and behind closed doors—David's fugitive years as a bandit and an outlaw, his stint as a mercenary in service to the enemies of Israel, his habit of seducing other men's wives.

Some of David's exploits seem so scandalous as to defy belief. Could it really be true that David once served as a mercenary under the detested Philistines and offered to go into battle against the rightful king of Israel? Did he really kill men, women, and children in order to eliminate the eyewitnesses to his crimes against the people of Israel? And what about the beautiful woman who was his principal wife and the mother of the crown prince—did he really conspire to murder her husband after he had lured her into his bed and then impregnated her with a bastard child?

The king whom the Court Historian served was, in fact, a bloodstained warrior who secured his crown through ruthless guerrilla warfare and cynical intrigue, a man of regal bearing but raw appetite, a man who did not hesitate to connive and even to kill in order to get what he wanted. And, remarkably, the Court Historian dared to set down in writing the whole truth as he knew it, leaving out no secret crime, no sin, and no scandal. Three thousand years later, the Bible brings us face-to-face with King David in all his complexity and contradiction.

Still, the formal biography of David in the Book of Samuel does not begin with David himself, and we will not encounter the man whom the Court Historian knew so well until much later in the biblical text. The story of David starts, appropriately enough, with a beguiling woman. Her name is Hannah, and she is only the first of many remarkable women who will figure crucially in his life.

A WOMAN OF SORROWFUL SPIRIT

Hannah, the Bible tells us, was heartbroken because she was childless—her affliction the same as the one visited emblematically upon the matriarchs Sarah and Rebekah and Rachel in the Book of Genesis. Hannah's husband tried to comfort her by declaring his love and suggesting that it ought to be enough: "Am I not better to thee than ten sons?" (1 Sam. 1:8) But Hannah was tormented by the sight of the children that his *other* wife had given him. So she made a pilgrimage to the temple of Yahweh and prayed for a son.

She prayed silently, moving her lips without uttering a sound, but with such fervor that the priest of the sanctuary decided that she was a common drunk.

"How long wilt thou be drunken?" the priest scolded Hannah. "Put away thy wine from thee."

"No, my lord, I am a woman of sorrowful spirit," she protested. "I have drunken neither wine nor strong drink, but have poured out my soul before the Lord."

Touched by Hannah's earnest words, the priest sent her away with a kind wish. "Go in peace," he said, "and the God of Israel grant thee thy petition." (1 Sam. 1:14–17)

Hannah returned to her home, joined her husband in bed, and "the Lord remembered her"—that is, Hannah conceived at last and later gave birth to a baby boy. The pious woman had promised God to dedicate any son she might bear to a lifetime of service in the temple, and she kept her promise. She named the child Samuel, which is understood to mean "He-who-is-from-God,"[1] and as soon as he was weaned she delivered him to the high priest.[2]

What Hannah did not know was that God had already singled out Samuel to play a unique role in the destiny of Israel. One night, as he slept in the sanctuary of Yahweh, the child heard his name called by a voice that he presumed to belong to the high priest. And Samuel responded with the same formulaic phrase that is repeated throughout the Bible when a human being is summoned to perform a task by God—first Abraham (Gen. 22:1), then Moses (Exod. 3:4), and now Samuel.

"Here am I!" said the boy.

"I called not," the old priest told Samuel when he harkened to the call. "Lie down again." (1 Sam. 1:5) (NEB)

The voice called to him twice more during that fateful night, and twice more Samuel answered "Here am I" (*Hineni*). At last the voice revealed itself to be the God of Israel, who now manifested himself before Samuel and spoke again. (1 Sam, 3:4–10) "Behold, I will do a thing in Israel," God told Samuel, "at which both the ears of everyone that heareth it shall tingle." (1 Sam. 3:11)[3]

Here, in the opening passages of the Book of Samuel, we find ourselves in a world of auguries and omens, priestcraft and prophecy, a world quite unlike the one inhabited by David himself. David, as we shall come to see, never actually *hears* the voice of God, and his biblical life story is strikingly modern precisely because we are shown how human beings use and abuse one another when God is silent and aloof. At the outset of Samuel, however, we are still in the "dreamtime" of the Judeo-Christian tradition, a time and place where a boy might be roused at midnight by a mysterious voice and suddenly find himself in the physical presence of God. Only later will David stride out of these mists and into the full light of history. For now, the Bible focuses on the crucial figure who is called by God to set into motion the chain of events that will one day put David on the throne of Israel.

SPIN DOCTORS

To understand why King David's life story begins with the calling of the prophet Samuel, we must first pause to consider some of the Bible's deepest mysteries: Who wrote the book that three faiths regard as Holy Writ? When and where did the biblical authors live and work? And why were they so much at odds with one another on matters of both theology and history? The answers to these questions reveal why the Bible is such a crazy-making book, so full of flaws and contradictions, so confusing in its depiction of who God is and what God wants that the Almighty comes across as a deity with a multiple-personality disorder. Above all, the answers reveal why the Bible celebrates a man like David—as sullied and sinful as any potentate of the ancient world—as "a man after God's own heart."

The Bible, according to the consensus of modern scholarship, is a patchwork of ancient texts that were composed and compiled by countless authors and editors, men and women alike, over a period of a thousand years or so. Among the strands of the biblical tapestry are history and biography, myth and legend, poetry and prayer, sacred law and secular law, rites of animal sacrifice and rituals of sympathetic magic, carpentry instructions and dermatological procedures, military tactics and dietary advice, and much else besides. The various biblical sources lived and worked at different times and places in the distant past, each one serving his or her own moral, political, and theological agenda, each one putting words into the mouths of biblical characters, and each one putting his or her own spin on the history of ancient Israel.

The oldest passages of the Book of Samuel, as we have seen, are generally attributed to the source known as the Court Historian, a man or woman who may have been an eyewitness to the reign of David and who dared to tell his remarkable life story with both deep compassion and brutal honesty. Later, the oldest passages of the Book of Samuel came to be overwritten with the work of other sources—priests and scribes, archivists and chroniclers, apologists and propagandists, bards and troubadours—who felt at liberty to embellish and edit the Court Historian's work.

The composite text was given a high polish by a source known as the Deuteronomistic Historian, a term used by Bible scholars to identify a school of priests and scribes who brought the Book of Samuel and other biblical books into line with the distinctive theology that is first announced in the Book of Deuteronomy. And the Bible as we know it today bears the fingerprints of one final set of editors known collectively as the Redactor (or "R"). Thus, the Bible is an elaborate tapestry rather than the work of a single author, human or divine, and we can tease out the strands that were woven into the narrative fabric by the various sources, each one putting a moral or political or theological coloration—or "spin"—on the text.

The opening passages of the Book of Samuel, for example, seem to be the work of an author who embraces the prophetic tradition of ancient Israel, an author from the same circles that produced the fiery theological manifestos of Isaiah and Jeremiah and Ezekiel.[4] Unlike the Court Historian, the prophetic author is not much interested in the realpolitik of ancient Israel or the sexual adventures of its princes and kings. The only real concern of the theological spin doctor who describes the calling of young Samuel is the profound and enduring mystery of how God works his will in history. So this author composed the prequel to the life of David that appears in the opening passages of the Book of Samuel. That is why we meet Samuel—one of those cranky, carping, God-inspired men and women whom we call prophets—long before we meet David himself. And that is why Samuel is presented as a man with grave misgivings about the very idea of monarchy.

In the Bible, as elsewhere in life and literature, nothing succeeds like success, and so David is forgiven for his sins and scandals by the Court Historian. But the prophetic sources lived long after the reign of David, and they witnessed the ultimate failure of kingship in ancient Israel. The dynasty founded by King David continued to reign for nearly five hundred years, but the Bible describes almost all of his successors as a sorry collection of apostates and blasphemers whose misconduct resulted in invasion and conquest, destruction and dispersion. For that reason, the first voice we hear in the Book of Samuel belongs to a biblical author who prefers holy men to kings and priests, and the tale opens with the prophet Samuel, the man whom God selects to make and break the kings of Israel.

THE WASTELAND

Samuel was born in the land of Canaan a couple of hundred years after its conquest by the coalition of twelve tribes known as *b'nai*

Yisrael, the Children of Israel, at a time when things had gone terribly wrong for the Chosen People. The Bible characterizes Canaan as the Promised Land, "a land flowing with milk and honey." (Exod. 3:8) But, as it turned out, Canaan was not a virgin paradise. Rather, the land promised to the Israelites teemed with tribes and peoples—"seven nations greater and mightier than thou," as God had warned the Israelites (Deut. 7:1)—who regarded Canaan as *their* homeland. Here begins the first and longest-lasting of the problems created by the disparity between what God promises and what God does in the Hebrew Bible.

At first God had vowed to cleanse the Promised Land of its native dwellers. "I will send my terror before thee," God promised Moses. "I will deliver the inhabitants of the land into your hand; and thou shalt drive them out before." (Exod. 23:27, 31) But he was so angry and disappointed with the "stiff-necked" Israelites, who were always so faithless and so defiant, that he changed his mind. "I will *not* drive them out from before you," God later told Joshua, successor of Moses and conqueror of Canaan, "but they shall be unto you as snares, and their gods shall be a trap unto you." (Judg. 2:3)

Indeed, the Israelites found the pagan gods and goddesses whom the Canaanites worshipped with orgiastic abandon to be far more alluring than the stern and censorious God of Israel. Yahweh was a bachelor father, a loner who disdained a female consort, but the Canaanite pantheon included an array of she-deities who were both erotic and maternal, thus answering the human need for a feminine object of worship. Once in Canaan, the Israelites turned to idolatry, sacred harlotry, and other ritual practices that the pious biblical source regards as too vile to describe. "And the children of Israel did that which was evil in the sight of the Lord," reports the Book of Judges in a phrase that is repeated like a mantra, "and forgot the Lord their God." (Judg. 3:7) Even David, as we shall see, kept a collection of idols in his own home.

So the Book of Judges seems to set up a theological rationale for the sorry fate that the Chosen People will endure. As a punishment for their faithlessness and infidelity, God now decreed that they would be humbled in battle against the people who shared their new homeland and the nations that surrounded it on all sides: "And the anger of the Lord was kindled against Israel, and He delivered them into the hands of the spoilers that spoiled them." (Judg. 2:14) Nor would the Israelites be capable of living in peace with one another. Although all twelve tribes claimed descent from the patriarch Jacob, a man also known as Israel, they bickered and battled with one another in a series of ruinous blood feuds that turned the Promised Land into a wasteland.

The moral decay reaches an appalling climax in a story that is preserved in the Book of Judges, a cautionary tale about a nameless woman who is gang-raped by her fellow Israelites. On a journey from Bethlehem to the hill-country of Ephraim, a man from the tribe of Levi and his concubine are forced to spend the night in a town that belongs to the tribe of Benjamin. A crowd of rowdy Benjaminites gathers around the house where they have taken shelter and demands that the guests be surrendered to them for their sexual pleasure. To spare himself, the frightened Levite pushes his concubine out the door and offers her to the mob in his place. All night long, while the Levite and his host cower inside the house, the woman is raped to death. Her body is left at the threshold.

But the carnage is not over yet. Demanding retribution, the outraged Levite hacks the woman's battered body into twelve pieces and sends the bloody chunks to the other tribes of Israel as a call to arms against the Benjaminites. All of Israel unites in a punitive war against the Benjaminites—men, women, and children alike—and the tribe is very nearly exterminated. At the last moment, the rest of the Israelites, suddenly remorseful at the prospect of genocide, spare the last six hundred Benjaminite men. But since none of the women has survived the slaughter, the Benjaminite men are sent by their fellow Israelites to Shiloh with instructions to seize the young virgins of the town and use them to repopulate the tribe of Benjamin. Thus the rape and murder of a single woman prompt the rape and abduction of six hundred more women, and only by these desperate and ugly means is the tribe of Benjamin preserved from extermination.

At this point in the Bible, however, we are reading the work of a biblical author who offers a political rather than a theological rationale for the ghastly state of affairs in ancient Israel. He is a covert propagandist who blames all the failings of the Chosen People on the simple fact that they were not yet ruled by a king. To the royal apologist, neither fidelity to God nor submission to priests and prophets was sufficient to break the cycle of apostasy and catastrophe that afflicted the Israelites. Indeed, the Book of Judges can be regarded as a parade of horribles intended to persuade the original readers of the Bible that only a king would be capable of putting an end to the chaos and imposing moral law and order on the unruly Israelites.

"In those days there was no king in Israel," writes the royal apologist by way of explaining the atrocities that are collected in the Book of Judges, "and every man did that which was right in his own eyes." (Judg. 21:25)

"GIVE US A KING!"

Two contending factions in the politics of ancient Israel can be glimpsed in these troubling passages of Judges. One faction preferred an old-fashioned theocracy—that is, the leadership of devout men and women who felt called upon by God to "judge" the people of Israel, as the Bible puts it. The other faction favored the newfangled institution of monarchy, and its members agitated for a king like the ones who reigned in the superpowers of the ancient world, Egypt and Mesopotamia. Remarkably, the Bible preserves the arguments for and against kingship as they were presented to its original readers, and we are able to see for ourselves how deeply they divided the people of ancient Israel. Indeed, the rivalry between theocracy and monarchy in ancient Israel was bitter enough to break God's heart.

Theocracy prevailed among the Israelites in the early period of the conquest. Deborah, the fiery prophetess who led the armies of Israel into battle against the Canaanites, was one of the first judges (Judg. 4–5), and Samson, who was famously seduced by a Philistine woman named Delilah and who then martyred himself by bringing down the walls of a pagan temple, was among the last. (Judg. 16–17) But the judges never succeeded in imposing divine law and moral order on the Israelites for very long. Again and again, the Israelites "hearkened not unto their judges, for they went astray after other gods, and worshipped them." (Judg. 2:17)

Even Samuel, the very last of the judges, failed in his efforts to save the Israelites from their own excesses—and his failure was a peculiarly intimate one. Under Samuel's leadership, the dreaded Philistines were defeated on the field of battle[5] and the corrupt priesthood of Israel was brought down. But Samuel was an ineffectual father whose sons rejected his pious ways, "turned aside after lucre, and took bribes, and perverted justice." (1 Sam. 8:3) So he forfeited the confidence of the elders of Israel, who fretted over what would happen when Samuel was gone and only his corrupt sons remained. At last the elders trekked out to confront Samuel at his home in Ramah, and they made a bold demand.

"Behold, thou art old, and thy sons walk not in thy ways," the elders declared. "Now make us a king to judge us like all the nations." (1 Sam. 8:5)

Their demand struck Samuel as unwholesome and even unholy—Israel was supposed to be a theocracy, not a monarchy. When they were still a mob of runaway slaves in the wilderness, Moses had revealed to the Israelites that they had been chosen to be "a kingdom of priests, and a holy nation," and their one and only sovereign was to be the invisible deity called Yahweh. "If you will hearken to my voice, and keep my covenant," God vowed, "then ye shall be mine own treasure from among all peoples." (Exod. 19:5, 6)[6] The rule of kings, according to the fundamental theology of the Five Books of Moses, was strictly for the goyim.[7]

Confounded by the sudden demand for a king, which he found so heartbreaking precisely because it was so ordinary and thus so unworthy of the Chosen People, Samuel sought guidance in prayer. And God, who had last addressed him when he was only a child, spoke again to Samuel. But now it was God who seemed childlike—Yahweh, so famously described in the Bible as a jealous god, seemed to regard the desire of the Israelites for a king as a personal insult. When he spoke to Samuel, his tone was resentful, petulant, even a bit whiny.

"Hearken unto the voice of the people," God instructed Samuel, "for they have not rejected thee, but they have rejected me, that I should not be king over them." (1 Sam. 8:7)

God, like the frustrated father of a stubborn and greedy child, was always ready to punish the Chosen People by the simple expedient of giving them exactly what they thought they wanted. During the years of wandering in the wilderness, for example, God fed the Israelites on the miraculous gift of manna, but when they tired of the monotonous diet of "bread from heaven" and yearned instead for roasted flesh, God provided them with quail in such abundance that the Israelites would be tempted to eat the stuff "until it comes out at your nostrils." (Exod. 16:4, Num. 11:19–20) Now God took a similar stance: if the people of Israel preferred a mortal king to the King of the Universe, God allowed, he would give them one—but they would live to regret it.

"YOUR SONS AND DAUGHTERS HE WILL TAKE"

At God's direction, Samuel delivered an oration to the people of Israel that fairly sizzled with contempt for the idea of monarchy. It was an indictment of kings that still reads like a revolutionary manifesto rather than pious prophecy. "This," warns Samuel, "will be the manner of the king that shall reign over you."

> He will take your sons to be his horsemen and to plow his ground and to reap his harvest, and to make his instruments of war, and they shall run before his chariots. And he will take your daughters to be perfumers, and to be

cooks, and to be bakers. And he will take your fields, and your vineyards, and your oliveyards, even the best of them. And he will take the tenth of your seed, and give to his officers. And he will take your men-servants, and your maid-servants, and your goodliest young men, and your asses, and put them to his work. He will take a tenth of your flocks, and ye shall be his servants.

(1 Sam. 8:11–17)[8]

Samuel's catalog of the sins of kings against their people seems strangely out of place in a book that celebrates the kingship of David. The Book of Judges, as we have already seen, can be understood as *"ex post facto* royalist propaganda,"[9] a series of atrocity stories that were meant to convince the original readers of the Bible that human beings cannot be trusted to govern themselves in the absence of a king. The core of both Judges and Samuel was composed by chroniclers of the Davidic kings who clearly regarded the coming of kingship as a wholly benign revolution—the Israelites were now sophisticated and sensible enough to throw off the rule of the tribal chieftains and charismatic holy men who had ruled them and to submit themselves to a national monarchy like the ones they saw all around them.

"Instead of the special theocracy [Samuel] has overseen to this point," writes Bible scholar Jan Wojcik, "the people now want sound economics, a strong military establishment, and a secure environment."[10]

But as we have seen, the Bible also preserves the fingerprints of authors who disdained the rule of kings. If David himself was capable of excessive and even outrageous conduct in both his public and private life, most of the kings who came after him were regarded with ever greater horror in the prophetic circles of ancient Israel. Indeed, the kings who succeeded David presided over a succession of political and military catastrophes that ended only with the destruction of Jerusalem in 586 B.C.E., when the Babylonians carried the ruling elite of the Davidic monarchy into exile. For that reason, some passages of the Book of Samuel may be regarded an "epitaph over the corpse of Israel buried in Babylon," as Bible scholar Robert Polzin puts it. "Kingship, despite all its glories, constituted for Israel communal suicide."[11]

That is why a tirade against kingship was put into Samuel's mouth by a later biblical source who had come to distrust and even detest earthly kings, a pious naysayer who still believed in old-fashioned theocracy rather than a newfangled monarchy. Long after David was dead and gone, this writer took the liberty of slipping a manifesto against monarchy into the same pages of the Bible where David, the greatest king of all, is celebrated with such ardor.

THE ANOINTED ONE

God gave the people of Israel the king they demanded—but his name was not David.

"I will send you a man out of the land of Benjamin," God told Samuel, "and you will anoint him to be prince over my people Israel, and he shall save my people from out of the hand of the Philistines." (1 Sam. 9:16)[12]

So it was that Yahweh chose a handsome but hapless fellow named Saul to ascend the throne of Israel as its first king, or so the Bible says. Saul may have been "young and goodly," and "a head taller than any of his fellows," but he was star-crossed from the beginning. (1 Sam. 9:2)[13] As a Benjaminite, he came from the smallest of the twelve tribes of Israel and the one responsible for the incident of gang rape and murder that nearly resulted in its extermination. Moreover, he belonged to the clan called Matri, "the humblest clan of all the tribe of Benjamin," as Saul himself put it, thus reminding us that the identity of an Israelite was still defined in terms of tribe and clan rather than nationality. (1 Sam. 9:21) (AB)

Saul's very first exploit, as reported in the Book of Samuel, encourages us to see him as something of a dullard. Sent by his father to find some stray asses from the family herd, Saul wandered aimlessly around the countryside until his provisions ran out. Finally Saul sought out a local seer in the desperate hope that *he* might know where to find the asses. The seer was Samuel.

"Here is the man of whom I spoke to you," God whispered to Samuel when Saul showed up. "This man shall rule my people." (1 Sam. 9:17) (NEB)

At dawn on the next day, Samuel roused Saul from sleep and anointed the young man who had come in search of his lost asses as the first king of Israel. The ceremony was simple and straight-forward, which may seem surprising when we begin to ponder the soul-shaking and history-making implications of the word "messiah," the familiar English rendering of *mashiach*, the Hebrew word for "the anointed one." From a small flask, probably fashioned of fired clay,[14] Samuel poured oil upon Saul's head—olive oil spiced with myrrh, cinnamon, cassia, and aromatic cane, according to a recipe for anointing oil found in the Book of Exodus (Exod. 30:22–25)[15]—and then bestowed a kiss upon Saul and intoned a few short pronouncements that began with a rhetorical question.

"Has not Yahweh anointed you prince over his people Israel?" recited Samuel. "It is you who will muster the people of Yahweh! It is you who will free them from the grip of their enemies all around!" (1 Sam. 19:1) (AB)[16]

Although the practice of anointing kings and their vassals may have been borrowed from the court rituals of ancient Egypt, the Bible confirms that the Israelites found a great many reasons and opportunities to anoint both people and things.[17] The altar of sacrifice was smeared with consecrated oil, and so were the tabernacle and the sacred paraphernalia used in ceremonies of worship. Aaron, the brother of Moses, was anointed as the first high priest of Israel, and anointment was the rite of initiation for the generations of high priests who came after him. (Exod. 40:10–12, 15) Even lepers were anointed with a "sevenfold" sprinkling of oil in a ritual of purification. (Lev. 14:15–18) Starting with Saul, however, the ancient ritual took on a new and enduring meaning for the people of Israel. Anointment became the essential and enduring symbol of kingship, a faintly magical rite in which the strength, wisdom, and power of Yahweh were symbolically conveyed to the mortal monarch.

God may have agreed to give the Israelites the king they had demanded, but Saul turned out to be the wrong one.

SAUL AMONG THE BAGGAGE

God's choice of Saul remained a secret until Samuel staged a convocation with the apparent purpose of drumming up public enthusiasm for the man whom he had privately anointed as king. Samuel summoned the people of Israel to Mizpah, one of the traditional gathering places and sites of worship in ancient Israel. The old man opened the proceedings by reminding the crowd of their clamor for a king and pointing out rather irritably why he still thought it was a terrible idea.

> Thus saith the Lord, the God of Israel: "I brought up Israel out of Egypt, and I delivered you out of the hands of all the kingdoms that oppressed you." But you have this day rejected your God, who himself saves you out of all your calamities and your distresses, and you have said unto him: "Nay, but set a king over us!"
> (1 Sam. 10:18–19)[18]

Then, curiously, Samuel conducted a drawing of lots among the twelve tribes of Israel with the apparent purpose of selecting the man who would be king.[19] Since God had already directed Samuel to anoint Saul as king,[20] the lottery was something of a sham. Still, the people watched as the first lot fell to the tribe of Benjamin, the second lot fell to the clan of Matri, and then the drawing of lots continued among the members of the clan, man by man, until the young man named Saul was finally selected, just as Samuel had known all along.

But at the moment of his selection, Saul was nowhere to be seen. As if to signal the sorry fate that awaits Saul, the biblical author gives us a moment of burlesque that makes Saul seem like a fool rather than an anointed king.

"Will the man be coming back?" a befuddled Samuel asked God.

"There he is," said God, "hiding among the baggage." (1 Sam. 10:22) (NEB)

At the very moment when he was to be acclaimed as the first king of Israel, Saul was cowering behind the baggage that was piled up around the encampment of the Israelites at Mizpah. Thus tipped to Saul's whereabouts by God himself, Samuel flushed the reluctant king out of his hiding place and presented him to the crowd.

"Do you see him whom Yahweh has chosen," asked Samuel, calling attention to the tall young man who now stood in plain sight and loomed head and shoulders above the rest of the crowd, "that there is no one else like him among all the people?"

"Long live the king!" cried the mob, satisfied at last to have a king of their own like all the other nations of the world. (1 Sam. 10:22–25) (AB)

Still, Saul was not acclaimed by every man among the people of Israel. Rabbinic tradition depicts him as a giant, tall and imposing, but we may suspect that some doubters in the crowd looked on him and saw only a gawky youth. The ancient rabbis regarded Saul as a model of humility because he hid from his own coronation, but some of the Israelites would have seen it as a sign of timidity or perhaps even cowardice. To them, the ass-herder who stumbled into kingship hardly seemed worthy of the honor.

"Saul went to his house in Gibeah, and there went with him men of valour, whose hearts God had touched," the Bible reports. "But certain base fellows said: 'How shall this man save us?' And they despised him." (1 Sam. 10:26–27)

THE SLAUGHTERED OXEN

Saul's kingship was quickly put to the proof by an act of aggression and a threatened atrocity from one of the traditional enemies of

Israel, the king of neighboring Ammon.²¹ The army of the Ammonite king boldly encamped outside Jabesh-Gilead, one of the frontier towns of Israel on the far side of the Jordan River, and the enemy king threatened to attack and destroy the town. Panic-stricken by the sight of the approaching army, the townspeople offered to submit to the rule of Ammon, but the enemy king responded with contempt to their offer to make peace through abject surrender.

"On this condition will I make it with you," the king of Ammon taunted, "that all your right eyes be put out." (1 Sam. 11:2)

The town elders begged for a respite of seven days in which to consider the grotesque offer, and the king of Ammon inexplicably consented. Messengers were promptly dispatched to Saul with a desperate plea for rescue. They found the newly crowned king at work in the fields of Gibeah, trudging behind a brace of oxen.

What King Saul did next offers a glimpse into the unsettled politics of ancient Israel in the earliest days of monarchy. Israel was still only a loose and informal confederation of tribes, not a national state, and the newly minted king could not count on mustering up an army by issuing a call to arms to the various tribes. So Saul chose to use threat and coercion to create a national army to go to the rescue of the besieged border town of Jabesh.

And he took a yoke of oxen, and cut them in pieces, and sent them throughout all the borders of Israel by the hand of messengers, saying: "Whosoever cometh not forth after Saul and after Samuel, so shall it be done unto his oxen."

(1 Sam. 11:7)

The same bloody gesture had been used once before to raise an army in Israel, when the Levite traveler hacked the dead body of his concubine into pieces in the very same town of Gibeah to incite a punitive campaign against the tribe of Benjamin. Now the first king of Israel—ironically, a Benjaminite—used a similar signal to raise a national army to go to war against the Ammonites. The grotesque call to arms had worked once before, and according to the Bible it worked again.

"And the dread of the Lord fell on the people," the Bible confirms, crediting the fear of God rather than the more palpable threat issued by Saul himself, "and they came out as one man." (1 Sam. 11:7)

"SHALL SAUL REIGN OVER US?"

An army of 330,000 soldiers rallied to the king's call. Saul, suddenly transformed from a plodding farmer into a daring battlefield commander, was inspired to send the embattled people of Jabesh a message that rang with kingly bravado. "Tomorrow, by the time the sun is hot," Saul promised them, "ye shall have deliverance." (1 Sam. 11:9)

Saul proved to be an able tactician. The enemy was put to rout by a surprise attack, "so that two of them were not left together." (1 Sam. 11:11) Yet even at the moment of triumph, Saul was reminded that his political adversaries remained at large in Israel. A crowd approached Samuel and demanded the blood of the Israelites who had dared to oppose Saul's kingship. "Who is he that said: 'Shall Saul reign over us?' " they railed at the old prophet. "Bring the men, that we may put them to death."

Saul himself silenced their call for vengeance, adopting the statesmanlike stance that a victor in battle can afford to strike. "There shall not a man be put to death this day," he declared, "for today the Lord hath wrought deliverance in Israel." (1 Sam. 11:13) Saul resolved to take advantage of the momentary surge of enthusiasm among the people: a second convocation was held, this time in the city of Gilgal, and "there they made Saul king before the Lord." (1 Sam. 11:15)*

---

*The twice-told tale of Saul's coronation may be an example of what scholars call a "doublet," that is, parallel accounts of the same incident by different biblical sources in slightly different versions. Doublets are regarded as key evidence of the multiple authorship of the Bible.

All of these ceremonials and convocations, of course, are profoundly at odds with what we have been taught to believe about the deity who is described in the Hebrew Bible. God is supposed to be all-powerful, but it turned out that his designation of Saul to be king of Israel was not enough to make it so—Samuel was obliged to engage in politicking and public relations in order to put Saul on the throne and keep him there. God is supposed to be all-knowing, but the Almighty apparently did not foresee that Saul would bungle the kingship that Samuel procured for him. God, it seems, is perfectly capable of making a mistake, and he made one when he instructed Samuel to anoint Saul. The twice-crowned king of Israel was already doomed.

A MAN AFTER GOD'S HEART

Saul's tactical victory in a skirmish with the king of Ammon did nothing to warn off the enemy that represented a far greater threat to Israel—the Philistines. The Bible suggests that the Philistines so dominated Israel that they were able to forbid metal-smithing lest the Israelites make swords or spears for themselves. "No blacksmith was to be found in the whole of Israel," the Bible reports. "The Israelites had to go down to the Philistines for their ploughshares, mattocks, axes, and sickles to be sharpened." Only Saul and his son Jonathan possessed proper weapons, and the rest of the Israelites were forced to content themselves with crude darts and flint-edged weapons. (1 Sam. 13:19–20, 22, 14:13) (NEB)

The kingdom of Saul, in fact, was occupied territory. Even Gibeah, the town where Saul lived and reigned, remained under the authority of a governor appointed by the Philistines. And Saul was unable or unwilling to engage in a war of liberation against the Philistines. He had dismissed the bulk of his army after the encounter with the Ammonites, and he commanded only three units of picked men. But his son Jonathan, brave but impulsive, acted on his own initiative and singlehandedly assassinated the governor of Gibeah. Word quickly reached the Philistines: "The Hebrews have revolted." (1 Sam. 13:3)

Jonathan's act of political terrorism forced his father's hand. Saul summoned the demobilized soldiers of his army to rally at a place called Michmash. But the Philistines fielded a far more powerful force, and Saul's fresh muster began to slip out of camp. At last, Saul found himself with an army of only six hundred men, and he faced three thousand charioteers, six thousand cavalrymen, and "an army like the sand on the seashore in number." (1 Sam. 13:5) (AB) To strengthen the resolve of the few who remained under his command, Saul decided to make a blood offering to Yahweh.

His pious impulse, however, took a bad bounce. Samuel had already instructed the king to await his arrival so that the holy man himself could officiate over the solemn ritual of sacrifice. Saul was to wait seven days, but a full week passed and Samuel had not yet arrived. So the king, full of anxiety and out of patience, acted on his own initiative. "Bring the holocaust[22] and the communion offering to me!" he ordered. (1 Sam. 13:9) (AB) And then, just as the victims of sacrifice were going up in smoke on the altar of Yahweh, Samuel showed up.

"What have you done?" Samuel demanded in horror at the sight of the burnt-offering.

"When I saw that the army had begun to drift away from me and that you did not come in the appointed number of days and that the Philistines were gathering at Michmash," the young king burbled in a desperate effort at self-justification, "I said to myself, 'Now the Philistines will come down against me at Gilgal—but I have not entreated the Lord's favor!' So I took it upon myself to offer up the holocaust."

"Thou hast done foolishly," scolded Samuel. If Saul had only heeded the command of Yahweh as conveyed by Samuel, his kingdom would have lasted forever. "But now thy kingdom shall not continue," the old prophet warned. "The Lord hath sought him a man after his own heart, and the Lord hath appointed him to be prince over his people." (1 Sam. 13:13–14)

The reign of King Saul was already in sharp decline, and those who had so recently anointed him—God *and* Samuel—were ready to abandon him. A man of God's own choosing, a man after God's own heart, his identity as yet unrevealed, would replace him on the throne of Israel.

The man who would be king is David.

"SPARE NO ONE!"

Saul and his army triumphed over the Philistines in the battle of Michmash in spite of his botched sacrifice to Yahweh and the dire words of Samuel. Saul then continued to campaign successfully against all the traditional enemies of Israel, not only the Philistines but also the armies of Moab, Edom, and Ammon,[23] three kingdoms that lay along the eastern frontier of the land of Israel. He fought, too, against the feared and hated Amalekites, a nomadic tribe of the Judean desert that had harried the Israelites during their wanderings in the wilderness. But as it turned out, Saul's campaign against the Amalekites was the occasion for one final blunder, and Saul forfeited the favor of God once and for all.

Samuel had passed along to Saul some very specific and exceedingly bloodthirsty instructions on how to wage war against the Amalekites. "I am resolved to punish the Amalekites for what they did to Israel, how they attacked them on the way up from Egypt," God instructed Samuel to tell Saul. "Go now and fall upon the Amalekites and destroy them, and put their property under ban." (1 Sam. 15:2) (NEB) The "ban" to which the biblical text refers—the Hebrew word is *herem*—was "the grimmest of the rules of Israelite holy war,"[24] and the functional equivalent of what the modern world calls genocide, as Yahweh himself made plain. "Spare no one," Samuel commanded Saul in the name of God. "Put them all to death, men and women, children and babes in arms, herds and flocks, camels and asses." (1 Sam. 15:2) (NEB)

Saul raised a new army—the Bible reports that the army of six hundred now swelled to some two hundred thousand men—and marched against the Amalekites. He dutifully and mercilessly put to the sword all but one of the Amalekites. But he was not dutiful or merciless enough to please the cranky and demanding Yahweh, and God's patience finally ran out.

First Saul allowed the Kenites, a tribe of nomadic copper-smiths who lived in the same precinct, to flee into the wilderness before the killing of the Amalekites began in earnest. Moses had married a Kenite woman and fathered his two sons with her, and now Saul recalled that the Kenites had "showed kindness to all the children of Israel, when they came up out of Egypt." (1 Sam. 15:6)[25] Next Saul spared the life of the king of the Amalekites, apparently recognizing a kindred spirit in a fellow monarch. Finally he set aside "the best of the flock and the herd—the fat ones and the young ones—and every good thing" as a prize of war for himself and his victorious army. (1 Sam. 15:9) (AB)

God was enraged by Saul's refusal to obey his plain order to kill *every* living thing among the Amalekites—men, women, and children, and their cattle, too. "I repent of having made Saul king," God confided to his prophet, "because he has turned his back on me and has not obeyed my commands." (1 Sam. 15:10–11) (NEB)

Samuel trekked out to find Saul and deliver the news of God's displeasure. As it happened, the unsuspecting king had just finished building a monument to himself and offering some of the booty he had seized from the Amalekites as a sacrifice to Yahweh. Foolish and vain, Saul had apparently talked himself into believing that he had been compliant enough to keep Yahweh's favor.

"May you be blessed by Yahweh!" Saul hailed the prophet. "I have carried out Yahweh's command." (1 Sam. 15:13) (AB)

"What then is this bleating of sheep in my ears? Why do I hear the lowing of cattle?" demanded a sarcastic Samuel, pointedly reminding Saul that he was supposed to have slain the very cattle that now idled in the pens where they were being kept for the pleasure of the king and his men. "The Lord sent you with strict instructions to destroy that wicked nation, the Amalekites; you were to fight against them until you had wiped them out.

Why then did you not obey the Lord? Why did you pounce on the spoil and do what was wrong in the eyes of the Lord?" (1 Sam. 15:18–19) (NEB)

"I have sinned," cried Saul. "Please, forgive my offense and come back with me, and I will bow low to the Lord."

"I will not go back with you," said Samuel, "for you have rejected the Lord's command, and the Lord has rejected you as king over Israel." (1 Sam. 15:24–29)[26]

Abruptly turning his back on Saul, the old man started to stride away. Abject and desperate, Saul seized the old man's robe and struggled to hold him back. But Samuel's garment tore away in the king's hand.

Here, we may imagine, the two men stood in tense silence for one long moment, each one contemplating the torn strip of cloth that Saul now held in his hand.

"The Lord has torn the kingdom of Israel from your hand today," said the prophet to the king, "and will give it to another, a better man than you." (1 Sam. 15:28) (NEB)

THE LONG, UNHAPPY REIGN OF KING SAUL

The received text of the Book of Samuel is so confused and distorted at certain crucial points that we cannot say exactly how long Saul sat on the throne of ancient Israel. "Saul was a year old when he began to reign, and he reigned two years over Israel," reads the Masoretic Text (1 Sam. 13:1), but some versions of the Septuagint* replace these nonsensical assertions with the report that Saul was thirty years old when he was crowned and that he reigned for twenty-two years.[27] Other versions of the Bible simply censor out the questionable numbers and leave blanks in the text: "Saul was . . . years old when he began to reign," goes the same

---

*The Septuagint is a Greek translation of the Hebrew Bible that was undertaken as early as the third century B.C.E. and is the version of the Hebrew Bible used in Christian tradition.

passage in the New Jerusalem Bible, and "he reigned over Israel for . . . years."[28] At best, the reign of Saul is "a guess," according to Bible historian John Bright, who goes on to assert that Saul remained on the throne for at least a decade.[29]

What is perfectly clear from the biblical account, however, is that God did nothing to hasten Saul's exit from the stage of history. Long after God admitted his mistake in anointing Saul and vowed to remove him from the throne, Saul continued to reign as king of Israel, wage war against the Philistines, and keep his rivals for kingship, real or imagined, at bay. Some scholars read the biblical text to suggest that Saul, who is depicted by the royal chroniclers of the Davidic kings as a bungler and a madman, may actually have been far more beloved by the people of Israel than his successor.[30]

The open-eyed Bible reader may wonder out loud why God waited so long to execute his harsh judgment on Saul, and why he allowed the hated Philistines to do his work for him. If Saul had forfeited God's favor early in his reign, why was he allowed to remain on the throne for so long?

The pious explanation for the delay in dethroning Saul and the way it was finally carried out can be summed up in the simple affirmation of William Cowper: "God moves in a mysterious way His wonders to perform."[31] That rationale explains why, for example, the Bible honors the Persian emperor Cyrus II, who conquered Babylon and thus put an end to the exile of the Jewish people, with the exalted title of messiah: if it took a pagan monarch from far-off Persia to restore the Jews to their homeland, the prophet Isaiah concluded, he must have acted with the blessing of the God of Israel. (Isa. 45:1) And by the same reasoning, God must have charged the Philistines with the task of putting an end to the life and reign of Saul, at least according to the implicit theological assumptions of the Book of Samuel.

Quite a different explanation suggests itself to those who approach the Bible as a work of history and biography. The passages in which God is shown to withdraw his blessing from Saul can be understood as an effort to put a retroactive theological spin on the recorded facts of history. If the Court Historian and other early sources were simply telling the truth as they knew it, they apparently felt compelled to report Saul's successes as well as his failures. They confirmed that Saul, not David, was the first king of Israel, that Saul won the first victories against the enemies of Israel, and that his reign was a long if unhappy one.

Above all, it is possible to read the oldest portion of their writings as an account from which God is mostly and notably absent. At the heart of the Book of Samuel is a tense and suspenseful account of the struggle for power between Saul and the man who would succeed him on the throne. Each one is depicted as ambitious, ruthless, and willful, and each one resorts to politics, intrigue, and violence to determine who will wear the crown. Only in retrospect does the Bible assert that God took sides in the contest between Saul and his successor.

THE EXECUTIONER

As if to signal the bloody fate that awaited Saul, the Bible provides us with a strange and unsettling coda to Samuel's grim prophecy that his kingship would pass to a better man than he. Samuel, we are told, resolved to carry out the bloodthirsty order that Yahweh had given and Saul had refused to obey.

"Bring ye to me Agag the king of the Amalekites," ordered the old prophet, and the defeated king was dragged before him in chains.

"Surely," observed the condemned man, "the bitterness of death is at hand."

"As thy sword hath made women childless," replied Samuel, reminding the Amalekite king of the Israelite blood that had already been spilled, "so shall thy mother be childless among women."

And then Samuel—seer, holy man, and prophet of Yahweh— roused himself to do what the warrior-king Saul had failed to do. Seizing a weapon in his own two hands, Samuel hacked the king of the Amalekites into pieces. (1 Sam. 15:32–33)

Now Samuel and Saul went their separate ways, the prophet to the shrine of Yahweh at Ramah, the king to the fortified household at Gibeah that served as the family home and the royal palace.

"And Samuel never beheld Saul again to the day of his death." (1 Sam. 15:35)[32]

Before Samuel passed away, however, God called upon him to anoint one more man as king of Israel. According to the deeply mystical vision of the prophetic source, the question of kingship in ancient Israel was already decided, and the divine plan that began when God planted the seed of Samuel in the womb of a grieving woman was about to be fulfilled.

Chapter Three

"HE IS THE ONE"

*Now so soon as David appeared at his father's
summons—a lad of ruddy colour, with piercing
eyes and in other ways handsome—Samuel
said softly to himself: "This is he whom it has
pleased God to make king."*

— JOSEPHUS, *JEWISH ANTIQUITIES*

Samuel was old and weary and ready to die, but he was called by
God for one more effort at kingmaking. As the holy man sat
alone in Ramah, fretting over the fate of King Saul, God roused
him with a sharp rebuke.

"How long will you mourn for Saul, seeing I have rejected him
from being king over Israel?" complained God. "Fill your horn
with oil, and go! I am sending you to Jesse of Bethlehem, for I
have chosen myself a king among his sons."

"How can I go?" protested a timid Samuel, mindful that Saul
might have fallen out of favor with Yahweh but was still king of
Israel. "If Saul hears it, he will kill me!" (1 Sam. 16:1–2)[1]

God apparently regarded Samuel's fear of Saul as well founded,
and he went to the trouble of cooking up a cover story. "Take a
heifer with you and say, 'I have come to sacrifice to the Lord,' "
God instructed Samuel. "Then call Jesse to the sacrifice, and I will
tell you what you shall do. You will anoint the one I point out to
you." (1 Sam. 16:2–3)[2]

So Samuel, ever obedient to God, trudged out to Bethlehem

with a heifer in tow. When he was hailed by the apprehensive city elders—"Is your visit peaceful, O seer?" they asked in quailing voices—the old prophet stuck to the cover story: "It is to sacrifice to Yahweh I have come." Then Samuel issued a special invitation to the man called Jesse, and pointedly insisted that Jesse bring his sons along, too. (1 Sam. 16:4) (AB)

Jesse showed up in the company of seven strapping sons. So striking was Eliab, the eldest, so tall and handsome, that Samuel promptly concluded he must be the one whom Yahweh had chosen to be king. But God set him straight. "Do not look upon his appearance or his stature—I have rejected him!" he whispered to Samuel. "For it is not as a man sees that God sees: a man looks into the face, but God looks into the heart." (1 Sam. 16:7) (AB)

Then Jesse paraded the rest of his sons in front of the old prophet, but God rejected each one in turn.

"Yahweh has not chosen any of them," said Samuel in consternation. Then he addressed a question to Jesse: "Are these *all* of your children?"

"There is still the youngest," allowed Jesse. "He is tending the flock."

"Send and fetch him," ordered Samuel.

The last and youngest son, of course, was David.

"Arise!" said God to Samuel when David arrived. "Anoint him, for he is the one!" (1 Sam. 16:10–12)[3]

Then, as David's father and seven older brothers watched in amazement, the old prophet raised his horn and poured the holy oil over the young man's head.

Thus did the God of Israel correct his mistake in the choice of a king. To emphasize that divine charisma had been withdrawn from Saul and bestowed upon David, one of the biblical sources insisted that "the spirit of Yahweh came mightily upon David from that day forward" and, at precisely the same moment, "the spirit of Yahweh departed from Saul." (1 Sam. 16:1–14)[4] Here is yet another fingerprint of the biblical author who embraced the prophetic tradition and piously attributed each event in the history of ancient Israel to God's will.

Still, if the theological overlay is lifted off, the older and grittier passages of the Bible make it clear that divine will alone was not sufficient to remove Saul from the throne of Israel and install David in his place. David may suddenly have been filled with "the spirit of Yahweh," but his worldly qualities—his will to power, his guile and cunning, his military genius and his utter ruthlessness in bringing it to bear on his enemies—will turn out to be crucial to his ultimate success against Saul. In a real sense, David was the creator of his own kingship.

THE FAIRY-TALE PRINCE

David's coming has been subtly anticipated from the opening passages of the Bible, when God is shown to promise Abraham that the land of Israel will one day reach imperial dimensions, an expansion that will be achieved only under David's rule: "From the river of Egypt unto the great river, the river Euphrates." As we have seen, the Book of Genesis is salted with stories that anticipate the more squalid incidents of his reign—incest and seduction, rape and rebellion. But only now, as he steps forward to be anointed by Samuel, is David named and depicted in the biblical text.

Our first glimpse of David is meant to convince us that he was an even finer specimen than Saul, not only a charismatic figure who inspired love and loyalty but also "a comely person," a man of compelling physical beauty: "Ruddy and attractive, handsome to the eye and of good appearance." (1 Sam. 16:12, 18) (AB) David, in other words, is presented as the archetypal fairy-tale prince, and that is exactly how we are encouraged to see him in these opening passages of his life story.

The Bible may pause to praise his "good appearance," but we are never actually told what David looked like. The Hebrew word conventionally rendered as "ruddy" suggests to some translators that David was a redhead,[5] and the Hebrew phrase translated as "handsome to the eye" is understood by others to mean both that

David was pleasing to behold and that David himself had beautiful eyes.[6]

The passages that describe David's physical appearance represent yet another strand of biblical authorship in the tapestry that makes up his life story. As a rule, the Bible is candid about the physical flaws of even the most exalted men and women in the sacred history of Israel—the matriarch Leah, for example, suffered from poor eyesight, and Moses was a stutterer—but now and then a biblical figure suddenly looms larger than life. Bible critic Robert Alter characterizes the more fanciful episodes in the Bible as "folkloric embellishments,"[7] and the life story of David is richly decorated with heroic exploits and romantic encounters that owe more to folklore and fairy tale than to history *or* theology.

For example, Samuel's search for the new king suggests the story of Cinderella and the glass slipper. Even the number of sons that Samuel ruled out before finally reaching David seems slightly fanciful: seven is a richly symbolic number throughout the Bible, and seven sons is a common motif in folk traditions.[8] And the sense that we are being told a tall tale is heightened by the contradictions that can be teased out of the biblical text; the Book of Samuel, for example, describes David as the youngest of *eight* sons of Jesse (1 Sam. 16:10–11, 17:12), but Chronicles refers to him as the *seventh* son. (1 Chron. 2:13–15) Clearly the various biblical authors did not know or could not agree on something so basic as how many brothers David had, and they supplied their own resonant numbers.

The fact that David is both the youngest *and* the worthiest of the sons of Jesse, by the way, is another example of an ironic subtext that runs throughout the Hebrew Bible. The principle of primogeniture, by which the firstborn or eldest son is supposed to succeed to his father's title and property, began in distant antiquity, and the Bible formally embraces the superior rights of the eldest son in the elaborate rules of law that are embodied in the biblical text. Yet the Bible can be understood as a saga about the surprising success of *younger* sons: Isaac prevails over his older half brother, Ishmael; Jacob over his earlier-born twin, Esau; Joseph over all of his older brothers. Each of these stories may have been intended to prepare the Bible reader for the successes of David. When we finally encounter him, we are not at all surprised that the last-born David beats out his six or seven older brothers for the blessing of God.

"And the elder shall serve the younger," God revealed to Rebekah about the fate of her twin sons, Jacob and Esau. (Gen. 25:23) The same will be true of David and his son and successor, Solomon.

All of the earliest exploits of David are filled with the sparkle and glow of a fairy tale. Soon enough we will begin to see David as an ambitious tribal chieftain at war with a reigning king, an outlaw who shakes down the wealthiest of his countrymen for protection money, a mercenary who puts himself in service to Israel's worst enemy. All of these personal characteristics seem historical rather than fanciful precisely because they are so much at odds with what we expect of a fairy-tale prince. For now, however, the Bible engages in a kind of narrative backing and filling to provide David with a tale of origin that fits his political and theological stature: "As often happens with great men, popular imagination supplied charming legends," observes Bible commentator Robert H. Pfeiffer, who points out that the incidents of David's early life create "an atmosphere of make-believe and the illusion of a mirage."[9] Or, as another scholar once wrote of Homer, "he was given suitable lives, not a true one."[10]

MELANCHOLIA AND MUSIC THERAPY

The very first encounter between Saul and David was the direct result of a terrible affliction that God visited upon Saul. "The spirit of God" may have departed from Saul, but he was not merely abandoned to his lonely fate. Rather, "an evil spirit from Yahweh" was sent to haunt and terrorize the doomed king.

Exactly what afflicted Saul has been debated since antiquity. Josephus, a Jewish general and historian who authored a "rewritten Bible" in order to explain Jewish law and tradition to a readership in the Roman Empire, insisted that Saul was "beset by strange disorders and evil spirits which caused him . . . suffocation and strangling."[11] More recent Bible critics understand Saul's affliction as fits of melancholia and madness that we would describe today as mental illness.[12]

The biblical author, however, regarded Saul's dementia strictly as a sign of divine disfavor.[13] And so the courtiers of the king turned to the traditional cure for spirit possession—a cure that was "common to every ancient society confronted by demons"—in a desperate effort to relieve Saul's suffering. The cure was the sound of music,[14] and the courtiers urged that Saul submit to the Bible-era equivalent of music therapy.

"Let our lord command his servants to seek out a man who is a skillful player on the harp," they proposed, "so that when the evil spirit comes upon you, he shall play with his hand and you shall be well."[15]

"Provide me a man that can play well," Saul agreed, "and bring him to me."

"Behold, I have seen a son of Jesse the Bethlehemite who is skillful in playing," piped up one of the courtiers. Then, as if to make the ironic point that David was more richly favored by God than Saul himself, the well-meaning courtier checked off the other admirable entries on the résumé of the young lyre player: "A mighty man of valor, a man of war, skilled in speech, and handsome—the Lord is with him." (1 Sam. 16:16–18)[16]

Saul dispatched a messenger to Jesse with a royal decree: "Send me your son David!" Jesse dutifully summoned David from the fields where he was tending the sheep, provided him with an ass to ride, provisioned him with bread and wine and a kid from the flock, and then sent his youngest son to serve King Saul.

Saul, like so many other men and women to follow, was suddenly and powerfully smitten with love for David at the moment he laid eyes upon him. Then and there, King Saul resolved to name young David as his weapons bearer, a position of unique intimacy and importance in the royal household.

"David shall remain in my service," went the king's message to the young man's father, "for he has found favor in my eyes." (1 Sam. 16:22) (AB)

Yet even though "weapons bearer" was David's new job title, Saul cherished him for a gentler skill: David alone was capable of easing the madness that came upon the king at odd moments and reduced him to raw terror. "And it came to pass, when the evil spirit from God was upon Saul, that David took the harp, and played with his hand, and so Saul found relief, and it was well with him, and the evil spirit departed from him." (1 Sam. 16:14–23)[17]

DAVID AND GOLIATH

The Bible tells two very different stories about the first meeting of Saul and David. Although the passage that introduces David as the royal lyre player is regarded by some scholars as "the oldest tradition available to us,"[18] the second story is far more familiar and more enduring. Indeed, it is the most vivid moment in the remarkable life story of David as it is preserved in the Bible, and it has been imprinted indelibly on our imagination through thirty centuries of high art and popular culture. When we think of David, we think of this story.

"Now the Philistines gathered together their armies to battle," the biblical tale begins, "and there went out a champion from the camp of the Philistines, named Goliath." (1 Sam. 17:1, 4)

The Philistines arrayed themselves on one hillside, the Israelites on the facing hillside, and Goliath stood in the valley between the two opposing armies, the Vale of Elah (Valley of the Terebinth).

"Choose you a man, and let him come down to me," Goliath

challenged. "If he be able to fight with me and kill me, then we will be your servants—but if I prevail against him and kill him, then you will be our servants, and serve us!" (1 Sam. 17:8–9)

No fairy-tale villain was ever described in more fanciful terms—Goliath was a giant "whose height was six cubits and a span," that is, nearly ten feet tall, according to the Masoretic Text. (1 Sam. 17:4)[19] As if his sheer height and bulk were not intimidating enough, Goliath was outfitted in full armor, fashioned of bronze—a helmet on his head, a coat of mail over his huge torso, and a pair of greaves on his thick calves. A shield was carried by a bearer who walked ahead of him on the battlefield. Against the improvised weaponry of the Israelites, Goliath was armed with a sword, a spear, and a javelin, all of the same impressive scale. Indeed, the Bible notes that the wooden shaft of his weapon was as thick as a weaver's beam[20]—one of the emblematic details used to identify Goliath in the biblical text—and the spearhead alone weighed "six hundred shekels of iron," that is, fifteen pounds. (1 Sam. 17:7)

As for Saul and the army of Israel, the mere sight of Goliath shattered their will to stand up and fight, which was precisely the intent of the Philistines in sending the fearful giant out to the front line. Morning and night for forty days, Goliath appeared and issued the same challenge. "Give me a man," Goliath taunted, "that we may fight!" Not a man among the Israelites was brave enough to face him in single combat, and so the Philistine giant was free to stand in the open and abuse the Israelites. (1 Sam. 17:10)

Among the soldiers who cowered behind Saul in the ranks of the Israelite army were the three eldest sons of Jesse. David, too young to serve in the army, stayed at home to tend his father's sheep in the fields around Bethlehem, but now and then Jesse dispatched him to the front with provisions—parched corn and loaves of bread—for his brothers and cheeses as a gift to the captain under whom they served. So it was that David approached the front on that momentous day and saw for himself how Goliath taunted the men of Israel. And David saw, too, that not a man among them was willing to take up the challenge.

"What are you doing here?" shouted his eldest brother, Eliab, when he spotted David among the soldiers at the front—a flash of sibling rivalry that may have been intended as a reminder of the earlier biblical account of Joseph and his brothers.[21] "And who have you left to look after those few sheep in the wilderness? I know you, you impudent young rascal—you have only come to see the fighting." (1 Sam. 17:28) (NEB)

But young David was undaunted by the scolding, and he lingered in defiance of his big brother. Just as we would expect in a well-told fairy tale, David seemed to understand that the opportunity to make his fortune would be found not among the sheep on his father's country estate but here on the battlefield among kings and giants.

THE HEAD OF GOLIATH

Certain of the familiar details that the biblical author uses to dress up the tale of David and Goliath are consistent with what we know about warfare in ancient and primitive societies. Champions were sometimes selected to engage in ritual battle with each other as surrogates for their respective armies.[22] And, remarkable as it seems to us in an era of smart weapons and standoff warmaking, a courageous man with a sharp tongue might attempt to demoralize an enemy with verbal abuse before the fighting began in earnest. In fact, Goliath's taunts have been likened by anthropologist Raphael Patai to the Arab tradition of the *hija*, "an insulting poem or diatribe," by which an enemy was verbally battered in anticipation of battle. So the sight of Goliath strolling back and forth in front of the army of Israel, shouting insults and provocations in preparation for single combat with a champion, is not entirely fanciful.

Other details, however, betray the overheated imagination of the biblical storyteller. The inventory of Goliath's armor and armaments, for example, turns out to be an unlikely hodgepodge of ancient weaponry, some defensive and some offensive, none of it distinctively Philistine. Goliath's sword is described with a term that suggests a curved, scimitar-like weapon of Asiatic design, his helmet is Hittite in origin, and his "coat of mail" appears to be patterned after Egyptian scaled armor.[23] The biblical author obviously cared less for getting his facts straight than for making a suitable impression on his original audience—Goliath, readers are meant to understand, was such a formidable enemy that his defeat in battle by a shepherd boy would be, quite literally, a miracle.

Indeed, the fairy-tale quality of the biblical tale of David and Goliath always asserts itself. Young David, for example, is made to overhear the soldiers who gossip about the prizes that would be bestowed upon any man brave enough to take up Goliath's challenge and survive: "It shall surely be that the king will enrich the man who kills him with great riches, and will give him his daughter, and make his father's house free in Israel." (1 Sam. 17:25)[24] Thus inspired by the prospect of such good fortune—yet another common motif in folklore across history and throughout the world—David boldly approached King Saul and offered to do what no man in the army of Israel had been willing to do.

"Let no man's heart fail within him," said young David, adding a subtle taunt of his own to those uttered by Goliath. "Your servant will go and fight with this Philistine." (1 Sam. 17:32)

King Saul, giving no sign that he had ever seen David before, scoffed at the idea of a shepherd boy in single combat with the mightiest warrior in the Philistine army. "You are only a lad," Saul said, "and he has been a man of war from his youth." (1 Sam. 17:33)[25]

At this point in the biblical account, however, the storyteller's voice falls away and we hear from the biblical theologian. David delivers a richly symbolic sermon in response to Saul's highly practical observation. He is only a humble shepherd, David boasts of himself, but he has rescued the sheep of his father's flock from ravening lions and bears, and now he would rescue the flock of Israel from the predations of the Philistines. Notably, David mentions nothing about the reward that he might expect—riches, a royal princess, and tax relief. Rather, he presents himself as pious and wholly pure of motive. God alone—not a sense of patriotism or raw self-interest—now motivates David to take up Goliath's challenge.

"Your servant smote both the lion and the bear, and this uncircumcised Philistine shall be as one of them, seeing he has taunted the armies of the living God," young David is made to say. "Yahweh, who delivered me out of the paw of the lion, and out of the paw of the bear, will deliver me out of the hand of this Philistine."

"Go," says Saul, convinced by the boy's zealous words, "and Yahweh shall be with you." (1 Sam. 17:36–37)[26]

The Bible gives us a final poignant encounter between Saul and David in the moments before the fateful battle, a moment so intense and so intimate that the scene is still capable of surprising the modern reader. The king suddenly strips off his own armor and weaponry—a helmet of bronze, a coat of mail, a belt and sword—and he dresses young David in them. The gesture is tender and solicitous, as if to express the love that wells up in the king toward the shepherd who offered to save his crown. But young David is too slender to bear the weight of the armor and lacks the experience to wield a heavy sword in battle—the biblical text suggests that he staggered under the heavy trappings of war, unable to walk, much less to fight! So David slips out of Saul's armor, lays down the king's sword, and chooses a very different set of weapons—the wooden staff of a shepherd and the slingshot that a boy raised in the country might fashion for his own amusement and defense.

"And he took his staff in his hand, and chose him five smooth stones out of the wadi, and put them in the shepherd's pouch," the Bible records, "and his sling was in his hand, and he drew near to the Philistine." (1 Sam. 17:40)[27]

The sight of David—"this handsome lad," the biblical author

pauses to note once again, "with his ruddy cheeks and bright eyes" (1 Sam. 17:42) (NEB)—moved Goliath to scornful laughter.

"Am I a dog, that you come to me with a stick?" Goliath taunted. "Come on, and I will give your flesh to the birds and the beasts." (1 Sam. 17:44) (NEB)

Once again, David is given an ornate sermon to deliver to Goliath.

"You come to me with a sword, and with a spear, and with a javelin, but I come to you in the name of Yahweh Sabaoth, the God of the armies of Israel, whom you have taunted," David retorted, invoking Yahweh by his formal title as a god of war—a reference to years of wandering in the wilderness and the conquest of Canaan. "This day will Yahweh deliver you into my hand, and I will smite you, and take your head off, and I will give the carcasses of the hosts of the Philistines this day to the birds and the beasts, so that all the earth may know that there is a God in Israel." (1 Sam. 17:45–46)[28]

The Philistine, enraged by the bold words of the boy who stood before him, lurched forward with an upraised spear. If Goliath thought that the foolish lad would scamper away at his approach, he was wrong. David ran forward and stopped short of the towering warrior. The next moment is perhaps the single most iconic in all of the Bible, a scene that can be seen today in both the art of the high Renaissance and thirty-second television spots for fast-food chains.

And David put his hand in his bag, and took thence a stone, and slung it, and smote the Philistine in his forehead; and the stone sank into his forehead, and he fell upon his face to the earth. So David prevailed over the Philistine with a sling and with a stone.

(1 Sam. 17:49–50)

David ran up to the fallen warrior, seized his sword, and delivered a coup de grâce, neatly separating Goliath from his head. At the sight of their champion's decapitation, the Philistines broke and ran, and the Israelites rose to pursue them.

Today the phrase "David and Goliath" refers to any struggle of unequal adversaries in which the underdog comes out on top. But the tale carried a specifically theological meaning for the original readers of the Bible. The shepherd who finds favor in the eyes of God and prevails over kings and armies is one of the most persistent, and most poignant, images in the Hebrew Bible. The Patriarchs were restless nomads who followed their herds and flocks throughout the ancient Near East. Moses was tending his father-in-law's sheep in the wilderness of Midian when he was called by God to lead the Israelites out of slavery in Egypt and deliver them to the Promised Land. So the image of the shepherd takes on exalted meanings throughout the Bible: the good shepherd becomes a metaphor for a king and a redeemer. Indeed, the notion of a god or a king as a shepherd and the people as his flock can be found not only in the towering figures of Judeo-Christian tradition— Abraham, Moses, David, and Jesus—but throughout the pagan faiths of the ancient Near East.[29]

"That man alone can be a perfect king who is well skilled in the art of the shepherd," wrote Philo, a Jewish chronicler who, like Josephus, explained the theology of the Hebrew Bible to the Roman Empire, "for the business of a shepherd is a preparation for the office of a king to any one who is destined to preside over that most manageable of all flocks, mankind."[30]

WHO *REALLY* KILLED GOLIATH?

As familiar as the story of David and Goliath may be, a careful reading of the biblical text reveals that it is riddled with flaws and inconsistencies that are "in contradiction both with what goes before," as the founder of modern Bible scholarship, Julius Wellhausen, put it, "and with what follows."[31] Between the theological flourishes and the "folkloric embellishments," the hard facts of

David's life seem to disappear in the passages that are best known to Bible readers.

Thus, although the Book of Samuel first introduces David as "a mighty man of valor, a man of war" who has been summoned by Saul from the household of Jesse and recruited for a lifetime of royal service as a weapons bearer and court musician (1 Sam. 16:18), David makes his second appearance as a country bumpkin and a total stranger to King Saul. "Whose son is this lad?" asks the bewildered Saul when he encounters David on the battlefield, and his general, Abner, replies with equal bafflement: "As thy soul liveth, O king, I cannot tell." (1 Sam. 17:55)[32] Then Saul is shown to recruit David a second time for royal service: "And Saul took him that day, and would let him go no more home to his father's house." (1 Sam. 18:2)

Another example of the confusion in the biblical text involves what actually happened to the severed head of Goliath, a large and rather unwieldy relic of David's miraculous victory. David is described as bringing the head as a prize of war to Jerusalem (1 Sam. 17:54)—but at this point in the biblical narrative Jerusalem still belonged to the native-dwelling tribe called the Jebusites, and the day when David would conquer Jerusalem by force of arms was still many years off. (2 Sam. 5:6–9) By then, Goliath's head seems to have disappeared; only his sword is preserved in a shrine of Yahweh as a war trophy. (1 Sam. 21:10)

Finally, the biblical account of David's single most famous exploit is undermined by a troubling line of biblical verse in the Second Book of Samuel, where a man called Elhanan is credited with the slaying of Goliath in a campaign against the Philistines that took place when Saul was long dead and David was king of Israel. As if to confirm the identity of the Philistine warrior who was slain by Elhanan, the biblical author assures us that he is, in fact, referring to Goliath, "the staff of whose spear was like a weaver's beam." (2 Sam. 21:19)

Much ingenuity has been brought to bear in solving the mystery of who killed Goliath, and the effort begins within the pages of the Bible. The author of Chronicles, whose self-appointed mission was to clean up the ancient text of Samuel several centuries after it was composed, insisted that the Philistine warrior whom Elhanan fought and killed was the *brother* of the famous Goliath, "the staff of whose spear was like a weaver's beam," and not Goliath himself. (1 Chron. 20:5) The ancient rabbis proposed a neat solution to the problem by suggesting that Elhanan and David were one and the same man: "The two names belong to the same person: David was called Elhanan, 'he to whom God was gracious.' "[33]

Some modern scholars have sided with the pious commentators in suggesting that David and Elhanan were the same man, although their reasoning is slightly different—perhaps, they suggest, "David" is the throne name adopted by the man called Elhanan when he ascended to kingship, just as a cardinal of the Roman Catholic Church will take a new and honorific name when he is raised to the papacy.[34] Others are willing to entertain the idea that Elhanan *did* slay Goliath, and "the deed of a lesser warrior has been transferred to David" by some royal biographer who sought to glorify the king.[35]

A very simple and compelling solution is available. Here again, the various biblical sources—or was it the imagination of the bards and chroniclers who came long before the biblical authors?—may have decorated the life story of King David with fairy tales and folktales, if only to fill in the blanks in an otherwise rich biographical record. The human imagination abhors a vacuum, after all, and seeks to fill in the blanks in a life or a history. The same impulse appears to be at work, for example, in the biblical life story of Moses, whose miraculous survival in a little boat of reeds may have been borrowed intact from a far more ancient tale told about an Akkadian king of the third millennium B.C.E. All of these tales—the ones told about Moses and David and much else besides—were preserved and embellished by the authors and editors who compiled the law, legend, and lore of ancient Israel into the patchwork that we have learned to call *the* Bible.

This simple notion of how the Bible was composed, which encapsulates the consensus of the last hundred years or so of biblical scholarship, helps us to resolve the other flaws and contradictions in the story of David and Goliath. One of the traditional tales of ancient Israel suggested that Saul and David first encountered each other on the day the young man arrived at the royal household to serve as court musician. Another tale suggested that their first meeting took place on the field of battle on the day when David fought Goliath. And the biblical source who compiled the various tales of ancient Israel chose to include *both* versions in the sacred history of Israel.

Intriguingly, the very fact that the Bible preserves multiple and contradictory versions of the same incident has been cited by scholars as evidence that the Bible accurately and reliably preserves the oldest folk traditions of ancient Israel—the priests and scribes who compiled and edited the sacred texts of ancient Israel felt obliged to include *all* of the oldest traditions even when they conflicted with one another. Even more intriguing, however, is the suggestion that the inclusion of two inconsistent versions of the same story is really a wink and a nod from the biblical author, a way of signaling the reader that *both* versions may be purely fanciful. The biblical author generally provides a single version of an incident when he is confident that it happened just that way, or so goes one theory of the function of doublets in the biblical text. When two or three versions of the same incident are included, the author means to signal us that he is not quite sure how it happened or whether it happened at all.

THE LOVES OF DAVID

With the defeat of Goliath, David is poised to emerge from the mists of myth and legend and step into the full light of history. The fairy-tale prince will shortly be revealed as the flesh-and-blood figure who is a fugitive, an outlaw, a soldier of fortune, a traitor, and much else besides. But the romantic glow that surrounds young David in the opening passages of his biblical life story lingers for a few more moments. The biblical author pauses to describe a series of passionate encounters between David and two of the adult children of Saul—first Jonathan, the king's eldest son, and later Michal, the king's daughter. Each one, like Saul himself, falls suddenly and deeply in love with David. Indeed, the love of Michal for David is "the only instance in all biblical narrative in which we are explicitly told that a woman loves a man."[36]

The name David has been interpreted by some scholars to mean "darling" or "beloved" in biblical Hebrew,[37] and love at first sight is exactly what David seems to inspire in everyone who encounters him. King Saul has already fallen under his thrall. "And David came to Saul," the Bible says of their first encounter, "and he loved him greatly." (1 Sam. 16:21) Once David had distinguished himself in battle, he endeared himself to the rest of Saul's family—Jonathan and Michal, too, "loved David." (1 Sam. 18:20) The charismatic David inspired the same passion in the general populace, not only his own tribe but the whole of the twelve tribes: "All Israel and Judah loved David." (1 Sam. 18:16) But it is the love between David and Jonathan that is the most intriguing of all.

Jonathan was a man wholly governed by his appetites and passions. He took it upon himself to assassinate the Philistine governor of Gibeah, as we have already seen, and he risked his life in a nearly suicidal commando attack on a Philistine fortress. On yet another occasion, Jonathan impulsively gorged himself on honey on the very day when Saul had ordered the army of Israel to fast, and his impulse nearly cost him his life—his father had been ready to put him to death, and he was saved only because the army rallied to his support. (1 Sam. 14:24 ff.) Now we see another and still more provocative expression of Jonathan's impulsive nature: he was smitten with love for David on the very day that David smote Goliath.

> The soul of Jonathan was knit with the soul of David, and Jonathan loved him as his own soul.
>
> (1 Sam. 18:1)

Jonathan entered into a "covenant" with David, the Bible reveals, "because he loved him as his own soul." To seal the bond between them, Jonathan stripped off his robe and the rest of his apparel—"even to his sword, and to his bow, and to his girdle"—and tenderly draped them on the handsome young man. Significantly, Saul had tried to do much the same thing for David only moments earlier, but David had rejected the offer of armor and weaponry from Jonathan's father. Now, the gesture was accepted and fully reciprocated.

What's more, it was not only his armor but his more intimate garments, too, that Jonathan removed from his own body and placed upon David's. Such details have not escaped the attention of artists and writers over the centuries; D. H. Lawrence, for example, depicted David and Jonathan as stripping down to a "leather loin-strap" before tenderly exchanging their clothing. "If a man from the sheep dare love the King's son," Lawrence's David says to Jonathan, "then I love Jonathan."[38] The nature of the love between David and Jonathan is one of the most tantalizing mysteries of the biblical life story of David.

Exactly what does the biblical author mean when he writes that "the soul of Jonathan was knit with the soul of David"? A pious reading insists that the biblical text offers "the classic description of genuine unselfish love."[39] A more worldly reading suggests that the covenant (b'rit) between David and Jonathan was not a love pact but a political arrangement by which Jonathan, son of the reigning king, pledged his loyalty to the man who would ultimately replace his father on the throne of Israel.[40] But something more heartfelt and more carnal may have characterized the love of David and Jonathan, even if the Bible dares not speak its name.

"We have every reason to believe that a homosexual relationship existed," argues Tom Horner, Bible scholar and Episcopal priest, with rare bluntness. "Seminary professors must consider it, as well as must the diagnostician of ancient male love."[41]

Later, the biblical author will cast the first encounter between David and Jonathan in a new and tantalizing light when he allows us to hear David's famous confession of love for Jonathan, so full of provocative meanings for the modern reader. "Wonderful was thy love to me," David will sing of Jonathan from the pages of

Holy Writ, "passing the love of women." Indeed, as we shall see, some imaginative readers of the Bible wonder whether David captured the heart of Saul, too, and maybe even Goliath! For now, however, the biographer of David hastens on, and the account snaps into much sharper focus as Saul's "love" for David suddenly turns into fear and loathing.

AND DAVID HIS TEN THOUSANDS

King Saul, we are told, elevated young David to a position of command over his "men of war," and David was no less competent and effective in his campaigns against the Philistines than he had been in single combat against Goliath. "Whithersoever Saul sent him, he had good success," the Bible emphasizes, "and it was good in the sight of all the people, and also in the sight of Saul's servants." (1 Sam. 18:5) From the first moment of his new military career, David was hailed by the people of Israel as a war hero on the strength of his victory over Goliath.

> And it came to pass as they came, when David returned from the slaughter of the Philistine, that the women came out of all the cities of Israel, singing and dancing, to meet the king, with timbrels, with joy, and with three-stringed instruments.
>
> (1 Sam. 18:6)

The same words and phrases are used earlier in the Bible to describe how the prophetess Miriam and the women of Israel celebrated the victory of the Israelites over the army of Pharaoh at the Red Sea. "Sing ye to Yahweh, for he is highly exalted," called Miriam in a transport of ecstasy, and the women responded as they danced around her: "The horse and his rider hath he thrown into the sea." (Exod. 15:20–21)[42] Perhaps the parallels between the two passages should be understood as evidence that circle dances and call-and-response songs were the traditional way of celebrating a victory in ancient Israel. Or, more intriguingly, Miriam's song and dance may have been written into the Bible by the biblical author as yet another foreshadowing of David.

But the two victory celebrations are very different in one telling detail. The song that Miriam sang praised God alone for the victory, even to the exclusion of Moses, but the song that the women of Israel sang after the victory over Goliath praised only flesh-and-blood warriors and did not mention God at all.

> And the women sang one to another in their play, and said:
> Saul hath slain his thousands,
> And David his ten thousands.
>
> (1 Sam. 18:7)

Just as Yahweh was a jealous deity, the Bible reveals, Saul was a jealous king. His dementia did not prevent him from parsing out the words of the victory song with care; indeed, the moments of paranoia only sharpened his perceptions. Saul did not fail to understand the subtle sting of the song that the women of Israel sang: they praised young David above the king himself, and they credited him with martial prowess that exceeded Saul's own by tenfold. So it was that King Saul marked the handsome young war hero as a man to bury rather than to praise, and so it was that the fairy-tale prince, even at his moment of triumph, fell into disfavor with the king he was destined to succeed.

"They have ascribed to David ten thousands, and to me they have ascribed but thousands," Saul muttered in bitter complaint. "All he lacks is the kingdom." (1 Sam. 18:8)

Abruptly, the fairy-tale glow of the biblical life story of David is extinguished, and something much darker asserts itself. "Saul eyed David from that day and forward," the Bible reports (1 Sam. 18:9), and the two men entered into a long and deadly chess match that would leave only one of them alive.

Chapter Four

INNOCENT BLOOD

FIRST DEMON: *Oh! What I should find most delightful,*
after a sleepless night, is a sherbet of anise with a liqueur.
SEVENTH DEMON: *As for me, I should rather hear David sing.*
SAUL: *God of David! Help me!*

—ANDRÉ GIDE, *SAUL*

On the very day after Saul first heard the women of Israel sing David's praises, according to the rather woozy biblical chronology, the young war hero was back in the court of the old king, plucking the strings of his lyre in an effort to soothe the suffering Saul. Then, suddenly, King Saul rose to his feet, seized a spear, and hurled the weapon at David's head with one mighty thrust.

"I will pin David to the wall!" vowed Saul.

Only by sidestepping the spear and fleeing from the palace did the spry David escape with his life. The weapon hurtled past the spot where he had stood a moment before and planted itself deep in the far wall. (1 Sam. 18:10–11) (AB)

Here, Saul's murderous rage is traced by the biblical author to God himself: "An evil spirit from God came mightily upon Saul, and he raved in the midst of the house." Even in the grip of madness, Saul understood that God was siding with David: "Saul was afraid of David, because the Lord was with him, and was departed from Saul." (1 Sam. 18:10, 12) Elsewhere, however, the biblical text suggests a wholly human motive for the attempted murder of David: Saul had already marked David as his rival for kingship in the overheated tribal politics of ancient Israel, and "so Saul became David's constant enemy." (1 Sam. 18:29) (AB) A third explanation for Saul's failed attempt at homicide is provided by a psychiatric reading of the same text: Saul, after years of intermittent manic depression, had finally slipped into plain homicidal madness.

"There were spooky, tempestuous spells," David says in Joseph Heller's *God Knows*, "in which killing me was just about the only thing Saul had on his rabid and demented mind, the poor fucking nut."[1]

Whether it was politics or madness or a meddlesome God—or all three at once—that turned Saul's love for David into hatred, the biblical author now describes an exercise in political games-manship so convoluted, so treacherous, so deeply soaked in con-spiracy that it reminds us of Shakespeare's *Richard III* or, for that matter, Richard Condon's *The Manchurian Candidate*. What seems especially and uncannily modern in the biblical life story of David is the sense of "fires within fires"—Arthur Miller's phrase for the paranoia that suffused the Salem witch trials. Just as conspiracy theories shaped politics and popular culture in America in the lat-ter part of the twentieth century, the court history of King David as we find it in the Bible fairly crackles with the same tension and suspicion.

Even if Saul was mad, he was also wily, as we shall soon see for ourselves. The king devoted considerable effort and ingenuity to eliminating David as a rival without bloodying his own hands or alienating the considerable number of men and women in his lit-tle kingdom, including his own adult children, who had fallen so deeply in love with David. But David would prove wilier still.

THE HAND OF A KING'S DAUGHTER

Saul's first ploy was to remove David from the royal household by raising him to a yet higher rank in the army of Israel—"captain over a thousand" (1 Sam. 18:13)—and sending him off to fight the Philistines in the hope that he would be killed in action. Later, David would use the same ploy to murder a man whose wife he had seduced and impregnated. For David, the scheme worked perfectly. Not so for the unlucky Saul. David was victorious in battle again, the people of Israel came to love the war hero with even greater fervor, and Saul himself "lived in fear of him." (1 Sam. 18:14–16) (AB)

So Saul made an even more calculating move against David. "Behold my elder daughter Merab," he declared to David. "Her will I give you to wife—only be valiant for me, and fight the Lord's fight." Saul figured that David would throw himself even more recklessly into the next battle with the Philistines if a royal princess was the prize of war. "Let not my hand be upon him," Saul muttered to himself, "but let the hand of the Philistines be upon him." (1 Sam. 18:17)

David now revealed a gift that would turn out to be even more central to his survival than his physical courage or his soldierly skills—he was a master of political intrigue, and he quickly grasped the motive behind Saul's new gambit.

"Who am I, and what is my life," said David to Saul in words so modest that they approach sarcasm, "that I should be son-in-law to the king?" (1 Sam. 18:18)

So David foiled Saul's plot by declaring himself unworthy to wed a woman of royal blood, and Merab was married off to another man. But soon a new opportunity presented itself to Saul: the king learned that his youngest daughter, Michal, had fallen in love with David. Once again, Saul sought to use the hand of his daughter as a way of putting David in harm's way, and his new plan was far less subtle than the first one.

"Speak with David secretly," Saul ordered one of his courtiers, "and say: 'Behold, the king hath delight in thee, and all his servants love thee—now, therefore, be the king's son-in-law.' " (1 Sam. 18:22)

David was not fooled by the king's latest words of flattery and entreaty, and he turned aside the marriage proposal with yet another declaration of his own unworthiness. "Does it seem to you a trifling thing to offer oneself as a son-in-law to the king?" he demurred to the king's emissary. "Well, as for me, I am poor and humble." (1 Sam. 18:24) (AB)

When David's refusal was reported back to Saul, the king took the plea of poverty to mean that David was unable to come up with a suitable "bride-price" (*mohar*), the dowry-in-reverse that a suitor was expected to pay his future father-in-law in ancient Israel. So Saul extricated David from his predicament by proposing a bride-price that required only courage in battle, which David possessed in plenty, and not a hoard of gold.

"The king desires no bride-price," Saul's emissary now told David, "but a hundred foreskins of the Philistines." (1 Sam. 18:25)[2]

If David took up the grotesque challenge, or so Saul calculated, he would certainly die by the sword of some Philistine soldier who refused to be separated from his foreskin. What else, after all, would better motivate a man in battle than the integrity of his own genitalia! But, yet again, Saul badly underestimated the willful young David, who may have declined to marry Merab but suddenly burned with desire for her younger sister.

The Bible does not explain his sudden change of heart, but David now relished the idea of sitting at Saul's table as the son-in-law of the king. Indeed, some scholars suspect that marriage to the daughter of the reigning king had always been David's first objective in his long, patient, ruthless plan to put himself on the throne of Israel.[3] So despite his earlier protestations of humility and poverty, David sallied forth in search of foreskins as a bride-price for Michal. Ever the overachiever, David returned with *two* hundred severed Philistine foreskins, twice as many as Saul had demanded.[4]

Saul, foiled again, was forced to welcome the man he detested to the point of madness into the most intimate circles of his family and his court: "And Saul gave him Michal his daughter to wife." (1 Sam. 18:27) But Saul had not yet resigned himself to his fate, and his efforts to do away with David only grew more frantic.

If the Philistines would not do the job for him, vowed mad King Saul, he would find a way to do it himself even if it meant defying the will of God.

"And Saul saw and knew that the Lord was with David, and Michal loved him," the Bible sums up. "And Saul was yet more afraid of David, and Saul was David's constant enemy." (1 Sam. 18:28–29)

A GAME OF CHESS

Saul could do nothing right, and David could do nothing wrong, for the simple reason that God willed it to be so—it was only a matter of time before his divine plan to unseat Saul and replace him with David was revealed, and David was elevated to his rightful place on the throne of Israel. Such is the subtext of the Bible as it has come down to us, a set of texts that were repeatedly "corrected" by successive generations of editors and redactors to put a theological seal of approval on King David and the dynasty that continued to reign in Jerusalem for five centuries.

But the pious account of David's rise to power, as we have already seen, may be read as an overlay applied to the older texts, a theologically correct effort by some later biblical source to rewrite history by attributing every act of human will to the hand of an unseen and unheard God. The core of the biblical text is much grittier, much bloodier, and much more suspenseful, as if the author was never quite sure of how it would all turn out. At the heart of the biblical life story of David are two men—each ambitious, willful, and ruthless—contending with each other for a crown. An open-eyed reading of the Bible permits us to conclude that David prevailed over Saul because of his superior skills in war and politics, not because God willed it so.

Saul's next move against David, for example, was a blunder. The hapless king confided to Jonathan that he intended to kill David at the first opportunity. Saul even spoke openly of his murderous intent within the royal household, which included both

Jonathan and Michal, David's wife. Saul ought to have known that his plan would be communicated to David, and so it was that Jonathan, who "delighted much in David," sought David out, urged him to remain out of sight, and warned him: "Saul my father seeks to slay you." (1 Sam. 19: 1–2) In the meantime, while David absented himself from the court, Jonathan sought to change Saul's mind.

"Sir, do not wrong your servant David, because he has not wronged you," urged Jonathan. "His conduct toward you has been beyond reproach. Did he not take his life in his hands when he killed the Philistine, and the Lord won a great victory for Israel? You saw it, you shared in the rejoicing. Why should you commit a sin of innocent blood by putting David to death without cause?" (1 Sam. 19:4–5)[5]

Jonathan's open praise of David seemed to succeed in softening Saul's anger, if only momentarily, perhaps because of Jonathan's earnest and eloquent words, or because his own mood had lurched once again from murderous rage to impulsive affection, or because he had decided to feign a change of heart.

"As the Lord lives," King Saul vowed, "he shall not be put to death." (1 Sam. 19:6)

So Jonathan conducted David back to the court of Saul. David took up residence with his new wife and resumed his duties as an officer in the king's army. Once again he marched off to war, and once again he marched back in victory over the Philistines. "He slew them with a great slaughter," the Bible reports, "and they fled before him." (1 Sam. 19:8) But David's victories in battle only stoked King Saul's mad rage.

"TOMORROW YOU WILL BE A DEAD MAN"

Now Saul's mood swings were more frequent and more violent, and the Bible describes yet another ugly incident in the palace. As David strummed the lyre, "an evil spirit from the Lord" came upon Saul and the king tried to pin David to the wall with his spear. (1 Sam. 19:9) David fled to his own house and locked himself inside with Michal. Saul dispatched a few of his soldiers to David's house with instructions to wait out the night and strike him down as soon as he emerged in the morning.

Michal, like her brother Jonathan, loved David despite their father's hatred for him—and it was she who contrived to thwart the king's latest attempt to murder him. She spotted the royal hit men who were waiting in ambush, and she alerted her husband. "If you save not your life tonight," she warned him, "tomorrow you will be a dead man." (1 Sam. 19:11)[6]

Then she put an artful but effective plan into action. Opening a window on an upper floor of the house, she lowered David down to the ground and watched as he slipped away into the darkness. Then, taking one of the household gods that the biblical author calls teraphim,[7] she placed the figurine in David's bed, arranged a tangle of goat's hair at its head, and covered it with a blanket. To anyone who spied into the darkened room, she calculated, it would look as if David were asleep. Then she sent word to the guards waiting outside that David was ill and bedridden.

The ploy was sufficient to fool the king's men, and they reported to Saul that his son-in-law was confined to a sickbed. Now Saul, his mind sharpened to a cutting edge by sheer paranoia, saw his opportunity. "Bring him to me, bed and all," ordered Saul, "so that I may slay him myself." (1 Sam. 19:15)[8]

So the soldiers returned to David's house, forced their way into his bedroom, and discovered the ruse. But it was too late—David was long gone and beyond easy capture. Only Michal remained to face her father's rage when she presented herself at the palace.

"Why have you played a trick on me," demanded Saul, "and let my enemy get safe away?"

Michal's cool reply betrayed a truly impressive measure of chutzpah. "He said to me," she lied, " 'Help me to escape, or I will kill you.' " (1 Sam. 19:17) (NEB)[9]

CRAZY QUILT

The episode of Michal's deception and David's getaway is salted with allusions to other passages in the Bible, some subtle and some pointed, all of which demonstrate how the crazy quilt of biblical text is stitched together. As bits and pieces of what we now call the Bible were compiled and collated, revised and redacted, and sometimes even censored by generation after generation of authors and editors, people and events were combined and conflated. The same story was sometimes told two or three times, each in a slightly different version; words, phrases, and whole passages were sometimes cut out, put aside, and restored in a different place. As a result, here and there in the biblical text we are able to glimpse a landscape that is profoundly at odds with the official theology of the Bible.

Michal's ruse faintly echoes an incident in the Book of Genesis—and both episodes reveal something shocking about the casual use of idols by the ancient Israelites. According to the tale in Genesis, the patriarch Jacob fled from his father-in-law, Laban, in the company of the two daughters whom he had taken as his wives, Leah and Rachel. Laban's daughters carried off their father's teraphim, and Rachel contrived to hide the stolen idols from her pursuing father by secreting them in the cushions of a camel saddle that had been carried inside their tent for safekeeping, seating herself on the saddle, and then telling her father that she could not rise from her seat because she was menstruating. (Gen. 31:34–35)[10]

Both of these stories feature a household idol that is used by a daughter to deceive her father, although the teraph that Michal used to simulate a sleeping David was apparently a mask or a statue of life-size proportions rather than a statuette. What is especially shocking and revealing about the episode is the fact that, as late as the lifetime of David in the early tenth century B.C.E., the Israelites were still keeping and using idols despite the oft-stated loathing of Yahweh for polytheism and paganism.

"Thou shalt have no other gods before me" is the first of the

Ten Commandments, and the second commandment is even more specific: "Thou shalt not make unto thee a graven image, nor any manner of likeness, [and] thou shalt not bow down unto them, nor serve them, for I the Lord thy God am a jealous God." (Exod. 20:3–5) God threatens plague and famine and exile as punishment of the Israelites for the sin of idolatry, and he decrees a holy war to expunge idol-worship by the non-Israelites who claimed the Promised Land as their homeland.

> Ye shall surely destroy all the places, wherein the nations
> that ye are to dispossess served their gods, upon the high
> mountain, and upon the hills, and under every leafy tree.
> And ye shall break down their altars, and dash in pieces
> in their pillars, and burn their Asherim[11] with fire; and
> ye shall hew down the graven images of their gods; and ye
> shall destroy their name out of that place.
>
> (Deut. 12:2–3)

Yet the Book of Samuel preserves a casual reference to the presence of graven images in the home of an Israelite couple—and no ordinary couple at that! Somehow, the biblical author who tells the tale of how Michal aided and abetted David in his flight from King Saul found nothing worthy of comment in the fact that the household of the king's daughter was supplied with teraphim or that Michal was perfectly comfortable in using them to trick her father and conceal her husband's escape. Thus, a stray line of biblical text confirms that "God's anointed" was at liberty to indulge in religious practices that are explicitly condemned in later passages of the Bible.

Some of the priests and scribes who were the custodians of Holy Writ in ancient Israel were scandalized by such details, and they censored the older texts—the Book of Chronicles, for example, is a cleaned-up version of David's life story in which the incident of the teraphim, along with much else, is simply left out. For that reason, if Samuel had been lost or suppressed and only Chronicles had survived, we would know nothing of David's sins and scandals, including his casual attitude toward idolatry. But the Book of Samuel was apparently regarded as so ancient and so authentic that, here and elsewhere in the life story of David, the final editors of the Bible felt obliged to preserve the text in its entirety.

DERVISHES

"Now David fled, and escaped," the Bible continues, "and came to Samuel." (1 Sam. 19:18)

The reunion of David and Samuel, the man who had secretly anointed him as the future king of Israel, is the occasion for yet another surprise—the scene is a kind of theological burlesque, a healthy reminder that the Bible sometimes takes itself less seriously than we take it.

The old prophet listened with concern to David's account of "all that Saul had done to him," and the two of them fled together from Ramah to a hiding place among the shepherds who pitched their tents on the outskirts of the town.[12] But some nameless informer betrayed them to King Saul, who promptly dispatched his soldiers to find and arrest David. Upon their arrival at the hiding place, however, the king's men came upon Samuel and a band of his fellow seers, all of them in a trance-state of spiritual ecstasy and all them uttering words of prophecy. The sight of so many holy men in the grip of mystical frenzy turned out to be infectious. "The spirit of God was upon the messengers of Saul, and they also prophesied." (1 Sam. 19: 20)

Word reached Saul that his death squad had been lifted into a state of ecstasy, which rendered them useless as killers. So Saul sent a second band of assassins, and they, too, fell into impotent gibbering. Then Saul sent yet another squad of killers, and they succumbed to the same sorry fate. The exasperated king resolved to do the job himself.

Saul set out in search of David, first in the city of Ramah where Samuel lived, then on a windswept height overlooking

Ramah, and finally among the tents on the outskirts of Ramah where David and Samuel were hiding. There King Saul found the man he sought to kill—and there, too, Saul fell under the same spell that had turned each of his soldiers into a whirling dervish.

"And he stripped off his clothes," the Bible reports, "and he prophesied before Samuel, and lay down naked all that day and all that night." (1 Sam. 19:24)[13]

The biblical author is openly derisive of Saul at this moment, picturing the warrior-king as a pathetic figure, writhing on the ground and speaking in tongues, wholly enraptured by the "spirit of God" and thus rendered utterly harmless. Even as we laugh at Saul, however, we are reminded that God's ulterior motive is being served—God is shown to use the gift of prophecy as an affliction rather than a blessing, a device to torment Saul and spare David. "That is why men say," the Bible notes dryly, and perhaps with a touch of sarcasm, " 'Is Saul also among the prophets?' " (1 Sam. 19: 24)[14]

"THERE IS BUT A STEP BETWEEN ME AND DEATH"

Still, God plays only an incidental role in the story of David's survival. More often, David relies on his own skills or the favors extended to him by the men and women who are so smitten by him. After Michal arranged his escape from the king's men, for example, David sought out her brother Jonathan and recruited him for service as a spy in the court of King Saul—but not before venting his anger and resentment toward Saul.

"What have I done?" David demanded of Jonathan when they met secretly in the countryside. "What is my sin before your father that he seeks my life?" (1 Sam. 20:1)[15]

David may have been protesting a bit too much. After all, he had already been told by Samuel that he was designated to replace Saul as king of Israel, and he appears to have harbored his own driving ambition for the throne. But he had not yet gone into open insurrection against the king, and so he was still able to protest his innocence with credible fervor.

Jonathan's response, too, was either insincere or ignorant. Contrary to everything reported in the Bible so far, Jonathan denied that his father wanted to kill David.

"Behold, my father does nothing either great or small but that he discloses it to me," Jonathan reassured David. "Why should my father hide this thing from me? It is not so!" (1 Sam. 20:2)[16]

"Your father knows well that I have found favor in your eyes, and he has said to himself: 'Let not Jonathan know this,'" David replied. "But truly as the Lord lives, and as your soul lives, there is but a step between me and death." (1 Sam. 20:3)[17]

These ominous words silenced Jonathan's defense of his father, and now Jonathan spoke solicitously to his beloved friend. "What does your soul desire?" he asked tenderly, "that I should do it for you?" (1 Sam. 20:4)

David knew exactly what he wanted of Jonathan, and he proposed an elaborate intelligence-gathering mission back at the court. The next day was the feast of the new moon,[18] when David would be expected to join Saul at the king's table for a festival that would be celebrated with three days of feasting. Jonathan was to observe Saul's reaction to the absence of his son-in-law; if Saul happened to miss him, Jonathan would explain that David had asked permission to return to his hometown of Bethlehem to participate in a ritual of sacrifice with his own clan. Then Jonathan was to report the king's response to David.

"If he says: 'Well and good,' then I will have peace," David explained to Jonathan, "but if he flies into a rage, you will know that he is set on doing me wrong." (1 Sam. 20:7)[19]

Then David, as if fearful of an act of treachery and betrayal by Jonathan, reminded his old friend of the solemn pact of love and loyalty that they had already sealed between them. "Keep faith with me!" he demanded. "Kill me yourself if I am guilty. Why let me fall in your father's hands?" (1 Sam. 20:8)[20]

"God forbid!" Jonathan cried, and the two young men solemnly renewed their bond of love. "Jonathan pledged himself afresh to David because of his love for him," the Bible relates, "for he loved him as himself." (1 Sam. 20:9) (NEB)

So David slipped away and sought refuge in the wilderness, and Jonathan returned to his father's house to take his place at the feast. Saul himself sat in his customary place against the wall—a telling detail that suggests the king's hypervigilance. Next to him sat Abner, Saul's favorite general, and Jonathan was seated on the opposite side of the table.[21] David's place, of course, was empty.

On the first day of the festival, King Saul said nothing about David's empty place at the table, thinking that David must have absented himself because of a ritual impurity and that he would show up when he was fit to do so.[22] On the second day, however, Saul asked Jonathan why David had missed two days of feasting at the king's table. When Jonathan recited the agreed-upon alibi, his father erupted into anger.

"You son of perverse rebellion!" Saul railed at Jonathan, enraged that his son was making excuses for David and concluding that Jonathan had sided with his rival for the throne. "Do I not know that you have chosen the son of Jesse to your own shame and the shame of your mother?" (1 Sam. 20:30)[23]

At this moment, the enraged Saul seems less like a paranoid—or a man possessed by an "evil spirit from God"—than a watchful, calculating, and intuitive ruler. After all, Saul was correct in asserting that Jonathan, like Michal, had allied himself with David. And Saul voiced the plausible anxiety that had turned him against David in the first place: David sought the crown that Saul now wore, the crown that Jonathan would wear one day unless David took it away from him. And, as if Saul could not say the name aloud, he referred to David only by his Hebrew patronymic, "son of Jesse."

"I see how it will be!" railed the king. "As long as Jesse's son remains alive on earth, neither you nor your crown will be safe. Send at once and fetch him unto me—he deserves to die!" (1 Sam. 20:31)[24]

"Deserves to die! Why?" protested Jonathan. "What has he done?" (1 Sam. 20:32) (NEB)

Jonathan's defiant words stung Saul, who now realized that his son was an active coconspirator of the man he feared and hated most of all. And so Saul reenacted his earlier encounters with David, seizing his spear and menacing his own son, as the rest of the courtiers watched in silent horror.

Jonathan rose from the table, more in anger at the public humiliation he had endured than in fear of death, and stalked out of the banquet chamber. So indignant was the crown prince, the Bible pauses to note, that he ate nothing on the second day of banqueting, "for he was grieved for David, and because his father had put him to shame." (1 Sam. 20:34) The next morning, Jonathan slipped out of the palace and headed for the distant hilltop where David was hiding.

An elaborate plan had been devised by the two men during their earlier rendezvous, and Jonathan carried it out with almost ludicrous precision. He brought along a young servant and pretended to be out for a morning of archery practice in the countryside, shooting arrows into an empty field and then sending the lad to fetch them back. David, hiding behind a hillock within earshot of the rendezvous point, was supposed to listen for Jonathan's instructions to his servant. If Jonathan called out that the arrows had fallen short of where the lad stood, it would signify that Saul had calmed down and David might safely return to court; if, however, Jonathan told the boy that the arrows had fallen beyond where he stood, it would mean that Saul was still enraged and David must run for his life. As for the lad himself, he was apparently expected to stand in the middle of the target range and take his chances on Jonathan's prowess with bow and arrow!

"Look, the arrows are beyond you," Jonathan called to the servant, making sure to shout loudly enough for David to hear— the words signaled David that Saul was still aggrieved. Then Jonathan again addressed his servant, but these words, too, can be understood as an urgent message to David: "Hurry! No time to lose! Make haste!" (1 Sam. 20:38) (NEB)

Jonathan handed his bow and quiver to the lad and sent him back to town, thus raising a nagging question as to whether the whole unlikely charade was necessary. Then David, alerted to the fact that Saul was still seeking his life, emerged from his hiding place.

As soon as the lad was gone, David rose from behind the mound, and fell on his face to the ground, and bowed humbly three times. Then they kissed one another, and wept with one another, until David's grief was even greater than Jonathan's.

When the two men stepped back from their lingering embrace, Jonathan spoke one last time.

"Go in peace," Jonathan said to David at their moment of parting. "We have pledged each other in the name of Yahweh, who is witness forever between me and thee, and between my seed and thy seed, forever." (1 Sam. 20:41)[25]

Then the two men rose and departed. Jonathan headed back to the city and David turned toward the wilderness. Neither one knew with certainty whether they would ever embrace each other again.

Chapter Five

DESPERADO

We were a self-centered army without parade or gesture, devoted to freedom, the second of man's creeds, a purpose so ravenous that it devoured all our strength, a hope so transcendant that our earlier ambitions faded in its glare.
—T. E. LAWRENCE, SEVEN PILLARS OF WISDOM

David is now a fugitive on the run. He has lost everything—his lofty rank in the king's army, his seat at the king's table, and the bed that he once shared with the king's daughter. Homeless and despairing, he lacks every resource that he would need to escape the king who is determined to kill him—food, money, weapons, comrades. But he possesses an indomitable will to survive—and willpower, it turns out, will be enough.

UNCOMMON BREAD AND A GIANT'S SWORD

After David parted from Jonathan, he made his way to the town of Nob,[1] one of the many places in ancient Israel where one might find a shrine for the worship of Yahweh. He rousted the local priest, a man named Ahimelech, who trembled with fear at the sight of David, a man of high station who now resembled one of the vagrants, so wretched and yet so threatening in their desperate poverty, who could be seen along the byways of ancient Israel.

"Why art thou alone," the priest asked in a quavering voice, "and no man with thee?" (1 Sam. 21:2)

David, for the first but not the last time in the Bible, does something that he apparently found quite easy and convenient.

He lied.

"I am under orders from the king," David told the priest. "I was to let no one know about the mission on which he sent me or what these orders were." (1 Sam. 21:3)

David spoke with perfect self-assurance and more than a bit of blarney as he improvised a cover story. "When I took leave of my men, I told them to meet me in such and such a place," he explained to the priest, and then he abruptly demanded: "Now, what have you got? Let me have five loaves, or as many as you can find." (1 Sam. 21:3–4) (NEB)

Was David now reduced to begging a country priest for a handout? Or was he extorting provisions for himself—and perhaps a few cohorts who were traveling with him—with an oblique threat of violence?

"There is no common bread under my hand, but there is holy bread," Ahimelech allowed, "if only the young men have kept themselves from women." (1 Sam. 21:5)

The holy bread—or "shewbread," as it is known in the antique English of the King James Version—consisted of twelve specially prepared loaves made with pure wheat flour and sprinkled with frankincense. On the Sabbath, the fresh-baked loaves of holy bread were put on display in two neat rows on a table in the sanctuary as a symbolic offering to God. The old loaves that had been removed from the sanctuary could be eaten—but only by consecrated priests, according to the strict rules of the Book of Leviticus. (Lev. 24:5–9)

The priest of Nob was not brave enough to reject David's demand for the holy bread straightforwardly on the grounds that he was not a consecrated priest. Instead, he made only a feeble attempt to refuse him by invoking an entirely different rule from the Book of Deuteronomy, one that applied to the ancient military practice of maintaining ritual purity before battle. (Deut. 23:9–11)

David and his men, the priest was asserting, could not partake of the holy bread if they had been rendered unclean by sexual contact with women.

"Of a truth, women have been kept from us these three days," David declared. Then he continued to improvise in an effort to get his hands on the holy bread: "The young men's bodies have remained holy, and how much more will they be holy today." (1 Sam. 21:6)[2]

Thus appeased—or perhaps intimidated—the priest of Nob agreed to bend the rules by handing over the supply of holy bread.[3] But David was not yet satisfied.

"Have you a spear or a sword here at hand?" he demanded. "I have no weapon with me because the king's business was so urgent." (1 Sam. 21:9)[4]

Remarkably, the priest now disclosed that a rare and cherished weapon was stored in the shrine of Yahweh. "The sword of Goliath the Philistine, whom thou slew in the vale of Elah," Ahimelech told David. "Behold, it is here wrapped in a cloth behind the ephod." (1 Sam. 21:10)

EXCALIBUR

Here again is a tantalizing glimpse behind the curtain of theological correctness draped over the Bible by its later editors and redactors.

The "ephod" to which the priest of Nob so casually referred was some kind of ritual object on display in the shrine of Yahweh, an object large enough to conceal the gigantic sword of Goliath. Elsewhere in the Bible, the same term, "ephod," is used to identify a priestly garment, perhaps a brief linen tunic or even a loincloth. Here, however, and in a few other passages of the Bible (e.g., Judg. 8:27), the term may refer to a graven image of Yahweh, fashioned of gold, or perhaps the bejeweled case in which it was stored. Ironically, the deity who so detested idolatry may have been the object of idol-worship at some point in the early history of ancient Israel.[5]

The presence of Goliath's sword in the shrine of Yahweh is curious for another reason, too. When last noted in the biblical narrative, the sword had been stashed in David's tent. (1 Sam. 17:24) Now, by remarkable coincidence—or was it the hand of God?—David happened upon the sword that he had taken from Goliath at the fateful battle that had set him on the path toward power.

"If thou wilt take that sword, take it," the priest said, "for there is no other weapon here." (1 Sam. 21:10)[6]

"There is no sword like it," David said, knowing better than anyone else how the weapon had been bloodied in battle. "Give it to me." (1 Sam. 21:10)

Thus armed with an Excalibur of his own, and provisioned with holy bread, David left the priest of Nob in peace. An agent of King Saul, a man named Doeg from the neighboring land of Edom, had observed David's encounter with the priest (1 Sam. 21:7), but Doeg did nothing to stop him. So David slipped back into the wilderness and continued to elude the men whom Saul sent in search of him. Still, he found himself harried out of Israel—or, rather, the fraction of Israel over which Saul actually enjoyed sovereignty. Much of the country was under occupation by the Philistines, and it is a measure of David's pragmatism that he now headed toward Gath, the hometown of Goliath and one of the five cities of ancient Israel that were under the occupation and rule of the Philistines.

If the king of Israel sought to kill him, David would not hesitate to place himself under the protection and at the service of Israel's old and bitter enemy.

"AM I SHORT OF MADMEN?"

According to one of the most bizarre tales in all of the Bible, "the sons of God"—or, more literally, "the sons of the *gods*" (*b'nai Elohim*)[7]—descended from heaven soon after the creation of the world and bedded the women who struck their fancy, thus siring a race of giants known as the Nephilim. (Gen. 6:2–4) Their descendants still lived in the land of Canaan when, countless centuries later, Moses sent spies ahead of the conquering army of Israel. "All the people that we saw in it are men of great stature," went the "evil report" of the defeatists, "and we were in our own sight as grasshoppers, and so we were in their sight." (Num. 13:32, 33) When the Israelites fought their way into Canaan under the generalship of Joshua, all but a few of these giants were exterminated. "Only in Gaza, in Gath, and in Ashdod did some remain," goes a brief report in the Book of Joshua, naming three of the five cities of Israel that were still dominated by the Philistines even after the conquest of Canaan. (Josh. 11:22)

David's link to Gath began when he defeated Goliath, whom the Bible depicts as not just a man of impressive stature but the distant offspring of the sexual union between gods and mortals.[8] Now David presented himself to the Philistine overlord who ruled Gath, a king named Achish, and pleaded for refuge against Saul. But David discovered that, even among the Philistines, he was regarded as a dangerous young man.

"Is not this David the king of the land?" the wary counselors of Achish warned their king, claiming for David a crown that was not yet his own and urging Achish, like Saul, to see David as a threat to his throne. "Did they not sing to one another of him in dances," they continued, stoking the king's fears, "saying: 'Saul hath slain his thousands, and David his ten thousands?' " (1 Sam. 21:12)

The peril in these whispered words was not lost on David, who "laid up these words in his heart and was sore afraid of Achish the King of Gath." (1 Sam. 21:19) And so David, always daring and quick-witted but never more so than when in danger, contrived to put the Philistines at ease.

And he changed his demeanor before them, and feigned himself mad in their hands, and scrabbled on the doors of the gate, and let his spittle fall down upon his beard.

(1 Sam. 21:13)

So David feigned lunacy to save his own life. Here is a moment that strikes Bible scholars as something new and remarkable—where else in the writings of the ancient world do we find a sacred history in which a God-chosen king turns himself into a drooling and gibbering idiot? Indeed, the scene depicts David as not merely undignified but cowardly. Yet David's ploy works and the king of Gath is utterly fooled.

"The man is mad!" complained Achish. "Am I short of madmen that you bring this one to plague me?" (1 Sam. 21:16) (NEB) So David was escorted out of the court to the king's dismissive cry—"Must I have this fellow in my house?"—and hustled out of Gath. (1 Sam. 21:16) (NEB) David was still on the run, but now he did not seek refuge amid the familiar comforts of a royal court. Rather, he sought refuge in a cave, more like a runaway slave than a man who would be king.[9]

DESPERADOES

Word of David's desperate predicament—and the whereabouts of the cave in which he had barricaded himself—reached his tribal homeland, the land of Judah. Not only his brothers and the rest of his family but hundreds of men from the tribe of Judah sought out David's stronghold among the hills near Adullam.[10] But David quickly saw that if he was no longer alone, he was also no longer in the company of kings.

> And every one that was in distress, and every one that was in debt, and every one that was discontented, gathered themselves unto him; and he became captain over them; and there were with him about four hundred men.
> (1 Sam. 22:2)

"Flotsam, ruffians, and desperadoes" is how John Bright describes the men who rallied to David, and "bandit chief" is the title he bestows upon David himself. Indeed, the blunt text of the Book of Samuel provokes the suspicion that the real David may have been someone far less exalted than the man we find in the pages of Chronicles or the Psalms.[11] About the best case that can be made for David during his fugitive years is that he was a soldier of fortune who relied on guerrilla tactics to survive and prevail against the reigning king of Israel.

TRIBES

One member of David's outlaw band was a man who is identified in the Bible as a prophet but seems to have been a master of guerrilla warfare. Like Mao Tse-tung and Che Guevara and Ho Chi Minh, the prophet Gad understood that even the strongest urban fortress is always at risk of being surrounded and cut off by a superior force, and thus a guerrilla army is always safest when it is on the move through the countryside.

"Abide thee not in the stronghold—depart and get thee into the land of Judah," Gad counseled. (1 Sam. 22:5)

David followed Gad's advice, moving himself and his band of partisans into the traditional homeland of the tribe of Judah, where he hoped to find support among his own people. Saul may have been elected to reign as the first king of the tribal confederation called Israel, but the Bible suggests that the loyalties to family, clan, and tribe were far older and far stronger than any sense of citizenship in the newfangled monarchy.

Saul himself played on the old tribal loyalties in his pursuit of David. As he presided over a council of war at his stronghold in Gibeah—sitting, spear in hand, under a tamarisk tree—Saul sought to convince his counselors and captains, all of them Benjaminites, that David, a man from the tribe of Judah, was their enemy, too. Surely, Saul suggested, David would favor Judah over Benjamin if he succeeded in defeating Saul and seizing the kingship.

"Hear now, ye Benjaminites, will the son of Jesse give every one of you fields and vineyards?" Saul demanded, still unable to speak David's name aloud and using only his patronymic. "Will he make you all captains?" (1 Sam. 22:7)

Even now, when he so desperately needed his clansmen's solidarity, Saul could not control his raging paranoia. Somewhere out there, at this very moment, David lay in wait for him—or so the king complained—but Saul would be forced to face him alone. "All of you have conspired against me," Saul railed. "There was none that disclosed it to me when my son made a league with the son of Jesse, and there is none of you that is sorry for me, or disclosed to me that my son has stirred up my servant against me." (1 Sam. 22:8)

Only one man spoke up—Doeg the Edomite, the man who had spotted David in conversation with the priest Ahimelech in the shrine of Yahweh at Nob. Perhaps glancing at the spear in Saul's hand, he sought to prove his loyalty to the king.

"I saw the son of Jesse coming to Nob, to Ahimelech," the man reported, using the king's oblique term of reference for David. "And he inquired of Yahweh for him, and gave him victuals, and gave him the sword of Goliath the Philistine." (1 Sam. 22:10)[12]

Doeg, of course, was embellishing the truth. Nowhere in the Bible does it say that the priest of Nob "inquired of Yahweh"—a phrase that refers to the practice of using tools of divination to seek guidance from on high and suggests that Ahimelech had assisted David by appealing to God on his behalf.[13] Perhaps Doeg was seeking to make Ahimelech appear as guilty as possible in order to distract Saul from the fact that Doeg had not disclosed a vital bit of intelligence sooner. If so, it worked. Saul was swept up in a new murderous frenzy, and he now turned his full attention to Ahimelech.

A DAY OF SLAUGHTER

King Saul summoned all of the priests of Yahweh who served in the sanctuary at Nob—Ahimelech and the rest of his family among them—to the royal court at Gibeah. Now it was their turn to endure the king's angry interrogation.

"Why have you conspired against me, you and the son of Jesse?" Saul ranted, accusing Ahimelech of treason. "You gave him bread, and a sword, and inquired of God for him, that he should rise against me, to lie in wait." (1 Sam. 22:13)[14]

"Who among all thy servants is so trusted as David, who is the king's son-in-law and the commander of thy bodyguard and is honorable in thy house?" answered the priest, reasonably enough—after all, who would have turned away the king's son-in-law? And as for seeking a divine oracle on David's behalf, Ahimelech exclaimed: "Be it far from me! Let not the king impute anything unto his servant, nor to all the house of my father, for thy servant knoweth nothing of all this!" (1 Sam. 22:14–15)[15]

Saul did not deign to argue with the accused priest. Rather, he simply pronounced Ahimelech guilty and sentenced him to death. "You will surely die, Ahimelech—you, and all of your father's house." (1 Sam. 22:16)[16]

Saul ordered the execution then and there: "Turn, and slay the priests of Yahweh!" he commanded the palace guard. Then, as if understanding that it would take more than an impulsive command to convince the soldiers to slay an ordained priest, Saul explained why the priests must die: "Because their hand also is with David, and because they knew that he fled, and did not disclose it to me." (1 Sam. 22:17)[17]

The soldiers, however, did not heed the king's bloody order. They stood in silence; their weapons remained at their sides. Saul, further maddened by their insolence and insubordination, looked in panic around the court. We can imagine he saw only blank faces, and his paranoia must have sharpened as he calculated that all of them—his courtiers, his palace guard, his own tribesmen—had sided with young David.

And then his eye fell on the man who had been willing to inform on Ahimelech, a foreigner who would not be so fussy about spilling the blood of men who were consecrated to a lifetime of service to the God of Israel.

"Turn thou," Saul said to Doeg, "and strike down the priests!" (1 Sam. 22:18)[18]

Unlike the men of Saul's own tribe, the Edomite did not hesitate to carry out the king's order—the informer-turned-executioner fell upon the priests and "slew on that day fourscore and five persons that did wear a linen ephod."[19] But the carnage did not end there: Saul ordered his death squad to descend on Nob itself. "And he smote Nob, the city of the priests, with the edge of the sword, both men and women, children and sucklings, and oxen and asses and sheep." (1 Sam. 22:19)[20]

Men in power have always resorted to terror and even mass murder to discourage a local populace from sheltering an enemy and to make an example of those who are suspected of doing so. Nob is only the first in a list that includes Lidice, the Czech town that Nazi Germany eradicated as a punishment for harboring partisans in World War II; Deir Yassin, the Arab village that was terrorized by the Irgun and the Stern Gang in the War of Independence that brought the modern state of Israel into existence; and My Lai, the Vietnamese village where civilians were slaughtered out of fear and hatred of the Vietcong. Saul may have been mad, but the message that he sent to the rest of Israel by ordering the murder of the men, women, and children of Nob was cool and calculated: anyone who trafficked with David, however innocently, was at risk of death.

One priest managed to escape the mass murder. His name was Abiathar, and he was one of Ahimelech's sons. Significantly, Abiathar managed to carry off an ephod—not a priestly garment but a tool of divination. The Bible does not disclose how he eluded the sword on that day of slaughter, but we know where he sought refuge from Saul: "Abiathar escaped, and fled after David, and Abiathar told David that Saul had slain the priests of Yahweh." (1 Sam. 22:21)

David listened to Abiathar's report of the massacre and re-called his visit to the shrine at Nob. "I knew on that day, when Doeg the Edomite was there, that he would surely tell Saul," David said, blaming himself for bringing down Saul's wrath on the innocent men, women, and children of the town. "I have brought about the death of all the persons of your father's house." (1 Sam. 22:22)

David, as we shall come to see, was capable of even greater acts of violence. Yet he was also susceptible to self-reproach and compassion. Indeed, a constant state of tension between ruthlessness and sentimentality was basic to his character. Now he was moved to the expression of concern, so eloquent and so heartfelt, that seemed to be his first impulse at moments of loss or danger.

"Abide thou with me, fear not," said David to Abiathar, offering the fugitive priest a place in his guerrilla army, "for he that seeketh my life seeketh thy life; for with me thou shalt be in safeguard." (1 Sam. 22:23)

A GREAT SLAUGHTER

David's little army of outcasts and malcontents increased as new men sought out his latest encampment and put themselves under his command, but the head count never exceeded six hundred. To sustain themselves in the wilderness, David and his men raided farms and towns and carried off food and wine and livestock, extorted protection money from the wealthier landowners, and now and then earned a few shekels as mercenaries for the Philistines. As it turned out, David was skilled in the brutal craft of banditry.

On one occasion, David led his men on a raid at a place called Keilah, a fortified town northwest of Hebron and south of Adullam. Significantly, Keilah was located within the boundaries of Judah, and thus its townspeople were fellow members of the tribe of Judah. The Philistines were reported to be terrorizing the local populace and stealing the wheat harvest right off the threshing-floors. David's men feared attacking a place deep inside the territory dominated by the Philistines, but he assured them that God had ordered the mission—and besides, the prospect of plunder made the effort worth the risk. So the Philistines were put to "a great slaughter," and David and his men "brought away their cattle," a crucial prize of war for an army that had to feed itself on what it was able to steal or extort from the populace. (1 Sam 23:2, 3, 5)

One of the biblical sources, seeking to put a favorable spin on the facts, insists that the raid on Keilah was an action against the Philistines rather than the townspeople—"Thus David *liberated* the inhabitants of Keilah" (1 Sam. 23:5) (AB)[21]—but the unmistakable subtext points to something less praiseworthy. If David regarded himself as the liberator of the people of Keilah, they felt no gratitude. Indeed, a close reading of the biblical passage reveals that men and women throughout the land of Israel—and even his fellow tribesmen in the land of Judah—regarded David with suspicion and sometimes even hatred.

David soon learned that Saul hoped to capture him by putting Keilah under siege. "God has delivered him into my hands," Saul exulted. "For he has walked into a trap by entering a walled town with gates and bars." (1 Sam. 23:7) (NEB) When told that Saul and his army were approaching, David resorted to the use of an ephod as a tool of divination, anxiously seeking an oracle from God.

"Will the men of Keilah deliver me up into his hand?" David asked.

"They will deliver thee up," the ephod confirmed. (1 Sam. 23:12–13)[22]

Thus warned of the treachery of the townspeople he had just "liberated"—and perhaps reminded by the guerrilla-prophet Gad that a walled town can be a deadly place—David and his men "arose and departed" from Keilah and slipped into the wilderness.

"And David abode in the wilderness and remained in the hill-country," the Bible reports. "And Saul sought him every day, but God delivered him not into Saul's hand." (1 Sam. 23:14)[23]

SHAKEDOWN ARTIST

From a new encampment in the Judean wilderness, within striking distance of the village of Carmel, David sent ten young men to the estate of a rich Calebite named Nabal.[24] "The man was very great, and he had three thousand sheep, and a thousand goats," the Bible notes, and David sized him up as a likely benefactor. The modern term for what David had in mind is "shakedown."

David carefully instructed his men on what to say to Nabal: David and his army had come across the rich man's flocks and herds in the wilderness, but they had taken none of his livestock and they had done no harm to the shepherds who tended them. The biblical text is heavy with the unspoken threat of violence— after all, why send *ten* men to deliver the message, and why deliver such a message at all? And, lest Nabal miss the point, David directed the young men to ask the rich man to show his gratitude for what David did *not* do to his sheep and his shepherds. (1 Sam. 25:2–8)

"All hail! and peace be both unto thee, and peace be to thy house, and peace be unto all that thou hast," one of the young men addressed Nabal in ornately respectful words, perhaps resting his hand ever so casually on the hilt of his sword. "For we come on a good day—give, I pray thee, whatsoever cometh to thy hand, unto thy servants, and to thy son David." (1 Sam. 25:8–9)

One phrase that fell from the lips of the young men—"For we come on a good day"—may have been a reference to the sheep-shearing festival then in progress on Nabal's estate, but the words might be taken as an unspoken threat: "You should see us on a bad day." Yet Nabal, whose name means "foolish" or "churlish," rejected their demand with bold but foolhardy contempt.[25]

"Who is David?" Nabal replied dismissively. "In these days, every slave who breaks away from his master sets himself up as a chief! Shall I then take my bread, and my wine, and the meat I provided for my shearers and give it to men who come from I know not where?" (1 Sam. 25:10–11)[26]

When these defiant words were reported back to David, he issued an order to his army—"Let every man strap on his sword!"— and four hundred of them set off in the direction of Nabal's estate. As they approached their target, David complained out loud about Nabal's appalling ingratitude and scolded himself for failing to take the flocks and herds when he first had the chance.

"He has repaid me evil for good," muttered David, as if to convince himself he was justified in carrying out the rough justice that he intended to visit on Nabal and his household.

The Bible depicts David as a man acting out of righteous necessity. God had anointed him to be king but had done nothing at all to put a crown on his head. Instead, David had been forced into flight by King Saul, and he was responsible for the sustenance of his men and their camp followers, including women and children. Nabal was a rich man with far more than he needed, and they were desperate fugitives who survived on what they were able to scare up.

At this moment, David appears as a kind of Robin Hood, or a Che Guevara. If the churlish Nabal will not give him what he needs to feed his people, David reasons, then he has no choice but to take it by force of arms. And it is a measure of David's charisma that the Bible reader is invited to see him as a heroic figure even when he is acting brutally and criminally. Even on a purely theological plane, David is depicted as a wholly sympathetic figure— after all, he did not *ask* to be anointed as the future king of Israel, and now he has been left to his own devices. To the biblical author who stamped a divine seal of approval on the life story of David, the ends always justify the means: "And David had great success in all his ways, and the Lord was with him." (1 Sam. 18:14)

Still, the bloodcurdling threat that fell from David's lips seems more appropriate to a bandit or terrorist than a man on a mission from God.

"God do the same thing to me and more," vowed David as he and his army approached the estate of Nabal, "if I leave alive until morning a single one who pisses against the wall!" (1 Sam. 25:22)[27]

HAREM

At least one person in the household was quick to grasp the point of the impending visit by David and his men—Nabal's wife, Abigail, a woman "of good understanding, and of a beautiful form." Without telling Nabal, she ordered a gift-offering to be prepared for the approaching raiders: "two hundred loaves, and two skins of wine, and five sheep, slaughtered and dressed, and five measures of parched corn, and a hundred clusters of raisins, and two hundred cakes of figs," all of it to be loaded on asses and sent ahead as if to encourage David and his men to just take the stuff and go away. (1 Sam. 25:18)[28]

Perhaps to mitigate the horror of the threatened atrocity, one of Nabal's shepherds is made to deliver an address justifying David's demands. "David and his men were very good to us, and we were not hurt, neither did we miss anything, when we were in the open country," the shepherd told his mistress, "they were as good as a wall around us, night and day, while we were minding the flocks." The real evildoer was Nabal, who "flew upon" David's men when they attempted to "salute our master" and solicit some humble gift in return for their protection. If David now approached the estate with evil intentions toward Nabal and his household, the fault lay with Nabal. (1 Sam. 25:14–17)[29]

"He is such a good-for-nothing," the shepherd complained, "that it is no good talking to him." (1 Sam. 25:17) (NEB)

Abigail's curiosity about David seems to have outweighed any fear she may have felt, and so she mounted an ass and rode out to greet him with the bounty she had prepared. Surely she already knew of his considerable reputation as a war hero and high-ranking officer in the king's army—ruddy, handsome, and fit—who had turned to banditry. There is something of Lady Chatterley in Abigail, who finds a dashing young outlaw more intriguing than her rich but stingy and ill-tempered husband. The fact that one of her servants felt free to refer to her husband as a "good-for-nothing" suggests that Nabal was held in contempt by everyone in his household. So the Bible allows us to understand that Abigail was already inclined to blame her husband and side with the outlaw. At first sight of David, she hastened toward him, alighted from her ass, and bowed her forehead to the ground in greeting.

"Let thine handmaid, I pray thee, speak in thine ears," pleaded Abigail in phrases that are both formal and yet flirtatious, "and hear thou the words of thy handmaid." (1 Sam. 25:24)

Abigail unburdened herself to David, calling her husband a "base fellow" and blaming him for insulting David. "Nabal is his name, and churlishness is with him," Abigail said. She was careful to let David know that *she* had not received the ten young men he had sent to their estate, as if to suggest that she would have shown generosity from the first.

"And now this present which thy servant hath brought unto my lord," she said, referring to the bounty she had prepared, "let it be given unto the young men that follow my lord." (1 Sam. 25:27)

Abigail now delivers a sermon that was surely scripted by one of the more pious biblical sources and inserted into the text to prefigure David's rise to kingship and, at the same time, to soften some of his rough edges. If only David would refrain from the slaughter he intended to carry out—"withhold thee from blood-guiltiness," as Abigail put it—and if, instead, he used his sword in "the battles of the Lord," he would be rewarded with "a sure house" and he would be raised to be "prince over Israel." The soul of David would be "bound in the bundle of life with the Lord thy God," she predicted, and "the souls of thine enemies shall he sling out, as from the hollow of a sling"—a flattering allusion to the humble weapon that David had used to defeat Goliath. (1 Sam. 25:25–31)

"And when Yahweh shall have dealt well with my lord," concluded Abigail, calling his attention back to her, "then remember thy handmaid." (1 Sam. 25:31)[30]

The florid language of Abigail's address to David cannot quite conceal the romantic and even erotic undercurrents of their encounter—and it seems that David was smitten, too.

"Blessed be Yahweh, God of Israel, who sent you to meet me this day," he replied, still speaking in the coarse tongue of a bandit rather than the exalted phrases of a psalmist. "If you had not come so quickly to meet me, not a single one of Nabal's household who pisses against a wall would have been left alive by morning."

David, handsome and dashing, was surely accustomed to the yearnful attention of flirtatious women, and he knew how to flirt back in a manly way. And he must have understood that some women would be aroused rather than put off by his swagger and his crude language. Abigail was one such woman.

"A blessing on your good sense," said David to Abigail, "a blessing on you because you have saved me today from the guilt of bloodshed." (1 Sam. 25: 32–35)[31]

David accepted Abigail's gift of food and wine, and then, signaling his men to turn back in the direction of his camp, he saluted her. "Go up in peace to thy house," he said. "I have harkened to thy voice, and I have accepted thy person." (1 Sam. 25:32–35)

That night, as David and his men feasted on Abigail's bounty somewhere in the wilderness, a celebration "like the feast of a king" was held in the grand house of Nabal. Abigail had not yet told Nabal of her encounter with David—so bold and so thrilling—and her husband must have congratulated himself on his own courage in turning away David's men: "Nabal's heart was very merry within him, for he was very drunken." (1 Sam. 25:36) But she burned to reveal to her foolish husband how close he had come to death, and how it was only her charm and savvy that had spared him from David's sword. And surely Abigail wanted her churlish husband to understand how little she thought of him, and how much she thought of David. So she waited until Nabal had slept off the effects of a night of feasting and drinking.

"And it came to pass in the morning, when the wine was gone out of Nabal, that his wife told him these things," the Bible reports, "and his heart died within him, and he became as a stone." (1 Sam. 25:37)

Ten days after his attack of apoplexy—or was it heartbreak

over his wife's infatuation with the bandit-chieftain?—Nabal was out of the way. "The Lord smote Nabal," the Bible reports, putting a proper theological spin on Nabal's convenient death (1 Sam. 25:38). David thanked God for his good fortune—and then he sent a hasty but confident proposal of marriage to his benefactress: "David has sent us to take you to be his wife," his messengers explained. Just as quickly, Abigail accepted. "And she arose, and bowed down with her face to the earth," the Bible reports, "and said: 'Behold thy handmaid is a servant to wash the feet of the servants of my lord' "—which David's messengers understood to mean "yes." (1 Sam. 25:41)

Then Abigail rose to her feet, mounted her ass, and rode away from her dead husband's estate in the company of David's men and five of her maidservants. Promptly upon her arrival at David's encampment, the widow Abigail and the handsome outlaw who had come so close to killing her first husband were wed.

Abigail was only the latest of David's wives—David was still married to Michal, whom he had left behind in Gibeah, and later he managed to pick up another wife in the nearby village of Jezreel,[32] a woman named Ahinoam. As befits a king, David was already assembling what would one day become his harem.

HIS SUBTLE WAYS

Now David and his band and their camp followers sought refuge in a place called Ziph, a remote stretch of wooded hill-country in the land of Judah. But the locals were no more enamored of David than Nabal had been, and they sent a delegation all the way to Gibeah to petition the king to rid them of him. They informed Saul exactly where David was hiding out—"The hill of Hachilah," they reported with military precision, "which is on the south of Jeshimon"[33]—and begged the king to march against him. (1 Sam. 23:19)

"O king, come down," pleaded the men of Ziph, "and our part shall be to deliver him up into the king's hand." (1 Sam. 23:20)

"Perhaps he is planning some trickery!" the king fretted to himself, and so he insisted on confirmation of David's where-abouts before committing himself to a campaign. (1 Sam. 23:22) (AB) "Go, I pray you, and make yet more sure, for it is told me that he deals very subtly," King Saul told the delegation. "Find out all the lurking-places where he hides himself, and come back to me—then I will go with you, and if he be in the land, I will search him out among all the thousands of Judah." (1 Sam. 23:23)[34]

Whether inspired by his old paranoia or his grasp of strategy and tactics, Saul's demand for a fresh intelligence report turned out to be a sound move. For just as Saul had feared, David had already slipped out of Ziph and headed into the wilderness of Maon.[35] When Saul learned of David's latest "lurking-place," he mustered three thousand picked men and marched toward the mountain stronghold.

The king's army approached the mountain from the side op-posite David's encampment. Saul divided his men into two units, sending them around both sides of the mountain in a classic pin-cer movement. Before he was able to close the circle and cut off any chance of escape, a courier from the royal headquarters ap-peared with an alarming message.

"Haste thee, and come," the messenger told Saul, "for the Philistines have made a raid upon the land."

With the capture of David so tantalizingly close, Saul was forced to break off his attack, turn his army around, and march back to face the Philistines. By the time he returned to the wilder-ness to resume his pursuit of David, the fugitive was on the run again. But, yet again, David's enemies among his own people be-trayed his whereabouts to the king.

"Behold," the latest informer addressed Saul, "David is in the wilderness of En-gedi."

En-gedi was (and is) an oasis near the western shore of the Dead Sea, an idyllic place where shepherds watered their sheep at the spring-fed pools of sweet water and wild goats gamboled among the cliffs and outcrops. There Saul ran David to ground, and the young man seemed within the king's grasp. (1 Sam. 24:3)

A coarse but colorful tale is preserved in the Book of Samuel about the encounter between Saul and David at En-gedi. At an awkward moment during the search-and-destroy mission, the king sought out a cave among the rocks in order to defecate.[36] By chance, David and his men were hiding in the deeper reaches of the same cave, and they watched in amazement as the king of Israel squatted on the cave floor and relieved himself in supposed privacy. How easy it would be for David to slip up behind the king at this vulnerable moment and strike him down once and for all!

"The day has come!" whispered David's henchmen in excitement. "Yahweh has put your enemy into your hands, as he promised he would, and you may do what you please with him!" (1 Sam. 24:5)

But David, in a sudden display of piety and integrity, declared himself to be shocked—shocked!—at the suggestion. "God forbid that I should harm my master," he scolded. "He is the Lord's anointed!" (1 Sam. 24:7)[37]

Here, as elsewhere in the Book of Samuel, one of the biblical sources has taken care to absolve David of any culpability, whether direct or indirect, for the fate of King Saul and his dynasty. Still, David was not too pure of heart to engage in a prank that can be seen as a tactic of psychological warfare. Sneaking up behind Saul as he was defecating, David drew his dagger, sliced off the hem of Saul's robe, and then slipped away unnoticed. Moments later, as Saul rearranged his garments and left the cave, David followed the king and called out to him.

"My lord the king!" David said. "Why do you harken to the ones who say: 'David seeks to hurt you'?" (1 Sam. 24:9)[38]

Saul must have been no less amazed at the sight of his fugitive son-in-law standing above him on a rocky crag than David had been only moments before at the sight of the king of Israel squatting in the cave.

"Behold, this day your eyes have seen how Yahweh delivered you into my hand in the cave," David continued. "Some bade me kill you, but I said: 'I will not put forth my hand against my lord, for he is Yahweh's anointed.' " Then David held up the strip of cloth that he had just sliced from the royal cloak. "My father, see the skirt of thy robe in my hand!" he cried. "I cut off the skirt of thy robe, but I killed you not!" (1 Sam. 24:11–12)[39]

Saul, always thrown off-balance by sudden upwellings of emotion, was overwhelmed by the tender words that fell from the lips of the man whom he regarded as a traitor and an assassin, a conspirator and a usurper, a bandit and an outlaw.

> "Is this thy voice, my son David?" And Saul lifted up his voice, and wept. And he said to David: "Thou art more righteous than I;[40] for thou hast rendered unto me good, whereas I have rendered unto thee evil."
>
> (1 Sam. 24:17–18)

The interlude, which reads like a fairy tale from first to last, ends abruptly and implausibly as Saul concedes his crown to David: "And now, behold, I know that you will surely be king, and that the kingdom of Israel will be established in your hand." Then the reigning king is reduced to begging the future king for mercy: "Swear now to me by the Lord that you will not cut off my seed after me." (1 Sam. 24:21–22)[41]

So the two bitter enemies part as friends in the biblical account of the encounter at En-gedi. But history reasserts itself when the narrative resumes a moment later: David is again on the run with Saul in pursuit, as if the encounter between the once and future kings of Israel at the fairy-tale oasis had never happened at all.

RETURN OF THE MADMAN

After so many hot pursuits and breathless escapes, David tired of the fugitive life and started to yearn for a more secure existence. "One of these days I shall be killed by Saul," he thought to himself, apparently calculating that his good fortune might not last forever. And the Bible is blunt about what David did next: "The best thing for me to do will be to escape into Philistine territory. Then Saul will lose all further hope of finding me anywhere in Israel, search as he may, and I shall escape his clutches." (1 Sam. 27:1)[42]

So once again David sought refuge with the hated enemy of his people. He resolved to offer himself and his skills as a soldier of fortune to the king of Gath, and so he returned to the court of King Achish, where he had once played the mad fool to save his own life. With six hundred armed men under his command, the battle-hardened guerrilla commander cut a considerably more formidable figure than the lone fugitive whom Achish had beheld on David's earlier visit. A bit of David's customary swagger can be detected in his bold words to Achish.

"Grant me a place in one of the cities in your country," he proposed. Then he posed a rhetorical question that was tinged with menace: "Why should I remain in the royal city with your majesty?" (1 Sam. 27:6)[43]

David and his army did not intend to leave the king and his city in peace unless they were given safe refuge elsewhere, or so his words implied. And the threat was not lost on Achish, who evidently decided that it would be better to comply with David's demand than to try to expel him from Gath by force of arms. So he gave David the town of Ziklag.[44] "That is why," the Bible notes in passing, "Ziklag still belongs to the kings of Judah to this day" (1 Sam. 27:6)[45]—an intriguing aside that suggests the passage was composed at a time when men with David's blood in their veins still reigned in ancient Israel. Harried out of his homeland by King Saul, forced to seek protection wherever he could find it, and perfectly willing to make a deal with the traditional enemy of his people, the future king of Israel was now a vassal of the Philistines.

David and his men marched out of Gath and set up a base of operations in Ziklag. They were soon joined by their wives and families, and the army in exile was fortified by Benjaminite defectors who had apparently lost faith in Saul, at least according to the revisionist account in the Book of Chronicles: "They were among the mighty men, his helpers in war." (1 Chron. 12:1) The escape from Judah into Philistia had accomplished precisely what David had hoped for: "And it was told to Saul that David was fled to Gath, and he sought no more again for him." (1 Sam. 27:4)

"SURELY HE HAS BECOME LOATHSOME TO HIS OWN PEOPLE"

Safely ensconced in the land of the Philistines under the patronage of the king of Gath, David and his men supplied themselves by raiding the nomadic desert tribes whose settlements and pasturages lay to the south of Gath in the direction of Egypt, "the Geshurites and the Gizrites and the Amalekites." (1 Sam. 27:8) The Bible suggests that he confined his predations to non-Israelites and left his own people unmolested, but confirms in plainspoken language that David was merciless toward his victims.

> And David smote the land, and left neither man nor woman alive, and took away the sheep, and the oxen, and the asses, and the camels, and the apparel.
>
> (1 Sam. 27:9)

Significantly, David no longer bothered to consult Yahweh about his choice of targets, and no longer did he dignify his raids as blows against the Philistines, as he did when he marched to the "rescue" of the townspeople of Keilah. Indeed, David dutifully reported back to his new liege, King Achish, with a daily accounting of his plunder.

"Where was your raid today?" the Philistine king would ask.

"Against the Negev of Judah," David would respond, naming the desert stretches of his own tribal homeland, "and against the Negev of the Jerahmeelites, and against the Negev of the Kenites." (1 Sam. 27:10)[46]

Here David was teetering on the verge of treason. According to the conventional reading of the biblical text by pious commentators, David's reference to "the Negev of Judah" was meant to deceive the king of Gath into believing that David was raiding the towns and villages of his tribal homeland as a loyal vassal of the Philistines when, in fact, he confined himself to murdering and plundering only the traditional enemies of his people, such as the Amalekites. But the text raises the unsettling notion that David was willing to make victims of his own people, too—an interpretation that would explain why many Judahites were so quick to inform on him to King Saul.

Whether or not David was a traitor in service to the Philistines may be debatable, but the Bible leaves no doubt at all that he committed the kinds of atrocities that we call war crimes. As if already considering the political repercussions of his banditry on his future efforts to gain the throne, David adopted a brutal policy of leaving no eyewitnesses to his deeds.

And David left neither man nor woman alive to bring them back to Gath, saying: "Lest they should tell on us."

(1 Sam. 27:11)

The biblical author seems to anticipate a gasp of horror from his readers—"You mean *David* did *that?*"—and so he affirms the accuracy of his account. "So did David," the Bible continues, "and so hath been his manner all the while he dwelt in the country of the Philistines." (1 Sam. 27:11)

Here David betrays a cynicism so deep that it still has the power to shock us: the man who had won the hearts and minds of all Israel is apparently willing to afflict his own people on behalf of their worst enemy, and he makes sure that no one will be left alive to testify against him later on. Achish's cynicism, however, was even deeper. "Surely he has become loathsome to his own people, Israel!" the king of Gath smugly observed. "I shall have him for a servant always!" (1 Sam. 27:12) (AB)

Achish's sense of mastery—"a slave of eternity" is the literal translation of the words (*obed olam*) he used to describe David[47]— was only strengthened when he put the mercenary general to a test of loyalty. When the armies of Philistia were mustered for yet another attack on the land of Israel, Achish summoned David to his court and questioned him closely.

"You know," Achish said to David, "that you and your men must take the field with me."

"Good," David answered smartly. "You will learn what your servant will do."

"Then I will make you my bodyguard for life!" snapped an exultant Achish in response to David's declaration of loyalty. (1 Sam. 28:1–2)[48]

At this bleak moment in the biblical narrative, the troubling question of David's nature and motives is left unanswered. Was he really so quick and so willing to take up arms against the king of Israel? According to the conventional reading of the Bible, David never meant to join the Philistines in battle against the Israelites but sought to deceive Achish by affirming his willingness to do so. After all, if David had declined to go to war with the Philistines, he would have put his own life at risk then and there. So he gave the answer that Achish wanted, thus passing the loyalty test for the moment, and he hoped that the king of Gath would not call his bluff by ordering him and his men to march against Saul and the army of Israel.

DOUBLETS

The exploits of David during his fugitive years are described with shocking candor by one of the original authors of his biography as we find it in the Bible. But an open-eyed reading suggests that another pen was at work on the same text, a pen in the hand of a spin doctor who tried to put every act of brutality and betrayal in the best possible light. Thus, the Bible has been decorated with "correctives" to the awkward passages where "the future king of Israel is depicted in the embarrassing role of a Philistine-hired mercenary," all in an effort to "explain away the facts of history."[49]

The best example is the spin that is put on David's raids in the ill-defined stretches of "the Negev of Judah." By parsing out the words and phrases selected by the biblical source, we are meant to conclude that David was seeking to deceive the king of Gath. "David, no traitor at heart and not wishing his fellow countrymen to think him such, continued to play a devious game," insists Bible historian John Bright. "While convincing Achish by false reports that he was conducting raids into Judah, he actually devoted himself to harrying the Amalekites and other tribes of the southern desert whose incursions had always plagued neighboring Israelite clans. . . ."[50]

Far less subtle is the biblical source who put a theological spin on the otherwise realistic episodes of David's outlaw years. When David is tutored in the art of guerrilla warfare by the prophet Gad, for example, it is a man of God rather than a man of war who acts as his mentor. (1 Sam. 22:5) David seeks permission from God before going into battle. "Shall I go and smite the Philistines?" he asks by means of divination, and God responds: "Go and smite the Philistines." (1 Sam. 23:2) When David cuts off the hem of King Saul's robe while he is relieving himself, David is shown to reproach himself for his prank: "Yahweh forbid that I should do such a thing to Yahweh's anointed!" (1 Sam. 24:7) (AB) And Saul, who is depicted throughout the Book of Samuel as a homicidal maniac, turns suddenly sweet and gentle when he discovers that David has spared his life, and he literally thanks God for his salvation. "The Lord handed me over to you and you did not slay me," he says. "May the Lord reward you with goodness for the goodness you have done for me today." (1 Sam. 24:19–10)[51]

Perhaps the best evidence that these passages consist of theological subtext rather than history or biography can be found in the "doublets" that appear in the text of Samuel. A doublet, as we have noted, is a tale that is preserved in the Bible in two or more versions—Saul is twice shown to learn of David's whereabouts from the men of Ziph; the king twice leads an army of three thousand men in pursuit; and, most notably, he is twice spared from death by David, first in the cave at En-gedi, and then, a few chapters later, when David and his men slip into the royal barricade at "the hill of Hachilah."

Significantly, the second doublet seems to flicker between military adventure and miracle story. David relies on his spy network to find out the location of Saul's war camp, and he uses his skills as a guerrilla fighter to infiltrate the camp by night. Yet the biblical text can be read to suggest that David is assisted by a rare instance of divine intervention: God has sent Saul and his men into a trancelike sleep called *tardema Yahweh* ("the slumber of Yahweh") (1 Sam. 26: 12), the same comalike state that Adam experienced when God extracted a rib in order to create the first woman. (Gen. 2:21)[52]

"God hath delivered your enemy into your hand," whispers Abishai, one of David's trusted commanders, in the second of the doublets. "Now let me smite him with the spear—one stroke, and I will not smite him a second time!" (1 Sam. 26:8)[53]

"Destroy him not, for who can put forth his hand against the Lord's anointed, and be guiltless?" says David, who explains that Saul will surely die, but only when God says so: "The Lord shall smite him, or he shall go down into battle and be swept away." (1 Sam. 26:9–10)[54]

So David is shown to leave the sleeping king undisturbed, pausing only to carry off his spear and a flask of water that lay at his side. Later, David hails the soldiers in the king's camp from a distance, and delivers a scolding to Saul's trusted general, Abner, for dereliction of duty. "Why have you not kept watch over your lord the king?" demands David, holding up the stolen spear and water flask to demonstrate how close he had managed to come to Saul. And when Saul awakens and overhears these taunts, he is struck with the same gush of sentiment he showed at En-gedi.

"Behold, I have played the fool," the king says. "Blessed be thou, my son David, thou shalt both do mightily, and shalt surely prevail." (1 Sam. 26:21, 25)

At the end of each of the doublets, the conflict between Saul and David is resolved, the two men are reconciled, and each goes his separate way. But the happy ending is paper-thin, and the sharp edges of history always poke through. David may be bold, handsome, and charismatic, but the Bible allows us to see him as an outlaw, a mercenary, even a mass murderer, and it raises the alarming notion that he was a traitor, too. Even if, as the Bible intends, we fall in love with David—even if we conclude that he acted with such brutality and cunning only because he was forced to do so by the aloofness of the Almighty and the homicidal rage of King Saul—the Bible never allows us to forget that he is a Robin Hood with bloodstained hands.

Chapter Six

GHOSTWIFE

1. WITCH: *When shall we three meet again*
   In thunder, lightning or in rain?

2. WITCH: *When the hurly-burly's done,*
   When the battle's lost and won.
   —SHAKESPEARE, *MACBETH*

At an odd moment in the account of David's outlaw years, the Bible records an event that signaled a sea change in the destiny of Saul and all of Israel.

> Now Samuel was dead, and all Israel had lamented him, and buried him in Ramah, his own city.
>
> (1 Sam. 28:3)[1]

The death of Samuel represented a blow to the newborn kingdom of Israel. After all, Samuel had once ruled the twelve tribes as the last of the judges. It was he who answered the people's call for a king of their own, and it was he who anointed the first two kings of Israel, the one who still reigned and the other who would reign if he managed to survive the first king's best efforts to kill him. Everyone in Israel, the Bible makes clear, felt a sharp sense of loss and dislocation. But for Saul, losing the man who had been his mentor, confessor, and father figure was a catastrophe. Ever since Saul had ordered the mass murder of the priests at Nob, no other man of God besides Samuel had been available to minister to the troubled king or to intercede with Yahweh on his behalf. Now that Samuel, too, was dead, Saul discovered that he had irredeemably forfeited the favor of God.

The revelation came at a moment of acute danger to Israel. The Philistines fielded an army at a place called Shunem, and the Israelites gathered at Gilboa.[2] But when Saul surveyed the battle lines and saw for himself the size of the enemy force, "he was afraid and his heart trembled greatly." (1 Sam. 28:5) The king yearned for a word of comfort or advice from on high, but he found not a single priest among his entourage. So Saul was forced to seek an oracle from God on his own initiative.

> And when Saul inquired of the Lord, Yahweh answered
> him not, neither by dreams, nor by lots, nor by prophets.
> (1 Sam. 28:6)[3]

God himself had fallen silent, and Saul realized that he was truly alone.

THE SACRED DIVINING BOX

God's silence is a pointed reminder that he had long ago withdrawn from direct communication with his Chosen People. A careful reading of the Book of Samuel confirms that no one—not Samuel, not Saul, not even David—is privileged to converse directly with God. Indeed, one of the strikingly modern notes in the life story of David is the fact that he does not speak with God at all.

Yahweh was not always so aloof. The Bible tells us that he had once walked and talked with the men and women he had created. In the Book of Genesis, God strolls through the Garden of Eden "toward the cool of the day," hoping for a chat with Adam and Eve but failing to find them. (Gen. 3:8) He shows up at the tent of Abraham "in the heat of the day" and sits down to an impromptu meal of chops and curds. (Gen. 18:1, 8) He engages in a wrestling match with Jacob—and loses! (Gen. 32:29) He routinely chats with Moses "face to face" and even "mouth to mouth, as a friend speaketh to a friend." (Exod. 33:11, Num. 12:8) But Moses is the last human being to enjoy the privilege of direct conversation with God.

"Hear now my words," God declared to Aaron and Miriam, Moses' brother and sister. "If there be a prophet among you, I the Lord do make myself known unto him in a vision, I do speak to him in a dream." (Num. 12:6)

The death of Moses may be regarded as the great divide in the sacred history of Israel, the point in time when myth and legend come to an end and real history begins. The biblical authors who composed David's life story allowed that God might have walked on earth and conversed "face to face" with human beings at some point in the distant, dreamy past, but they did not entertain the notion that their contemporaries might hear the voice of God with their own ears or see him with their own eyes. A prophet like Samuel might hear from God, but only in dreams and visions and trance states. The rest of humankind—even "a man after God's own heart" like David—was restricted to the crude machinery of divination.

Divination by the casting of lots is an ancient, universal practice. Even if we now regard it as crude and superstitious, lot casting survives in the form of tossing a coin or plucking the petals of a daisy for decision making. According to the Bible, the ancient Israelites consulted Yahweh in exactly the same manner, using the Ark or the ephod or the mysterious ritual objects called the Urim and Thummim. Robert H. Pfeiffer characterizes the Ark as a "sacred divining box" and John Lindblom calls the ephod an "oracle-instrument"; each was more elaborate and ornate than a coin toss but no different in function.[4]

Divination is often mentioned but the paraphernalia are never described with clarity in the Bible. The lots were probably pebbles, sticks, arrows, or other objects marked with words and images and cast like dice or drawn at random from a container by the person who performed the ritual. The Urim and Thummim may have been lots fashioned out of precious stones instead of river pebbles. The Ark and the ephod were probably used as containers for the lots, and so was the priestly mantle called "the breastplate of judgment," where the Urim and Thummim were stored. (Exod. 28:30, Lev. 8:8)

An illuminating example of divination by lot casting appears in the Book of Samuel. Saul had decreed a day of solemn fasting on the eve of a battle with the Philistines, but Jonathan, unbeknownst to his father, violated the decree by eating on the fast day and encouraging the men in Saul's army to do the same. On this earlier occasion, too, God failed to respond to Saul's urgent plea for tactical advice from on high: "Shall I go down after the Philistines? Wilt thou deliver them into the hand of Israel?" (1 Sam. 14:37) Saul took the refusal to answer as a sign of God's displeasure, but he was baffled about the cause. So he ordered that the Urim and the Thummim be used to find out who had angered God. Was it Saul himself? Was it Jonathan, who had sampled some wild honey in the forest in defiance of Saul's decree? Or was it some other malefactor among the people of Israel?

"If this guilt lie in me or in my son Jonathan, O Lord God of Israel, let the lot be Urim," Saul asked. "If it lie in thy people Israel, let it be Thummim." (1 Sam. 14:41) (NEB)[5]

Urim originally meant "condemned" and *Thummim* meant "acquitted," according to one scholarly surmise.[6] So Saul posed his question, the lots marked as Urim and Thummim were drawn at random, Urim was selected, and thus the guilty one was either Saul or Jonathan. Now the king asked the next crucial question. "Cast between me and Jonathan, my son!" he ordered. "Let him whom Yahweh takes die!" (1 Sam. 14:42) (AB)

"Let it not be so!" cried the soldiers, but Saul insisted—and the casting of lots identified Jonathan as the wrongdoer. (1 Sam. 14:42)[7]

Once Jonathan's guilt was established by the casting of lots, he confessed to his sin. "I did certainly taste a little honey," he declared. "Here am I—I will die." (1 Sam. 14:44) Saul sentenced his son to death, but the army rallied to his defense: "So the army rescued Jonathan, and he died not." (1 Sam. 14:45)

The trial-by-divination of Saul and Jonathan had taken place long before God withdrew his blessing from Saul and anointed David as the next king of Israel. Since then, God's only direct contact with Saul had been the "evil spirit from Yahweh" that occasionally possessed him and literally drove him mad. Now Saul desperately sought an oracle from God on the eve of a crucial battle with the Philistines—and Saul was reminded that one might "inquire of God" and receive no answer at all.

GHOSTWIFE

"Thou shalt not suffer a witch to live," God had decreed to Moses long ago on Mount Sinai, and all of the black arts were flatly condemned as "abomination to the Lord" in biblical law: "There shall not be found among you one that useth divination, a soothsayer, or an enchanter, or a sorcerer, or a charmer, or one that consulteth a ghost or a familiar spirit, or a necromancer." (Exod. 22:17, Deut. 18:10–12)[8]

Saul had dutifully enforced the divine law against practitioners of magic, and he "banished from the land all who trafficked with ghosts and spirits." (1 Sam. 28:3) But now he was in despair and close to panic. If God on high would not answer him, he resolved, he would find someone to summon up a familiar voice from the spirit world, even if it meant his own damnation.

"Seek me a woman that divines by a ghost," Saul ordered his courtiers, "that I may go to her, and inquire of her." (1 Sam. 28:7)

"Behold, there is a woman that divines by a ghost at En-dor," his dutiful courtiers replied.

The Bible does not explain why his courtiers had neglected to inform the king before now, but Saul was glad to discover that at least one diviner had escaped his purge. By long tradition in biblical translation and commentary, she is known as the witch of En-dor, but there is another and even spookier way to render the original Hebrew text: "ghostwife."[9] Disguising himself in commoner's clothes, Saul waited until nightfall to call upon her.

"Divine unto me, I pray thee, by a ghost," demanded Saul from behind the cloak that he wore to hide his face, "and bring up the man I shall name." (1 Sam. 28:8)[10]

Perhaps the wily woman was fooled by his disguise—or perhaps not. Her coy response may have been intended to signal Saul that she knew exactly who he was.

"Behold, thou knowest what Saul hath done, how he hath cut off those who speak with ghosts and spirits," she said self-righteously. "Why then layest thou a snare for my life, to cause me to die?" (1 Sam. 28:9)[11]

"As Yahweh lives," Saul vowed, "no punishment will fall upon you for this thing." (1 Sam. 28:10)[12]

His words were doubly ironic. As Saul knew—as perhaps both of them knew—the king could hardly put the woman to death for doing exactly what he asked of her. What's more, his vow to protect a witch in the name of Yahweh was itself a blasphemy—after all, it was God who condemned every practice of the occult. But as the witch of En-dor could plainly see, Saul simply did not care that he was breaking his own law and damning himself.

"Whom shall I bring up unto thee?" asked the woman. (1 Sam. 28:11)

"Bring me up Samuel," said the king, and his words were surely a cry from the heart.

Here is yet another moment when the theological niceties seem to evaporate and we glimpse something that is deeply forbidden. Elsewhere, the Bible regards the occult as not only sinful but utterly false and useless. "The faith of the Old Testament carried on . . . warfare with special bitterness . . . against belief in the spirits of the underworld, against demons and spirits of the dead, against soothsaying and necromancy," writes the venerable Bible scholar Gerhard von Rad.[13] He is seconded by the philosopher Martin Buber: "That is the religion of Moses, the man who experienced the futility of magic."[14] Yet black magic is shown here to be fully effective, and the witch of En-dor succeeds in summoning up the spirit of the dead Samuel just as Saul had demanded.[15]

No eerier scene is presented anywhere in the Hebrew Bible. We can only imagine what Saul saw as he watched the woman— did she groan and babble, sway and keen, and mutter strange spells and incantations in order to conjure up a ghost from the spirit world? But the Bible allows us to understand that the woman herself was suddenly seized with remorse, bewilderment, and plain terror as Samuel struggled up from the grave at her command.

"Why hast thou deceived me?" she moaned aloud as she worked her magic. "For thou art Saul."

"Be not afraid," said Saul to the witch of En-dor in another ironic reversal of roles. "What seest thou?"

"I see a god," she whispered in astonishment, "coming up out of the earth."

"What is his appearance?" Saul asked.

"An old man cometh up," she answered as if in a trance, "and he is wrapped in a robe." (1 Sam. 28:12–14)[16]

Now it was Saul who was suddenly terror-stricken, and he fell to the floor of the old woman's hut, burying his face in the ground in obeisance to the ghost he had summoned up. And yet the scene suddenly shifts from terror to burlesque: the spirit of Samuel has been roused from its ghostly slumber and is none too happy to find itself back among the living.

"Why hast thou disturbed me by bringing me up?" complained the resentful ghost.

"I am sore distressed," whined Saul, who apparently lifted himself from the floor to recite his bad-luck story, which Samuel surely knew as well as anyone. "The Philistines make war against me, and God is departed from me and answers me no more, neither by prophets nor by dreams, and so I have called upon you that tell me what I should do." (1 Sam. 28:15)[17]

"Why then do you ask of *me*," said Samuel, "seeing the Lord is departed from thee and is become thine enemy?" (1 Sam. 28:16)

Now it was the ghost of Samuel who recited a familiar litany, reminding Saul that he had forfeited God's favor when he failed to kill the king of the Amalekites and thus forced the old prophet to finish the job himself. "Thou didst not harken to the voice of the Lord and didst not execute his hot wrath upon Amalek," Samuel said in rebuke. (1 Sam. 28:18) And then he issued one more chilling prophecy before returning to his ghostly rest.

The Lord will deliver Israel into the hand of the Philistines, and tomorrow shalt thou and thy sons be with me.
(1 Sam. 28:19)

Saul was so shattered by the unequivocal prophecy of his own death that he fell once again to the ground, not in obeisance but in simple terror. The Bible pauses to note that he had eaten nothing for a day and a night, perhaps in a ritual of purification to prepare himself for the séance, and now he was drained of energy, courage, and even the will to live.

The sight of the ruined Saul stirred a maternal compassion in the witch of En-dor.

"I listened to what you said and I risked my life to obey you," she said with surprising tenderness. "Now listen to me: let me set before you a little food to give you strength for your journey." (1 Sam. 28:21–22) (NEB)

"I will not eat," answered Saul. (1 Sam. 28:23)

But the woman, more like a Jewish mother than a trafficker in dead souls, urged Saul to take some nourishment. The two servants who had accompanied Saul on his midnight adventure joined in the chorus: "Eat, eat," we might imagine them to say. Slowly and perhaps a bit sulkily, King Saul picked himself up from the floor, seated himself on the edge of the woman's bed, and waited while she killed a fatted calf and kneaded a measure of unleavened flour, whipping up a meal of veal cutlets and matzah.

Fortified by her food and comforted by her kind words, Saul departed from the ghostwife's cottage and returned to the encampment where his army waited. To the credit of the crazy old king, Saul did not allow Samuel's prediction of his imminent death to dissuade him from going forth once more to do battle with the Philistines.

"WHAT ARE THESE HEBREWS DOING HERE?"

Across the border in Philistia, David, too, was caught up in the preparations for war. "And the lords of the Philistines passed on by hundreds and by thousands," the Bible reports, and David's battle-tested guerrillas followed at the rear of the mighty column. But the odd sight of a contingent of Israelites in the ranks of the vast Philistine army troubled a few of the warlords.

"What are these Hebrews doing here?" the princes demanded of David's patron, King Achish of Gath. (1 Sam. 29:3)[18]

"Is this not David, the servant of Saul, king of Israel, who has been with me these days and years?" replied Achish, who was ready to vouch for David's loyalty. "I have found no fault in him from the day he defected to me unto this day." (1 Sam. 29:3)[19]

The Philistine generals did not share Achish's credulity. They refused to believe that David was earnest in his defection—surely he would turn on his Philistine allies in order to put himself back into the good graces of King Saul. "He shall not fight side by side with us, or he may turn traitor in the battle," they protested. "What better way to buy his master's favour than at the price of our lives?" (1 Sam. 29:4–5) (NEB)

Above all, the Philistines still feared the military prowess and sheer ruthlessness of the young mercenary.

"Is this not David," the lords of Philistia asked the king of Gath, "of whom they sang one to another in dances, saying:

> Saul hath slain his thousands,
> And David his ten thousands?
> (1 Sam. 29:5)

So Achish, dutifully but regretfully, summoned the man he regarded as his faithful vassal to his war tent and ordered him back to his fiefdom in Ziklag.

"As Yahweh lives, you have been upright—I have not found evil in you since the day of your coming," he said to David, oddly invoking the God of Israel rather than one of the gods and goddesses of the Philistine pantheon. "Nevertheless, the Philistine lords favor you not." (1 Sam. 29:6)[20]

Remarkably, David did not take advantage of Achish's order, which offered him an opportunity to avoid open warfare against his own countrymen. Rather, as the Bible plainly reveals, David urgently reasserted his loyalty to the Philistine cause. Any enemy of the king of Gath, David insisted, was his enemy, too.

"But what have I done," David pleaded, "that I may not go and fight against the enemies of my lord the king?" (1 Sam. 29:8)

"I know you are as good in my sight as an angel of God," Achish said, again invoking the Israelite deity. "But the Philistine commanders have said: 'He shall not go up with us to the battle.' So rise up early in the morning, and as soon as you have enough light, depart." (1 Sam. 29:10)[21]

David obeyed the order, rising early with his men and leading them back into Gath as the Philistine army formed up into ranks and columns and marched toward Jezreel, where Saul and Jonathan had positioned the army of Israel in battle array. When the Philistines and the Israelites finally crossed swords, David and his men had already retreated to safety deep in enemy territory.

DAVID AND THE MYSTERY OF THE HABIRU

An intriguing clue to David's origin and character may be found in the question that the lords of Philistia put to King Achish on the eve of battle: "What are these *Hebrews* doing here?" (1 Sam. 29:3) The Bible generally refers to the twelve tribes who descended from the patriarch Jacob as "Israelites" or, more precisely, the Children of Israel (*b'nai Yisrael*).[22] But the Philistines use a very different term for the same people—"Hebrews" (*ivrim*), a word that may have been used to identify David and his men as renegades.

Nowadays, of course, "Hebrew" is the word used to described the *language* of the Bible and, in its updated form, of the modern state of Israel. But the Bible uses the term to identify a *people*, not a language, and only in very specific circumstances. "Hebrews" is used for the Israelites only in biblical passages where non-Israelites such as the Philistines or the Egyptians are speaking about the Israelites, or where the Israelites are distinguishing themselves from non-Israelites. The distinction between "Hebrews" and "Israelites," however, remained a mystery until the late nineteenth century, when archaeologists began to uncover references to a people called the Habiru in extra-biblical texts of the ancient Near East.

The Habiru, for example, are mentioned in a cache of diplomatic correspondence dating back to the fifteenth century B.C.E. that was unearthed at a site in Egypt known as Tell el-Amarna. The clay tablets were covered with writing in the cuneiform alphabet of the Akkadian language that was used in international diplomacy and commerce in the ancient Near East, and they included intelligence reports from the chieftains of Canaan about newly arrived marauders called Habiru (or "Apiru," as the term is sometimes rendered in English) who were waging a war of conquest throughout Canaan.

"The Apiru plunder all the lands of the king," complains the Canaanite chieftain of Jerusalem in one of the Amarna letters, pleading with the Pharaoh for protection against the plunderers. "If there are archers here in this year, the lands of the king, my lord, will remain intact; but if there are no archers here, the lands of the king, my lord, will be lost!"[23]

To the glee of early Bible scholars, who saw the Habiru and the Hebrews as one and the same people, the Amarna letters seem to prove, once and for all and with solid documentary evidence, that the Bible is a work of history rather than a sacred myth. But the initial enthusiasm was tempered when it was discovered that the word *habiru* is found in writings from other sources, too, including the ancient Mesopotamian archives found at Mari, a site on the Euphrates River in modern Syria. As used by these far-flung archivists and chroniclers of the ancient world, *habiru* apparently referred to *any* people who lived outside a settled community rather than to a specific tribe or nation.

Today, *habiru* is probably best understood as a term for "fugitives" or "refugees" who might show up as bandits or brigands in one place, soldiers of fortune in another, or what we today would call illegal aliens almost anywhere in the ancient Near East during the second millennium B.C.E. The most desperate among them might have sold themselves into slavery for the simple expedient of a place to sleep and a daily meal, but most of the *habiru*, like the ones mentioned so tantalizingly in the Amarna letters, were marauders who descended upon towns and farms that offered the prospect of easy plunder.[24] Thus, the word *habiru* certainly applies to David and his little army of malcontents, and that may be what the lords of Philistia meant when they used the word recorded in the Bible as "Hebrews."[25]

An oblique but intriguing glimpse into the ways of the *habiru*—and the real life of David—is afforded by a much more recent phenomenon, the so-called *klephts* of nineteenth-century Greece. The *klephts*, according to historian Paul Johnson, were "bands of debtors, jailbirds, fugitives, misfits, victims and adventurers who could not flourish in society but took to the hills to live by violence." They tended to leave shepherds unmolested, since many of them had been shepherds themselves, but they "robbed unguarded travelers [and] sometimes carried out mass attacks on villages." The bands were exclusively male, and members may have engaged in homosexuality among themselves. A "successful bandit," who had "built up a band that was strong in reputation, men and sheep," might be able to put himself in service to the governing authority as a *kapitanos*, an officer in charge of a paramilitary unit, thus passing "the frontier from illegality to legality."[26]

On every point, the *klephts* bear a striking resemblance to the Habiru of the ancient world and to David and his men during their fugitive years. David started out as a shepherd, but he literally "took to the hills" when he forfeited the favor of King Saul. He prided himself on his generosity toward the shepherds who served the rich Nabal, but he did not hesitate to shake down the rich man himself. He routinely led his men in "mass attacks on villages," and then he relied on his fearsome reputation to put himself in service to the king of Gath. His declaration of love for Jonathan suggests that he may have shared the tastes of the *klephts* in matters of the heart. "Local folk songs often told the tale of how a bandit became a famous and rich kapitanos," Johnson writes of the *klephts*[27]—and the same might be said of the Bible and its heroic account of David's ascent from bandit to king.

The Bible presents David as a lordly figure who moved in the loftiest circles of power and privilege in ancient Israel, the son of a landowner from Bethlehem and the son-in-law of King Saul. Later, he will marry into other royal families, and the biblical genealogists will contrive a long and honorable family tree for him. And yet the Bible also depicts David as a fugitive, an outcast, a mercenary. So we may wonder if David was, in fact, an outsider who bullied and insinuated his way to power and then inspired his royal biographers to rewrite history in order to cast him in a heroic and romantic light. Perhaps the notion of David as a *habiru* is closer to the truth—and, if so, it helps to explain the bloodthirsty exploits of his fugitive years and the ruthlessness that figures so crucially in his character.

DAVID'S PLUNDER

Classic Bible commentary holds that David was only bluffing when he offered to go to war against Saul, and insists that he meant all along to act loyally to the nation of Israel. The troubling question of what David would have done if his Philistine masters had called his bluff is left unanswered. But now, as if to sweeten the sour taste that the whole episode leaves in the reader's mouth, the biblical author hastens to credit David with an act of courage that counterbalances his apparent treachery.

Three days after leaving the Philistine army, David and his men finally reached Ziklag, but they found only empty, smoking ruins. In David's absence, the dreaded Amalekites had raided the place, setting the town afire and carrying off the women and children. Even the wives of David, Abigail and Ahinoam, were gone.

Then David and the people that were with him lifted up their voice and wept, until they had no more power to weep. The soul of all the people was grieved, every man for his sons and for his daughters, but David strengthened himself in the Lord his God.

(1 Sam. 30:4)[28]

But even as David mourned his missing wives, his men began to blame *him* for the folly of leaving Ziklag undefended. "David was in a desperate position," the Bible concedes, "because the people, embittered by the loss of their sons and daughters, threatened to stone him." (1 Sam. 30:6) (NEB) Here we are reminded that David, no matter how charismatic the Bible makes him out to be, was forced to contend with naysayers like any other leader. The people of Judah had been willing to betray him to Saul, and now his own men were ready to rise up and put him to death.

As if to divert the attention of the mutinous army, David announced that he would seek an oracle from Yahweh on what to do next. So he called for Abiathar, the only priest to escape the slaughter at Nob, and bade him to bring along the ephod he had managed to snatch from the shrine of Yahweh. David had used the same ploy once before when his men declared themselves too frightened to carry out a raid on the Philistines at Keilah, and it worked again to silence the mutineers at Ziklag.

The casting of lots, as we have already seen, yielded only simple answers to the questions posed to God—"Yes," "No," and sometimes "No comment"—but here the biblical author asks us to imagine the encounter as an intimate conversation between Yahweh and David.

"Shall I pursue?" David inquires. "Shall I overtake them?"

"Pursue" is Yahweh's simple reply by means of lot casting, but then the biblical author suggests that God elaborated upon his answer: "For thou shalt surely overtake them, and shalt without fail recover all." (1 Sam. 30:8)

Thus reassured of victory by the ultimate authority, David's men forgot all about stoning their commander. Instead they lined up behind David as he set off in search of the Amalekite raiding party. Finding the enemy in the trackless wilderness, however, was not so easy. After all, the Amalekites were camel-mounted no-mads moving through familiar terrain, and they enjoyed a head start of several days. David needed some intelligence on the whereabouts of the raiding party, and his source turned out to be a young Egyptian slave whom the Amalekites had abandoned in the desert when he fell ill.

To restore his strength and loosen his tongue, the Egyptian was given water and food—"a cake of figs and two clusters of raisins," the Bible reports with convincing detail—and then David himself began to question him. (1 Sam. 30:12) After the fearful young man extracted David's promise to "neither kill me nor turn me over to my master," he agreed to lead David and his men to the Amalekite camp. (1 Sam. 30:15)[29] As they ap-proached, David saw that the raiders were raucously celebrating their victories, "eating and drinking and feasting because of all the great spoil that they had taken out of the land of the Philistines and out of the land of Judah." (1 Sam. 30:16)

At twilight David and his men charged the camp, and the fighting continued without pause "unto the evening of the next day." Four hundred of the Amalekites were able to mount their camels and escape, but the rest of the raiders were slain without mercy. As the oracle of Yahweh had promised, all of the captives—David's two wives and the rest of the women and children—were recovered alive and unharmed, and the flocks and herds of the Amalekites were taken as spoils of war.

"This is David's plunder!" cried the men who had been ready to stone him only a few days before, thus crediting their com-mander with the ultimate destruction of the Amalekite raiders. (1 Sam. 30:20) (AB)

SPOILS OF WAR

Any chance to spill the blood of an Amalekite, the ancient and emblematic enemy of the Israelites, made for good public relations. "Thou shalt blot out the remembrance of Amalek from under heaven," Moses had declared in the name of God. "Thou shalt not forget."(Deut. 25:19) And the fresh supply of plunder gave David an opportunity to make generous gifts to the opinion makers of Judah and the people whose lands he had once raided, thus rehabilitating himself in the eyes of his countrymen. Accordingly, from this moment forward, the Bible subtly revises its depiction of David: he is presented more as a savvy politician seeking to build a constituency than as a renegade guerrilla captain.

First, against the protests of the frontline soldiers, David insisted on sharing the spoils of war with some two hundred men who served in the rear guard during the attack on the Amalekites. "The share of him that goes down to the battle, so shall be the share of him that tarried by the baggage—they shall share and share alike," David decreed. "And it was so from that day forward," the biblical author pauses to note, "that he made it a statute and an ordinance for Israel unto this day." (1 Sam. 30:24–25)[30]

Next, David allotted a portion of the plunder as gift-offerings to "the elders of Judah" and his other "friends" in towns and cities in the land of Judah: "To them that were in Beth-el, and to them that were in Ramoth," begins the long list preserved in the biblical text, "and to all the places over which David himself and his men had ranged." (1 Sam. 30:27, 31) Even a few non-Israelite tribes who lived within the tribal homeland of Judah were favored with gifts—the Kenites, for example, and the Jerahmeelites. Significantly, the places that David favored with gifts were located within the vicinity of Hebron, a place regarded as sacred in the legend and lore of ancient Israel and a seat of political authority in the tribal homeland of Judah.[31]

"Behold, a present for you," went the message from David that accompanied each gift, "of the spoil of the enemies of the Lord." (1 Sam. 30:26–31)

At this moment, the soldier of fortune and bandit-king is eclipsed by the politician and the statesman. Clearly, the biblical author is preparing his readers for David's elevation from fugitive to monarch, but we are also able to mark a change in David himself: he is older and wiser, battle-hardened but somehow mellowed by his exploits in war. His youthful swagger has been replaced by a more regal bearing, and his taste for rough justice has been softened by more generous impulses. David's long exile from the land of Israel is now coming to an end, and when he next sets foot in Hebron, he will be ready to claim the crown of kingship.

THE KING IS DEAD

The crown that David sought still rested on the head of King Saul, but not for much longer. The king's army, outnumbered and outfought by the Philistines, spilled down the slopes of Mount Gilboa in open rout, and Saul found himself in great peril. "And the Philistines followed hard upon Saul and upon his sons," the Bible reports (1 Sam. 31:2), a reminder that ancient kings customarily went to war with their armies, and they were the first targets of the enemy forces that sought to decapitate an army by killing its commander in chief. (1 Sam. 31:2)

Jonathan was the first to fall into the hands of the Philistines, and then two more sons of Saul were taken—all three of them were slain where they stood. Now Saul found himself cut off by a platoon of Philistine archers, an arrow in his belly. (1 Sam. 31:3)[32] At that desperate moment, the Bible suggests, the king of Israel imagined himself riddled with arrows, tortured to death on the battlefield, his body handled like carrion and put on display for the pleasure of the jeering Philistines—and the prospect of an ignoble death was more painful to Saul than death itself.

"Draw your sword, and run me through," Saul ordered his armor-bearer, "so that these uncircumcised brutes may not come and taunt me and make sport of me." (1 Sam. 31:4) (NEB) But the armor-bearer was "sore afraid" to obey and so he refused to draw his sword, choosing to defy the king's last command rather than stain his own hands with the king's blood. (1 Sam. 31:4)

"Therefore Saul took his sword, and fell upon it," the Bible reports. "And when his armor-bearer saw that Saul was dead, he likewise fell upon his sword and died with him." (1 Sam. 31:4–5)

Thus was Samuel's prophecy fulfilled at long last, and Saul's death ended the torment that he had suffered since the day that God withdrew his blessing and abandoned him to his fate. "So Saul died, and his three sons, and his armor-bearer, and all his men, that same day together." (1 Sam. 31:6) But the peace that now soothed old Saul was denied to the people of Israel. When word of the carnage began to spread, the towns in the vicinity of Mount Gilboa emptied as the Israelites fled in panic. "And the Philistines came," the Bible says of the deserted houses of Israel, "and dwelt in them." (1 Sam. 31:7)

Saul's final paranoid vision of his own death came to pass. The next day, as the Philistine soldiers picked their way among the dead on the battlefield, pausing here and there to strip a corpse of any valuables they might find—yet another realistic detail of warfare in the ancient world—they came upon the body of King Saul.

And they cut off his head, and stripped off his armor, and sent into the land of the Philistines round about, to carry the tidings unto the house of their idols, and to the people.

(1 Sam. 31:9)

Just as Saul had feared, he was disgraced in death even as he had been tormented in life: the royal armor that he had worn in his final battle was displayed in a temple of Ashtaroth, one of the pagan goddesses of the ancient Near East, and his headless body was nailed to the town wall at a place called Beth-shan,[33] where it might remind the Philistines of their triumph and the Israelites of their defeat.

THE CROWN OF THE SLAIN KING

On the third day after David's return to Ziklag from his skirmish with the Amalekite raiding party, a stranger appeared at his camp. His clothes were ripped, dirt was sprinkled in his hair—both traditional signs of a man in mourning—and when he was ushered into the presence of David, the man fell to the ground and prostrated himself in submission.

"From where do you come?" David asked.

"Out of the camp of Israel, I have escaped," the man explained.

"How went the matter?" David asked, eager to know how Saul and his army had fared against the Philistines. "I pray thee, tell me."

"The people are fled from the battle, and many of the people are fallen and dead," answered the stranger. "Saul and Jonathan, his son, are dead, too." (2 Sam. 1:3–5)

Here at last was the moment that David had been awaiting ever since Samuel had anointed him as Saul's successor to the throne of Israel. Since then, David had managed to survive the mad king's effort to murder him, first when he was still at court, then during his fugitive years in the wilderness, and finally as a mercenary in service to the Philistines. All the while, we may imagine, he must have wondered whether the holy oil that Samuel had poured over his head so many years before had been a blessing or a curse.

But David dared not rejoice at the word of Saul's death, and he continued his interrogation. The stranger was courageous (or foolish) enough to identify himself as an Amalekite—surely he risked sudden death by doing so!—and then he proceeded to tell a remarkable tale about the last moments of Saul's life, a much different version from the one just provided by the biblical author.

The man had happened upon Saul on the slope of Mount Gilboa in the heat of the battle. Though mortally wounded, the king still leaned on his sword as the chariotry and cavalry of the Philistines pressed down upon him. And then Saul cried out to him. "Stand beside me, and slay me," begged the king, "for the throes of death have seized me, but there is still life in me yet." The stranger complied, putting Saul to the sword as an act of simple mercy.

"I took the crown that was upon his head, and the bracelet that was on his arm," the stranger disclosed to David, "and I have brought them unto my lord." (2 Sam. 1:9–10)[34]

The notion that the crown of Israel was put into David's hand by an Amalekite who confessed to slaying King Saul must have shocked and perhaps even outraged the original readers of the Bible. Yet the Bible, which gives two versions of the battlefield death of Saul, offers no other explanation for how the symbols of kingship once worn by Saul came into David's possession. So we are left to wonder which version of Saul's death is true—did Saul fall on his sword or was he put out of his misery by a passing Amalekite?—and what role, if any, David played in this mysterious episode.

Of course, the inconsistent accounts of Saul's death could be yet another pair of doublets, each originating with a different source and both used by a biblical editor who did not bother to harmonize them. Another explanation is that the Amalekite was simply telling a lie—perhaps he had plundered the king's dead body and then made up a tale to tell David in the belief that he would reward the man who had finished off his rival and brought him the royal insignia. If so, the Amalekite badly misjudged David.

"How is it that you were not afraid to put forth your hand to destroy the Lord's anointed?" David asked in pious rage. "Go," he told one of his own men, "and fall on him." (2 Sam. 1:14–15) Then, as David witnessed the hasty execution of the last man to see King Saul alive, he uttered a cold benediction.

"Your blood be upon your own head," he said, "for your own mouth has testified against you." (2 Sam. 1:16)

A less wholesome meaning can be detected in the same text, a crack in the wall of apologetics that has been thrown up around the figure of David by the biblical sources. The Court Historian, presumably an insider at the court of the Davidic kings and perhaps even an eyewitness to some of the events he describes, made every effort to show David as wholly pure of motive. Never does David openly covet the crown or actively conspire against Saul. Not once but twice, David declines to slay him when he has the chance to do so. Again and again, David declares his love and loyalty to the rightful king of Israel. Yet the biblical author feels obliged to address the awkward question of how the royal crown and bracelet ended up in David's hands so soon after Saul's death.

Surely the original readers of the Bible—no less than the modern reader who is inclined to see conspirators under every bed—must have wondered whether David played a more active and more sinister role in these curious events. Did the king of Gath, for example, carry the crown back to David with the intent of putting his trusted vassal on the throne of Israel as an ally and even a quisling? Or is it possible that David went to war with the Philistines after all and plundered the dead body of Saul with his own hands? The Amalekite's story, conveniently enough, acquits David of any such treachery and was meant to put an end to such scandalous speculation.

"As for Saul's regalia, the present narrative shows that David came by it innocently and by an agent acting on his own initiative," explains Bible scholar P. Kyle McCarter, Jr. "So there is no genuine reason, we are to believe, to suspect David of any wrongdoing in the matter of Saul's death."[35]

If we seek an answer to the question that asks itself—*Cui bono?* Who benefits?—the response is plain enough: David is the one whose path to the throne was cleared of a crucial obstacle by Saul's death. And, as we shall see, the death of Saul is only the first occasion on which David distances himself from a political murder that works to his advantage. But the Bible does not preserve any evidence of David's culpability, whether because no such evidence ever existed or because it has been concealed from us.

Indeed, David betrayed no pleasure or relief at the news of Saul's death. Rather, the man who had begged the Philistines for the opportunity to go into battle against Saul and the army of Israel now rent his garments in a public display of grief, and his men followed his example. "And they wailed and wept and fasted until evening," the Bible reports, "for Saul, and for Jonathan, his son, and for the house of Israel, because they were fallen by the sword." (2 Sam. 1:12) The face that David showed to the men around him, the face he showed to the people of both Judah and Israel, was one of unrelieved grief and despair.

"Thy beauty, O Israel, upon thy high places is slain!" David began to rhapsodize. "How the mighty are fallen!" (2 Sam. 1:19)

"PASSING THE LOVE OF WOMEN"

The death of Saul and Jonathan moved David to eloquence, and here we find the first appearance of verses by "the sweet singer of Israel," as David is later called in the Bible. (2 Sam. 23:1)

Saul and Jonathan, the lovely and the pleasant,
In their lives, even in their death, they were not divided.
They were swifter than eagles,
They were stronger than lions.

(2 Sam. 1:23)

The biblical author seeks to authenticate David's famous words of praise for Saul and Jonathan by claiming to rely on a long-lost source that is supposedly even more ancient than the Bible itself. "Behold," the Bible says of David's eulogy, "it is written in the Book of Jashar." (2 Sam. 1:18) The undeniable grace and power of the elegy inspired the pious tradition that David was the author of the Psalter in its entirety. "As Moses gave five books of laws to Israel," goes a midrash in the Talmud, "so David gave five Books of Psalms."[36] Although modern scholarship allows only that a few psalms in the Book of Psalms may date back to "the Davidic period,"[37] the elegy for Saul and Jonathan inspires considerably more enthusiasm.

"His authorship is unquestionable," writes Robert H. Pfeiffer.

"The deep pervading emotion shows that it was composed immediately after the battle of Gilboa, under the first shocking impression of the calamity."[38]

Even if the eulogy can be attributed to David, the fact remains
that the pretty sentiments found here are not much more truthful
than the platitudes that are uttered over graves nowadays. Saul
and Jonathan were bitterly divided over David: Jonathan loved
him, Saul hated him, and Saul even tried to murder his own son
and successor because he felt betrayed by Jonathan's love for
David. But now David was ready to rewrite their history—and his
own—in the words that he uttered so memorably: "In their lives,
even in their death, they were not divided."

Still, a certain sly irony can be detected in the eulogy. Perhaps
mindful of the raw envy that burned in Saul when he heard the
women of Israel declare their preference for David in song
and dance—"Saul hath slain his thousands, and David his ten
thousands"—David now admonished the women of Israel to
honor Saul in death even if they preferred David in life.

> Ye daughters of Israel, weep over Saul,
> Who clothed you in scarlet, with other delights,
> Who put ornaments of gold upon your apparel.
> (2 Sam. 1:24)

Even now, the words and phrases that fall from David's lips
betray an appeal to the senses and an appreciation for the "de-
lights" of dressing and undressing. David had experienced such
pleasures at the hands of both Saul *and* Jonathan, each of whom
stripped off his own apparel and armament and dressed David in
them. And now, in one of the most provocative moments in the
Bible, David openly declared the passion that he felt toward
Jonathan.

> I am distressed for thee, my brother Jonathan.
> Very pleasant hast thou been unto me,

Wonderful was thy love to me,
Passing the love of women.

(2 Sam. 1:26)

To pious Bible readers of many centuries, these words have reflected the wholesome affection of a man toward his friend and comrade in arms. For others, however, the same words raise a tantalizing question.

WAS DAVID GAY?

Much effort has been expended in explaining away David's declaration of love for Jonathan, a declaration that suggests an undeniable homoerotic subtext. Commentators in all three Bible-based religions insist that what passed between David and Jonathan was something pure and pious. "The classic description of genuine unselfish love," is how Rabbi Israel H. Weisfeld puts it,[39] and Robert H. Pfeiffer vouches for David's machismo by pointing out that his grief over Jonathan is "intense and sincere, but nonetheless virile."[40]

More recent scholarship proposes a political motive for the vows of love exchanged by these two men. The Hebrew word for love (*aheb*) may refer to "genuine affection between human beings, husband and wife, parent and child, friend and friend," concedes Bible scholar J. A. Thompson, but the same word is used with "political overtones" in the Bible and in various ancient texts from elsewhere in the Near East. "In this context, the verb *love* expresses more than natural affection," Thompson argues. "It denotes rather the kind of attachment people had to a king who could fight their battles for them."[41]

So perhaps we are meant to see only a political alliance, and not a pledge of love, when Jonathan declares his "love" for David. After all, Jonathan offered to renounce his claim to the throne and to support David's bid for kingship only if David promised to protect him and his family when Saul was dead or gone. "I know that as long as I live you will show me faithful friendship, as the Lord requires," Jonathan bargained with David, "and if I should die, you will continue loyal to my family forever." (1 Sam. 20:14)[42]

But the passion in David's elegy cannot be overlooked, and the plainspoken references to love between men cannot so readily be explained away. "Male homosexuality was rampant in Biblical times," insists anthropologist Raphael Patai. "The love story between Jonathan, the son of King Saul, and David, the beautiful hero, must have been duplicated many times in royal courts in all parts of the Middle East in all periods."[43] That's why, for example, we find intimacies between men in the Epic of Gilgamesh, the creation myth of ancient Sumeria, and that's why some open-minded commentators are willing to entertain the notion that the Israelites were not shocked to hear of one man's love for another man.

"Homosexuality was both dignified and manly—in fact, often associated with heroes—in the cultures that surrounded Israel," argues Bible critic Tom Horner. "And how could Israel not have been influenced by these cultures? How could it have adopted an entirely different sexual ethic, living as close as it did to foreign influences?"[44]

Of course, the essential message of the Bible is that God's Chosen People were supposed to be different from the rest of humankind—a "holy nation," as God puts it. (Exodus 19:6) The sexual practices of the non-Israelites among whom they lived are routinely condemned as an "abomination." But we have already seen that the Israelites, like everyone else in the world, were never quite capable of living up to God's lofty expectations. The best evidence was their stubborn demand for a king of their own, which may have disgusted God and his prophet, Samuel, but proved that the Israelites aspired to be just like everyone else, only more so, in the words of an old Jewish joke. Perhaps, then, the Bible preserves the evidence of a sexual dalliance between two men that would not have shocked anyone in the classical world.

"There can be little doubt," Horner concludes, "except on the part of those who absolutely refuse to believe it, that there existed a homosexual relationship between David and Jonathan. They were simply well-rounded men who acted fully within the standards of a society that had been dominated for two hundred years by an Aegean culture—a culture that accepted homosexuality."[45]

Once our eyes are opened, homoerotic moments and meanings can be detected throughout the life story of David. When Saul complains about Jonathan's relationship with David, the cause for Saul's complaint gets a political spin in most translations. "I know that you side with the son of Jesse," Saul rails at Jonathan, "to your shame, and to the shame of your mother's nakedness!" (1 Sam. 20:30) (New JPS) But some scholars detect "a slight textual corruption" in the original Hebrew text that distorts the meaning of Saul's words. Rather than scolding Jonathan for *siding* with David in a political dispute, Saul may have been expressing his shock and horror at Jonathan for *sleeping* with David. For that reason, some suggest that the ancient Greek versions of the Bible preserve a more accurate reading of Saul's words: "For, do I not know that you are an *intimate companion* to the son of Jesse?" is how some scholars would render the same text.[46]

The same sexual tension has been detected by artists and writers over the centuries. André Gide was tempted to see in King Saul himself a "possessive desire for the beautiful young shepherd who joins his court," and to explain Saul's efforts to slay David not as a matter of madness or politics but rather as "an attempt either to repress his homosexual longing by killing its inspiration or to revenge himself on a beloved who spurns him."[47] Even Goliath is depicted as hopelessly smitten with young David in a poem by Richard Howard, "The Giant on Giant Killing": "My eyes . . . fell upon David like a sword."[48]

The subtitle of Howard's poem is "Homage to the Bronze *David* of Donatello (1430)," and it reminds us that David inspired contradictory emotions in the artists and poets of the

Renaissance. To Peter Martyr, David and Jonathan offered an example of chaste male friendship that he considered superior to the pairings in the pagan myths of Greece and Rome, perhaps because he did not believe them capable of expressing physical love for each other. To Abraham Cowley, their friendship on earth was exalted into something mystical. "The reward of their perfect love for each other," Bible scholar Ted-Larry Pebworth explains, "is the eternal contemplation of God in the person of primal, absolute love."[49] But for artists such as Donatello and Michelangelo, who are said to have recruited their own young lovers as models for statues of David, the handsome warrior was the object of intense sexual yearning. And the same yearning can be teased out of the biblical text that inspired them—David was clearly a man given to carnal pleasure, and nothing in the Bible rules out the possibility that he took his pleasure with both men and women.

LONG LIVE THE KING!

The most telling detail in the biblical account of David's eulogy for Saul is what happened *after* the elegy was spoken and David turned his thoughts to matters of pure politics. The death of Saul and the defeat of the Israelites created a vacuum of power in ancient Israel and an opportunity for David to fill it. By surviving Saul's efforts to kill him, David had triumphed over the king, and now he was ready to claim the throne as yet another spoil of war. So David considered whether now was the right time to sever his allegiance to the Philistines, return to his tribal homeland in Judah, and put himself in play for the kingship. The biblical author works out these calculations in the metaphor of an oracle, thus putting the divine imprimatur on matters of realpolitik, but David is clearly thinking like a politician now.

"Shall I go up into any of the cities of Judah?" David inquires of Yahweh, presumably by consulting the "sacred divination box" or one of its many equivalents.

"Go up," God responds.

"Whither shall I go up?"

"Unto Hebron," God answers, naming the traditional capital of Judah and one of the most sacred sites in ancient Israel.

And so David abandoned the refuge that had been provided to him by the king of Achish and repudiated the fiefdom that had been granted for his faithful service. The exodus from Ziklag was complete: David and his wives, Abigail and Ahinoam, and the whole of his little army, "every man with his household," trekked out of Philistia and crossed the border into the land of Judah.

Surely it was a moment of anxiety for David. After all, his vassalage to the Philistines had lasted "a full year and four months"—the Bible is precise (1 Sam. 27:7)—and he had spent several years before his arrival in Ziklag at large in the countryside as a *habiru*. As he now trod the bloodied soil of his homeland, David must have wondered whether his belated gifts of Amalekite plunder to the elders of Hebron would be enough to restore him to their affections.

It turned out that David need not have worried. The Bible reports that he was welcomed as a favorite son, and any lingering resentment was erased by the death of Saul and the prospect that a man of Judah, rather than one of those detested Benjaminites, would now reign over the tribal homeland.

> And the men of Judah came, and they there anointed David king over the house of Judah.
>
> (2 Sam. 2:4)

The prize that Yahweh had set aside for young David when he was just a lad tending his father's flocks was now within his grasp—but, for the moment, David was king of Judah only. Even as David was crowned by acclamation of his own tribe, a man named Ishbaal, one of Saul's surviving sons,[50] was being conducted to a safe refuge in the forest of Gilead on the far side of the Jordan by Abner, a first cousin of Saul and general of his army. Abner took the bold initiative of crowning Ishbaal as king over a shaky coalition of peoples and tribes—the people of

Gilead and Geshur and the Jezreel Valley, and the Israelite tribes of Benjamin and Ephraim[51]—but he was sufficiently astute in matters of politics to dub the hapless son of Saul "king over all Israel." (2 Sam. 2:9) Thus, at the very moment of his coronation, David found himself in a civil war, and the crown of Israel was at stake.

Chapter Seven

"SHALL THE SWORD DEVOUR FOREVER?"

*". . . and the rest rose to their feet, the sceptred kings,
obeying the shepherd of the people, and the army
thronged behind them."*

—HOMER, *THE ILIAD*

David reigned as king of Judah in Hebron for exactly seven and a half years, but he ruled only a tribe and not the nation of Israel. Although Saul was dead, his dynasty survived in the person of his eldest son, a forty-year-old nebbish whom the Bible sometimes calls Ishbaal and sometimes Ish-bosheth. So long as a king from the house of Saul still reigned, David would remain only a tribal chieftain, and his path to the throne of all Israel would still be barred.

Sound political instincts had prompted David to send gifts to the tribal elders in his campaign for the crown of Judah. Now he made much the same effort to win the more glorious crown of Israel. Indeed, the Bible suggests that David embarked on a Machiavellian enterprise, forging alliances with the various tribes of Israel, currying favor with their elders, and acquiring a harem worthy of a great monarch, thus making himself an even more plausible candidate for the kingship of all Israel. Of course, David was ready to go to war for the crown, but his preparations for war were rooted in politics.

What prompted his next public gesture was an exploit by the men of Jabesh-Gilead. Upon hearing that the Philistines had hung the bodies of the slain Saul and his sons from the walls of Beth-shan, the pious heroes of Jabesh decided to do something about it.[1] They infiltrated Beth-shan by night, lifted the mangled corpses from the wall, and spirited them back to Jabesh, where the remains were cremated with honor under a sacred tamarisk tree. (1 Sam. 31:11–13) David had played no part in their exploit—but as king of Judah he saw fit to honor the men who had honored Saul.

"Blessed be ye of the Lord," went the message that David sent to the people of Jabesh, "and the Lord show kindness and truth to you, and I also will requite you this kindness, because you have done this thing." (1 Sam. 2:5–6)

But, even as he honored the people of Jabesh, David issued a warning. "Now let your hands be strong, and be you valiant, for Saul your lord is dead," his message continued, "and also the house of Judah has anointed me king over them." (1 Sam. 2:5–7)[2] His point was unmistakable: David, king of Judah, aspired to the throne of all Israel, and a civil war between Judah and the house of Saul seemed inevitable. And so the people of Jabesh, like everyone else in the land of Israel, would be forced to take sides.

MAN ON MAN

The incident that turned the mounting tribal rivalries into a clash of arms starts out as a slightly comical encounter.

The army of Ishbaal, under the command of Abner, marched out of the stronghold in Gilead, while the army of David, under the command of Joab, marched out of Hebron. The two generals and their men encountered each other at the pool of Gibeon,[3] Abner on one side and Joab on the other side.

Abner was Saul's first cousin, and Joab was David's nephew, and so the bond between each king and his general was a matter of blood rather than politics—a reminder that loyalty to family, clan, and tribe was still more crucial in ancient Israel than any sense of citizenship in a tribal confederation.[4] Indeed, the fact that Abner and Joab each supported a different candidate for the kingship of Israel did not yet make them open adversaries, and they were comfortable in chatting with each other across the pool of Gibeon.

"Let some of the young men take the field," Abner called to Joab, as if suggesting an impromptu game of football, "and play before us."

"Let them take the field," Joab answered in the same spirit of sportsmanship. (2 Sam 2:14)[5]

As the two generals and the rest of the soldiers watched from the edge of the pool, twelve of Abner's men and twelve of Joab's approached each other to "play," each man lining up face-to-face with his opposite as if for a scrimmage in a game of touch football. A similar scene is recorded in the history of the Third Crusade, when a few warring Franks and Saracens declared an impromptu truce, rested together, and set the young boys from the two sides in mock combat with each other. But according to the biblical account, this contest suddenly escalated from a sporting match into bloody combat.

> And they caught every one his fellow by the head, and thrust his sword in his fellow's side; so they fell down together.
>
> (2 Sam. 2:16)

One reading of the biblical text suggests a deadly irony at work: the soldiers on both sides were Israelites, members of the same tribal confederation and worshippers of the same God, and yet they turned their weapons against each other with tragic consequences. The same text, however, can also be understood as the report of a gladiatorial contest rather than a game that spins out of control. Josephus, a soldier and a scholar, describes the incident as purely a military encounter from the first moment—the two generals "wished to discover which of them had the braver soldiers, and it was agreed that twelve men from either side should meet in combat"[6]—and his modern counterpart, Yigael Yadin, also a soldier and a scholar, comes to the same conclusion. The young men, Yadin writes, were apparently selected to engage in a series of single combats, man on man, just as David had once taken up the challenge of Goliath to engage in a duel that would decide a battle.[7]

Whether it began in jest or in earnest, the incident at the pool of Gibeon symbolizes the futility and tragedy of civil war among the tribes of Israel: each man was killed in the act of killing his adversary, and so it was a battle with no victors. The site of the tragedy came to be called the Field of the Flints in apparent reference to the flint-bladed weapons that the men had used.[8] Once the twenty-four men had fallen, the rest of the soldiers closed with each other in force: "And the battle was very sore that day." (2 Sam. 2:17)

"SHALL THE SWORD DEVOUR FOREVER?"

David's army was the victor in the skirmish at the pool of Gibeon, the first battle of the civil war between Judah and Israel. But the biblical author pauses to relate another incident that helps us understand the highly personal nature of combat in the ancient world and, especially, the terrible intimacy of civil war. Although Abner served as commander in chief of Israel's army, he found himself face-to-face with the enemy when a foot soldier named Asahel, the brother of Joab, singled him out on the battlefield. Abner broke and ran, and Asahel followed.

"Turn aside from following me," Abner pleaded as he struggled to escape his pursuer. "Why should I smite you? How then should I hold up my face to Joab, your brother?" (2 Sam. 2:21–22)[9]

Abner's plea to Asahel reminds us that the combatants were related to each other by blood, and they were mindful of the ancient tribal code of vengeance that obliged a man to avenge the death of a near relation—the Arab word for "clan," to take an example from a similar culture, can be rendered more literally as "blood revenge group."[10] Thus, Abner was hesitant to slay Asahel precisely because he feared that Joab would regard the death of his brother not as a casualty of war but as an insult to family honor that required the taking of a life in exchange.

But Asahel continued his deadly pursuit, and so Abner executed a deft maneuver, thrusting his spear backward as he ran from Asahel and impaling him with such force that the spearhead passed through his groin and came out through his back. And, just as Abner had feared, what had begun as a death in the heat of battle was now the cause of a blood feud—Joab and another one of his brothers, Abishai, took up the chase.[11] By nightfall, Abner and his men found themselves trapped on a hilltop, surrounded by Joab and his army.

"Shall the sword devour forever?" Abner called to Joab in a line of biblical text that rumbles with augury. "Do you not know that it will be bitterness in the end? How long shall it be, then, before you bid your troops to stop the pursuit of their kinsmen?" (2 Sam. 2:26)[12]

Abner may have been begging for mercy, but his words were also statesmanlike. The people of Israel ought to look beyond the old loyalties to family, clan, and tribe, he suggested, and instead regard themselves as citizens of the nation of Israel and subjects of its king, Ishbaal. And, significantly, Joab heeded Abner's desperate but earnest words—he gave up his effort to avenge his slain brother and signaled a cease-fire by sounding a note on the ram's horn. At the sound of the shofar, which was used for both military and ritual purposes in ancient Israel, "all the people stood still, and pursued after Israel no more, neither fought they anymore." (2 Sam. 2:28)

"As God lives," Joab called out to Abner, "if you had not spoken, the soldiers would not have given up the pursuit of their kinsmen until the morning." (2 Sam. 2:27)[13]

Both Abner and Joab ordered their men on night marches—Abner fled across the Jordan River to put himself beyond striking distance in case Joab suffered a change of heart, and Joab hastened to reach Hebron by first light to announce his victory to David. Unlike the fantastic body counts that are often reported in the Bible, the number of casualties of the battle at the pool of Gibeon is entirely credible: David's army suffered only twenty deaths, including Asahel's, and "three hundred and three-score" of the men in Abner's army were slain in battle. But it was only the first skirmish in the civil war between Judah and the rest of the Israelites: "Now there was long war," the Bible confirms, "between the house of Saul and the house of David." (2 Sam. 2:32, 3:1) David had been right in warning the men of Jabesh to prepare for war. A price would be paid in blood for the crown that he sought, but not the blood of David.

A DOG'S HEAD

The life of David and the history of ancient Israel, as described in Samuel, were compounded of sex and politics, and sometimes it is impossible to say where sex leaves off and politics begins. One example is an incident that took place within the house of Saul in the aftermath of the old king's death. Once again, the biblical author is foreshadowing an even more sordid incident of the same kind that will soon arise within the house of David.

Abner had contrived to put Saul's son on the throne of Israel—but Abner was the hand that worked the puppet named Ishbaal, and only once did the puppet admonish the puppetmaster. Abner had availed himself of the sexual favors of a woman named Rizpah—a concubine of Saul and the mother of two of Ishbaal's half brothers—or so the new king had somehow come to believe. Intimacy with a royal concubine was regarded in ancient Israel not only as a violation of a sexual taboo and an insult to the reigning king, but—even more ominously—as an act of treason.

"To lie with a monarch's concubine," explains Bible scholar An-son Rainey, "was tantamount to usurpation of the throne."[14]

"Why have you lain with my father's concubine?" Ishbaal de-manded of Abner, surely surprising himself no less than Abner with his sudden audacity.

"Am I a dog's head that belongs to Judah?" said the defiant Abner. "I have been loyally serving the house of Saul, and I have not delivered you into the hand of David, and yet you reproach me over a woman!" (2 Sam. 3:8)[15]

The cagey Abner never actually confirmed or denied Ishbaal's accusation, and the Bible does not tell us whether the charge was true or false. If, in fact, Abner had summoned a royal concubine to his bedchamber, it would have confirmed that the kingmaker held the king in contempt or, even worse, that he aspired to re-place Ishbaal on the throne. Indeed, the fact that the fearful Ish-baal dared to make such an accusation reveals how little he trusted his own general. In any event, Abner responded to Ish-baal's question with a bold and unambiguous threat: "May God do thus and more to Abner if I do not do for David as the Lord swore to him—to transfer the kingship from the house of Saul, and to establish the throne of David over Israel and Judah from Dan to Beersheba." (2 Sam. 3:9–10) (New JPS)

The hapless king fell silent at Abner's self-righteous speech. "And he could not answer Abner another word," the Bible reports, "because he feared him." And, true to his threat, the treacherous general promptly sent a message to David, offering to betray the son of Saul. "Make league with me," Abner proposed, "and, be-hold, my hand shall be with you to bring over all Israel unto you." (2 Sam. 3:11, 12)

David was willing to accept Abner's offer, but he had a griev-ance of his own to settle before he would make a deal. Years ear-lier, when David was still a fugitive, King Saul had annulled the marriage of David and Michal and married his daughter to a man named Paltiel. Since then, of course, David had collected a half-dozen more wives—not only Abigail and Ahinoam, whom we have already encountered, but Maacah and Haggith and Abital and Eglah, too, all of whom had borne him sons. But now David wanted Michal back, if only to enhance his kingly stature and to strengthen his claim on Saul's throne by putting a royal princess back into his own harem. (2 Sam. 3:2–5)[16]

"One thing I require of you," David sent word back to Abner. "You shall not see my face except you first bring Michal, Saul's daughter, when you come." (2 Sam. 3:13)[17]

Another measure of David's determination to reclaim Michal—and a measure, too, of David's characteristic guile—is found in the fact that he sent much the same message to Ishbaal. "Deliver to me my wife Michal," David admonished the son of Saul, "whom I betrothed to me for a hundred foreskins of the Philistines." Nothing in the law or tradition of ancient Israel entitled David to make such an audacious demand, but the threat of David's army was enough to frighten Ishbaal into compliance. And it was Ishbaal, always unsure of his grip on the crown and always deferential to more forceful men, who took his sister from her second husband and sent her to David as a kind of peace-offering.

The incident raises a question about David that will loom larger as the eye of the biblical author seeks out ever more intimate places in his life story. The Bible shows us, again and again, that David was a man who loved women. Indeed, the defining moment in his long and troubled life will result from his mortal weakness for one woman in particular. But it is also clear that David was capable of using and even abusing women. Here, for example, David did not seek to remarry his first wife out of tender emotions; rather, he calculated that Michal, a daughter of Saul, would be a valuable political asset in his campaign for the throne of Israel.

Michal's needs and desires in the matter do not enter into the equation. As a young woman, of course, she had declared her love for David. But did David love Michal? "That is precisely what the text leaves unsaid," writes feminist Bible scholar J. Cheryl Exum, "suggesting that David's motives are . . . purely political," both at the time of their first marriage and at the time when he reclaimed Michal.[18] In fact, the whole incident raises the unsettling notion that Michal was forcibly separated from her second husband, Paltiel, and sent back to David's harem against her will. And as we shall see, her life as one of David's many wives was utterly loveless.

Perhaps the best evidence that Michal was taken by force is a poignant note that has been injected into the biblical account of these otherwise political proceedings. As Michal was escorted back to the court of David, Paltiel followed her in abject misery, "weeping as he went." Only when the unhappy parade reached the outskirts of Hebron—Michal followed by her sobbing husband, and both of them under guard—did Abner turn the heartbroken man around and send him back home.

"Go, return," the general ordered. "And he returned." (2 Sam. 3:14, 16)

The sad story of Michal is the first, but not the last, example of a woman whom David takes for his sexual pleasure or political advantage without bothering to consider whether she is a willing consort.

"ALL THAT YOUR SOUL DESIRES"

Once Michal was restored to her first husband, Abner renewed his courtship of David. To ingratiate himself, he began to agitate on David's behalf within the tribe of Benjamin and among the elders of Israel. David still reigned only in the land of Judah, but Abner now campaigned for his elevation to the throne of all Israel. Even though the prophet Samuel had anointed David in secret, Abner seemed to know of David's claim of divine favor, and he piously invoked the God of Israel to justify his sudden change of colors.

"The Lord has spoken of David, saying: By the hand of my servant David I will save my people Israel out of the hand of the Philistines and all their enemies," Abner said. "In times past you sought for David to be king over you—now do it." (2 Sam. 3:17–18)[19]

The Bible does not disclose why Abner experienced a change of heart. Perhaps he concluded that David was destined to take the crown away from Ishbaal, and he wanted to put himself on the winning side. Perhaps he resented Ishbaal's accusation of sexual scandal, whether or not he was guilty as charged. In any case, Abner's declarations of loyalty persuaded David that he was now an earnest ally, and so David granted Abner the audience he had long sought. Abner arrived in Hebron with twenty of his men—all blooded in battle against David's army—but David welcomed his former enemies with a royal feast. As Abner's men drank and dined at the king's table, the turncoat general coolly offered to betray the man he had once championed.

"I will arise and go, and will gather all Israel unto my lord the king," Abner said, "that they make a covenant with you, and that you may reign over all that your soul desires." (2 Sam. 3:21)

David accepted Abner's pledge of loyalty without a moment of self-caution. If the renegade general of a rival king was willing to come over to David's camp, he was ready to embrace his new ally without questioning his motives or his bona fides. The deal was done, and Abner "went in peace." (2 Sam. 3:21)

Not everyone in David's inner circle was quite so trusting of Abner, who had changed his colors once and might change them again. David's own general, Joab, still nursed a highly personal grudge against the man who had killed his brother in battle. When Joab returned to Hebron after his latest foray against the Israelites to discover that Abner had come and gone with David's blessings, the headstrong general charged into the throne room and confronted David.

"What have you done?" Joab cried out. "Abner came to deceive you, and to learn all about your movements and to find out what you are doing!" (2 Sam. 3:24–25)[20]

The Bible does not tell us whether David answered these insolent words, but the scene suggests that Joab was unimpressed by the crown that David now wore and unintimidated by the man he had known as a comrade in arms long before David made himself king of Judah. Indeed, Joab was never willing to defer to his uncle's authority, and now he took it upon himself to exact revenge on Abner without bothering to ask for permission—he dispatched his own messengers to summon Abner back to Hebron, "but David knew it not." (2 Sam. 3:26)

When Abner appeared once again at the gates of Hebron, perhaps a bit bewildered by his sudden recall, Joab called him aside and asked for a moment "to speak with him quietly." The unsuspecting Abner drew close to Joab and, we might imagine, inclined his head to hear what his former adversary had to say. And then Joab drew his dagger and delivered a deathblow to Abner, striking him in the groin, the very same spot where Abner's spear had penetrated the body of his dead brother. Asahel's blood cried out for revenge, as Joab saw it, and now revenge had been taken.

Surely David the outlaw would not have been shocked at the rough justice that Joab inflicted on Abner. David the king, however, could not afford to be implicated in the blood feud that raged between the clans of Abner and Joab. Just as he had done when the Amalekite reported the slaying of Saul, David disavowed the slaying of Saul's general. Although both deaths were ultimately to his benefit, David refused to alienate the people of Israel by acknowledging any role in these useful murders.

"I and my kingdom are guiltless before the Lord forever from the blood of Abner," David mused aloud. "Let it fall upon the head of Joab, and upon all his father's house." (2 Sam. 3:28–29)

A public funeral for Abner was held in Hebron. David himself followed the bier and delivered the eulogy, whipping the crowd into a frenzy of grief. "And the king lifted up his voice, and wept at the grave of Abner, and all the people wept," the Bible reports, describing a display of political showmanship that seems eerily modern. "Know you not that there is a prince and a great man fallen this day in Israel?" David cried. Ignoring the entreaties of his own courtiers, he made a point of refusing to take food on the day of the funeral: "God do so to me, and more also, if I taste bread or anything else till the sun be down." (2 Sam. 3:32, 35, 38)

And his public display of grief had precisely the effect that David had intended.

"And all the people took notice of it, and it pleased them," the Bible records. "So all the people and all Israel understood that day that it was not the king's will to slay Abner." (2 Sam. 3:36)[21]

Back in the palace at Hebron, David complained to his courtiers about the ruthlessness of Joab and his brothers—"These men are too hard for me!"—and he piously called upon Yahweh to punish them. "Reward the evil-doer," he prayed, "according to his wickedness." But he recognized, too, that a hard man can be good to find in the treacherous world in which he lived. Joab, who has been described by modern scholars as a "good Machiavellian courtier" and the "toughest of ancient Near Eastern mafiosi," was too valuable to the ambitious king of Judah to be sacrificed for the sake of public relations. (2 Sam. 3:39)[22]

And so David ordered Joab to join in mourning the man he had killed—"Rend your clothes, and gird you with sackcloth, and wail before Abner" (2 Sam. 3:21, 39)—but he neither dismissed Joab from his service nor punished him for slaying Abner. The day might come when a man of Joab's skills and temperament would turn out to be crucial to winning and keeping the throne. If Joab ever became dispensable, David must have resolved, he would dispense with him. And until then, Joab would remain in service to David as the general of his army and, from time to time, the royal hit man.

BEHOLD THE HEAD OF THE KING

When word of Abner's assassination reached the court of King Ishbaal in far-off Gilead, "his hands became feeble, and all the Israelites were affrighted." Abner had been the real power in the rump kingdom, and now Abner was dead and gone. How then could the cowering Ishbaal, who has been dismissed by Bible scholars as "an ineffectual weakling" and "a thoroughly unkingly invertebrate," stand up against the ruthless king of Judah who so clearly wanted to claim the crown of all Israel? (2 Sam. 4:1)²³

Ishbaal's terror was wholly justified. Two captains in his army, Baanah and Rechab, following the example of their dead general, sought to win favor with David by delivering Ishbaal's head. So shabby was the court of King Ishbaal that he was attended only by a woman who busied herself with sifting wheat as she sat outside his door while he took his customary midday nap—and, fatefully, she had fallen asleep at her chore. The two conspirators walked right past her into the king's bedchamber, where they stabbed the sleeping man to death. (2 Sam. 4:5) (NEB)

The assassins paused only to hack off the king's head, and they carried it with them as they slipped out of the palace and fled toward the frontier. All night long they traveled in the direction of Judah, cradling the gruesome evidence of the favor they had done for David, urging each other on with speculation about how richly they would be rewarded for it.

"Behold the head of Ishbaal, the son of Saul, your enemy, who sought your life," the killers addressed David as they held up the severed head. "Yahweh has avenged my lord the king this day of Saul and of his seed." (2 Sam. 4:8)

The boastful assassins may have been well pleased with their deed, but David declared that he was not. "When one told me: 'Behold, Saul is dead,' as though he brought good tidings, I took hold of him and slew him instead of giving a reward for his tidings," David responded. "How much more, when wicked men have slain a righteous person in his own house upon his bed, shall I not now require his blood of your hand, and take you away from the earth?" (2 Sam. 4:10–11)

So, as he had done so many times before, David issued a death sentence. His soldiers fell on the two men, "and they slew them, and cut off their hands and their feet, and hanged them up beside the pool in Hebron." The severed head of Ishbaal was given an honorable burial in the same grave that held the corpse of Abner, the man who had made him king of Israel and who had been ready to unmake him. Buried along with their mangled remains was the brief dynasty that Saul had founded.

"WE ARE THY BONE AND THY FLESH"

Years had passed since David was first called out of the fields by his father to meet a strange old seer named Samuel. On that day, the prophet had poured oil over his beautiful young head and promised him the throne of Israel as a gift from Yahweh. But over the years David must have wondered when the promise would be fulfilled. Of course, he did not wait in idleness for God to put a crown on his head, nor does the Bible suggest that God intended him to do so—David made his own destiny, both by force of arms and by backroom intrigue. Now at last David was rewarded with the prize that he had sought for so long, with such craft and cunning, and with such bloodthirsty ambition. At the age of thirty-seven, after seven and a half years on the tribal throne in Hebron, David was raised by popular acclaim to the kingship of both Judah *and* Israel.

We can imagine David's satisfaction when one of his courtiers announced that a delegation of distinguished men, the elders of all Israel, had appeared at the gates of his palace in Hebron and now awaited his pleasure.

"Behold," the elders of Israel proclaimed to the king of Judah, "we are thy bone and thy flesh." (2 Sam. 5:1)

These diplomatic words were perhaps intended to veil the ugly truth that all of them knew: David was the king of Judah, and Judah was at war with the rest of the twelve tribes of Israel. Indeed, the very notion of a blood relationship between David and the rest of the Israelites is seen by scholars as a late insertion in the original Hebrew text. Still, the elders of Israel were willing to put an end to the bloody civil war by conceding defeat, making a covenant with David, and acclaiming him as "king over Israel."

"In the past, while Saul was still king over us, you led the forces of Israel to war and you brought them home again," the elders declared by way of obeisance, acknowledging David's heroism in war and his good standing with God, "and Yahweh said to you: 'You shall be shepherd of my people Israel, and you shall be their prince.' " (2 Sam. 4:2) (NEB)

The long and glorious reign of David, king of Israel, had begun.

Chapter Eight

CITY OF DAVID

Stories about Jerusalem should not be dismissed because they are "only" myths: they are important precisely because they are myths.

—KAREN ARMSTRONG, *JERUSALEM*

David's first act as king of Israel was to select a new royal capital for the united kingdom over which he now reigned. As a battle-tested military strategist, he wanted a place that was centrally located and easily defensible. As a savvy politician, he wanted a place that belonged to none of the twelve tribes. The capital was to be regarded as an island of national identity in a sea of tribal rivalries—a symbolic function not unlike that of the District of Columbia in the early history of the United States. So David chose as his new capital a fortified hill-town in the heart of ancient Israel, a place that had always belonged to the Jebusites, one of the native-dwelling tribes of Canaan, a place called Jerusalem.

Jerusalem has long been regarded in pious tradition as a place of surpassing holiness. According to the the Talmud, Jerusalem was the place where Adam offered the first sacrifice to God, where Noah erected an altar after the Flood, where Abraham was called to slaughter Isaac.[1] So sacred was Jerusalem that in one rabbinical fairy tale David refuses to mount a military assault on its defenses. Instead, he orders Joab to climb to the top of a cypress tree near the city wall; the tree is pulled back with ropes and then allowed to spring back into place, and Joab is catapulted over the high wall and into the heart of Jerusalem. The surprised Jebusites surrender to Joab without a fight, and the city wall lowers itself to allow David to stride into Jerusalem.[2]

The truth, as recorded in the Book of Joshua, is rather more brutal. Unlike the other cities of Canaan, Jerusalem had beaten back the Israelite armies under the command of Joshua during the invasion and conquest that first established Israelite sovereignty: "And as for the Jebusites, the inhabitants of Jerusalem, the children of Judah could not drive them out." (Josh. 15:63)[3] To make Jerusalem the capital of his new monarchy, David would have to succeed where the mighty Joshua had failed.

"You will never get in here!" the Jebusites taunted David and his men from the ramparts of Jerusalem. "Even the blind and the lame will turn you back." (2 Sam. 5:6) (New JPS)

But the Jebusites badly underestimated David's cunning and ruthlessness. He sent a squad of commandos to infiltrate the fortifications and surprise its defenders, issuing an order of shocking brutality.

"Whoever smites a Jebusite," David ordered his men, "let him strike at the windpipe, for David hates the lame and the blind!" (2 Sam. 5:8) (AB)

THE LAME AND THE BLIND

The blood-shaking command of David has been the source of much consternation over the centuries. What, after all, are we to make of the fact that God's chosen king declares his hatred for "the lame and the blind" with such callousness and cruelty? The question is even more frustrating because the biblical text itself is so "troubled" and even "corrupted" that we cannot know with certainty what the biblical author meant to convey with these words.[4] Still, the mighty efforts of scholars and theologians to explain away David's death sentence on the disabled is significant in itself—King David is ultimately so charismatic that sympathetic Bible readers have come up with some highly inventive arguments to excuse his less savory words and deeds.

Thus David's order to "strike at the windpipe," as P. Kyle McCarter, Jr., renders the Hebrew text of 2 Samuel 5:8 in the Anchor Bible, may mean only that David was urging his men to kill rather than maim the enemy in the assault on Jerusalem—he was a pragmatic soldier, and he did not want to be burdened with wounded prisoners of war once he had conquered Jerusalem.[5] Indeed, the seemingly bloodthirsty order may be understood as evidence of David's compassion: he was expressing a preference for a clean kill in battle, McCarter proposes, out of respect for "religious scruples against the mutilation of living human beings, a violation of the sanctity of the body to which David finds killing preferable."[6]

Other scholars suggest that the phrase is a metaphor that reveals how David managed to penetrate the defenses of Jerusalem. The Hebrew word for "windpipe" (*sinnor*) also means "water pipe" in postbiblical usage and may refer to a gutter or conduit that ran through the city walls to the nearby Spring of Gihon, the principal source of fresh water supplies for Jerusalem. Thus, some translators suggest that David ordered his men to penetrate the defenses of Jerusalem by crawling up the waterworks: "Getteth up to the gutter" is how *The Holy Scriptures According to the Masoretic Text* (JPS) renders the same phrase.[7] Still others regard *sinnor* as a kind of grappling hook, which is the meaning of a similar word in Aramaic, and thus the New English Bible translates the same text in a much different way: "Let him use his grappling-iron to reach the lame and the blind, David's bitter enemies."

Of course, none of these theories account for the unsettling fact that David is said to *hate* "the blind and the lame," and a heroic effort has been made over the centuries to explain it away. Medieval commentators imagined that the Jebusites had posted images of a blind Isaac and a lame Jacob on the ramparts of

Jerusalem to demoralize the Israelites.[8] One especially imaginative sage of the late Middle Ages proposed that "the lame and the blind" were water-powered robots, and he explained David's supposed attack on the waterworks of Jerusalem as a way of disabling them by cutting off their power supply!

Modern scholars have proposed more reasonable, if not necessarily more accurate, approaches to the same troubling text. Maybe "the lame and the blind" were "taboo cultic personnel of the Jebusite shrine" who were stationed on the fortifications in the hope that David and his men would break off their attack for fear of violating the taboo.[9] Or "perhaps [the Jebusites] paraded the blind and the lame of the city on the walls, as was the custom of the Hittite army, to warn any soldier who dared to penetrate the stronghold of his fate."[10] Each of these scholarly arguments, no less than the fanciful tales offered by the Talmudic storytellers, is intended to give us a kinder and gentler David than the ruthless warrior-king who is depicted in the Book of Samuel.

The most straightforward reading of the text does not require such exertions. The Jebusites taunted David—"Even the blind and the lame will turn you back"—and David replied with a taunt of his own: "David hates the lame and the blind." Even if this exchange of threat and counterthreat was merely an example of battlefield rhetoric, full of sarcasm and perhaps a bit of bluff, it rings true of David. He had always been willing to act ruthlessly against anyone he regarded as an enemy or a security risk, and nothing he said or did during the conquest of Jerusalem would have come as a surprise to those who knew him before he was king of Israel.

THE CITY OF DAVID

A second and entirely different version of the conquest of Jerusalem appears in the Book of Chronicles. As we have already seen, the Chronicler is always quick to censor the scandalous details of David's life. He betrays no knowledge of David's brutal sentiments toward "the lame and the blind," nor does he report a commando attack on the waterworks of Jerusalem. Rather he gives an antiseptic account that focuses on an act of daring and courage by Joab.

"And David said: 'The first man to kill a Jebusite shall become chief and captain,' " goes the account of the Chronicler. "And Joab went up first, and so he was given the command." (1 Chron. 11:6)[11]

Chronicles is a much later—and much fussier—source than the Book of Samuel, and that's why scholars are tempted to regard the older work as the more authentic one, especially when the two are at odds. The Chronicler's tale, for example, suggests that Joab first achieved his high rank in David's army by his feat of arms in the conquest of Jerusalem. The Court Historian, by contrast, assigns Joab a prominent role throughout the civil war that brought David to the throne. Both sources, however, agree that Joab was a crucial figure in David's life; indeed, Joab is "second only to David and Absalom in frequency of reference," as Bible scholar Joel Rosenberg points out, and he will come to play a fateful if ultimately tragic role in preserving David's monarchy.[12] In fact, some scholars suspect that the greater role allowed to Joab by the Chronicler is evidence that David's rough-and-ready henchman may have been an even more prominent figure in ancient Israel than the Court Historian was willing to admit.

"Joab is a sympathetic figure," explains Rosenberg, "decisive when the king is vacillating, loyal to David throughout his reign and the interregnum, active where the king is sedentary, performing the work that the king finds odious, deferring to the king where credit is to be claimed for victories, and, in general, devoted to the civil peace, or at least, like any good Machiavellian courtier, devoted to the economy of violence."[13]

For the moment, David still regarded the conquest of Jerusalem as a personal triumph, and rightfully so. According to the Court Historian, David devised the strategy for penetrating the defenses, and he led his own men in the successful assault. Significantly, he neither asked for nor required any assistance from the tribal militia that had served King Saul—David conquered Jerusalem with only the picked men of his own army.

"The capture of Jerusalem was entirely a private affair of David's," observes Gerhard von Rad,[14] and Frank Moore Cross, another luminary in biblical scholarship, points out that Jerusalem is depicted as "the personal possession of the king by right of conquest, providing the king with an independent power base over which he exercised absolute sway."[15] Accordingly, David promptly named the city he had conquered—or, at least, the citadel at the center of Jerusalem—after himself.

"And David dwelt in the stronghold," the Bible reports, "and called it the City of David." (2 Sam. 5:9)

Here we can discern two different explanations for the same event: the Court Historian credits the flesh-and-blood David with the victory over the Jebusites, but more pious biblical sources insist that the credit belongs to God alone. Shrugging off David's military genius and the sheer guts of the men who served him, one of the later biblical authors puts a theological spin on the Court Historian's battle report—the conquest of Jerusalem ought to be seen as the fulfillment of the promise that God had made to David so many years before.

"David kept growing stronger, for Yahweh, the God of Armies, was with him," goes one characteristic passage that has been written into the Court Historian's account. "Thus David knew that Yahweh had established him as king over Israel and had exalted his kingship for the sake of his people Israel." (2 Sam. 5:10, 12)[16]

The same tension between history and theology, of course, can be detected throughout the biblical life story of David. Some Bible readers, like some of the biblical sources, will entertain the idea that David succeeded on the strength of his own brilliant but thoroughly mortal gifts and powers. Others see David's successes as the working out of God's will in history. Not a few Bible readers and Bible scholars are able to hold both thoughts in their minds at once—David was both gifted *and* God-inspired, and that is why he survived and prevailed against every enemy and every defeat that stood between him and the glorious kingship described in the Bible.

In either case, David was now ready to take on the momentous task of nation building, which both God and David saw as his destiny and which Bible historians praise as his greatest accomplishment. The obstacles that he faced were daunting: the twelve tribes of Israel were not yet a unified people, and David would have to overcome their tendency toward blood feuds and civil war. Indeed, the Israelites were not far removed from their origins as pastoral nomads, and they lacked the resources of the powerful monarchies and empires that surrounded them on all sides—a powerful king with a cabinet of ministers and counselors, an efficient bureaucracy, a professional army equipped with state-of-the-art weaponry, and the other elements of what we would today call infrastructure.

But it is exactly here and now that David reveals his stature as a leader, a mover and shaker, the maker of a nation and an empire. Significantly, he is shown to embellish his new capital in a manner befitting a great and glorious king. Under the Jebusites, Jerusalem centered around a hilltop citadel, but David pushed to the outer limits of the site: "And he built the city from around the Millo to the surrounding wall." (1 Chron. 11:8) (AB)[17] David received emissaries from the king of neighboring Tyre, Hiram, who sent him a supply of the rare and prized lumber from those famous cedars of Lebanon and a contingent of carpenters and masons whose skill and sophistication was unmatched in tribal Israel.[18]

Once construction of the palace was under way, David began filling the royal harem with fresh young women and the royal nursery with more children. Perhaps to ingratiate himself with the Jebusites over whom he now ruled—Jerusalem was, after all, a conquered and occupied city—David "took him more concubines and wives out of Jerusalem," and his new wives turned out to be blessedly fertile: "And there were yet sons and daughters born to David," eleven of whom are named at this point in the Bible. (2 Sam. 5:13)[19]

David was now firmly seated on the throne of Israel, and he

was approaching those sublime heights of power and glory toward which he had long struggled. "And David perceived that the Lord had established him king over Israel, for his kingdom was exalted exceedingly, for His people Israel's sake," the Chronicler exults. "And the fame of David went out into all lands, and the Lord brought the fear of him upon all nations." (1 Chron. 14:17)

One nation, however, did not yet fear David—the Philistines. And, ironically, it was David's former ally who would put him to the first and crucial test of his kingship.

MAN OF WAR

None of the grand exploits attributed to David escaped the attention of the Philistines, or so the Bible suggests. As long as David was merely king of Judah, the Philistines might have regarded him as a vassal and even an ally—after all, he had served them faithfully as a soldier of fortune! But whoever wore the crown of a united Israel would surely be regarded as an enemy of Philistia, and so it was that the Philistines declared war on King David. The army that marched on Jerusalem to dethrone King David was the very same army in which he had once sought to serve in the campaign against King Saul. But now it was David, not Saul, whose kingship was at risk.

The Philistines sent a task force to search out David and his men—but David, too, had his sources of intelligence. When he learned that a Philistine army was on the move, he went to ground in what the Bible calls "the stronghold," presumably the City of David in Jerusalem but possibly his old stronghold at Adullam. Soon the enemy appeared in the lowlands of Rephaim, which lay on the approaches to Jerusalem and positioned the Philistines to split the northern and southern regions of David's united monarchy. Thus the old guerrilla fighter was faced with the same tactical decision that figured so crucially in his war with Saul—should he stay in his stronghold and and hope to survive a siege, or should he sally forth and fight?

"Shall I go up against the Philistines?" he inquired of God, presumably resorting to the casting of lots. God answered: "Go up!" (2 Sam. 5:18–19) (AB)

David and his men engaged the Philistines and succeeded in driving them off. Indeed, the Philistines fled in such haste that they left behind their own array of idols, which David and his men seized as spoils of war. The taking of an enemy's ritual paraphernalia was a common practice in ancient warfare—it was thought to humiliate the defeated enemy and celebrate the superior power of the god or gods of the victor. In fact, the Philistines had once taken the Ark of the Covenant, if only briefly, in an earlier battle with the Israelites. (1 Sam. 4:1–11) Lest we suspect that David and his men actually *used* the abandoned idols, the fussy author of Chronicles (but *not* the author of Samuel) insists that "David gave instructions and they burned [them] with fire." (1 Chron. 14:12) (AB)

The first skirmish with the Philistines, as it turned out, was only a tactical victory. The Philistines regrouped and appeared again at the approaches to Jerusalem, and David resorted again to the tools of divination to seek instruction from God. Now, however, Yahweh is shown to give rather more elaborate advice than could plausibly have been extracted with a series of yes-or-no questions. God, displaying the tactical insights of a Napoléon or a von Clausewitz, now ruled out a second frontal assault on the Philistine lines. "Circle around them," God said, ordering David to execute a flanking maneuver and carry out an assault on the undefended rear of the enemy. To express the tactical advantages of the maneuver, the biblical text slips into a kind of martial rhapsody.

"Then, when you hear the sound of the wind in the asherahs," God tells David, referring to the upright poles by which the goddess Asherah was venerated, "look sharp, for Yahweh will have marched out ahead of you to attack the Philistine camp!" (2 Sam. 5:23–24)[20]

Here we find the kind of metaphorical flourish that is so often used by the biblical authors to depict a physical manifestation of the ineffable God of Israel—Yahweh will manifest himself as a kind of storm god, and the sound of the wind is the evidence of God's physical presence. The very fact that God is shown to express himself in ornate prose rather than the yes-or-no answers of divination suggests that the passage is of late authorship. But the kernel of military intelligence that can be found within the husk of theology makes it clear that David's generalship was the decisive factor in defeating the Philistines once and for all.

"David did as the Lord had commanded him, and he smote the Philistines from Gibeon to Gezer." (2 Sam. 5:25)[21]

Gibeon, of course, was the place that figured so prominently in the civil war that followed the death of Saul. It was here that twelve men of Ishbaal's army and twelve men of David's army managed to kill each other off in a single round of ritual combat. Gezer was a frontier town on the border between Israel and Philistia, and so the biblical author is suggesting that David finally succeeded in driving the Philistines out of the heartland of Israel and confining them to a narrow coastal strip along the Mediterranean. The expulsion of the Philistines from Gibeon was a notable achievement because it was in the nearby town of Kiriath-jearim[22] that the most sacred ritual object in all of Israel was located—the gilded wooden chest known in the Bible as the Ark of the Covenant.

GOLDEN TUMORS AND GOLDEN MICE

The Ark was a tactile symbol of both history and theology in ancient Israel. According to the Bible, the Ark was fabricated by a master carpenter named Bezaleel during the forty years of wandering in the Sinai. Moses himself provided the specifications—"two cubits and a half was the length of it, and a cubit and a half the height of it," all of it fashioned out of acacia-wood, covered with pure gold, and fitted with rings and staves that allowed the Ark to be carried by the Israelites wherever they went. (Exod. 25:1 ff.)

Within the Ark were stored the two stone tablets on which

Moses was believed to have inscribed the sacred law of Yahweh on Mount Sinai. (Deut. 10:1) Atop the Ark were two gold-wrought figures of cherubim—fierce sphinxlike beasts rather than the fat angels of contemporary Christmas cards—and God himself was imagined to have ridden on their outstretched wings as he led the Israelites through the wilderness: "Yahweh Seated-upon-the-Cherubim" is one of the many names of the God of Israel. (2 Sam. 6:2) (AB) Indeed, the Ark was carried into battle by the Israelites precisely because it was imagined to be the throne and footstool of Yahweh Sabaoth, that is, Yahweh in his fearsome role as the God of Armies.[23]

How the Ark first came to the town of Kiriath-jearim is the point of an especially bizarre tale preserved in the Book of Samuel. Twenty years earlier, when David was still a lad tending his father's sheep in Bethlehem, the Philistines had succeeded in capturing the Ark in battle, but later they insisted on restoring it to the defeated Israelites when they found themselves afflicted with an infestation of mice and a plague of tumors.[24] To make amends to Yahweh over the hijacking of the Ark, and to persuade him to lift the plague, the Philistines struck on the idea of fashioning five mice and five tumors out of pure gold; they loaded the Ark and the golden offerings on a cart drawn by milk cows and sent the driverless cart in the direction of the Israelite border, where it finally came to halt in a village called Beth-shemesh.

The surprised locals, busy at work on the wheat harvest, greeted the Ark with an impromptu round of burnt-offerings, but their exultation did not last long. When a few of the curious reapers dared to peak inside the Ark, God promptly struck them dead, and, lest anyone miss the point, he smote fifty thousand others, too. So the people of Beth-shemesh hastened the Ark on its way—"Who is able to stand before Yahweh, this holy God? And to whom shall it go up from us?"—and it finally came to rest in the private house of the local priest in Kiriath-jearim, where the Ark remained for the next twenty years. (1 Sam. 6:20–7:2)

So long as the district around Kiriath-jearim remained under occupation by the Philistines, the Ark was inaccessible to the people of Israel. Now David had evicted the Philistines, but he was not content to leave such a rare and precious relic in a backwater town. Indeed, some scholars suggest that David was a conqueror rather than a liberator of Kiriath-jearim, and he seized the Ark as a spoil of war![25] In any event, David resolved to bring the Ark from its humble setting in Kiriath-jearim to Jerusalem, where it would symbolize the centrality of the City of David in the newly reunited kingdom of Israel.

The Ark may have been regarded as a relic of the greatest sanctity in ancient Israel, but David was determined to use it for political purposes. The presence of the Ark in Jerusalem would attract worshippers from all over the land of Israel; it would link his new-minted crown and his newfangled capital to the most ancient traditions of the twelve tribes; and it would demonstrate to any doubters or dissidents that King David, unlike Saul or any of his sons, was the master of his own fate and the fate of all Israel.

THIRTY THOUSAND PICKED MEN

David's army had numbered only six hundred during his years as a freebooter and an outlaw, but now the king of Israel summoned thirty thousand picked men from throughout the land of Israel to serve as a guard of honor in the solemn procession that would bring the Ark into Jerusalem.[26] Ranks of musicians filled the air with "the sound of all kinds of cypress-wood instruments," as the Bible describes the scene, "with lyres, harps, timbrels, sistrums, and cymbals." (2 Sam. 6:5) (New JPS) The Ark was loaded on a cart fashioned out of virgin lumber and pulled by a brace of oxen, and two men—the sons of the priest in whose home the Ark had been sheltered—were detailed to walk alongside and guide the cart on the road to Jerusalem. David himself led the procession, leaping and dancing with ecstatic abandon.

So holy was the Ark, however, that even the pious showmanship of David was not sufficient to soothe the God of Israel, or so the Bible allows us to understand. At one awful moment, as the cart passed a threshing-floor on the road to Jerusalem, the oxen stumbled and one of the attendants, a man named Uzzah, reached out to steady the Ark. His only motive was to make sure that the throne of invisible Yahweh did not tumble to the ground. But the mere touch of a mortal hand was apparently an offense to Yahweh, because "the anger of the Lord was kindled against Uzzah, and God smote him there for his error, and there he died for his error." (2 Sam. 6:7)

David, always so bluff and brave, so rough and ready, was badly rattled by the incident at the threshing-floor. "David was afraid of Yahweh that day," the Bible reports, and he wondered whether Uzzah's death meant that God was symbolically withdrawing his imprimatur on David's kingship by preventing the Ark from being installed in the City of David. "How can I let the Ark of Yahweh come to me?" fretted David. So he ordered a halt to the procession, dispersed the soldiers and the musicians, the singers and the dancers, and stashed the Ark in a house on the road to Jerusalem, the residence of a man called Obed-edom, where it remained for the next three months. (2 Sam. 6:9)[27]

Only when David was assured that the auguries were good— "Yahweh has blessed Obed-edom's house and all that belongs to him because of the Ark of God"—did he try again to bring the Ark to the City of David. "I'll bring the blessing back to my own house!" he figured. (2 Sam. 6:12) (AB)[28] But now he took even greater precautions to soothe the temper of the mercurial Yahweh and, not incidentally, to put on an even more spectacular display for the tens of thousands of Israelites who had gathered to see their king as he brought the holiest relic of Israel into the city he had named after himself. (2 Sam. 6:12)[29]

The spectacle is eerie and even grotesque. Slowly and solemnly, the oxcart bearing the Ark began to roll in the direction of Jerusalem once again, guarded by soldiers, attended by singers and musicians, watched by thousands of awed onlookers who lined the road. Every six steps, the whole procession halted as David himself offered up an ox and a fatling sheep, an orgy of sacrifice that must have left the road to Jerusalem soaked in blood.

To demonstrate his piety—and, we might imagine, to make sure that every eye was on him alone—David had shed all of his royal apparel and wore only the brief linen ephod that was the customary garb of a consecrated priest. Thus attired in nothing more than a loincloth, the handsome king capered and whirled like a dervish as the ram's horn shrieked, the cymbals clanged, the woodwinds droned, and the crowds reveled in a pious frenzy.

"And David danced before Yahweh with all his might," the biblical author writes. "So David and all the house of Israel brought up the ark of Yahweh with shouting and with the sound of the horn." (2 Sam. 6:14–15)[30]

At last the solemn procession reached the walls of Jerusalem, passed through the open gate, and came to a halt inside the fortified citadel known as the City of David. Here David presided over yet another public spectacle that resonated with sacred meaning and political showmanship.

First David pitched a tent and placed the Ark inside—a gesture that invoked the most cherished traditions of the Israelites, a nation whose sacred writings celebrate their origins as of tent-dwelling nomads and depict a tent as God's preferred meeting place with his greatest prophet. Then David once again arrogated to himself the role of high priest, sacrificing "burnt-offerings" and "peace-offerings" to Yahweh and pronouncing a blessing over the people of Israel in the name of Yahweh Sabaoth, the fierce and punishing aspect of God. Finally David did what kings have always done to ingratiate themselves with their subjects: he hosted a public feast, handing out to each man and each woman "a loaf of bread, a cake made in a pan, and a raisin cake." Only then, after a day of both bread and spectacle, did the people of Israel disperse, "every one to his house." (2 Sam. 6:18–19)[31]

On the day when Saul had been acclaimed as the first king of Israel, the crowd had included a sprinkling of doubters and dissenters. "How shall this man save us?" they muttered at the sight of him. (1 Sam. 10:27) Today, by contrast, the masses were smitten by the handsome young king, or so the Bible suggests. Indeed, we may imagine how the men and women of Israel chattered excitedly among themselves as they wandered back to their homes, munching on raisin cakes and buzzing about the eye-grabbing dance that David had performed. If such was the word on the streets of Jerusalem, then King David's audacious gesture had been wholly successful.

THE WOMAN IN THE WINDOW

One woman had watched the whole remarkable spectacle with special care, but only at a distance from the crowds. From a high window in the royal palace, Michal—the daughter of King Saul and the first wife of King David—looked down into the street just as David and the Ark passed. But unlike the rest of the crowd, she was neither pleased nor impressed by what she saw.

"Michal looked out of the window and saw King David leaping and dancing before Yahweh," the Bible pauses to note, "and she despised him in her heart." (2 Sam. 6:16)

What so distressed the queen of Israel was the fact that the king had danced with such abandon that his brief linen garment repeatedly flew up and exposed his genitals to the crowd. By the time David showed up back at the palace, her anger had reached the flash point. So David, flush with excitement at the adoration of the crowds, found himself greeted not as an exalted king but as a husband in deep trouble with his wife.

"Didn't the king of Israel do himself honor today," complained Michal as soon as David appeared at the palace, "exposing himself today in the sight of his subjects' slave-girls like some dancer!" (2 Sam. 6:20)[32]

David's high spirits evaporated in the heat of her harsh words, and he lashed out with equal rancor. "In Yahweh's presence I *am* a dancer!" he retorted. "Blessed be Yahweh, who chose me instead of your father and all his family, and appointed me ruler over Yahweh's people Israel." (2 Sam. 6:21)[33]

Thus did David pointedly remind Michal that he was king and her late father was not; if she still lived in a royal palace, it was because of him alone. What's more, if she felt humiliated by his promiscuity—if she was jealous of the powerful sexual allure that he worked on the other women of Israel—David vowed to punish her with more of the same.

"I will dance before Yahweh and dishonor myself even more," he taunted, "but among the slave-girls that you speak of I will be honored." (2 Sam. 6:21–22)[34]

The scene fairly sizzles with sexual tension and echoes with the bitter emotions of an estranged husband and wife. The Bible, as we have already seen, suggests that Michal had been forcibly separated from her second husband, Paltiel, and sent back to King David against her will. Now the Bible goes on to imply that David and Michal had already stopped sleeping with each other and never did so again: "And Michal the daughter of Saul had no child unto the day of her death." (2 Sam. 6:23)

Like much else in the life of David, the estrangement of David and Michal can be viewed from the perspectives of theology, politics, and intimate human relations. The pious reading of the text holds that God punished Michal for her insolence toward the anointed king with the curse of childlessness, the worst fate that can befall a woman in the biblical hierarchy of values. A more worldly reading suggests that David simply shunned Michal from that day forward, contenting himself with the sexual favors of his many other wives and concubines and thus denying Michal a child. But from either perspective, Michal's childlessness changed the politics of succession in ancient Israel. King David sired many sons, and, as we shall see, they fought bitterly with each other for the throne. Since Michal, daughter of King Saul, did not produce a son, none of the potential successors could claim to bear the blood of *two* kings, Saul and David. The house of Saul reached a dead end in the marriage of David and Michal.

Above all, the fact that a moment of theological grandeur—the bringing of the Ark to Jerusalem—is linked so intimately to a moment of marital squalor reveals something telling about the Bible and, especially, the biblical life story of David. As we have seen, David is first and always a human being rather than a plaster saint, and the biblical author who knows and loves David best is the one who is fascinated by the dirty little secrets of the king of Israel.

A HOUSE OF CEDAR

"The Lord had given him rest from all his enemies," goes a brief notice in the Bible, and David's thoughts turned from matters of war and politics to the matter of God. So begins a curious passage in the Bible—"the theological highlight" of the Book of Samuel[35] according to one scholar, or "monkish drivel"[36] according to another, but one that casts a shadow over the rest of the Bible and the whole of the Judeo-Christian tradition.

The scene opens in the royal palace that King Hiram of Tyre built for David in Jerusalem. To counsel him on his duties to Yahweh, David has summoned not a priest but a prophet named Nathan, a uniquely commanding figure in the life of David whom we meet here for the first time. The troubled king muses out loud to the prophet about the ironic fact that David himself, a mere mortal, enjoys the comforts of a palace while the Ark of the Covenant, the throne and footstool of the King of the Universe, is sheltered only in a rude tent. (2 Sam. 7:1)

"See now that I dwell in a house of cedar," said the king, "but the ark of God dwells within curtains." (2 Sam. 7:2)

That very night Nathan was granted a vision in which Yahweh explained it all.

First Yahweh reaffirmed the fundamental credo of the Israelites, a people that began as a tribe of shepherds and goatherds and always cherished the nomadic ideal of wandering and tent-dwelling.

"Shalt thou build me a house for me to dwell in?" said God in Nathan's vision. "For I have not dwelt in a house since the day that I brought the children of Israel out of Egypt, even to this day, but I have walked in a tent and in a tabernacle. In all the places wherein I have walked among all the children of Israel, spoke I a word with any of the tribes of Israel, saying: 'Why have ye not built me a house of cedar?' " (2 Sam. 7:5–6)

After instructing Nathan to reassure David that he need not feel guilty about his royal digs, God next told Nathan to remind David of the special favor that he enjoyed.

> I took thee from the sheepcote, from following the sheep, that thou should be prince over my people, over Israel. And I have been with thee whithersoever thou didst go, and have cut off all thine enemies from before thee; and I will make thee a great name, like unto the name of the great ones that are in the earth.
>
> (2 Sam. 7:8–9)

Next God promised that David, unlike the judges and kings who had ruled over Israel before him, would be the founder of a dynasty—a "house," as the Bible puts it. The house of Moses ended with his death, and so did the house of Saul, but the house of David would produce generation after generation of kings.

> When thy days are fulfilled, and thou shalt sleep with thy fathers, I will set up thy seed after thee, that shall proceed out of thy body, and I will establish his kingship.
>
> (2 Sam. 7:12)

Finally God pronounced a blessing on the house of David that is unprecedented in all of the Bible, an unconditional promise of divine protection that no other mortal—not Adam, not Noah, not Abraham, Isaac, or Jacob, not even Moses—was ever granted. Here is what Bible scholar Matitiahu Tsevat calls the "blank check of unlimited validity made out to the house of David."[37]

"He shall build a house for my name, and I will establish the throne of his kingdom forever," God said of David's successor to the throne of Israel without pausing to specify which of his many sons he had in mind. "I will be for him a father, and he shall be to me for a son; if he commit iniquity, I will chasten him with the rod of men, and with the stripes of the children of men, but my mercy shall not depart from him." (2 Sam. 7:13–14)

God, in other words, might punish the kings who came after David for their wrongdoings, but he vowed that he would never abandon them as he had abandoned the house of Saul.

THE BLESSING AND THE CURSE

God's promise of eternal kingship to the house of David was something wholly new in the official theology of the Bible. God had entered into covenants with Noah and Abraham and Moses, but never before had he given such a sweeping promise of divine favor. Indeed, the deal that Moses is shown to broker between God and Israel was strictly an "if-then" proposition. "Behold, I set before you this day a blessing and a curse," Moses announced to the Israelites in the name of Yahweh. "The blessing, if ye shall hearken unto the commandments of the Lord your God, which I command you this day, and the curse, if ye shall not hearken unto the commandments of the Lord your God." (Deut. 11:28) But God's vow to the house of David was perpetual and unconditional.

And thy house and thy kingdom shall be made sure for
ever before thee; thy throne shall be established forever.
(2 Sam. 7:16)

The biblical source that contributed Nathan's prophecy to the Book of Samuel is generally understood to be one of the priests who served the Davidic monarchy in Jerusalem several centuries after David's reign. The royal theologian's motive was to put the divine seal of approval on the house of David, which continued to provide kings to rule over the southern kingdom of Judah for nearly five hundred years. So the prophecy of Nathan as we find it in Samuel can be understood as an artful work of propaganda that was composed and written into the Bible long after the supposed lifetime of King David.

"Actual history is telescoped in 2 Samuel 7," explains Frank Moore Cross. "While the promise was made to David, it is the house of David and the house of Yahweh that were bound together and promised eternity."[38]

Indeed, one sure sign that a later author or editor reworked the text of Samuel can be found in the distinctly schizoid quality of Nathan's prophecy. At one point, God is shown to reassure David that he does not want or need a "house of cedar" for the Ark of the Covenant, his throne and footstool on earth, because he prefers to dwell in a tent like the earliest ancestors of the Israelites. Then, abruptly, God changes his mind and demands a temple instead of a tent—but he specifies that David's *son*, rather than David, will provide one: "*He* shall build a house for my name, and I will establish the throne of his kingdom forever."[39]

The first idea expressed in the prophecy of Nathan—God prefers a tent to a temple—is based on the simple and unavoidable fact that David did *not* build a temple to Yahweh in Jerusalem, a fact that the biblical author felt obliged to explain in theological terms. So he insisted that David did not build a temple because God specifically told him not to do so. But, at the same time, the biblical author reaffirms an article of faith that dates back to the earliest history of the Israelites: Yahweh, the God of Israel, preferred a tent to a temple because, like his Chosen People, he was a restless wanderer, a nomad, a tent-dweller.

The idea of Yahweh as "a god of the way," a wandering god who accompanies his people from place to place, is believed to express the original theology of the Israelites. God favored a tribe of pastoral nomads as his Chosen People, according to the sacred history recorded in the Bible, and he rode along with them atop a portable shrine, the Ark of the Covenant, that served as his throne and footstool. The same idea may be preserved in the Ten Commandments, where the Tenth Commandment—"Thou shalt not covet thy neighbor's house"—may have started out as a rejection of *all* houses by a tent-dwelling people. (Exod. 20:14) "It is the brief expression of the 'desert-ideal,' the tenacious adherence to the forms of nomadic life that alone were considered worthy of men and pleasing to God," writes Bible scholar Elias Auerbach, drawing an analogy between the original Israelites of distant antiquity and the Bedouin tribes of more recent times.[40]

The second sentiment in Nathan's prophecy—God requires a temple, and David's son will build it—reflects the historical reality of ancient Israel as the later biblical authors knew it. Jerusalem was the site of the central sanctuary of ancient Israel, an opulent temple that was first built by David's son and successor and later rebuilt after its destruction by the Babylonians. According to the Book of Deuteronomy, God accepted worship and sacrifice only from a single central sanctuary—"the place which the Lord your God shall choose to cause His name to dwell there" (Deut. 12:11)—and that place was the Temple at Jerusalem.[41] So the original version of Nathan's prophecy was "written over" to make it clear that God had wanted a temple all along.[42]

Still, a hard knot of contradiction remains in the text—if God wanted a temple, then why did he tell David not to build one? No clear answer is given in the troubled and troubling text of the Book of Samuel, but the author of the Book of Chronicles came up with one of his own. According to the Chronicler, David knew that it would be necessary to build a "house of God" in Jerusalem, one that "must be exceeding magnificent, of fame and of glory throughout the world." So he assembled a supply of building materials—stone, cedar, brass, iron—and a corps of foreign stonemasons to work the stone. But, as David would later reveal to Solomon, his son and successor, God had told David that he was unworthy to build the temple because his hands were so bloodstained.

> My son, as for me, it was in my heart to build a house unto the name of the Lord my God. But the word of the Lord came to me, saying: "Thou hast shed blood abundantly, and hast made great wars; thou shalt not build a house

unto my name, because thou hast shed much blood upon the earth in my sight."

(1 Chron. 22:7–8)

No such explanation, however, appears in the prophecy of Nathan as reported in the Book of Samuel. At the end of the fateful encounter between the prophet and the king, David left his palatial house of cedar and entered the tent where Yahweh was understood to dwell, and he delivered a long and ornate prayer of thanksgiving.

"Thou has promised a good thing unto thy servant," said David. "Thou, O Lord God, hast spoken it, and through thy blessing let the house of thy servant be blessed forever." Significantly, the word "forever" appears seven times in the seventh chapter of the Second Book of Samuel, where the eternal promise of kingship is woven deeply and vividly into the biblical tapestry.

Then the king rose and returned to the palace in the City of David. But his sense of well-being would not last long. War and rebellion, conspiracy and deception, murder and mayhem, sexual adventure and sexual assault—all depicted with brutal candor by the biblical authors—would soon put his life and throne at risk even in the face of God's unconditional promise of divine favor. At the worst moments to come, David would surely wonder whether God could be trusted to keep his promise at all.

Chapter Nine

AT THE TIME WHEN KINGS GO FORTH TO BATTLE

War is the trade of kings.
—JOHN DRYDEN, *KING ARTHUR*

Davivd was now approaching the high-water mark of his kingship. Secure on the throne, safely established in his own fortress-city, and afire with a kind of pious bravado, David set out to accomplish what Saul had tried but failed to do. In a series of brutal military campaigns and elegant diplomatic initiatives, David pacified the traditional heartland of ancient Israel and expanded its borders, transforming the land and people of Israel from a ragged coalition of feuding tribes into an empire. Under King David, *Eretz Yisrael* reached from the "river of Egypt unto the great river, the river Euphrates," just as God had once promised the patriarch Abraham so long ago. (Gen. 15:18)

"And Yahweh gave victory to David," the Bible devoutly (and repeatedly) notes, "wherever he went." (2 Sam. 8:14)[1]

First he "smote the Philistines and subdued them," apparently driving the last of the Philistines out of central Israel and confining them, once and for all, to the coastal strip that constituted the land of Philistia. (2 Sam. 8:1) Then, leading his army across the Jordan River on Israel's eastern frontier, he campaigned as far afield as Damascus and the Euphrates River. As his army ranged through the ancient Near East, David subdued all of the traditional enemies who had long threatened the very existence of the land of Israel—the Moabites, the Ammonites, the Edomites, the Amalekites—and the smaller tribes and peoples submitted without a fight. After each victory, David left behind garrisons to occupy the defeated nation, and he carried tribute and plunder back to Jerusalem—"vessels of silver, and vessels of gold, and vessels of brass." (2 Sam. 8:10)

"And David reigned over all Israel," the biblical author sums up, "and David executed justice and righteousness unto all his people." (2 Sam. 8:15)

Still, there is a strange but significant imbalance in the biblical account of David's successes at statecraft and empire building. David is praised for his administration of "justice and righteousness," but we are never shown or told exactly what he did to earn such praise. Similarly, the military and diplomatic achievements of David's early reign are hastily summarized in a few sketchy passages of the Book of Samuel. Far more attention is paid to what happens around the royal banquet table and behind the closed doors of the royal bedchamber.

Indeed, only a few of David's exploits are reported at all, and these brief reports are entirely consistent with the proud and ruthless warrior whom we already know David to be. After defeating the Moabites in battle, for example, David lined up the survivors in three groups, and he ordered the men in each line to lie on the ground, "two lines to put to death, and one full line to keep alive." (2 Sam. 8:2) When David defeated the massed chariotry and cavalry of an obscure kingdom called Zobah, "a thousand and seven hundred horsemen," he made sure that he would not face them in battle again by ordering all of the chariot horses to be hamstrung. (2 Sam. 8:4) When he withdrew from the land of Edom, he left behind a series of garrisons, "and all the Edomites became servants to David." (2 Sam. 8:14) On the banks of the distant Euphrates, David erected a monument of stone bearing his name to mark the farthest reach of his empire. (2 Sam. 8:3, 13) (AB)

Still, the Bible makes no real distinction between the private affairs of King David and the public policy of the kingdom of Israel. Both aspects of the life story of David are so intertwined that they are not meant to be teased apart, and—as far as the more pious sources are concerned—both are meant to reflect the workings of God's will in the world of mortal men and women. All of these factors come into play in the curious tale of how King David suddenly resolved to do something to honor the memory of Saul and Jonathan. One day, abruptly and rather perversely, David was struck with the notion of canvassing Israel in an effort to find a man in whose veins ran the blood of King Saul.

"Is there yet any that is left of the house of Saul," asked David, "that I may show him kindness for Jonathan's sake?" (2 Sam. 9:1)

BLOOD GUILT

Saul was long dead. So were Jonathan and two of his brothers, all of whom had died in battle with the Philistines, and Ishbaal, the puppet-king who had been assassinated by his own officers. And, according to a grotesque incident that is revealed only much later in the biblical text, seven other sons and grandsons of Saul had been sacrificed by order of King David.[2] So David would find it difficult to search out yet another son of Saul, and his interest in doing so must have seemed odd and ominous to the courtiers who knew well the fate that had befallen the house of Saul.

Indeed, the fate of Saul's children at the hands of David is one of the strangest episodes in all of the Hebrew Bible. At some unspecified point during David's reign, the Book of Samuel reports, the land of Israel suffered a famine that lasted for three years, and David sought a divine oracle to explain why.

"Blood guilt rests on Saul and his family," God revealed, "because he put the Gibeonites to death." (2 Sam. 21:2) (NEB)

The Gibeonites had lived in an enclave in the tribal homeland of Benjamin under the protection of the Israelites ever since the original conquest of Canaan by Joshua. (Josh. 9:19–21, 27) Saul's supposed crime against the Gibeonites is never actually described, but David now wanted to atone on behalf of Saul—"the man who massacred us," as the Gibeonites described him, "and tried to exterminate us." (2 Sam. 21:5) (New JPS) David offered to bestow upon the Gibeonites a bounty of silver and gold, but they wanted only blood-vengeance.

"Let seven men of his sons be delivered unto us," the Gibeonites demanded, "and we will hang them up unto Yahweh." (2 Sam. 21:4–6)

"I will deliver them," David replied. (2 Sam. 21:4–6)[3]

David turned over two of Saul's sons and five of his grandsons to the Gibeonites, who promptly put them to death in a public execution. Exactly how the seven descendants of Saul died is not clear—the original Hebrew text has been interpreted to suggest that the men were "flung down" from a mountain (NEB), or "impaled" (New JPS), or "dismembered" (NJB), and the Anchor Bible boldly reports that they were "crucified"—which, if accurate, is the only reference to crucifixion in the Hebrew Bible.[4] Significantly, however, the Bible does specify that the men were killed "at the time of the barley harvest," which suggests a ceremony of human sacrifice rather than a judicial execution. (2 Sam. 21: 9)

What is actually going on here, some scholars speculate, is the offering of royal blood to propitiate an angry god who has punished the people of Israel with famine, a ritual of human sacrifice that may have been borrowed from the practices of the pagan Canaanites and one that plainly violates the official theology of the Bible. Even if David cannot be fairly characterized as a participant in human sacrifice, the very notion that he surrendered the sons of Saul to the Gibeonites for "hanging" is shocking enough. After all, each one of the victims was the son or grandson of King Saul and, therefore, a potential rival for the throne of Israel. The whole incident is so unsettling that some scholars suspect that the passage was censored out of the sacred texts of ancient Israel and restored later by one of the compilers and redactors who were the final editors of the Bible, which may explain why the passage pops up so late in the Book of Samuel.

Only one male descendant of Saul now survived, or so the Bible says, and he was an unfortunate cripple named Mephibosheth,[5] son of Jonathan and grandson of Saul. The boy had been only five years old when his father and grandfather died in battle, and his nurse had taken him into hiding, apparently fearful that Saul's enemies were seeking to slaughter everyone in the line of succession. Indeed, she may have worried that David himself represented the greatest threat to the child's life. "And it came to pass," the Bible reports, "as she made haste to flee, that he fell, and became lame." (2 Sam. 4:4) Now, as David canvassed his kingdom for any surviving member of the house of Saul, it was the crippled Mephibosheth who was found.

A DEAD DOG

Mephibosheth was fetched back to Jerusalem and ushered into David's throne room, where he promptly fell on his face in abject terror. David, as we have seen, had been careful to distance himself from the battlefield deaths of Saul and Jonathan and the assassination of Ishbaal. Even when seven prospective claimants to the crown of Saul were put out of contention in a single mass execution, David preserved a kind of plausible deniability—the Gibeonites, not David, spilled their blood. But surely poor Mephibosheth, the last known survivor of the house of Saul, must have ached with anxiety when David summoned him out of hiding.

"Fear not," said David to the crippled man who now groveled in front of him, "for I will surely show you kindness for Jonathan thy father's sake, and will restore to you all the land of Saul, and you shall eat bread at my table." (2 Sam. 9:7)

Mephibosheth, however, continued to cower.

"What is thy servant," said Mephibosheth to the king, "that thou shouldest look upon such a dead dog as I am?" (2 Sam. 9:8)

But David did exactly as he promised. The lands and houses that had once belonged to King Saul were put under the custody of an old retainer named Ziba, who was charged with the duty of managing the estate for King Saul's grandson. "But Mephibosheth dwelled in Jerusalem," the Bible carefully notes, "for he did continually eat at the king's table." (2 Sam. 9:13) The biblical author would have us believe that David was acting out of love for Jonathan; after all, Jonathan had extracted a solemn promise from David to care for his survivors. "I know that as long as I live you will show me faithful friendship," Jonathan had said, "and if I should die, you will continue loyal to my family for ever."

But surely the irony was not lost on the original readers of the Bible: Mephibosheth is one of "the lame and the blind" who "are hated of David's soul." (2 Sam. 4:8) Yet now David insisted that the lame grandson of King Saul "shall eat at my table as one of the king's sons." (2 Sam. 9:11) Perhaps David was concerned only with public relations. "Did David hope by this theatrical act of kindness to a descendant of Saul," wonders Robert H. Pfeiffer, "to offset the silent indignation of the Israelites after the slaughter of Saul's sons?"[6]

Even so, we know enough about David by now to imagine a more calculated reason for keeping Mephibosheth within his intimate family circle. As a man well acquainted with conspiracy, both as a practitioner and as a target, King David wanted the last survivor of the house of Saul where he could keep a watchful eye on him.

THE INVENTION OF BIBLICAL ISRAEL

An intriguing glimpse into David's inner circle is offered in a few spare lines of the Bible that describe the men who served in his royal cabinet. On these brief and oblique observations by the biblical author, modern Bible scholarship has come up with a description of how David worked a revolution in ancient Israel. With the assistance of these confidants and commanders and henchmen, David reinvented the army, government, and religion of ancient Israel, dragging the people out of their primitive tribal existence and showing them how a modern cosmopolitan state of the tenth century B.C.E. ought to function.

The Bible reports, for example, that Joab was placed in charge of the army of Israel, presumably the tribal musters that rallied to the king in times of war. But, significantly, David did not rely only on the tribal militia to protect his life and his throne—a man named Benaiah commanded the corps of foreign mercenaries who served as David's praetorian guard. (2 Sam. 8:18) And David's standing army included a few especially distinguished warriors who pledged their loyalty to him—these were the "mighty men," as the King James Version renders the Hebrew term *gibborim*, who served in elite units designated as "the Three" and "the Thirty." (2 Sam. 23:8, 13 ff.)

King David was attended by both a chronicler (literally, a "remembrancer") and a scribe, both of whom may have prepared and preserved the very annals on which significant portions of the biblical account are based. (2 Sam. 8:16–17) According to later notices in the Book of Samuel, the cabinet included a privy counselor known formally as "the Friend of David" (2 Sam. 15:37) (AB), and a man who served as overseer of the corvée, a program of labor conscription that supplied the king with the manpower to build his palaces and fortifications. (2 Sam. 20:24) Two men shared the office of high priest in King David's court—Abiathar, the lone survivor of King Saul's slaughter of the priests at Nob, and the mysterious Zadok, a man of dubious origins who may not have been an Israelite at all.

The cabinet of King David was something entirely new in the history of ancient Israel. For that reason, David can be seen as a reformer and a modernizer, the man who invented biblical Israel by turning twelve nomadic tribes into a single nation with all the appurtenances that could be found in the imperial courts of Egypt and Mesopotamia. Indeed, some scholars argue that David aped the rituals and institutions of the pagan peoples and nations that surrounded the land of Israel. Just as the developing nations of the twentieth century sought armament and constitutions and popular culture from the West, Israel in the tenth century B.C.E. may have found a role model in the superpowers of its day.

THE WOMAN AT THE WINDOW

The so-called Jebusite hypothesis, for example, holds that David borrowed freely from the Jebusite and Canaanite rituals of court and temple. "The main source of this borrowing," writes Bible scholar R. E. Clements, "would seem to have been Jerusalem, where David took over the tradition and authority of the Jebusite kingdom."[7]

The solemn processional by which David brought the Ark of the Covenant into Jerusalem—and even the marital spat that it prompted—are seen by some as evidence that the faith of ancient Israel was deeply suffused with pagan borrowings. When a nearly naked David dances in "the grip of cultic ecstasy," the biblical author may be echoing an ancient Canaanite text that describes the sacred marriage of El, the supreme god in the Canaanite pantheon, and his consort, Asherah. The raisin cake that David distributed to the crowds was the symbol of the cult of Baal, yet another Canaanite deity. The slave-girls who were said to "honor" David with sexual favors may have been temple prostitutes of the kind described in another pagan text from an important Canaanite archaeological site at Ras Shamra.[8]

Even the scene in which Michal watches David's antics has been likened to an ancient Near Eastern motif known as the Woman at the Window—an image of Astarte or some other goddess of love and fertility in the guise of a harlot showing herself at an open window. Similar images carved into Phoenician ivories have been recovered from archaeological sites in northern Israel, where they were apparently used as pagan icons. When David returns to the palace at the climax of the public ritual, ready to "bless" his house, as the Bible put it, perhaps we are meant to see a symbolic reenactment of the sacred act of intercourse between

El and Asherah. Significantly, Michal's punishment for spurning David is lifelong childlessness.

Indeed, some scholars see Michal as the pious believer in the God of Israel and David as an overenthusiastic innovator who borrowed a bit too heavily from pagan rites and rituals. When the Bible reports Michal's disgust at the dance that David performed, we may be witnessing not a wife's response to her husband's "sexual impropriety" but the shock and horror of a true believer at the "cultic innovation" that her husband was bringing to the strict Yahwism that was the faith of ancient Israel. "The linen ephod, the ecstatic dancing, and the apparent ritual nakedness of the king are motifs of ancient Near East mythology and priestly liturgies," one scholar observes. "David's role . . . bespeaks changes in Israel—a return, perhaps, to the sense of king and temple that prevailed in the heyday of pagan culture in the land."[9]

THE FRIEND OF DAVID

Just as David seems to have mimicked the pagan practices of the Canaanites, he appears to have modeled his cabinet after the court of Egypt or the "Egyptianized" monarchies of Canaan and Phoenicia. A "rational and bureaucratic mode of statecraft," proposes Joel Rosenberg, "is David's specific innovation."[10]

Thus the duties of the man described in the Bible as a "re-membrancer" may have been comparable to those of his Egyptian counterpart—"a master of ceremonies and foreign minister"—and the scribe may have been comparable to "the personal secretary of the pharaoh and his *chef de bureau*."[11] The "Friend of David" may have been a kind of privy counselor and marriage broker pat-terned after an Egyptian courtier with the formal title of "the Friend of the King,"[12] and David's corvée resembles the program of forced labor by which the pharaohs built their mighty temples and pyramids. Even the soldiers known as the Thirty may hark back to the "royal cortege" of thirty men who served in the court of Ramses II of Egypt three hundred years before the supposed lifetime of David.[13]

David, who had sown the seeds of more than one tribal blood feud during his years as a bandit and a mercenary, learned a practical lesson from the pagan kings whom he had served. Thus, he chose to surround himself with a personal bodyguard that consisted entirely of foreigners[14]—the "Cherethites" and "Pelethites" whose duty was to protect David from his own people are understood to have been "Sea Peoples" who, like the Philistines, came to the land of Israel from Crete or elsewhere in the Aegean. Some scholars propose that the Pelethites were, in fact, Philistines, and the Bible itself confirms that David's foreign mercenaries included a contingent of Gittites, that is, men from the Philistine city-state of Gath, the hometown of Goliath. (2 Sam. 15:18)

Even something so fundamental to the biblical history of ancient Israel as the "twelve tribes" may have been an innovation of King David. A fundamental assumption of the biblical authors is that the twelve tribes originated with the twelve sons of the patriarch Jacob, but the "twelveness" of the tribes is not always in evidence in the Bible—a close reading reveals that the total number of tribes ranges from ten to thirteen.[15] So the conventional wisdom of biblical scholarship—and the Bible itself—holds that David's single greatest achievement of statecraft was to forge the clans and tribes known loosely as "Israelites," including his own tribe of Judah, into a single nation called "Israel" and to place the nation under the governance of a king, an army, and a royal bureaucracy.

"Israel was no longer a tribal confederacy led by a charismatic *nagid* who had been acclaimed king, but a complex empire organized under the crown," explains John Bright. "While David's court was no picture of sybaritic luxury, it was hardly the rustic thing that Saul's had been."[16] Indeed, David proved himself to be a daring and energetic leader who constructed "a fully imperial conception of kingship," and did so "out of whole cloth."[17]

WHEN KINGS GO FORTH

Here then is King David as the biblical authors wished to remember him—and, more important, as they wished *us* to remember him. He reigned over not only a kingdom but an empire. He commanded the conscripted labor of his own people to build roads and cisterns, fortresses and palaces, and he accepted tribute from conquered kings and peoples throughout the ancient world. He was cherished by his loyal subjects for the "justice and righteousness" that he dispensed, and he was feared by his defeated enemies for the ruthless and powerful army that served him. He was attended by a royal court that resembled and perhaps even rivaled that of the pharaoh of Egypt, and his harem teemed with wives and concubines and children. Above all, according to the Bible, he enjoyed not only the favor of God but the divine promise of eternal kingship for his sons and successors.

And yet, as the Court Historian makes no effort to conceal, the zenith of power passed quickly and tragically.

The first sign of David's subtle turn of fortune was an ugly diplomatic rebuff by one of his new tributaries, the kingdom of Ammon. David had subjugated the Ammonites, as we have seen, and their king had become his vassal. When the old king died, David sent emissaries to the new king of Ammon to comfort him on the death of his father. "I will show kindness unto Hanun, the son of Nahash," David thought to himself, "as his father showed kindness unto me." (2 Sam. 10:2) But the counselors of the Ammonite king agitated against David. "Do you suppose David means to do honour to your father when he sends you his condolences?" they whispered. "These men of his are spies whom he has sent to find out how to overthrow the city." (2 Sam. 10:3) (NEB)

So on the orders of the king of Ammon, the royal messengers from Jerusalem were subjected to a series of indignities—half of each man's beard was shaved off, and each man's garment was cut halfway up from the ground so that his buttocks were laid bare, a public humiliation that McCarter compares to "symbolic castration."[18] Then all the emissaries were sent back to King David as living symbols of Ammonite defiance.

When David learned of how his emissaries had been abased and disfigured, he resolved to punish the insolent Ammonites with a new campaign—and, in the meantime, he ordered the messengers to remain in Jericho until their beards grew back, thereby sparing himself *and* his ambassadors any further embarrassment. The people of Jerusalem, at least, would not see the contempt with which the new king of Ammon regarded the king of Israel.

Realizing that "they had fallen into bad odor with David," the Ammonites fully expected a punitive expedition, and so they began recruiting soldiers of fortune from the land of Aram and other neighboring kingdoms. Against the Ammonites and their mercenaries David sent an Israelite army under the command of Joab. "Be of good courage," Joab declared, echoing the words that Moses spoke to Joshua, the original conqueror of Canaan, "and let us prove strong for our people, and for the cities of our God." (2 Sam. 10:12) So impressive was the sight of David's army that the Arameans and then the Ammonites broke and ran, and Joab returned in victory to Jerusalem.

The victory, however, was only temporary. The Ammonites regrouped, recruited a fresh supply of Aramean mercenaries from beyond the Euphrates, and marched in the direction of Israel again. At news of the renewed threat from the insolent Ammonites, David placed himself at the head of the army and led the fighting men of Israel across the Jordan River to engage the enemy on its own soil. Again the Arameans were put to rout, and David followed to inflict a bloody punishment on the fleeing soldiers: seven hundred charioteers and forty thousand infantrymen of the mercenary army from Aram were slain on David's orders. (2 Sam. 10:18)

"When all the vassal kings saw that they had been worsted by Israel, they sued for peace and submitted to the Israelites," the Bible concludes. "The Arameans never dared help the Ammonites again." (2 Sam. 10:19)[19]

As for the Ammonite king himself, however, David resolved that further punishment was necessary. He would bring the war to the gates of Rabbah, the royal capital of Ammon, and he would extract a price in blood for the shaved beards and exposed buttocks of his couriers. But the Court Historian pauses here to note an odd and somehow ominous fact: the army of Israel would go to war, but David, the warrior-king who had been blooded in so many battles, would stay home.

> And it came to pass, after the year was expired, at the time when kings go forth to battle, that David sent Joab, and his servants with him, and all Israel; and they destroyed the children of Ammon, and besieged Rabbah. But David tarried still at Jerusalem.
>
> (2 Sam. 11:1) (KJV)

Some of the old fire had gone out of David, or so the Bible seems to suggest. He was now well into middle age, and apparently he was no longer willing to endure the discomforts and dangers of a long march and a hard campaign in enemy territory. So he sent Joab and the army to fight, and he remained behind in the royal palace in Jerusalem. But as it turned out, David still burned with the white-hot sexuality that had always made him so compelling to both men and women. So it was that King David, idle and alone, embarked upon a sexual adventure that turned out to be at once the greatest love of his life and the scandal that signaled a sea change in his once-glorious destiny.

Chapter Ten

THE DAUGHTER OF
THE SEVEN GODS

His captain's heart,
Which in the scuffles of great fights hath burst
The buckles on his breast, reneges all temper,
And is become the bellow and the fan
To cool a gypsy's lust.

—SHAKESPEARE, *ANTONY AND CLEOPATRA*

The turning point in the life of David—and, in a real sense, the whole sweep of biblical history—is described in a single sentence that throbs with unresolved sexual tension and acute moral peril.

> And it came to pass at eventide, that David arose from his bed, and walked upon the roof of the king's house, and from the roof he saw a woman bathing, and the woman was very beautiful to look upon.
>
> (2 Sam. 11:2)

The Bible suggests that David rose from an afternoon nap and idled on the rooftop of his palace in order to catch a cool evening breeze. But we might also imagine that David woke from his slumber in a state of agitation and perhaps even sexual arousal. And perhaps he wondered whether he might be able to spot some willing woman from his observation point atop the palace—the Bible suggests that the king's bed was placed on the rooftop, at least during the warm seasons of the year, and more than one alluring woman may have displayed herself within sight and reach of the king, so handsome and so powerful! And so, when David spotted a naked woman at her bath on a nearby rooftop, he may have found exactly what he was looking for.

And here the biblical life story of David hangs in suspense for one exquisite moment. Will David, the anointed of God, turn away from the tantalizing sight of the bathing woman and return to his own bed, alone or in the company of one of his many consecrated wives? Or will he plunge forward into a new adventure in forbidden carnality? Will he spurn temptation in the way we would expect of "a man after God's heart," or will he yield to the demands of his own mortal heart?

A moment later, the suspense is over. King David chooses pleasure over piety, and both king and country will pay a terrible price.

THE SEVENTH WELL

The Bible does not disclose whether the beautiful and beguiling woman who bathed on the next rooftop was an innocent victim of David's voyeurism or a calculating exhibitionist who sought to catch the king's eye. Either or both may be true. But it does confirm that David moved quickly to recruit the object of his desire for his bed—"And David sent and inquired after the woman" (2 Sam. 11:3)—and his courtiers reported back with all the particulars.

Her name was Bathsheba, the courtiers told the king, and she was the wife of a man called Uriah the Hittite, a member of David's military elite, "the Thirty," and one of the many men of foreign ancestry who served in the army of Israel. (2 Sam. 23:13, 39)[1] Bathsheba, too, may have been a non-Israelite. Her name was interpreted by one early medieval exegete to mean "seventh well" or "brimming well," a metaphor used elsewhere in the Bible to indicate a fertile woman.[2] But as Bible historian Karen Armstrong proposes, Bathsheba's name "may originally have been 'Daughter of the Seven Gods,'" a polytheistic name in use among the Jebusites or other pagan tribes of Canaan.[3] Intriguingly, the Chronicler gives her name as "Bathshua" (1 Chron. 3:5), which was also the name of the Canaanite wife of Judah, a distant ancestor of David and founder of the tribe of Judah. And so the king's eye fell on a woman who was doubly forbidden to him—Bathsheba was married to another man, and she may have been one of those seductive strangers whom the Bible routinely accuses of luring Israelite men into "harlotry and other abominations."

Conveniently enough, Uriah was serving at the front in David's war on Ammon, and so it was easy for the king to summon Bathsheba to the royal bedchamber without worrying about interference from a cuckolded husband. The courtship of David and Bathsheba, such as it was, is described in a single blunt line of biblical text, but it is enough to confirm that David was a man accustomed to using the high office bestowed upon him by God for unholy purposes.

> And David sent messengers, and took her; and she came in unto him, and he lay with her.
>
> (2 Sam. 11:4)

At the moment of their adultery, Bathsheba "was purified from her uncleanness," or so the biblical author pauses to note in a moment of stinging irony. (2 Sam. 11:4) Under biblical law, a woman was considered "unclean" during her menstrual period, and a man was forbidden to engage in sexual intercourse with her until her period was over and she was "purified" by immersing herself in a ritual bath. (Lev. 15:19 ff.) David may have engaged in a forbidden sexual encounter with someone else's wife, but the biblical author assures us that his sex partner was not—God forbid!—ritually impure at the moment of their fornication.

Bathsheba's menstrual cycle is significant for other reasons, too. The fact that her period had already ended when she encountered King David suggests that she was likely to be ovulating, a detail that was recognized and remarked upon by the medieval sages whose commentaries are preserved in the Talmud. Thus the biblical author is subtly suggesting that Bathsheba was indeed a "brimming well," a woman ready to conceive, when David summoned her to his bed.

WARRIOR AND CUCKOLD

At the moment of creation, according to an apologetic tale from the Talmud, God decrees that Bathsheba is destined to be the beloved wife of David. But God later resolves to postpone the day of their wedding because of some wrongdoing by David—in one version of the tale, David displeases God by offering Bathsheba to Uriah, a non-Israelite, as a reward for his assistance in the battle with Goliath.[4] Ultimately God bestows Bathsheba upon David, as he had always intended to do, and "so [David] took only what was rightfully his."[5] Thus the rabbis invite us to regard David's relationship with Bathsheba as the great love of his life, a union sanctioned by God, even if the biblical author insists on presenting it as an illicit and ill-fated sexual encounter.

Still, the first spasm of sexual pleasure was brief, according to the Bible, and Bathsheba promptly returned to her own home. But like countless cheating couples before and after, David and Bathsheba were confronted with the most awkward possible evidence of their adultery. "And the woman conceived," the Bible reports, "and she sent and told David, and said: 'I am with child.' " (2 Sam. 11:5) And David, so skilled in the arts of deception, decided that the only way to hide their adultery was to make it appear that the bastard child in Bathsheba's womb had been fathered by her husband, Uriah.

Here we see yet another reason why the biblical author is so specific about the timing of Bathsheba's last period. Since Uriah had left Jerusalem for combat duty in far-off Ammon *before* Bathsheba's last period, he could not be credited with paternity of the child unless he returned to Jerusalem and slept with his wife *after* her period. Both David and Bathsheba—and, significantly, the biblical author, too—understood the implications of her menstrual cycles, and that is why David saw the necessity of putting the faithful soldier into bed with his unfaithful wife before the pregnancy manifested itself for all to see.

Thus begins a conspiracy that starts out as a bedroom farce and ends in darkest tragedy. First David sent word to his trusted general and confidant, Joab: "Send me Uriah the Hittite." (2 Sam. 11:6) The loyal soldier hastened back to Jerusalem, surely baffled at the strange summons from the king, and he must have been even more confounded after he was ushered into the throne room and listened to the king's prattling. "David asked if Joab was well and if the army was well and if the war was going well," the Bible reports, and Uriah, perhaps still wary of the king's purpose, replied noncommittally: "Yes, well." (2 Sam. 11:7) (AB) After only a few moments of such aimless chitchat, David abruptly dismissed him with a pointed suggestion.

"Go down to thy house," David said to Uriah, "and wash thy feet." (2 Sam. 11:10)

The washing of feet might suggest only a long soak in the tub to modern readers, but David meant something much more intimate. The Hebrew word for "feet" or "legs" (*raglayim*) was sometimes used in biblical Hebrew as a euphemism for genitalia, and the thrust of David's suggestion was that Uriah should avail himself of the opportunity to clean himself up and join his wife in bed for some well-deserved "rest and recreation." Then, of course, David would be able to plausibly deny that he was the father of the child that Bathsheba already carried.

But David badly misjudged Uriah by attributing to him the same uncontrollable sex drive and the same lack of moral restraint that were so prominent in his own nature. Uriah left the palace with the gift of food that David had thought to bestow upon him, but he did not return to his own house. Instead, the ever-faithful Uriah spent the night at the door of the palace. With

Uriah on guard at the king's door, of course, neither her husband nor her lover joined Bathsheba in bed that night.

"Why did you not go down to your house?" David asked Uriah the next day, astonished that the man would not avail himself of the comforts of his own bed and his own wife—and not a little aggravated, too.

"Israel and Judah are under canvas, and so is the Ark, and my lord Joab and thy majesty's officers are camping in the open on the battlefield," Uriah protested. "Shall I then go into my house, to eat and to drink, and to sleep with my wife? As thou livest, as thy soul liveth, I will not do this thing." (2 Sam. 11:11)[6]

Uriah's words carried a subtle reproach. He was reminding David of God's demand that soldiers refrain from sexual contact with women while at war. (Deut. 23:9–11) Ironically, David had once invoked the same rule of sexual purity to trick the priest of Nob into giving him holy bread.* Now, however, David was too desperate to be deterred by Uriah's pious words.

"Tarry here today," the king ordered Uriah, "and tomorrow I will let you depart." (2 Sam. 11:12)[7]

Then David insisted that Uriah join him for a feast at the royal banquet table, where the king urged cup after cup of wine on the soldier. A drunken Uriah, David calculated, would surely yield to temptation.

But David guessed wrong again. Even drunk on the king's wine, Uriah continued to put duty before pleasure. At last he fell asleep among the servants who bedded down at the king's door, where the whole court of King David was witness to the fact that Uriah had not lain with his wife. So it was that the king's attempt to concoct a cover story for Bathsheba's pregnancy was unwittingly foiled by the remarkable sense of piety, loyalty, and duty of a cuckolded warrior.

*See chapter 5.

THE DEVOURING SWORD

On the next morning, David woke up with a new thought. He decided to abandon his plan to put Uriah in bed with Bathsheba and instead to send the faithful soldier back to the front. But he asked Uriah to do him the favor of carrying a confidential message to his commander, Joab, who was directing the siege of Rabbah. And David counted on the faithful Uriah to carry the letter without opening it. If Uriah had peeked inside the sealed letter, he would have discovered that he was carrying his own death warrant.

"Put Uriah in the forefront of the hottest battle and then fall back," David had written to Joab, "and leave him to meet his death." (2 Sam. 11:15)[8]

Joab did not question the king's strange order, nor did he shrink from carrying it out. "That old watchdog of the monarchy"[9] was always ready to kill in the service of David and his kingship even when David himself was suffering from a failure of nerve. Joab had been studying the defenses of Rabbah, and he knew exactly where the Ammonites would offer the stiffest resistance to attack. And so, when he opened the letter that Uriah had handed him, Joab knew what to do to carry out the king's command.

Joab assigned Uriah to a skirmishing party that he sent into action at one of the strong points along the city wall. Sure enough, the Ammonites sallied out en masse to engage the attackers while the archers on the high wall fired down on them, and Joab's men began to fall under the fierce counterattack. Amid the chaos of battle, presumably at a moment when Uriah found himself face-to-face with the enemy and fighting for his life, Joab ordered the rest of the men to withdraw. Just as David had intended, the Ammonites struck down Uriah and left him dead on the battlefield.

Then Joab dispatched a courier to Jerusalem with a report on the war in Ammon—but he carefully instructed the messenger on how to break the news of Uriah's fate. "Thy servant Uriah is dead also," the man was ordered to say, as if it were an incidental detail. (2 Sam. 11:21) And David, upon hearing of the only casualty that mattered to him, responded with a few words of comfort for Joab that betray a chilly indifference to Uriah's death.

"Do not let this distress you—the sword devours one way or another," David ordered the messenger to tell Joab. "Press home your attack on the city, and you will take it and raze it to the ground." (2 Sam. 11:25)[10]

Bathsheba, too, showed neither relief nor satisfaction at the death of her husband. She observed the customary period of ritual mourning—but when the formal display of grief was done, David and Bathsheba wasted no more time on appearances.

"David sent for her and brought her into his house," the Bible reports. "She became his wife and bore him a son." (2 Sam. 11:27)

Surely the royal courtiers were careful not to mention the unfortunate cuckold or name the real father of the child within earshot of King David and his new queen—but it is just as certain that the whole scandalous affair was the subject of hot gossip throughout the palace and beyond. Indeed, the very fact that we find the story of David and Bathsheba within the pages of Holy Writ is the best evidence that David's wrongdoing was so much a matter of common knowledge that the Court Historian could not leave it out.

Nor did the affair escape the attention of Yahweh. The all-seeing and all-knowing God of Israel is notably absent from the biblical life story of David, especially in these tales of love and war, but now God is shown to bestir himself and make it known that "the thing that David had done displeased the Lord." (2 Sam. 11:27) Significantly, God did not speak directly to David as he had spoken to Moses. He expressed his displeasure through one of those cranky old men whom we know as the prophets. And, as David was about to discover, a God-inspired prophet in ancient Israel felt perfectly free to scold a king.

"THOU ART THE MAN"

King David, long accustomed to the company of brutal men and beguiling women, some of them highborn and some of them only *habiru*, but all of them worldly-wise, suddenly found himself confronted by Nathan, a man of God who presented himself at court with a message from Yahweh. The king granted Nathan an audience and listened in silence as the old man insisted on telling him a tale.

"Pass judgment on this case for me," Nathan began. "There were two men in a certain city, one rich and one poor." (2 Sam. 12:1) (AB)

The rich man was blessed with abundant herds and flocks, Nathan said, but the poor man had nothing at all except a single little lamb that he cherished as if it were human. "It grew up together with him, and with his children," Nathan continued, "and drank of his own cup, and lay in his bosom, and was unto him as a daughter." (2 Sam. 12:3)

One day, a traveler appeared in town and asked the rich man for provisions. Of course, the rich man would not have missed a kid or a lamb from his own herds and flocks, but instead he seized the poor man's single lamb to satisfy the stranger's appetite. The rich man slaughtered the lamb, dressed it, and turned the butchered meat over to the traveler to be eaten.

David, depicted here in a rare moment of naïveté, was apparently under the impression that Nathan had reported a real case and was asking him to judge the rich man for his crime.

"As the Lord lives, the man who has done this deserves to die," an outraged David declared, "and he shall restore the lamb fourfold, because he did this thing and he had no pity." (2 Sam. 12:6)

To which Nathan promptly replied: "Thou art the man!" (2 Sam. 12:7)

Now the prophet allowed the king to understand that the tale of the poor man's lamb was a parable rather than an actual case. The rich man was meant to represent David, whose harem was filled with willing women, and the poor man represented Uriah, who could comfort himself with but a single wife. And David listened in abject silence to the scolding that Nathan now delivered.

"I anointed thee king over Israel, and I delivered thee out of the hand of Saul, and I gave thee thy master's daughter, and I made his wives lie down in thine embrace," railed the prophet, mouthing words that he attributed to God.* "I gave thee the daughters of Israel and Judah, and if that were too little, I would give thee that many again. Why then hast thou despised the word of the Lord, to do that which is evil in my sight?' " (2 Sam. 12:7–9)[11]

Lest David mistake his meaning, Nathan spoke aloud what God already knew about David's secret crime. "Uriah the Hittite thou has smitten with the sword, and his wife thou hast taken to be thy wife," said Nathan. "Now, therefore, the sword shall never depart from thy house." (2 Sam. 12:9–10)

God's disappointment with the failings of humankind is perhaps the single most persistent theme of the Bible. The same punishing despair is found in the story of the Flood, where God resolves to exterminate the whole of his human creation save Noah and his family; and in the tale of Sodom and Gomorrah, where God destroys five cities filled with evildoers for the want of ten righteous men; and in the saga of the Exodus, where he threatens to slaughter the Chosen People and start all over again with Moses. Now, however, God reassured David that he would not suffer the ultimate penalty for his sins. "Thou shalt not die," Nathan told David, thus reminding him of God's special favor toward his anointed king (2 Sam. 12:13).

Still, God singled out David for a strikingly intimate affliction, a kind of rough justice in which the punishment was made to fit the crime.

---

*Nowhere does the Bible confirm Nathan's remarkable suggestion that Saul's wives ended up in David's harem. To explain the accusation, the Talmud speculates that Ahinoam of Jezreel, one of David's wives (1 Sam. 27:3), was the same woman identified as "Ahinoam the daughter of Ahimaaz," the only woman actually named in the Bible as a wife of Saul. (1 Sam. 14:50)

Behold, I will raise up evil against thee out of thine own
house, and I will take thy wives before thine eyes, and give
them unto thy neighbour, and he shall lie with thy wives
within the sight of this sun.

(2 Sam. 12:11)

The curse begins in the hazy language of metaphor but ends
with an explicit threat: David will be forced to watch another
man engage in sexual intercourse with his wives, and not only
David but the whole of his kingdom will witness their sexual violation and his public humiliation. "For thou didst it secretly,"
Nathan warned, again mouthing the words of God, "but I will do
this thing before all Israel, and before the sun." (2 Sam. 12:11) As
we shall come to see, God meant everything he said in the most
literal sense.

Finally, God announced his intention to deliver a coup de
grâce for the crime of David and Bathsheba—a death sentence,
not on the star-crossed lovers, but rather on the wholly innocent
victim of their fornication.

"The child that is born unto thee," warned Nathan, "shall
surely die." (2 Sam. 12:14)

THE THIRD MAN

The encounter between David and Nathan reveals something
unique about the theology and politics of ancient Israel. David may
have been the single most powerful man in ancient Israel—God's
anointed king of Judah and all Israel, a man with the power of life
and death over his subjects—but David still felt obliged to heed the
words of the prophet who scolded him for his most intimate sins. A
king might order the mass murder of *priests*, as Saul did when he exterminated the priests of Nob, but a *prophet* was sacrosanct. Here is
something wholly new in human politics, something wholly different from what came before or after in the long history of kingship.
Kings and priests, of course, have always contested with each

other for both moral and political authority—the murder of Thomas à Becket on the order of King Henry II in the cathedral at Canterbury is an old and memorable example, and the dethronement of the Shah of Iran in a theocratic revolution led by the Ayatollah Khomeini is a more recent one. But kings and priests alike recognized a third force in the politics of ancient Israel—the God-inspired men and women that the Bible knows as prophets (*neviim*). Just as Saul deferred to Samuel, and David deferred to Nathan, the kings of Judah and Israel always found themselves confronted and condemned by fearless truth-tellers who cared not at all for the trappings of royal authority, or, for that matter, the equally ornate trappings of the priesthood that presided over the Temple.

"The flow of charismatic energy in Israel," as Bible scholar William F. Albright puts it, was channeled through the prophets rather than kings or generals or priests. "From David's time on, the prophetic mission was closely associated with moral and political reform as well as purely religious revival." [12]

Moses was the first prophet, according to biblical tradition, and he set the example for all who came after him when he boldly confronted the mighty pharaoh of Egypt, condemning him for his evildoing and threatening him with divine punishment in the form of the Ten Plagues. Moses was privileged to speak with God "face to face, as a man speaketh unto his friend," even "mouth to mouth." (Exod. 33:11; Num. 12:8) When Moses died, Yahweh cut off any further direct conversation with mere mortals. Thereafter, as we have seen, kings and priests alike were allowed to consult God only by casting lots and asking for answers to yes-or-no questions. But the men and women whom God designated as his prophets would be granted the opportunity to hear the "dark speeches" of Yahweh and relay the message from on high to kings, priests, and commoners.

Hear now my words: if there be a prophet among you, I the Lord do make myself known unto him in a vision, I do speak with him a dream.

(Num. 12:6)

The biblical prophets who found themselves filled with "the spirit of Yahweh" have been likened to the ecstatics and diviners of other times and places, not only the mystics and wonder-workers who were active in pagan cults throughout the ancient world but also the Hasidim, dervishes, and Pentecostals of today. As with the shamans and seers of indigenous cultures who carry messages from the spirit world, no ordination was required to be a prophet—men and women received the word of God through the medium of "visions and oracles delivered in a state of trance."[13] "Ecstatic practices of an orgiastic type"—singing, dancing, speaking in tongues, perhaps even self-flagellation and self-mutilation—are some of the expressions "which, taken collectively, are called 'prophesying,' " as P. Kyle McCarter, Jr., concludes.[14]

But the prophet also served as a "sober mediator" between God and humankind.[15] The Bible depicts the prophets as a moral counterweight to both royal and priestly authority in ancient Israel, and the prophetic books still represent the beating heart of its ethical teachings. Samuel, the first of the "classical" prophets, was literally called by God as a young child—called by name and called by night—to the task of making and breaking both kings and high priests. His abiding faith in God and his fierce commitment to social justice can be traced to Isaiah and the other prophets of the Hebrew Bible. Indeed, the unbroken thread runs all the way down to John the Baptist, and, arguably, Jesus of Nazareth; all denounced kings and high priests in the name of God.

"I SHALL GO TO HIM"

Just as Nathan had prophesied, the nameless child of David and Bathsheba fell desperately ill: "And the Lord struck the child that Uriah's wife bore unto David." Still, it is a measure of David's character—both his audacity and his sheer willpower—that he refused to accept the decree and sought to bend God's will to his own. "David besought God for the child," as the Bible puts it, keeping a prayer vigil night and day, fasting, and sleeping on bare earth in a display of remorse and repentance. (2 Sam. 12:15, 16)

The illness of David's newborn son was not merely a family matter—after all, a king who grieved so deeply was incapable of attending to affairs of state—and so the elders rallied to King David, urged him to eat, tried to raise him up from the ground and restore him to the throne. But David refused all of their entreaties, and he continued to afflict himself day after day as the child grew weaker. When the child's short life came to an end on the seventh day of his illness, the servants of the royal household feared that news of the death would break David's spirit once and for all.

"While the boy was alive, we spoke to him, and he did not listen to us," they fretted among themselves. "How can we now tell him that the boy is dead? He may do something desperate." (2 Sam. 12:18) (NEB)

But as it turned out, David spared his courtiers the unpleasant task of breaking the news. When he saw them whispering in the corridor, the king was quick to grasp the reason for their concern.

"Is the boy dead?" he asked.

"He is dead," the courtiers replied.

Abruptly David rose from the ground, washed himself, and dressed in fresh clothes. Then he anointed himself, walked to the tent-shrine of Yahweh, prostrated himself, and prayed one more time.[16] The words that he uttered to Yahweh are not recorded, but the biblical author tells us that David promptly asked for food and then sat down to his first meal in seven days.

"What is this?" his servants dared to ask. "While the child was alive, you fasted and wept and kept a vigil for him, but now that the child is dead, you rise up and eat."

"While the boy was yet alive I fasted and wept, for I said: Who knows whether Yahweh will not be gracious to me, and the child may live?" answered David in matter-of-fact words that seem at odds with his earlier antics. "But now that he is dead, why should I fast? Can I bring him back again?" (2 Sam. 12:21–23)[17]

Then David spoke words of such world-weariness and resignation, such fatalism and even cynicism, that they seem eerily modern. Unlike his famous tribute to the slain Saul and Jonathan, the elegy for his own son was short and blunt, if no less eloquent or poignant.

"I shall go to him," said David of the dead infant, "but he will not return to me." (2 Sam. 11:23)

David had sought mightily to persuade God to spare the innocent child through fasting and prayer, but when the child died in spite of his pious exertions, David could only shrug. Of course, a pious reading of the text suggests that David was at last deferring to the superior and mysterious power of God. But the same scene has been given a psychological and even an existential reading by some Bible commentators—David here reveals "a revolutionary new attitude in the psychic history of Israel," argues J.P.E. Pedersen,[18] and he is shown to be a "fully responsible, fully free man," according to Walter Brueggemann. David, in other words, is a worldly-wise man who refuses to blame God when his own prayers are unavailing.[19] No matter how devout David is made to seem in the pages of the Bible, the man who shines through the biblical text is one who, like most modern readers of the Bible, lives wholly in the here and now and neither beseeches nor blames God for his lot in life.

"BEHOLD, A SON SHALL BE BORN"

Of Bathsheba's grief, the Bible has little or nothing to say. "David comforted Bathsheba," the Bible observes, but he did not confine himself to whispering words of condolence. Rather, David "went in unto her, and lay with her," according to the literal translation of the euphemistic biblical Hebrew in the King James Version, or "had intercourse with her," according to the plain-spoken New English Bible. (2 Sam. 12:24) The fertile Bathsheba quickly conceived a second son, and the child was born healthy and strong.

Curiously, the child is named twice. The prophet Nathan, acting on instructions from God, dubs him Jedidiah, "beloved of the

Lord," to signal his divine favor and his future greatness. But Bathsheba insisted on calling him Solomon, which is traditionally understood to derive from the Hebrew word for peace, *shalom*.[20] "Behold, a son shall be born to thee," God announces to David in the Book of Chronicles. "For his name shall be Solomon, and I will give peace and quietness unto Israel in his day." Characteristically, the Chronicler makes no mention whatsoever of the doomed bastard who was born to David and Bathsheba, but he exults over Solomon. "He shall be to me for a son," God is reported to say, "and I will be to him for a father." (1 Chron. 22:9–10)

Nothing else is said of Bathsheba until the very end of the biblical life story of David, when she will emerge from obscurity to play a decisive role in the choice of David's successor to the throne. Indeed, as we shall see, Bathsheba was a woman who refused to be ignored.

"RAPED BY THE PEN"

So troubled were the rabbis and sages by the story of David and Bathsheba that they concocted a whole array of improbable excuses and far-fetched exculpatory tales to soften the impact of the frank biblical report.

Bathsheba was to blame for provoking David's lust, they asserted, "by taking off her dress where she knew he would see her."[21] Nor was David technically guilty of adultery when he succumbed to her seduction—Uriah, like other soldiers in biblical times, gave his wife a bill of divorcement before going off to fight so that she would be properly divorced if he went missing in combat, and so "Bath-sheba was a regularly divorced woman." What's more, Uriah was to blame for his own death, they insisted, because he refused "to take his ease in his own house, according to the king's bidding." Above all, the whole nasty affair was God's doing in the first place: God decreed that David should summon Bathsheba to his bed before they were properly married so that he could later serve as a shining example of moral redemption.

"Go to David," God would thereafter say to sinners, "and learn how to repent."[22]

One rabbinical fairy tale told in the Talmud insists that Satan, rather than David or Bathsheba, was to blame for their adultery. Bathsheba took the precaution of bathing behind a wicker screen that blocked her from view, thus sparing David from temptation. But Satan, seeking to ruin them both, assumed the shape of a bird and alighted on the screen. David shot an arrow at the bird, just as Satan had intended, but the arrow missed the bird and knocked down the screen. Once Bathsheba's naked body and long hair were revealed, "the sight of her aroused passion in the king," a passion so powerful that he could not have been expected to resist it—and didn't. For failing to avoid Satan's trap, David spent twenty-two years as a penitent, eating his bread mixed with ashes and weeping for a full hour each day.[23]

Yet, as earnest and imaginative as the Talmudic sages may have been, they tended to overlook one awkward but unavoidable fact: David himself and the other powerful men around him never seemed to court a woman or consult her about her wishes before "taking" her, as the Bible puts it. The Bible allows us to *imagine* that Bathsheba yearned for David with the same passion that he felt toward her, but the Bible never *says* she did. The plain text of the Bible—"And David sent messengers, and *took* her" (2 Sam. 11:4)—can be read to suggest that Bathsheba engaged in sexual intercourse with David under compulsion and perhaps even under the threat or use of physical force.

"This is no love story," argues J. Cheryl Exum. "The scene is the biblical equivalent of 'wham bam, thank you, m'am': he sent, he took, she came, he lay, she returned."[24]

Indeed, the most militant Bible critics resent the very intimacy of the scene that is presented in the Bible. "Raped by the pen" is how Exum describes Bathsheba at the hands of the biblical author. "By introducing Bathsheba to us through David's eyes, the narrator puts us in the position of voyeurs," Exum argues. "Is not this gaze a violation, an invasion of her person as well as her privacy?" After carefully parsing out the biblical text, Exum draws a pointed comparison between the depiction of Bathsheba in the Bible and one of the obligatory images in modern erotica. "Art, film, and pornography provide constant reminders that men are aroused by watching a woman touch herself," she concludes. "And if Bathsheba is purifying herself after her menstrual period, we can guess where she is touching."[25]

Not every reader, of course, comes away from the Bible with the impression that Bathsheba was an abused and exploited woman. Some modern Bible scholars, not unlike the Talmudic sages, condemn Bathsheba as a willful seducer, a woman "whose unchecked animal appetites had tragic consequences for him, his family, and the community he governed."[26] Perhaps she was "not as blameless as a first reading of the text might suggest," argues J. Blenkinsopp, who wonders out loud whether her rooftop bath was intended all along to snag the king. If so, her blunt report to David—"I'm pregnant" (2 Sam. 11:5) (AB)—might be seen "as more a cry of triumph than an SOS." And even if "we simply do not know whether she was a silent accomplice in the death of her husband," Blenkinsopp concludes, "there is no indication that her new situation was distasteful to her."[27]

Or perhaps David and Bathsheba were simply and truly in love with each other, as novelist Joseph Heller concluded after reading the biblical depiction of their affair. "We trysted secretly," David explains in *God Knows*, "embraced on the way to the couch, made giddy jokes and laughed excessively, and enjoyed every other kind of cozy, intimate hilarity together until the day the roof caved in with the news that she was pregnant."[28] In fact, the Bible confirms that David was so smitten with Bathsheba that he would one day yield to her in the most fundamental matters of state.

Still, even if Bathsheba was a willing sex partner, as most of us prefer to believe, we cannot deny that plenty of other women in King David's court were conscripted for sexual duty to kings and generals without their consent. David's first wife, Michal, is dragged from her second husband and restored to David's harem merely because David demands it, and, as we shall shortly see, the concubines of David's royal harem are sexually humiliated en masse and in public. Each of these outrages is less a matter of sexual pleasure than of political advantage—yet another reminder that, in the Bible as in life, sex and politics cannot be teased apart.

CITY OF JOAB

So distracted was David by all of these upheavals in the royal household that it fell to Joab alone to campaign against the king of Ammon and conquer the royal city of Rabbah. But Joab was loyal enough to reserve the final triumph for his old comrade, even if his message carried a barb of reproach to the king who had called his own capital the City of David.

"I have fought against Rabbah, yea, I have captured the citadel. So muster the rest of the army, encamp against the city, and capture it yourself," warned Joab, "lest I take the city, and it be called after *my* name." (2 Sam. 12:28)[29]

David finally stirred from his palace, placed himself at the head of an army, and marched out to pluck the apple of victory before it dropped of its own weight into Joab's hands. The city fell, and David enjoyed the special pleasure of lifting the bejeweled golden crown from a statue of Milcom, god of the Ammonites, and placing it on his own head. Then he ordered the plunder of Rabbah and the destruction of its defensive fortifications. At last, "David and all the people returned unto Jerusalem," the Bible notes.

What lay before David and his people on the king's return to Jerusalem was not a golden age of imperial glory, even if some Bible historians delight in depicting his reign in precisely that way. Rather, just as Nathan had warned, the house of David would come to be a snake pit of sexual predation and political conspiracy, deception and betrayal, blood feuds and blood-vengeance.

The first blow to David's kingship—his dalliance with Bath-sheba and its tragic aftermath—had been entirely self-inflicted, unless the pious reader is willing to follow the Talmudic rabbis in putting the blame on Bathsheba, Uriah, Satan, and God, too. Soon enough, a second blow would fall on the house of David, but this next one would originate wholly within David's intimate family circle.

Chapter Eleven

THE RAPE OF TAMAR

Oh miserable men, who destroy your own species through those pleasures intended to reproduce it, how is it that this dying beauty doesn't freeze your fierce lusts?
—JEAN-JACQUES ROUSSEAU, *THE LEVITE OF EPHRAIM*

Two women named Tamar figure crucially in the life of King David. The first Tamar was a Canaanite who disguised herself as a harlot in order to seduce her father-in-law, Judah, so that she might conceive a child.* She was a remarkable woman, beautiful and beguiling, assertive and brave. Despite her sins of incest and fornication and prostitution, the Bible pronounces her a righteous woman. David was a distant but direct descendant of Tamar and Judah, founder of the tribe of which he was king, and her passionate blood ran in his veins.

At first glance the linkage between Tamar and David may seem odd and off-putting to the devout reader of the Bible. Is it not ironic that David—God's anointed, king of all Israel, and progenitor of the Messiah—traced his ancestry back to the bastard son of a foreign woman who played the harlot with her own

---

*See *The Harlot by the Side of the Road*, Chapter 7, "The Woman Who Willed Herself into History."

father-in-law? By now, however, we know enough about David to realize that his bloodlines are perfectly appropriate. The very qualities that enabled the first Tamar to survive and prevail against the stern patriarchy of tribal Israel are the same qualities that allowed David to survive and prevail in the cutthroat political landscape of royal Israel—boldness and courage, guile and willfulness, and a taste for sexual adventure.

The second Tamar was the daughter of King David, the only one actually named in the Bible, and surely he was mindful of the exploits of the first Tamar when he chose the name for the baby girl. Tamar, like her father, earned a rare word of praise for her physical beauty from the biblical author—"a fair sister" is how she is introduced (2 Sam. 13:1)—and, as we shall see, she was no less desirable than the Canaanite woman whose name she carried. But the daughter of David was doomed to a tragic fate; her intimate sexual encounter with a near relation would be sordid rather than sublime, and it would end in tragedy rather than exaltation.

LOVE HURTS

Among the admirers of the fair Tamar in King David's court was a man named Amnon, the crown prince of Israel and Tamar's half brother. Amnon, firstborn son of David, was destined to replace his father on the throne one day, and the Bible allows us to understand that he was pampered by a doting father and feared by his many siblings. Perhaps that is why Amnon felt free to satisfy his every urge and impulse, no matter how grotesque or even criminal, and perhaps that's why nothing cautioned him against the longing he felt for his half sister.

"Amnon the son of David loved her," the Bible reports. "And Amnon was so distressed that he fell sick because of his sister Tamar; for she was a virgin, and it seemed hard to Amnon to do anything unto her." (2 Sam. 13:1–2)

The Bible may call it "love," but what Amnon felt for Tamar

was only lust, a demanding sexual hunger that he was unable to repress. So besotted was Amnon with unwholesome yearning for his half sister that he lost his appetite—his appetite for food, that is—and he began to grow thin and wan.

Soon enough, Amnon's pale face and shrunken frame and sulky mood caught the attention of his cousin and constant companion, a man named Jonadab.

"Why, O son of the king," Jonadab asked his cousin, "are you so low-spirited morning after morning?" (2 Sam. 13:4)[1]

"I love Tamar, my brother Absalom's sister," Ammon replied, identifying his half sibling by reference to Tamar's full brother, Absalom, as if to downplay the fact that he himself and Tamar were brother and sister. (2 Sam. 13:4)

Jonadab was "a very subtle man," as the biblical author tells us, and he devised a diabolical plan to put Tamar within reach of Amnon. (2 Sam. 13:3) "Take to your bed and pretend to be ill," Jonadab suggested. "When your father comes to see you, say to him: 'Let my sister come, I pray thee, and give me my food. Let her prepare it in front of me, so that I may watch her and then take it from her own hands.' " (2 Sam. 13:5–6)[2]

Amnon did exactly as his cousin had suggested—"Let my sister come, I pray thee," he begged of his father, "and make a few cakes in front of me"—and King David did exactly as his favorite son asked.

"Go now to thy brother Amnon's house," the king ordered Tamar, "and prepare a meal for him." (2 Sam. 13:6–7)[3]

"COME LIE WITH ME, MY SISTER"

At the command of her father the king, Tamar dutifully presented herself at the house of her half brother and set to work preparing food for Amnon as he watched from his sickbed. The Bible pauses to describe the making of the meal in detail—we are hearing a woman's voice, perhaps, and it is the voice of a storyteller who knows how to stoke the fear and anticipation of the reader.

And she took dough, and kneaded it, and made cakes in his sight, and did bake the cakes. And she took the pan, and poured them out before, but he refused to eat.

(2 Sam. 13:8–9)

Amnon, agitated and aroused but not by the meal his sister had prepared for him, suddenly ordered the rest of his household to leave: "Have out all men from me." When he was alone with his half sister—just as he had intended—Amnon instructed Tamar to bring the cakes to his bedside "that I may eat of thy hand." And when she approached his bed, Amnon seized her and spoke out loud what he had really wanted of her all along.

"Come lie with me, my sister." (2 Sam. 13:9–11)

The phrase that Amnon spoke was a standard biblical euphemism for sexual intercourse, although the literal translation that appears in most English-language Bibles is attenuated and oblique. Tamar would have understood the sexual demand that Amnon was making upon her. And Tamar, unwilling to submit herself to her half brother's pleasure, argued passionately and eloquently to change Amnon's mind.

"No, my brother, do not force me, for no such thing ought to be done in Israel," she protested. "Do not behave like a beast!" (2 Sam. 13:12)[4]

Unable to resist Amnon's superior physical strength, Tamar resorted to her own powers of speech—she tried to talk Amnon out of raping her. Both of them, she argued, would be disgraced by what he proposed to do: "Where could I go and hide my disgrace? And you would sink as low as any beast in Israel." (2 Sam. 13:13)[5] And she improvised an ingenious argument to save herself from forcible rape by holding out the tantalizing prospect that Amnon could have what he wanted if he only asked their father for permission. "Why not speak to the king?" she urged. "He will not refuse you leave to marry me." (2 Sam. 13:13)[6] But Amnon ignored her desperate plea.

"Being stronger than she," the biblical author bluntly reports, "he forced her, and lay with her." (2 Sam. 13:14)

Once Amnon had spent himself atop his sister, his self-proclaimed "love" turned suddenly to hatred—or perhaps more accurately, his lust turned to disgust. To explain Amnon's sudden change of heart, which makes an ugly scene even uglier, the Talmudic sages speculated, remarkably enough, that "Amnon hated Tamar because, when he raped her, he became entangled in her pubic hair and injured himself." Perhaps more credible and convincing is a truism about human nature. "A number of poets and psychologists could be cited on the readiness with which love . . . turns to hatred," observes P. Kyle McCarter, Jr., "and the intensity of the hatred thus produced."[7] The Bible, without pausing to explain exactly why, merely confirms Amnon's change of heart. "The hatred wherewith he hated her," the biblical author observes, "was greater than the love wherewith he had loved her." And so Amnon threw his sister out of the bed in which he had just raped her. (2 Sam. 13:15)

"Arise," said Amnon, suddenly unable to stand the sight of the woman he had just raped. "Be gone." (2 Sam. 13:15)

A WAR OF WORDS

At this ugly moment, among the most repugnant in all of the Bible, the biblical author allows us to see that Amnon and Tamar are truly the children of David, if only because Tamar shares some of his best traits and Amnon some of his worst. Amnon, like David, is a man driven by his sexual appetites and willing to use violence to get what he wants. And Tamar, again like David, is beautiful to behold and gifted with an eloquent tongue, which she has used here in a desperate effort to prevent her half brother from raping her.

Indeed, several of the pivotal women in David's life are shown to use sexual allure or artful speech—perhaps the only kind of armament available to a woman in biblical Israel—to protect and vindicate themselves and their loved ones. Even if feminist Bible scholarship bewails the victimhood of women in the Bible, and especially the women in David's life, the fact remains that more than a few heroic women refused to remain silent and compliant in the face of superior male strength and authority. And, significantly, words were their only weapons.

Abigail prevailed upon David to refrain from the slaughter of her husband, Nabal, and his household with an ornate speech. Bathsheba will change the course of history by persuading David to choose her son as his successor to the throne of Israel. And Tamar defended herself from rape as best she could by resort to words alone, appealing first to Amnon's higher nature—"You would sink as low as any beast"—and then to his self-interest— "Speak to the king. He will not refuse you leave to marry me." (2 Sam. 13:13)

The notion that a woman might try to talk a rapist out of raping her is plausible enough to the modern reader, but the last argument that Tamar offered in defense of her virtue seems outlandish and incredible—would Amnon seriously consider *marrying* his own sister rather than raping her? After all, the Bible plainly and sternly prohibits all manner of incest. "None of you shall approach to any that is near of kin to him, to uncover their nakedness," the God of Israel, using a standard biblical euphemism for sexual relations, decreed in the laws handed down to Moses. "The nakedness of thy sister, the daughter of thy father, or the daughter of thy mother, whether born at home, or born abroad, thou shalt not uncover." (Lev. 18:6, 9)

The biblical law against incest, in fact, lists every variation and permutation of forbidden sexual conduct. Indeed, incest between a brother and his half sister—"the daughter of thy father" (Lev. 18:9)—is specifically ruled out by the set of laws known as the Holiness Code. (Lev. 17 ff.) And so Tamar and Amnon must have known, even in the hottest moments of his sexual assault on her, that a marriage between siblings was beyond the power of the king to approve because it was strictly forbidden by ancient taboo and the law of Moses, too.

Or was it?

SISTER AND WIFE

On the strength of Tamar's single urgent plea to Amnon, Bible scholarship has constructed the surprising argument that marriage and sexual relations among siblings were *not* forbidden during the supposed lifetime of King David, despite the laws against incest and other sexual misconduct that can be found throughout the Bible. Perhaps Tamar meant exactly what she said when she held out the tantalizing prospect that King David would consent to a marriage between his daughter and his son.

The ancients, as it turns out, were far less concerned about incest than the modern readers of the Bible. Contrary to what we have been taught by Sigmund Freud, the taboo against incest was not primal and universal, and the biblical world regarded incest with far less horror than we might suppose by reading the parade of sexual atrocities in the Book of Leviticus. Throughout the ancient Near East, and down through history, sex and marriage among close relations have been not merely tolerated but actually celebrated. And, it has been argued, the cosmopolitan court of King David was both familiar and comfortable with such practices.

The ancient Egyptians, for example, embraced the notion of incestuous marriage both in religious myth and common practice. Because property passed from a mother to her eldest daughter, rather than from father to son, an Egyptian father might marry his own daughter, or a son might marry his sister, in order to prevent the family wealth from falling under the control of a son-in-law or a brother-in-law.[8] The reigning pharaohs customarily married their own sisters in pious imitation of the myth of Isis and Osiris, the sibling-lovers with whom the kings of Egypt identified. Although a prohibition against sexual intercourse between a father and his daughter is literally chiseled in stone in the Code of Hammurabi, the sacred myths of ancient Mesopotamia depicted gods and goddesses in sexual couplings with their own offspring and siblings. And the people of the land of Canaan, among whom the Israelites lived throughout their long history, told a tale in which the god called Baal engaged in sexual union with his sister, Anat.[9]

If the court of King David was "Egyptianized" and "Canaanized," as scholars have surmised, then the notion of marriage between Amnon and Tamar might not have seemed so bizarre. Moreover, his court may have embraced the practices of neighboring kingdoms in an effort to distinguish the new monarchy in Jerusalem from its tribal origins. "These are the first Israelite brood," writes Joel Rosenberg, referring to the adult children of King David, including Amnon and Tamar, "among whom the more complex and sophisticated aristocratic marriage patterns in Egypt and Mesopotamia are capable of being taken seriously."[10]

In fact, at certain vivid moments, the Bible betrays an easygoing attitude toward incest in general and the marriage of brother and sister in particular. For example, the daughters of Lot, a nephew of the patriarch Abraham, ply their father with wine and then sleep with him in order to conceive, all without condemnation or punishment of any kind. (Gen. 19:1–38) Indeed, since Lot's daughters apparently believed that the rest of humankind had been destroyed along with Sodom and Gomorrah, they are praised in biblical tradition for acting courageously to preserve human life on earth by the expedient of sleeping with their father.

Elsewhere in the Bible, the Patriarchs pass off their wives as their sisters—not once but three times! When Abraham and Sarah journey to Egypt in search of food during a famine in Canaan, Abraham masquerades as Sarah's brother out of fear that any lordly Egyptian who took a fancy to Sarah would be more likely to slay her spouse than her sibling in order to get his hands on her. In a rare biblical "triplet"—that is, the same story told in three different versions—Abraham resorts to the same ploy in an encounter with a Philistine king called Abimelech, and so does his son Isaac. Sarah is recruited for the harem of the pharaoh of Egypt in the first version and that of the king of the Philistines in the second. Rebekah, too, ends up in the bed of the same Philistine king in the third version (Gen. 12:10–20, 20:2–10, 26:1–10), and in all three versions it is only divine intervention that prevents these foreign kings from sleeping with the Matriarchs.

The motive of Abraham and Isaac in passing off a wife as a sister is the same in each incident: "He feared to say: 'My wife,' " the biblical author writes of Isaac, " 'lest the men of the place should kill me for Rebekah, because she is fair to look upon.' " (Gen. 26:7) Yet, intriguingly, Abraham is shown to insist that his claim to be Sarah's brother was not merely an act of deception: "She is the daughter of my father," riddles Abraham, "but not the daughter of my mother." (Gen. 20:12)[11] Perhaps Abraham was merely engaging in yet another lie when he claimed that Sarah was both his wife and his half sister—or perhaps, as some scholars have speculated, he was telling the truth. If so, the Bible may preserve evidence that the ancient Israelites, like other peoples of the ancient world, did not object to marriage between siblings after all.

In fact, the early Israelites may have been influenced by the folkways of an ancient people known as the Hurrians, who customarily identified their wives as their sisters in order to invoke "the safeguards and privileges" that were available to a man's sister but not his wife. By the time the oldest tales and traditions of ancient Israel were collected, the authors and editors who created what we know as the Bible simply did not remember or recognize the Hurrian practice of wife-as-sister.[12] But David and his household, who are believed to have lived a thousand years before the final canonization of the Bible, may have remembered and honored these oldest of traditions.

WHAT TAMAR KNEW AND WHEN SHE KNEW IT

Of course, at the terrible moment when Tamar was facing forcible rape, she did not pause to parse out these legal and anthropological niceties. Whether or not sex between siblings was forbidden in Jerusalem of the tenth century B.C.E., Tamar may have held out the prospect of a consecrated marriage just to deter her half brother from assaulting her. But there is another and more surprising explanation for Tamar's bold proposal. She did not heed the stern commandments of Leviticus, some scholars argue, because she had never heard of them.

According to the formal chronology of the Bible itself, the strict and wide-ranging legal codes that are found in Exodus, Numbers, Leviticus, and Deuteronomy were dictated by God to Moses during the years of wandering in the wilderness, long before the conquest of Canaan and long before David ascended the throne. By the time of David's supposed life and reign, the Bible insists, the so-called Five Books of Moses functioned as the constitution of ancient Israel. For that reason, the laws against incest in the Book of Leviticus would have been well known to David and his offspring and would have ruled out a marriage between Tamar and Amnon.

The last century or so of modern Bible scholarship, however, suggests a very different chronology. The core of the life story of David, including the heartbreaking encounter between Amnon and Tamar, was probably composed long before the law codes of the Torah. Indeed, the Book of Samuel is thought to embody some of the oldest passages in all of the Hebrew Bible. By contrast, even the oldest codes of law probably did not find their way into the Bible until the priests and scribes of ancient Israel fixed the text of the Five Books of Moses in their final form as late as the fourth century B.C.E. Precisely for that reason, the Bible has been called "a veritable anthology of Israelite covenant law representing seven hundred years of development, yet all of it introduced by words such as 'And the Lord said to Moses. . . .' "13

If so, the men and women of ancient Israel, including Tamar, would have been wholly ignorant of the laws of Leviticus, which would not be set down in writing for another two or three hundred years. In fact, the cosmopolitan princes and princesses of King David's court may have been far more familiar—and more comfortable, too—with the royal traditions of Egypt and Canaan than with the priestly law of the Israelites.

HER GARMENT OF MANY COLORS

Once Amnon had satisfied himself, Tamar was reduced to begging her brother for mercy of a very strained kind—she did not want to be thrust out of Amnon's house, where she might at least conceal her shame, into the street, where all would know by her appearance that she had been sexually abused by her own brother.

"No! It is wicked to send me away," Tamar protested. "This is harder to bear than all you have done to me." (2 Sam. 13:16) (NEB)

Amnon, his sexual appetite sated to the point of disgust, found no such mercy in his heart. "Put out this woman from me," he ordered one of his servants, who had apparently been within earshot throughout the sexual assault, "and bolt the door after her." (2 Sam. 13:17)[14]

"Put out this *woman*" is how Amnon's words are rendered in standard English translations, but the original Hebrew text reveals that Amnon no longer regarded his half sister as a human being: "Put out this *thing*" is the literal translation of his words.[15] And the servant did as he was told: Tamar suddenly found herself in the street, and we may suppose that she attracted the stares of all who passed Amnon's house as she was pushed out the door.

Her hair was disheveled, or so we may imagine. Her clothing was in disarray and her face, perhaps, was battered. And the Bible confirms that Tamar, at the moment of her public humiliation, was readily recognizable as the daughter of King David. "Now she had a garment of many colors upon her," the biblical author pauses to point out, "for with such robes were the king's daughters that were virgins apparelled."

The Hebrew phrase that is used to describe Tamar's "garment of many colors" is the same one used for Joseph's famous "coat of many colors." (Gen. 37:3) But the familiar wording of the King James Version, which is derived from the Septuagint, is nowadays regarded as purely fanciful. "A long-sleeved robe" is how the same garment is described in the New English Bible, and the term may have been borrowed by the Israelites from an Akkadian phrase that referred to "a ceremonial robe which could be draped about statues of goddesses."[16] Even without such pagan symbolism, the garment would have identified Tamar as someone "associated with the highest social or political status."[17]

Thus, as Tamar rose to her feet and stumbled off, anyone who saw the bruised young woman would readily know that she was not only a victim of rape but, shockingly, a daughter of the king.

A DAMAGED WOMAN

Tamar understood from the very moment that Amnon commenced his assault—"Come lie with me, my sister!"—that her life would be changed forever if he succeeded in having his way with her. No longer a virgin, Tamar was now unacceptable as a wife even if she was the daughter of the king. According to tradition in ancient Israel, as in so many other times and places, no man would marry a woman who had been deflowered by another man, whether with or without her consent.

Indeed, the tragic fate of Tamar helps to explain why the penalty for rape under biblical law was the marriage of the rapist to the woman he had raped, at least if the victim so desired. (Deut. 22:28–29) As shocking as it may seem to the modern reader, the compulsory marriage of the rapist and his victim was understood as a form of reparation—since the rapist had rendered his victim unmarriageable, the only way to repair the damage was to marry her.

And yet if we share the assumption of the biblical author that the law against the marriage of siblings was fully in effect, Tamar understood that a marriage to Amnon was out of the question. So as she fled from her brother's house, Tamar regarded herself as a woman damaged beyond repair. She solemnly performed the ancient rituals of mourning as if in grief for something within herself that had died.

> And Tamar put ashes on her head, and rent her garment of many colors that was on her, and she laid her hand on her head, and went her way, crying aloud as she went.
>
> (2 Sam. 13:19)

Significantly, Tamar did not seek refuge in the house of her father, nor did she tell the king what her half brother had dared to do to her. Instead she stumbled through the streets of the City of David toward the house of her brother, Absalom. Only there, sheltered by a young man with whom she shared both a mother and a father, did Tamar expect to find shelter.

WHAT DID DAVID KNOW
AND WHEN DID HE KNOW IT?

Exactly what was David's role in the rape of Tamar, his daughter, by Amnon, his son? King David, a man who was governed by his sexual impulses and was an expert at guile and deception, may have understood without being told that Amnon wanted more than tender loving care from his half sister when he asked that she come to his sickbed and feed him. Indeed, David may have been tipped off to Amnon's real intention by the very word used by the crown prince to describe the food that he wanted his sister to prepare.

The Hebrew word that Amnon used, *lebibot*, is usually translated into English as "bread" (JPS) or "cakes" (KJV) or "dumplings" (AB). But these mundane words fail to capture the sensual overtones of the Hebrew word that fell from Amnon's lips. Feminist Bible scholar Phyllis Trible, for example, calls *lebibot* an "erotic pun" that derives from the Hebrew word for "heart" and suggests arousal and pleasure.[18] "Libido cakes" is how another Bible commentator renders the word in order to convey the sexual demand that Ammon intended to make on Tamar,[19] and P. Kyle McCarter, Jr., concedes that "[Amnon] is privately anticipating more than the restoration of his health."[20]

So the question must be asked: Did David understand Amnon's intentions when he sent his daughter into Amnon's bedchamber? One scholar suggests that David was not only tacitly approving Amnon's sexual claim on his sister but actually "delivering her into the hands of . . . her rapist."[21] Another finds it "difficult to believe that David, himself the author of much subtler intrigues, would have been completely taken in by such transparent designs as this one."[22] The charge laid against David in contemporary Bible scholarship, where he is regarded as an unindicted coconspirator in the rape of his own daughter by his son, is so disturbing that even the conspiracy to murder Uriah seems rather ordinary by comparison.

Still, the Bible has already allowed us to see an aspect of David's personality that is perfectly consistent with the charge of conspiracy in the rape of Tamar. At certain unsettling moments, David is presented as a shadowy figure, a manipulator, a conspirator. The "kingly style of David," according to Joel Rosenberg, has always been characterized by "his movement within a cloud of agents, henchmen, and informers." By the time his children are fully grown, David seems "tired, vague, jaded, long used to (and dependent on) the ten thousand small acts of evasion and self-forgiveness, the royal loopholes and exculpations, that the king, as arbiter of the sacred and the profane, is empowered to wield."[23]

What's more, the aging King David showed himself to be a softhearted and sentimental father, sometimes dangerously so, when it came to a favorite son. Clearly, David doted on Amnon, his eldest son and his designated heir, and he complied with Amnon's demand for the services of his half sister without a moment of inquiry or reflection. So David may have allowed himself to be co-opted into Amnon's transparent plot out of his own conspiratorial habits and reflexes, his inability to say no to his firstborn son, and his ability to blind himself to something that he did not wish to see.

A DESOLATE WOMAN

Once she has passed into the house of her brother, the second Tamar disappears from the pages of the Bible. "So Tamar remained desolate in her brother Absalom's house," the Bible discloses (2 Sam. 13:20), and that is the last we hear of her. Given the limited roles available to a woman in biblical times—a virgin daughter in the house of her father, a consecrated wife in the house of her husband, or a widow in the house of her son—we may gather that Tamar remained hidden away in the house of her brother, a desolate woman until the day of her death.

"Keep this to yourself," counseled Absalom, who seemed to understand the treacherous family politics behind the rape. "He is your brother—do not take it to heart." (2 Sam. 13:20) (NEB)

But Absalom did not forget the insult that Tamar had suffered. He may have spoken soothing words to Tamar, but his own heart was afire with hatred for Amnon, and he burned for revenge against his sister's rapist. Still, Absalom checked his own impulse toward blood-vengeance and waited to see what King David would do about the crime that the crown prince had committed against his daughter.

Absalom himself said not a word to Amnon, the Bible reports, "neither good nor bad." (2 Sam. 13:22) Instead, he waited and watched to see what King David would do to punish the rapist within his own household. But Absalom waited in vain: David did nothing at all. "When King David heard the whole story, he was very angry," the Bible reports, "but he would not hurt Amnon because he was his eldest son and he loved him." (2 Sam. 13:21) (NEB)[24]

Time passed and King David seemed to behave as if the ugly incident had never happened. Tamar may have disappeared from the king's table, but Amnon still idled around the palace with all of his power and privilege fully intact. All the while, Absalom swallowed his anger and resentment until he could no longer stomach it. At last, Absalom vowed to do what David refused to do.

The third and final blow to the house of David was about to fall.

Chapter Twelve

"BLOODSTAINED FIEND OF HELL!"

My soul disclaims the kindred of her earth;
And, made for empire, whispers me within,
"Desire of greatness is a godlike sin."
—John Dryden,
"Absalom and Achitophel"

Two years had passed since the rape of the Tamar, but David had done nothing to punish Amnon, and Absalom still seethed with hatred for the man who had despoiled his sister. So Absalom resolved to take the matter into his own hands. To lure Amnon into his trap, Absalom invited King David and the royal household to a festival on his estate outside Jerusalem—"a feast fit for a king." (2 Sam. 13:28) (NEB) It was early spring, the season when the sheep were gathered for shearing, and a traditional occasion for feasting and drinking and merry-making.

"Let the king, I pray thee, and his servants go," Absalom said to his father. (2 Sam. 13:24)[1]

"No, my son, let us not all go," demurred David, his suspicions aroused by Absalom's sudden amiability, "lest we be a burden to you." (2 Sam. 13:25)[2]

"If not, I pray thee," Absalom persisted, "let my brother Amnon go with us." (2 Sam. 13:26)

"Why should he go with you?" David asked, abandoning all

pretense of concern for overtaxing Absalom's hospitality. (2 Sam. 13:27)

Absalom persisted. He implored the king to send *all* of his sons, including the crown prince, even if the king himself declined to go. Ever a sentimental father, David may have convinced himself that Absalom was finally ready to forgive Amnon for the rape of Tamar and resign himself to Amnon's eventual kingship. At last David consented to send all of his sons to Absalom's estate. And so the royal princes of Israel, the crown prince among them, mounted their mules and headed out of Jerusalem on the northerly road to Absalom's estate at Baal-hazor.

"STRIKE!"

Absalom arranged for an abundance of food and drink—the Hebrew word used in the biblical text *(misteh)* suggests that the banquet was to be "a drinking-bout"—because he counted on getting Amnon drunk.[3] Just before the festivities were about to begin, he summoned a few of his most trusted servants and issued one last instruction.

"Bide your time, and when Amnon is merry with wine, I shall say to you, 'Strike!' " said Absalom to his men. "Then kill Amnon." (2 Sam. 13:28) (NEB)

Absalom understood the political implications of assassinating the crown prince of Israel: David would surely regard the murder not only as fratricide but as treason. And so he sought to reassure the men he had charged with the task of killing his half brother.

"Fear not," he told them. "For I myself have given the command! Be courageous, and be valiant!" (2 Sam. 13:28)[4]

Absalom, we can imagine, must have greeted Amnon warmly and watched him attentively during the banquet, perhaps smiling at the crown prince from across the room to reassure him that all had been forgiven. The lilting music, the sizzle of roasting lamb, and the sloshing of red wine as cups were raised and filled again and again must have lulled Amnon and the other princes into thinking that Absalom's bitter hatred was spent and peace would now be restored within the royal family.

And then, suddenly, Absalom gave the signal—"Strike down Amnon!"—and his men fell on the unsuspecting prince, stabbing him with daggers and short swords, and leaving him dead where he sat. (2 Sam. 13:28)[5]

"Then all of the king's sons arose," the Bible reports, "and every man got him up upon his mule, and fled." So chaotic and confused was the scene of Amnon's murder that the first report to reach King David in Jerusalem described a general slaughter. "Absalom has slain *all* the king's sons," the first breathless messenger reported to King David, "and there is not one of them left." (2 Sam. 13:30)[6]

"THE KING'S SONS ARE COME"

Upon hearing the first report, David rose from his throne, tore his royal mantle, and threw himself to the ground, moaning and keening in an open display of grief. All but one of the courtiers followed his example and set to tearing their clothing, too. Only Jonadab, the same coolheaded young man who had conspired to put Tamar into Amnon's bed in the first place, stood apart and spoke calmly to the king.

"Let not my lord suppose that they have killed all the young princes," Jonadab told David. "Only Amnon is dead." (2 Sam. 13:32)[7]

The Bible does not explain how Jonadab obtained this crucial bit of intelligence, but clearly the biblical author has assigned him the task of explaining to David why his firstborn son was dead.

"By the anger of Absalom, this has been determined since the day Amnon forced his sister Tamar," said Jonadab, silent on his own role in the affair, as he calmly urged David to put the matter into perspective. "Your majesty must not pay attention to a mere rumor that all the princes are dead—only Amnon is dead." (2 Sam. 13:32–33)[8]

At that moment, one of the sentries at the royal palace raised a cry—a small crowd was ascending the hill on which the City of David stood and approaching the palace.

"Behold, the king's sons are come," said Jonadab. "As thy servant said, so it is." Then all of them "lifted up their voice, and wept bitterly." (2 Sam. 13:36)[9]

"And David mourned for his son every day," the Bible discloses, momentarily leaving us to wonder whether he wept for the dead Amnon or the missing Absalom. A few lines later, the biblical author makes it clear that David quickly reconciled himself to the death of Amnon and shifted his affection and concern to the son who stood next in line for the throne—Absalom.[10]

"David failed with longing for Absalom," the Bible reports, "for he was comforted concerning Amnon, seeing he was dead." (2 Sam. 13:37, 39)

Here is the same attitude of acceptance, so pragmatic and so fatalistic, that David displayed when he learned of the death of Uriah—"The sword devours one way or another"—and the death of his own child—"I shall go to him, but he will not return to me." Indeed, we can safely surmise that David was less interested in the dead-and-buried Amnon than in Absalom, whose vengeance-taking raised an urgent political crisis in Israel—Absalom was next in the line of succession, but the crown prince of Israel was on the run.

A CROWDED HOUSE

Absalom sought refuge in the kingdom of Geshur on the far side of the Jordan River. The choice was a natural one: Absalom and Tamar were the children of one of David's wives, a woman named Maacah, who was the daughter of the Geshurite king. (2 Sam. 3:3) Although "David's heart went out to him with longing" (2 Sam. 13:39) (NEB), the still-embittered king refused to allow him to return to Jerusalem. Three years passed as Absalom lingered in exile in the court of the king of Geshur.

The scene is rich with irony. David had sent Amnon into the

fatal trap set by Absalom just as he had once sent Tamar into the sexual ambush laid by Amnon, perhaps unwittingly but perhaps not. Now Absalom, just like his father before him, was a fugitive from royal justice. Indeed, the Court Historian suggests a fateful symmetry in the lives (and deaths) of the men and women whose stories are told in the vast biblical saga. "I will raise up evil against thee out of thine own house," Nathan had prophesied, and so it was that the intimate sins of David now afflicted the royal household in equally intimate ways. When it comes to a king, the Bible confirms, even a family crisis is a matter of politics, too.

"We sense the seemingly *crowded* nature of the royal house, its casual mingling of public and private life, the steady access of court and household to one another," observes Joel Rosenberg, who points out that David's "almost promiscuous accumulation of wives and children" has turned out to be "a time-bomb in the midst of the supposedly peaceable kingdom he labors to create."[11]

Only one man in the court of King David saw that the integrity of the state and not merely the repair of a family was at stake, and he alone sought to defuse the ticking time bomb.

THE THEATER OF POLITICS

Joab, the nephew of David who served not only as commander of his army but also as a henchman and political fixer, took it upon himself to bring Absalom back to Jerusalem. And the politico Joab, not unlike the prophet Nathan, resorted to a bit of theater to prick the conscience of the king. Just as Nathan had once made up a tale about a rich man who stole a poor man's lamb, Joab now arranged for David to hear the tale of an old woman who was supposedly grieving over her two sons, one of whom had been murdered by the other. Joab recruited a woman from the village of Tekoa to play the role of the mourning mother, told her exactly what to say, and sent her to David on the pretense of asking for advice from the wise king of Israel. Indeed, the "wise woman" of

Tekoa, as she is called in the Bible (2 Sam. 14:2), may have been a kind of professional actress, "specially skilled in speech" and trained to deliver her lines with the calculated moral impact that Joab now sought.[12]

"Thy handmaid had two sons," the old woman began, "but one struck the other and killed him." The rest of the family was pressing the old woman to surrender her surviving son "that we can put him to death for taking his brother's life." But if she did so, she would be left with no sons at all and, more to the point, no heir: "They will stamp out my last ember." And she begged the king to intervene: "Let your majesty call on the Lord your God to prevent his kinsmen bound to vengeance from doing their worst and destroying my son." (2 Sam. 14:6–7, 11)[13]

"As the Lord lives," declared King David, duped once again, "there shall not one hair of thy son fall to the earth." (2 Sam. 14:11)

But the old woman persisted. "May I add one more word, your majesty?" she asked, and then continued with the script that Joab had given her. "How then could it enter your head to do this same wrong to God's people? Out of your own mouth, your majesty, you condemn yourself—you have refused to bring back the man you have banished." (2 Sam. 14:13)[14]

This pointed reminder of the king's hypocrisy was an audacious act, even coming from a woman who was supposedly beside herself with grief, and David now recognized its real author.

"Is the hand of Joab behind you in all this?" David demanded, and the woman promptly confessed that Joab "put the whole story into my mouth." (2 Sam. 14:19) (NEB)

David confronted Joab over the deception—but, fatefully, he agreed to allow Absalom to return from the land of Geshur and dispatched Joab to bring him back. Still, even after Absalom was back in Jerusalem, David refused to receive his errant son at court. "Let him return to his own house," David commanded, "but let him not see my face." Two more years passed while Absalom lived in the City of David but did not see his father. (2 Sam. 14:24)[15]

At last Absalom sent an invitation to Joab to call on him, hoping the king's closest counselor would intervene once again on his behalf, but Joab did not show up at Absalom's house. Twice he was called, and twice he refused to come, although the Bible does not specify why. So Absalom resorted to a gesture he knew that Joab, "that toughest of Near Eastern mafiosi,"[16] would understand and appreciate.

"See, Joab's field is near mine, and he has barley growing there," Absalom told his servants. "Go and set it on fire." (2 Sam. 14:30)[17]

Sure enough, the arson was enough to rouse Joab, and soon he appeared at Absalom's house to confront Absalom—but Absalom ignored Joab's complaint.

"Why did I come from Geshur?" he demanded. "It would be better for me to be there still—let me now see the king's face, and if there be any guilt in me, let him kill me." (2 Sam. 14:32)[18]

Seven years had passed since Tamar disappeared into Absalom's house, an exile by reason of her rape, and five years had passed since Amnon was made to pay for his crime with his life—time enough, it seems, for David to relent at last. And so, when Joab appealed to David to receive his beloved son, the king consented.

> And when he had called for Absalom, he came to the king, and bowed himself on his face to the ground before the king, and the king kissed Absalom.
>
> (2 Sam. 14:33)

But the tenderness of the father-and-child reunion was short-lived. Absalom regarded the king as a man in decline, a man who was governed by his heart rather than his head, and he saw no reason to wait until his father's death to wear a crown of his own. The time bomb that had begun to tick when David allowed Amnon's crime to remain unpunished was now ready to explode.

A CHARIOT AND HORSES AND FIFTY MEN

The biblical author, as we have seen, makes much of David's good looks, and now he gushes even more enthusiastically over David's son. "Now in all Israel there was none to be so much praised as Absalom for his beauty," the Bible reports. "From the sole of his foot even to the crown of his head there was no blemish in him." Absalom's greatest glory was his full head of hair, so luxuriant that it weighed out at two hundred shekels—two or three pounds— when he submitted to his annual haircut. (2 Sam. 14:25) Absalom looked like a man who was destined to be a king, the Bible suggests, and he was already playing the role.

Absalom had procured for himself "a chariot and horses and fifty men to run before him," and he ventured out into the streets of Jerusalem with an entourage worthy of a king. Rising early each morning and placing himself near the city gate—not unlike the modern congressional candidate greeting voters on their way to work—Absalom boldly addressed any man who approached the palace to seek King David's judgment on a matter in dispute.

"I can see that you have a very good case, but you will get no hearing from the king," Absalom would say. "If only I were appointed judge in the land, it would be my business to see that everyone who brought a suit or a claim got justice from me." (2 Sam. 15:3–4) (NEB)

Such words might be characterized as an act of lese majesty and maybe even open treason, but the aging David, passive and aloof, did nothing to stop his son's politicking, and Absalom soon began to build a constituency. When those whom Absalom intercepted on the way to the palace began to prostrate themselves before him, the king's son acknowledged their obeisance by extending his hand so that they might kiss it. With David lingering inside the palace and young Absalom working the crowds outside, the son of the king began to seem more kingly than the king himself.

"So Absalom," the Bible confirms, "stole the hearts of the men of Israel." (2 Sam. 15:6)

Indeed, the prophecy of Nathan was approaching its fulfillment. The earliest sign of David's decline had been his refusal to lead his army to war against Ammon. Then came his scandalous affair with Bathsheba, a sexual adventure that might be seen as the impulsive act of a man in a midlife crisis. Next came his soft-hearted refusal to punish Amnon for the rape of Tamar. And now David's passivity in the face of Absalom's open play for power suggests fatigue and a certain lassitude—the years of struggle, the hard-fought campaigns and conspiracies, and the burdens of high office had taken a toll on King David.

When Absalom turned forty, he took steps to turn his campaign for the throne into a coup d'état. He decided to take up residence in Hebron, the capital of the tribal homeland of Judah, where David himself first reigned as king. And he offered David a feeble excuse for his sudden desire to relocate: while in exile in Geshur, Absalom insisted, he had vowed to "serve Yahweh" at Hebron if he were permitted to come home. But David either failed to mark, or failed to protect himself against, the predations of his ambitious son. (2 Sam. 14:7)[19]

"I pray thee, let me go and pay my vow in Hebron," said Absalom.

"Go in peace," said the king—and his words crackle with irony in light of what is about to happen. (2 Sam 14:7, 9)

THE SOUND OF THE HORN

Now Absalom followed his father's example by arranging to wear the crown of Judah in a kind of dry run for his claim on the crown of all Israel. He recruited one of David's most trusted counselors, a man named Ahitophel, to join his conspiracy. He took a sizable entourage with him to Hebron—some two hundred unsuspecting men whom he would later call upon to serve as his bodyguard and courtiers—and he sent spies throughout the land of Israel with instructions to rally the people in support of his kingship when he launched his coup d'état. The signal for the coup would be the piercing blast of the shofar.

"As soon as you hear the sound of the horn," Absalom briefed his agents, "then you shall say: 'Absalom is king in Hebron.'" (2 Sam. 15:10)

When at last a messenger revealed to David that Absalom had risen up against him and captured the loyalty of the people—"The hearts of the men of Israel are after Absalom" (2 Sam. 15:13)—David reverted to the same impulse that had seized him when he was dodging spears in the court of King Saul.

"Arise and let us flee," David ordered his courtiers at the first news of Absalom's uprising. "Make speed to depart, lest he overtake us quickly, and bring down evil upon us, and smite the city with the edge of the sword." (2 Sam. 15:14)

THE FUGITIVE KING

Some of David's courtiers, the comrades in arms who remembered his old brass and derring-do, declared themselves willing to stand and fight if only the king asked them to do so. "As your majesty thinks best," they told him. "We are ready." But David's only thought was to break and run. "And the king went forth," the Bible reports, "and all his household after him." David had already learned that Ahitophel had joined his renegade son in rebellion, and he no longer knew whom he could trust among his fellow Israelites. For that reason, he refused to rely on the tribal militia to defend him against Absalom, and he brought along only the foreign mercenaries who had long served as his private army, the Cherethites and the Pelethites and the men of Gath, a spare force of six hundred men in all (2 Sam. 15:15, 18).[20]

In his haste to escape from the royal palace, however, David abandoned the ten concubines who had once attended to his famous sexual appetites. The women were left behind "to keep the house," according to an apologetic passage in the Bible, but the relinquishment of the royal harem can be seen as yet another measure of the defeatism that had seized David. And, as we shall see, it would have calamitous results both for the women themselves and for the integrity of David's kingship. (2 Sam. 15:16)

Clambering after the king and his court came a small crowd of clergymen—the two men who shared the office of high priest in Jerusalem, Zadok and Abiathar, and the Levites who attended the tent-shrine of Yahweh and assisted in rituals of sacrifice. They carried with them the Ark of the Covenant, surely believing that David would prevail against Absalom if the Ark was in his arsenal. But once again David showed himself to be in the grip of a crippling fatalism.

"Carry back the ark of God to the city," he ordered, assigning the task to Zadok and Abiathar. "If I shall find favor in the eyes of the Lord, he will bring me back, but if he say thus: 'I have no delight in thee,' behold, here I am, let him do to me as seems good unto him." (2 Sam. 15:25–26)

David's flight from Jerusalem was the nadir of his reign and marked the near destruction of a man who had once inspired adulation among the Israelites. From the heights of imperial power and glory, he was once again a fugitive, commanding an army no larger than the guerrilla band he had led in his youth. We may imagine that David was showing signs of age, his hair turning silver and thinning on the crown of his head, his once-taut belly now sagging just a bit, his skin turning leathery. And the biblical author confirms that the sight of the fugitive king in desperate flight from the City of David was heartbreaking even to those who might be ready to hail Absalom as their new king.

> And all the country wept with a loud voice, as all the people passed over; and as the king passed over the brook Kidron, all the people passed over, toward the way of the wilderness.
>
> (2 Sam. 15:23)

David crossed the brook of Kidron, which marked the traditional boundary of Jerusalem (1 Kings 2:37), and headed up the slope to the very peak of the Mount of Olives, "where God was wont to be worshipped." (2 Sam. 15:32) The phrase itself is odd and provocative—the only sacred site on the Mount of Olives was the so-called Mount of Corruption, where King Solomon would later erect a series of shrines for the pagan gods and goddesses who were worshipped by his hundreds of foreign wives, "for Ashtoreth the detestation of the Zidonians, and for Chemosh the detestation of Moab, and for Milcom, the abomination of the children of Ammon," as the biblical author, full of contempt and disgust, puts it. (2 Kings 23:13) Perhaps the nightmare landscape that David now crossed was a place of pagan worship rather than a sacred site of Yahwism, and the passing reference to the God of Israel represents the effort of one biblical source to overwrite the older tradition.

As David ascended the Mount of Olives and headed toward the wastes of the Judean desert, his own elegiac words for the slain Saul and Jonathan must have haunted him. At that bitter moment, David must have cast his memory back to his glory days, and surely we are intended to do so—the day when Samuel rejected David's seven brothers and called the youngest one to be anointed, the single combat between the shepherd boy and the Philistine giant, the fairy-tale romance with a king's daughter and the freebooting years when he always succeeded in besting old king Saul, the final campaign that brought David ever upward toward kingship and empire. Here the Bible preserves the very moment when David teeters at the edge of despair: the king of all Israel, a man after God's own heart, was now reduced to a refugee, barefoot and weeping.

> And David went up by the ascent of the mount of Olives, and wept as he went up; and he had his head covered, and went barefoot; and all the people that were with him covered every man his head, and they went up, weeping as they went up.
>
> (2 Sam. 15:30)

The scene is, in a real sense, one of the defining moments of the Bible. The people of Israel—and, more particularly, the descendants of the tribe of Judah who will one day be called the Jews—will experience for themselves the terror of flight and the pain of exile in the millennia to come. But it is here that the Bible offers the first glimpse into that terrible future as David flees into the wilderness.

A FRIEND OF THE KING

Yet something stirred in David at this moment of defeat, some spark of the survival instinct that had kept him alive against the best efforts of his enemies to kill him off, some resurgence of the strong will and the agile mind that had allowed him to prevail against them until now. At the darkest moment in his life, David seemed to assert himself against all those who conspired to put an end to his kingship.

On the peak of the Mount of Olives, David encountered a man called Hushai, who is identified in the Bible as "the Friend of David." (2 Sam. 15:37) (AB) The phrase, as we have seen, is reminiscent of an ancient Egyptian title, "the Friend of the King," and may have identified Hushai as a privy counselor of special intimacy.[21] Hushai, too, was reduced to despair—his garment was rent and his head was sprinkled with earth in the ancient signs of mourning. And yet, at the sight of his friend, the old fighting spirit reasserted itself in David, and the king suddenly saw a way to use Hushai to fight back against his renegade son.

"If you come with me, you will only be a burden to me," David told Hushai, suddenly displaying his old savvy as a guerrilla fighter. "But if you return to the city, and say to Absalom: 'I will be thy majesty's servant, as I have been thy father's servant in time past,' then you can help me frustrate Ahitophel's plans." (2 Sam. 15:33)[22]

The espionage apparatus that David put into place is a sign

that he had not lost his cunning and ruthlessness after all. Hushai would insinuate himself into Absalom's inner circle and then serve as a double agent. Whatever intelligence Hushai managed to gather within the court of Absalom would be passed along to the two high priests, Zadok and Abiathar, who would use their own trusted sons to convey the intelligence reports to David. And, even more crucially, Hushai would be in a position to neutralize whatever good advice Ahitophel might give to Absalom. If Ahitophel counseled a particular policy or a plan of action, then Hushai would seek to turn Absalom's mind against it.

"O Lord, I pray thee," implored David, "turn the counsel of Ahitophel into foolishness." (2 Sam. 15:31)

THE LAME PRINCE

Absalom was not the only man in Israel who burned with ambition to depose King David and make himself king. Amid the chaos created by Absalom's coup d'état, the plotters showed themselves. Saul's lame son, Mephibosheth, was now ready to claim the crown, as David discovered when he crossed the path of Ziba, the old servant of King Saul and the man into whose care David had placed Mephibosheth and his estate.

Ziba was leading a string of asses loaded down with food and drink: "Two hundred loaves of bread, and a hundred clusters of raisins, and a hundred of summer fruits, and a bottle of wine." Another sign of David's renewed vigor was his sudden demand to know what Ziba meant to do with the supplies—David understood the value of such provisions to a guerrilla army, and he apparently intended to "liberate" the asses and all they carried to supply his own army. Just as David had once shaken down the household of Nabal during his years of banditry, now he did the same to Ziba. Unlike Nabal, Ziba knew and feared David, and he quickly complied with the unspoken demand. (2 Sam. 16:1)

"The asses are for the king's household to ride on," Ziba said, improvising a gesture of support to assuage David, "and the bread and summer fruit for the young men to eat, and the wine that such as are faint in the wilderness may drink." (2 Sam. 16:2)

"And where is your master's son?" David now demanded of Ziba.

"Behold, he abides at Jerusalem, for he said: 'Today the Israelites are going to give me back my father's kingdom,' " Ziba declared, thus betraying Mephibosheth as readily as he had surrendered the supplies intended for his master. (2 Sam. 16:2)[23]

David now played on what he calculated to be Ziba's greed and faithlessness. He declared Ziba to be free of any duty to serve Mephibosheth, and authorized Ziba to seize the property that he held in trust for Saul's only surviving son.

"Behold," said David to Ziba, "you shall have everything that belongs to Mephibosheth." (2 Sam. 16:4)[24]

So the expert plotter was back in play. With a few deft words, David managed to separate Mephibosheth from his lifelong servant and his only real ally, thus neutralizing one contender in the mad scramble for power that Absalom had set into motion. Now amply provisioned, surrounded by a corps of mercenaries who owed allegiance only to him, and wired into Absalom's inner circle through a network of spies and double agents, David marched into the wilderness with renewed strength and a freshened spirit. No longer was it a rout; rather the old guerrilla fighter was returning to the style of warfare that he knew intimately and had used successfully against Saul and his other enemies. Now he would bring the same skills to bear against an enemy in whose veins his own blood flowed.

"YOU BLOODSTAINED FIEND OF HELL!"

David's old fighting spirit was stirring again, but the fact remained that Absalom, not David, was now the charismatic leader to whom the people of Israel turned. Here we are reminded that God's favor and public acclaim are two very different things: Saul may have forfeited the affection and confidence of Yahweh, but he never faced a general rebellion against his kingship. Here and now, all the old grudges were boiling up against David, and the notion that he was God's anointed king seemed to matter not at all to the general populace. The fact that the people of Israel rallied so readily to Absalom confirms that David may have been beloved of God, but he was despised of men.

As David passed through the village of Bahurim on the outskirts of Jerusalem, he discovered for himself not only how little he was loved but also, perhaps more important, how little he was feared by the people of Israel. A man called Shimei, a blood relation of Saul, charged out of his house at first sight of the fleeing king and his entourage. Undaunted by David or the soldiers who flanked him, Shimei boldly approached, cursing bitterly and casting stones at all of them, both the king and his men.

"Begone, begone, you scoundrel! You man of blood!" cried Shimei. "The Lord has returned upon you all the blood of the house of Saul, whose throne you have stolen!" (2 Sam. 16:7)[25]

"Man of blood" is how Shimei's words of abuse toward David are generally translated into English from the original Hebrew text, but even this rich and resonant phrase may not convey the gall that boiled up in Shimei at the sight of the deposed king. So P. Kyle McCarter, Jr., offers an alternate and perhaps more accurate translation of the same phrase in the Anchor Bible: "You bloodstained fiend of hell!"

Shimei proceeded to scold King David publicly in the harsh language of a man who is either fearless or mad. David, he declared, had bloodied his own hands in the course of claiming the kingship of Israel. The Bible does not specify what bloody deeds Shimei had in mind, but scholars have speculated that he condemned the king for some or all of the very deeds from which the biblical authors have so carefully distanced King David—the death of Saul and Jonathan in battle against David's former masters, the Philistines; the assassination of Saul's son, Ishbaal, and Saul's general, Abner, both of whom were killed by men who sought to curry favor with David; and the hanging of seven other sons and grandsons of Saul by the Gibeonites. Unlike the biblical apologists, who insist that David is guiltless in all of these deaths, Shimei condemned David as a mankiller who was being punished by God for his bloody deeds.

"The Lord has given the kingdom to your son, Absalom!" Shimei railed. "Behold, you murderer, see how your crimes have overtaken you!" (2 Sam. 16:8)[26]

The old soldiers who accompanied David—the "mighty men" (*gibborim*), as they are known in the King James Version and other translations (2 Sam. 16:6)—were astounded at Shimei's words, and their first impulse was to silence him with the sword.

"Why should this dead dog curse my lord the king?" asked Abishai, Joab's brother, the impulsive killer who would have struck down King Saul himself during their bandit years if he had not been restrained by David. "Let me go over, I pray thee, and take off his head." (2 Sam. 16:9)

But David once again refused to let Abishai draw his sword. "What have I to do with you, ye sons of Zeruiah," complained David, distancing himself from the bloodthirsty brothers, Abishai and Joab. Perhaps David was reluctant to order the execution of a close relative of King Saul; perhaps he was suffering from the sentimentality that sometimes blunted his old ruthlessness; or perhaps he was simply confident enough in his own renewed strength that he felt no need to punish a deranged old man for his lunatic words. In any event, David spared Shimei. (2 Sam. 16:10)

"Let him curse," said David, who wondered aloud whether God himself had not bidden Shimei to deliver the public scolding. "Perhaps the Lord will mark my sufferings and bestow a blessing on me in place of the curse laid on me this day." (2 Sam. 16:10, 12) (NEB)

So David moved on, and his little army followed him. David may have regained some of his old confidence, but he was still a man on the run. And it is a measure of his lingering fatalism and defeatism that David attributed Shimei's bitter curse to God himself.

"If someone curses in that way, it's because Yahweh has said to him: 'Curse David!' " (2 Sam. 16:11)[27]

Indeed, God's anointed now believed himself to be under a curse of divine origin. "To the ancient mind, the curse had real efficacy," explains John Bright, and the notion of blood-guilt "was no figure of speech."[28] Indeed, David may have felt himself doubly betrayed—first by his own son, who had deposed him from the throne, and now by his God, who had instructed an old man to put him under a curse. As David and his band moved off in search of a new refuge, Shimei trailed after them, still cursing, still throwing stones, still casting fistfuls of dust at the once and future king.

Chapter Thirteen

"O ABSALOM,
MY SON, MY SON!"

Now it is war indeed—
  Now there is room for a spy!
O Peoples, Kings and Lands, we are awaiting your commands—
What is the work for a spy?
                    —RUDYARD KIPLING, "THE SPIES' MARCH"

Absalom and his army marched into the City of David in muted glory—David had fled, Jerusalem was undefended, and so the new king of Israel claimed the ultimate prize without so much as drawing his sword from its scabbard. Now he turned to his father's former advisor, the turncoat Ahitophel, a man so revered that a question put to him by a king was "as if a man inquired of the word of God." (2 Sam. 16:23)

"Give your counsel what we shall do," said Absalom, as if he was surprised at how easy it had been to depose King David and confused about what to do next. (2 Sam. 16:20)

Ahitophel knew that Absalom needed to make a public display of his authority. Since he had not been forced to fight for the throne, and had not distinguished himself in battle, the self-crowned king must do something to show that he was now the man in charge. So Ahitophel came up with an audacious and even shocking idea, one that would convey a clear message to the army and the rest of Absalom's supporters that there was no turning back for any of them.

"Have intercourse with your father's concubines," Ahitophel counseled the new king, "and all Israel will come to hear that you have given great cause of offence to your father, and this will confirm the resolution of your followers." (2 Sam. 16:21) (NEB)

AN ORGY ON THE PALACE ROOFTOP

The whole point of Ahitophel's plan was for Absalom to take his pleasure with David's ten concubines in a public place where all of his subjects would be able to watch. A pavilion was erected on the roof of the royal palace—the same place, ironically enough, where David had first spotted Bathsheba. Then each one of the concubines was escorted to the pavilion, where she submitted to a sexual encounter with Absalom "in the sight of all Israel." (2 Sam. 16:22)

The public spectacle depicted in the Bible can be seen as yet another lurid episode in the soap opera that King David's life so often resembled. But it is also evidence of the moral example that David had set for his sons. Thus, for example, David's sexual conquest of Bathsheba may have led Amnon to believe that he could take his half sister, Tamar, for his own pleasure without consequence. The fact that the rape of Tamar went unpunished by David prompted Absalom to take revenge against Amnon—and David's apparent weakness and lack of resolve encouraged him to go into open rebellion against his father.

The incident is yet another example, too, of what J. Cheryl Exum means by the phrase "raped by the pen." Nowhere is it reported in the Bible that the ten women of David's harem were forced to submit to Absalom—and yet neither is it suggested that they had the right or the opportunity to say no to the king's son. Just as David apparently enjoyed a kind of droit du seigneur—the right of a lord to make a sexual claim on any of his subjects—over Bathsheba, Absalom seems to have taken it for granted that the women of the harem were sexual functionaries whose job it was to service the man who happened to wear the crown, father or son.

God is nowhere to be seen or heard in these ugly affairs, and men and women are perfectly capable of making trouble for each other and themselves without divine intervention. But as we have noted, at least one of the more pious biblical authors intends us to see the hand of God at work throughout David's long ordeal, and even in the sexual humiliation of ten innocent women on the palace roof. Long ago, when the prophet Nathan had boldly condemned King David for his dalliance with Bathsheba and pronounced a curse on the house of David in the name of Yahweh—"I will raise up evil against thee out of thine own house"—he was quite specific in describing what kind of evil was to befall David: "I will take thy wives before thine eyes, and give them unto thy neighbour, and he shall lie with thy wives in the sight of this sun." According to the theological overlay that can be discerned throughout the Book of Samuel, the rebellion of Absalom in all of its ugly particulars was the will of God and the fulfillment of Nathan's prophesy. (2 Sam. 12:11–12)

Still, the theological spin on the life story of David can be off-putting to some Bible readers. God may have intended to humble and humiliate David for sinning with Bathsheba—but what did the ten women in David's harem do to merit sexual humiliation at the hands of Absalom? To the modern eye, the scene suggests forcible rape of a weirdly ritualized kind—one woman after another is escorted to the rooftop of the palace for an act of intercourse with the king in front of an audience—and it is uncomfortable to imagine that a God whom we praise for justice and mercy was the author of such a lurid scene. Yet just as the bastard child of David and Bathsheba was made to die as punishment for David's sin, ten innocent women were forced to submit to public sexual humiliation for the same reason.

SPY AND AGENT PROVOCATEUR

Among those who welcomed Absalom to Jerusalem was Hushai, once "the King's Friend" to David and now turned agent provocateur. Just as David had instructed, Hushai sought to ingratiate himself with Absalom and insinuate himself into the royal court. "Long live the king!" cried Hushai to Absalom.

"Is this your loyalty to your friend?" Absalom asked, referring to Hushai's formal title and clearly suspicious about his sudden change of allegiance. "Why did you not go with him?"

"Because I mean to attach myself to the man chosen by the Lord, by this people, and by all the men of Israel," Hushai replied, sounding wholly sincere. "I will serve you as I have served your father." (2 Sam. 16:16–19) (NEB)

Absalom was persuaded by Hushai's lie and he welcomed the old man into his inner circle of counselors. Indeed, he immediately invited Hushai to participate in a council of war to decide how and when to deal with the potential threat that David, even in exile, represented to his kingship. Absalom may have succeeded in chasing his father out of Jerusalem, but David was not yet defeated.

Ahitophel proposed a decisive military operation against David: he would raise a strike force of twelve thousand picked men and lead them against David's little band of soldiers. The key to Ahitophel's plan was speed—Absalom must attack while David was still demoralized by the sudden loss of the throne and fatigued by the hasty flight from Jerusalem.

"Let me go in pursuit of David tonight," Ahitophel implored. "I will come upon him while he is weary and weak. I'll surprise him, so that the entire army that is with him will desert, and I shall kill no one but the king." (2 Sam. 17:2)[1]

Then Ahitophel waxed rhapsodic with visions of a quick and painless victory over David. "I will bring all the people over to you as a bride is brought to her husband," he promised Absalom in a curiously tender metaphor, "and all the people will be in peace." (2 Sam. 17:3)[2]

Absalom and his counselors were ready to send Ahitophel in pursuit of the old king. But then Absalom, perhaps unsettled at the prospect of ordering his father's death, or perhaps only because he was curious about what Hushai thought of Ahitophel's bold plan, consulted his newest advisor. And Hushai, whose job it was to undermine Ahitophel, denounced the plan and offered one of his own.

Instead of striking a preemptive blow against David with a hastily assembled force under Ahitophel's command, Hushai advised, Absalom ought to wait until he had raised a vast army from every corner of Israel, "from Dan even to Beersheba, countless as grains of sand on the seashore." Then Absalom himself ought to lead the army into battle against David. (Sam. 17:11)

To make the case for his plan of operations, Hushai reminded Absalom of his father's ferocity and cunning. "You know that your father and his men are hardened warriors, and as savage as a bear in the wilds robbed of her cubs," Hushai said. "Your father is an old campaigner, and even now he will be lying hidden in a pit." (Sam. 17:8)[3] David, like a cornered bear, would surely put up fierce resistance to Ahitophel's preemptive strike, and word of the early casualties would demoralize the rest of Absalom's men. "Anyone who hears the news will say, 'Disaster has overtaken the followers of Absalom,' " Hushai warned. "The courage of the most resolute and lionhearted will melt away, for all Israel knows that your father is a man of war." Then Hushai conjured up a vision of Absalom's ultimate victory. "We will light upon him as the dew falling on the ground," he assured the king, "not a man of his family or his followers will be left alive." (2 Sam. 17:8, 10, 12)[4]

Hushai's advice was bad, and intentionally so. The Bible confirms that Ahitophel had offered "good counsel," while Hushai's plan was calculated to help David and hurt Absalom. A quick strike against David's small and disordered band of refugees and runaways offered the chance of an early victory, and any delay in attacking David would allow him to find a safe refuge beyond the reach of Absalom, strengthen his own fighting force, repair his political alliances within Israel, and recruit, among the neighboring kingdoms, allies to whom he was related by blood and marriage. Indeed, David was an expert at guerrilla warfare—we might even say he invented it!—and he knew how to defeat a large conventional army of the kind that Hushai recommended with the same hit-and-run tactics he had used against Saul.

Why did Absalom reject the "good counsel" of Ahitophel and embrace the intentionally bad advice of Hushai? The biblical author himself appears to be astounded at Absalom's boneheaded decision to listen to Hushai and ignore Ahitophel, and he explains it with a characteristic theological shrug. "The Lord had ordained to defeat the good counsel of Ahitophel," the Bible reports, "to the intent that the Lord might bring evil upon Absalom." (2 Sam. 17:14) But we might wonder whether Absalom, acting out of some kind of primal fear, was reluctant to issue a death sentence on his own father.

THE FIFTH COLUMN

Now Hushai sought out Zadok and Abiathar, the high priests whom David had left behind in Jerusalem as fifth columnists, and gave them an urgent intelligence report to convey to the fugitive king.

"Do not spend the night on the plains of the wilderness," went Hushai's message, which was apparently prompted by his concern that Absalom would, in fact, do exactly what Ahitophel had proposed, "but cross the river at once, lest the king be swallowed up, and all the people that are with him." (2 Sam. 17:16)[5]

The biblical author, writing several millennia before John le Carré and Len Deighton, pauses here to give his readers a tense account of the Bible-era spycraft practiced by David's espionage apparatus. The high priests in Jerusalem entrusted the message from Hushai to a maidservant, who carried it secretly to a safe house on the outskirts of Jerusalem where their sons, Jonathan and Ahimaaz, were stationed. The two young men were detailed to act as couriers and bring the message to David. But they had been spotted by some watchful lad in service to Absalom, who had betrayed their whereabouts to the king.

The couriers reached the town of Bahurim—the place, by the way, where Shimei had denounced David as a "bloodstained fiend of hell." Fearing that they would be tracked down and arrested before they could reach David's camp, they sought refuge at a house along the road. And to conceal themselves from the king's patrols, they lowered themselves into a well in the courtyard. The kindly woman who lived in the house placed a cover over the mouth of the well and sprinkled it with grain to suggest that the well had not been opened recently.

"Where are Ahimaaz and Jonathan?" demanded the king's guard when they arrived at the house.

"They are gone over the brook of water," the intrepid woman lied. (2 Sam. 17:20)[6]

The soldiers headed off in the direction of the brook, but they found nothing and returned empty-handed to Jerusalem. Meanwhile, Jonathan and Ahimaaz clambered out of the well and hurried to David's camp, where they delivered Hushai's message: "Arise, and pass quickly over the water," they said, "for this is how Ahitophel has given counsel against you." Thus warned, David roused his men and marched them down to the river's edge, where they crossed to safety on the eastern bank of the Jordan. (2 Sam. 17:21)[7]

"By the morning light," the Bible reports, "there was not a straggler who had not gone over the Jordan." (2 Sam. 17:22)[8]

CAPTAINS OF THOUSANDS

Just as Hushai had hoped and Ahitophel had feared, Absalom's delay in making war on his father allowed David both time and space to make preparations for the decisive battle to come.

Ahitophel fell into a deadly despair over Absalom's lack of faith in his advice. Perhaps he felt personally disgraced, or perhaps he was fearful of the fate that would surely befall him if

David returned to Jerusalem in triumph. Indeed, he was unwilling to wait and see whether David or Absalom would be the ultimate victor. "And when Ahitophel saw that his counsel was not followed, he saddled his ass, and arose, and got himself unto his city, and set his house in order," the Bible discloses, "and strangled himself, and he died." (2 Sam. 17:23)

Meanwhile, David set up a base of operations at a place called Mahanaim—ironically, it was the same place that briefly served as the seat of government for the rump kingdom of Ishbaal, the son of Saul. Unmolested by Absalom, David used the respite to strengthen and supply his army, mustering fresh recruits and "setting captains of thousands and captains of hundreds over them." Allies, old and new, rallied to his support, and he began to collect arms and provisions from kings and comrades in arms. (2 Sam. 18:1) "Beds, and basins, and earthen vessels, and wheat, and barley, and meal, and parched corn, and beans, and lentils, and parched pulse, and honey, and curd, and sheep, and cheese of kine," goes the redolent biblical inventory, "for David, and for the people that were with him, to eat." (2 Sam. 17:28–29)

At last David was ready to move against Absalom, who had raised an army and was now encamped in the nearby land of Gilead on the eastern bank of the Jordan River. But the seasoned and savvy guerrilla fighter refused to engage Absalom and his much larger forces in a set-piece battle. Instead David divided his army into three units, each one under the command of a trusted captain—Joab; Abishai, his brother; and a man called Ittai, an old cohort who hailed from the Philistine city-state of Gath. David's plan was to strike at Absalom's army in the forest of Ephraim, the kind of broken country ideally suited for the hit-and-run tactics that David had used so successfully against Saul.

David, old in years but eager to lead his men into battle as he had done in his glory days, declared his intention to put himself on the front line: "I shall surely go forth with you myself." Perhaps he recalled the moral catastrophe that had befallen him when he stayed behind in Jerusalem while Joab had campaigned against the Ammonites, or perhaps he was rejuvenated by his return to the life of a guerrilla captain. But his comrades in arms prevailed on David to remain behind lest he fall into the hands of Absalom. "If half of us die, will they care for us?" argued his lieutenants. "But thou art worth ten thousand of us." David yielded to their demands, and he agreed to remain behind. (2 Sam. 18:2–3)

Success in battle depended on a ruthless and decisive strike against Absalom's much larger fighting force, and David surely knew it as well as any man in either army. Still, on the very eve of battle, David experienced an upwelling of fatherly sentiment, the same love of a father for a son that had stayed his hand against Amnon after the rape of Tamar. Here again, David betrayed the tenderness that was at once one of his most endearing qualities and one of his greatest weaknesses as a leader. David gathered his commanders, Joab and Abishai and Ittai, and issued one last order as the army watched and listened.

"Deal gently for my sake with the young man Absalom," said David in an order that was partly a king's command and partly a father's plea. (2 Sam. 18:5) (NEB)

Then the army rose, divided into three columns, and marched off in the direction of the forest of Ephraim. David watched from the city gate as "the entire army marched out by hundreds and thousands." (2 Sam. 18:4) (AB) Now it was up to them, David must have realized, to decide whether father or son would wear the crown of Israel.

THE DEVOURING FOREST

On that day of battle, David's little army conducted "a great slaughter" in the forest of Ephraim. The landscape favored David's guerrilla tactics, and his small units moved more easily over the terrain than the much larger army fielded by Absalom. Twenty thousand men fell in battle—and, as the biblical author confirms, "the forest devoured more people that day than the sword devoured." (2 Sam. 18:8)

Absalom rode into battle at the head of his army, but he, too, was defeated by the dense forest—and, as it turned out, by his own lovely head of hair. As envisioned by the Talmudic sages and the ancient chronicler Josephus—although never stated outright in the Bible—Absalom, on his mule, passed under the boughs of a tree in the forest of Ephraim, and his long hair was caught fast in a low-hanging branch.[9]

"He was taken up between the heaven and the earth," is how the Bible lyrically describes the mishap, "and the mule that was under him went on."

One of David's men saw Absalom hanging helplessly—and, we may imagine, in pain—from the branch of the tree, and he promptly reported the sighting to Joab. (2 Sam. 18:9)

"Why did you not strike him to the ground?" Joab wanted to know. And, despite David's order to spare his son, Joab suggested that he had placed a bounty on Absalom's head: "I would have had to give you ten pieces of silver, and a belt." (2 Sam. 18:11)[10]

"If you were to put a thousand pieces of silver in my hand, I would not lift a finger against the king's son," the soldier replied, "for we all heard that the king charged you and Abishai and Ittai, saying: 'Beware that none touch the young man Absalom.'" (2 Sam. 18:11–12)[11]

David might be softhearted toward his own son, but Joab always seemed to be capable of clearer thinking and more ruthless action. As long as Absalom lived, Joab knew, he remained a threat to David, and it was only by killing him that Joab would be able to crush the insurrection and preserve the integrity of the monarchy that David had created.

So Joab dismissed the reluctant soldier, picked up three darts,[12] assembled ten of his own men, and went in search of the tree in which Absalom was caught up. The scene would be comical if it were not so pitiful: Absalom "was yet alive in the midst of the terebinth," dangling "between the heaven and the earth," when Joab himself struck him "through the heart" with the darts. Apparently Absalom survived Joab's three sharp blows—did he groan in pain? did he beg to be put out of his misery?—and so the ten young men who accompanied Joab set upon Absalom with their own weapons to finish the job, and they "smote Absalom, and slew him." (2 Sam. 18:15) Or perhaps Absalom was already dead, and the wily Joab was only seeking to make it more difficult to pin the death of the king's son on one man.

Then Joab sounded the ram's horn to signal a cease-fire, and the army of David broke off the slaughter. As word of the death of their king and commander spread through the ranks, Absalom's army fell into open rout: "All Israel fled, every one to his tent." The corpse of the slain Absalom was cut down from the tree, cast into a pit in the forest, and buried under a heap of stones—a traditional form of burial for a villainous and despised enemy. The biblical author pauses here to note that Absalom left no son "to keep [his] name in remembrance"—a signal that Absalom's claim on the kingship ended with his death. (2 Sam. 18:18)

GOOD TIDINGS

David waited at the gates of his stronghold, and a watchman stood atop the city wall. At last the watchman spotted a lone runner approaching from the distance, and he reported what he saw to the king.

"If he be alone, then he has tidings," mused the king, who knew that many men on the run was a sign of an army in rout, but a single runner meant only that a message had been sent from the front. (2 Sam. 18:25)[13]

In fact, Joab had dispatched two runners to relay the news to King David. One was a black-skinned man from Ethiopia—a Cushite, as the Bible puts it—who was apparently serving along with the other foreign mercenaries in David's army. The other was Ahimaaz, son of the high priest Zadok, who had begged Joab for the privilege of telling the king "that the Lord hath avenged him of his enemies." Joab, however, knew that David was unlikely to share the young priest's enthusiasm when he learned that

Joab had defied his command to spare Absalom. (2 Sam. 18:19) Indeed, Joab may have remembered the fate of other men who had hastened to tell David that an enemy had been slain in battle!

"Why will you run, my son," said Joab, "seeing that you will have no reward for the tidings?"

"Come what may," the young man answered, "I will run." (2 Sam. 18:22–23)[14]

Now the watchman on the city wall spotted the second runner, too, and he was able to make out that one of the two men was Ahimaaz.

"He is a good man," said David hopefully, "and comes with good tidings." (2 Sam. 18: 27)

"All is well," called Ahimaaz as he trotted up to the gate. He bowed to the king, pressing his forehead to the ground, surely breathless with exultation as well as exertion. "Blessed be the Lord thy God, who hath delivered up the men that lifted up their hand against my lord the king." (2 Sam. 18:28)

But David did not pause to join in thanksgiving to God. He did not ask for details of how the battle had been won. He did not utter a word of congratulation or celebration. Rather the king asked the courier a single question, the only question that really mattered to him.

"Is all well with the young man Absalom?"

"I saw a great commotion," mumbled Ahimaaz, perhaps realizing the enormity of the blow he was about to deliver and finding himself unable to give the king a straight answer, "but I did not know what had happened." (2 Sam. 18:29) (NEB)

Now the Cushite approached the gate.

"Tidings for my lord the king," declared the second messenger. "The Lord has avenged you this day on all those who rebelled against you." (2 Sam. 18:31)[15]

Thus does the biblical author play out the suspenseful account, denying the truth to David long after we have witnessed the fate of Absalom. Now, once again, King David asked the only question that seemed to matter to him.

"Is all well with the young man Absalom?" David asked the second messenger.

"May all the king's enemies and all rebels who would do you harm," burbled the Cushite, "be as that young man is." (2 Sam. 18:32) (NEB)

David puzzled out the bitter truth that was concealed within these ornate but oblique phrases—and his heart broke.

> And the king was much moved, and went up to the chamber over the gate, and wept, and as he went, thus he said: "O my son Absalom, my son, my son Absalom! Would that I had died for thee, O Absalom, my son, my son!"
>
> (2 Sam. 19:1)

VICTORY INTO MOURNING

Word soon reached Joab that David had been shattered by the news of Absalom's death. The king spent the day with his head in his hands, weeping and moaning in a public display of grief. Instead of a triumphal march from the front to the stronghold where David waited, the soldiers slipped back into the city "by stealth," as if they were cowards running away from a defeat rather than conquering heroes returning from battle to reclaim the royal capital. "And the victory that day," the Bible notes, "was turned into mourning unto all the people." (2 Sam. 19:3)

Joab was made of tougher stuff. The old soldier reacted to the king's grief over Absalom—the man who had done his best to kill *him* first—not with sympathy but with rage and disgust, and he did not hesitate to tell David so.

"You have put to shame this day all your servants, who have saved you and your sons and daughters, your wives and your concubines," ranted Joab at the cowering king. "You love those that hate you and hate those that love you! For it is plain that if Absalom were still alive and all of us dead, you would be content." (2 Sam. 19:6–7)[16]

David may have been God's anointed and, once again, king of all Israel, but Joab recalled their freebooting days too well to regard him as anything but a mortal man. So Joab barked out orders to David, a general commanding a king, reminding him of where his duties lay.

"Arise, go at once, and give your servants some encouragement," Joab told David. "If you refuse, I swear by the Lord that not a man will stay with you tonight, and that will be worse than all the evil that has befallen you from your youth until now." (2 Sam. 19:8)[17]

A chastened David rose at Joab's command, perhaps wiping his tear-filled eyes. David took his rightful seat at the city gate, the traditional gathering place where the judges and high priests of ancient Israel had conducted public ceremonies and exercised the power of high office. "Behold, the king doth sit in the gate," the people said to one another, as if to confirm that the king was back in his right mind, the shattered monarchy was repaired, and all was as it should be. (2 Sam. 19:9)

But nothing would ever be the same for David or the kingdom he had created. "The king ceases to be king," points out Bible critic David M. Gunn. "From this point on, he is simply and essentially man."[18] Against all his political wiles, his ruthlessness in battle, and his will to power—or, for that matter, the favor of the God of Israel—David was now helpless in the face of a loss that neither politics nor theology was able to soothe.

Chapter Fourteen

AN ANGEL AT THE
THRESHING-FLOOR

. . . angels in the architecture . . .
—Paul Simon, "You Can Call Me Al"

The sight of King David at the gate of his capital-in-exile re-assured the loyalists who had rallied to his banner in the war against Absalom. The land of Israel, however, was still in crisis. Now that Absalom was dead, and while David still lingered in his distant stronghold, no king reigned in Jerusalem. And the Israelites, leaderless and fearful, reverted to their old tribal feuds and rivalries.

"And all the people were at strife throughout all the tribes of Israel," the Bible notes. "The entire army was complaining to all the staff-bearers of Israel: 'So now why have we no plans for bringing the king back?' " (2 Sam. 19:10–11, 12)[1]

The old king, it seems, was sulking. David had not forgotten that Absalom's rebellion had begun in Hebron—the capital of the tribal homeland of Judah and the place where David himself was first crowned a king—and he resented the disloyalty of his own tribe in rallying to Absalom's kingship. Indeed, he marked the fact that the other tribes of Israel had clamored for his return to Jerusalem but his own tribe of Judah remained insultingly silent.

"Ye are my brethren, ye are my bone and my flesh," went his petulant message to the elders of Judah. "Why are ye the last to bring the king back to his house?" Standing on protocol, David refused to return to Jerusalem until he was accorded the proper expression of remorse and respect from his own tribe. At last the elders of Judah sent the message that David had demanded—"Return thou, and all thy servants" (2 Sam. 19:15)—and the people of Judah thronged to the banks of the Jordan River "to meet the king, to bring the king over the Jordan." (2 Sam. 19:15, 16)

The king's homecoming to the City of David is described in the Book of Samuel in a phantasmagorical scene, and the matter-of-fact quality of the earlier narrative is replaced by a blend of symbolism and surrealism. The other biblical sources, so plainly fascinated with the hard facts of military history or the intimate scenes of a family in crisis, are joined here by an author who is caught up in a kind of fever dream. Now and then, the flesh-and-blood David seems to disappear in a swirling mist of myth and memory.

The scene opens on the banks of the Jordan River. A ferryboat "passed to and fro to bring over the king's household." Suddenly, the humbled enemies of King David—all the men who had cursed him to his face or plotted behind his back—began to appear, one by one.

First came Shimei, who had once condemned David as a "bloodstained fiend of hell." Now he fell to the ground before the restored king, buried his face in the earth, and begged for his life.

Next came Ziba, the servant whom David had assigned to care for Mephibosheth, Saul's only surviving son. In his haste to abase himself before the returning king, Ziba did not wait until David had stepped out of the boat but instead waded into the swirling waters of the Jordan to greet him.

Finally, Mephibosheth, the last potential claimant to the throne once occupied by King Saul, appeared at the riverside. And just as David had once tried to convince the king of Gath of his harmlessness by feigning madness, Mephibosheth shambled up to David like a homeless lunatic. "He had neither dressed his feet, nor trimmed his beard, nor washed his clothes," the Bible reports, "from the day the king departed until the day he came home in peace." (2 Sam. 19:25)

The sight of these old enemies offended Abishai, Joab's brother, who believed that their betrayals merited nothing less than the ultimate punishment. "Shall not Shimei be put to death for this," asked Abishai, "because he cursed the Lord's anointed?" (2 Sam. 19:22)

But David only shushed Abishai. "What have I to do with you, ye sons of Zeruiah?" he asked yet again. The king was in an expansive mood, and he impulsively declared a general amnesty: "Why should any man be put to death this day in Israel? I know now that I am king of Israel." (2 Sam. 19:23) (NEB)

"My lord the king is as an angel of God," said Mephibosheth, whose mind was not so disordered that he could not engage in a bit of ornate flattery for the man who had just spared his life. (2 Sam. 19:28)

David's largesse symbolizes the urgent interest of the biblical sources in the healing of old wounds. The house of David must be put back in order, and a nation in disarray must be united again. Blood-vengeance and tribal feuds must end, and the self-perpetuating cycle of insult and injury must be broken once and for all. And so David, mild and forgiving, is made to serve as a symbol of theological law and order—God's anointed was back where he belonged, and the time had come for healing rather than vengeance.

WIDOWS WITH THEIR HUSBAND ALIVE

David soon discovered, however, that the wounds of war were too deep to be healed with a few gracious words. Indeed, the strife in David's life was always double-edged, cutting into the flesh of his loved ones and the flesh of the body politic at the same time. And now David was forcefully reminded of the stain on his honor and the breach of royal protocol that had taken place while he was absent. When he returned to his palace he came upon the ten concubines whom he had left behind when he fled from Jerusalem, the women whom Absalom had taken to the rooftop for an orgy "in the sight of all Israel."

Absalom, as we have seen, committed a double sin when he engaged in a public orgy with the women of his father's harem—he violated the taboo against incest, and he committed an act of treason. The women were now fleshly symbols of the failed rebellion of a usurping son, and whether we look at them from the perspective of biblical theology or royal politics or Freudian psychology, they were untouchable. For David—and for the biblical author, too—it was simply unthinkable for the rightful king to take his pleasure with these twice-tainted women, and so now he simply shunned them.

The king's very first decree upon resuming the throne in Jerusalem was to shut the women away where he would never lay eye or hand upon them again. David "provided them with sustenance," the Bible notes, "but went not in unto them." (2 Sam. 20:3) He tended to be generous toward his enemies at the moment of triumph, but even the biblical author seems to concede the sting of injustice in the fate of these ten women: "So they were shut up unto the day of their death in widowhood, with their husband alive." (2 Sam. 20:3)

"EVERY MAN TO HIS TENT, O ISRAEL!"

The estrangement of the king from his concubines was repeated on a larger scale across the land of Israel, and the old rivalries between Judah and the other tribes of the Israelite confederation still sputtered. David himself was the flash point.

"Why have our brethren, the men of Judah, stolen thee away?" complained the Israelites, who resented the fact that David had been first welcomed back from exile by his fellow Judahites.

"Because the king is near of kin to us," retorted the men of Judah, asserting a claim on David by reason of his roots in Judah.

The bickering exploded into a new civil war when a man

named Sheba, a rabble-rouser from the tribe of Benjamin, rallied the Israelites to make war on Judah. Unlike Absalom, who challenged David for the kingship of all Israel, Sheba was a secessionist who sought to break up the delicate tribal coalition over which David reigned. (2 Sam. 19:42–43)

"We have no portion in David," cried Sheba to the rebel army he had raised. "Every man to his tent, O Israel!"(2 Sam. 19:42)

To punish Sheba and crush the uprising, David issued a new call to arms. But instead of relying on his own trusted generals, Joab and Abishai, David summoned a man called Amasa to lead the army into battle. The choice was surprising and rather perverse—Amasa had served as the commander of Absalom's army in the abortive campaign to dethrone David. Amasa had been pardoned for his act of treason during the general amnesty that followed the victory over Absalom, and now David entrusted him with the crucial task of raising an army in Judah and going in pursuit of Sheba. David specified that the tribal muster should be complete within three days so that the rebel army could be tracked down and destroyed before securing a stronghold in one of the fortified cities of Israel.

Amasa, however, quickly forfeited the confidence of King David when three days passed and he still tarried somewhere in Judah. With Amasa nowhere to be found, David turned to his kinfolk and comrades in arms, Joab and Abishai. And rather than order a tribal muster from Judah, David put them in command of the foreign mercenaries who served as his bodyguard, the Cherethites and the Pelethites. Then the hastily assembled task force moved out in search of Sheba and his rebel army.

BLOOD ON THE HIGHWAY

On the way to search out and destroy Sheba, Joab came upon the missing Amasa and his men. Unlike the king, who had been willing to entrust an army to Amasa, Joab saw him only as a renegade and a traitor. The two men had commanded opposing armies during the rebellion of Absalom, and it must have galled Joab twice over to see him pardoned and then named as a general of David's army. Now Joab resolved to satisfy his old grudge.

"Is it well with thee, my brother?" called Joab, apparently greeting him in friendship. (2 Sam. 20:9)

Then, curiously, "Joab took Amasa by the beard with his right to hand to kiss him"—and as he pulled Amasa into an embrace, Joab loosed his sword from its sheath.[2] "Amasa took no heed to the sword that was in Joab's hand," and he was neatly disemboweled, falling down dead and "wallowing in his blood in the midst of the highway." (2 Sam. 20:9–10, 12)

Refusing to waste any time or tears on their old enemy, Joab and Abishai marched off in pursuit of Sheba while Amasa lay in a pool of his blood and bowels. The militiamen who had accompanied Amasa, however, were stunned by the sight of their slain commander.

"He that is for David," cried one of Joab's lieutenants to Amasa's men, "let him follow Joab!" (2 Sam. 20:11)

But the men refused to move. So the resourceful young officer dragged Amasa's body into the adjacent field and covered it with a garment, thus hiding the ghastly corpse from the green recruits who found the sight of blood so unsettling. Only then did the reluctant men of the tribal muster begin to put one foot in front of the other and move off numbly after Joab.

Sheba was finally cornered at a place called Abel, where he sought refuge behind the high wall of the fortified city. Joab promptly besieged the town, and his men began to pile up a mound of earth to span the moat and reach to the top of the wall. As they prepared for a final assault, a woman's voice was heard from within.

"Come near that I may speak with thee!" she called to Joab, and he consented to palaver with her before ordering his men to destroy the city. (2 Sam. 20:16)

Like the woman of Tekoa once recruited by Joab to put Absalom's case to King David, her counterpart in Abel may have been an advocate selected by the townsfolk "by reason of her skills of speech and persuasion." Armed only with the power of artful speech, the woman of Abel went to work on the old soldier.[3]

"We are peaceable and faithful," declared the wise woman of Abel, as she is called in the Bible. "Seekest thou to destroy a city and a mother in Israel?"

"Sheba has lifted up his hand against the king," Joab replied coolly. "Deliver him only, and I will depart from the city."

"Behold," the woman said, no less coolly, "his head shall be thrown to thee over the wall."

The woman, "a mother in Israel," returned to the townsfolk who cowered behind the wall and, "in her wisdom," she told them exactly what they needed to do to save their lives. Moments later, the severed head of Sheba came hurtling high over the wall and landed in the camp of the besieging army. And Joab, having achieved what he came to do, sounded the ram's horn to signal a retreat, and headed back to Jerusalem to report his latest victory to the king. (2 Sam. 20:22)

THE SWEET SINGER OF ISRAEL

On the day of David's final victory—"the day that the Lord delivered him out of the hand of all his enemies," as one biblical author puts it—the king sang a song of thanksgiving to the God of Israel, or so the Bible says. In the biblical account, he stops abruptly and delivers a long, ornate, deeply pious sermon in which he credits God for each one of his successes in life. Here, as elsewhere in Samuel, the work of the Court Historian has been overwritten by a biblical author whose interest in David is strictly theological.[4]

"The Lord is my rock, and my fortress, and my deliverer," begins the first of the many praise-songs and psalms traditionally credited to David. "My savior, thou savest me from violence." (2 Sam. 22:3)

The song that has been written into the Book of Samuel at this point is repeated in a slightly different version as Psalm 18 in the Book of Psalms. "In both places it is attributed to David," writes Bible scholar Mitchell Dahood, who goes on to argue that "there is no internal evidence militating against such an attribution."[5] Indeed, it is here that the Bible identifies David as "the sweet singer of Israel," a gentle soul whom we first met during those golden days of his youth when he was able to soothe King Saul by plucking the strings of his lyre.

To be sure, at certain sublime moments in the Bible, David is depicted as a singer and a dancer, a poet and a musician. His famous elegy for Saul and Jonathan is what convinces Harold Bloom that a flesh-and-blood David may have been the author of the literary efforts that are attributed to him in pious tradition. "It is . . . possible that David indeed was a poet," allows Bloom, "and that the lament for Jonathan and some of the Psalms began as his work."[6]

And yet the words mouthed by David at this moment are profoundly at odds with the ironic and measured lyricism of his elegy to Jonathan—and, for that matter, with the man whom we have come to know so intimately. In fact, virtually nothing in David's song of thanksgiving rings quite true.

DELIGHT

God, for example, is almost always an aloof and indistinct figure in the biblical life story of David. Unlike Abraham, with whom God sat down for an impromptu meal of curds and chops, or Moses, with whom God chatted "face to face," David is never granted a manifestation of Yahweh that he can perceive with his own eyes or ears. But the praise-song that David now sings depicts God as a deity who reveals himself in urgent, unmistakable, and highly theatrical ways, rather like the storm god whom we encounter in the Book of Exodus:

> Smoke arose up in his nostrils,
> And fire out of his mouth did devour,

Coals flamed forth from him.
He bowed the heavens also, and came down;
And thick darkness was under his feet.
                                        (2 Sam. 22:9–10)

On the rare occasions when God does offer advice to David, he communicates through the oracles of the Urim and Thummim or, at best, in the dreams and visions of prophets like Samuel, Nathan, and Gad. Throughout the ordeal that the king had endured—the rape of Tamar, the assassination of Amnon, the rebellion of Absalom—David did not hear from God at all. But here we find a very different version of David's relationship with God.

"Yea, I called my God, and out of his temple he heard my voice," David sings. "The Lord thundered from heaven, and the most high gave forth his voice." (2 Sam. 22:7, 14)

Significantly, the theology of David's praise-song simply does not mesh with what we have already learned about his attitude toward the role of God in the lives of mortals. God might or might not favor him, David seemed to believe, and there was simply nothing David himself could do about it, one way or the other. When his prayers for the life of his bastard child went unanswered, David summed up his own theology with a fatalistic shrug. "I shall go to him," David said of the dead infant, "but he will not return to me." (2 Sam. 11:23)

The same fatalism can be seen at his moments of greatest physical and moral peril during the rebellion of Absalom. David declined to arm himself with the Ark of the Covenant, the throne and footstool of the God of Armies, and insisted on sending the relic back to Jerusalem. Indeed, he was never quite sure whose side God was on—perhaps, David allowed, Shimei's blood-shaking curse had been placed on him at the specific command of God himself! And so David never bothered to implore God to intervene in his desperate struggle with his own son; he relied on himself to preserve his life and his kingdom.

Now, however, David is shown to praise God for intervening

on his behalf and to credit God for his every victory in battle against his enemies—a theme that will be repeated throughout the Book of Psalms.

> He sent from on high, he took me,
> He drew me out of many waters;
> He delivered me from mine enemy most strong,
> From them that hated me, for they were too mighty for me.
>
> (2 Sam. 22:17–18)

Most striking of all is the off-putting note of pious self-praise that can be heard in David's first psalm. "He delivered me because he delighted in me," David sings, referring to his special favor in the eyes of God. "The Lord rewarded me according to my righteousness," he continues, incredibly enough. "According to the cleanness of my hands hath he recompensed me." (2 Sam. 22:20–21) And he is made to claim a degree of moral rectitude that we already know to be wholly unmerited.

> For I have kept the ways of the Lord,
> And have not wickedly departed from my God.
> For all his ordinances were before me;
> And as for his statutes, I did not depart from them.
> And I was single-hearted toward Him,
> And I kept myself from mine iniquity.
>
> (2 Sam. 22:22–24)

How can we reconcile the cloying piety of David's psalm of thanksgiving with the rough-and-ready quality of the life he actually lived? The simple answer, of course, is that David did not speak the words attributed to him here. Rather the psalm was fabricated by one of the later biblical sources and put into the mouth of David at a time when the man himself was long gone. In fact, a close study of the text convinces some Bible scholars that it was cobbled together out of two older poems. "Like the two spires of a cathedral," writes Bible scholar Artur Weiser, "the two parts of the mighty hymn soar to heaven."[7]

Indeed, the appearance of the psalm at this point in David's life story can be taken to exemplify how the biblical authors and editors went about creating the Bible out of the raw materials available to them. "It was a common literary practice in ancient Israel to place a long poem or 'song' (*shirah*) at or near the end of a narrative book," explains Robert Alter, who diplomatically concedes that David's authorship of the text "cannot be categorically dismissed" but deems it "unlikely."[8] And the late biblical editors were apparently undeterred by the fact that David's theological assumptions and rhetorical style, both so restrained and so spare in earlier passages, now seemed suddenly bloated, overdecorated, and out of character.

The real motive of the biblical author who composed the psalm—and the editor who added it to the sacred texts that ultimately became the Bible—is betrayed in the next passage of Samuel. Suddenly, the Bible harkens all the way back to the "theological highlight" of Samuel, the passage in which God is shown to make an eternal and unconditional promise of kingship to the house of David.[9] "Now these are the last words of David," insists the biblical author by way of introduction to one final burst of biblical poetry, even though David is still very much alive and his life story is not yet fully told. (2 Sam. 23:1)

> For is not my house established with God?
> For an everlasting covenant He hath made with me,
> Ordered in all things, and sure;
> For all my salvation, and all my desire,
> Will he not make it to grow?
>
> (2 Sam. 23:5)

David may be yet alive, but the mortal David is already being eclipsed by the transcendental David, the shimmering theological icon who will loom so large in the messianic yearnings of both

Judaism and Christianity. As far as the late biblical author is concerned, David is as good as dead already, and only the symbolic David really matters. But as we shall see, the Bible is not quite ready to bury the flesh-and-blood David.

ANGELS AND DEVILS

One final act of kingship was reserved for the aging King David: the taking of a census to determine the population of Israel. A census may seem like an unremarkable function of government to the modern reader, but the ancient Israelites regarded the notion as something monstrous, if only because a head count would assist the king in imposing the hated burdens of conscription and taxation on the populace. What's more, David's simple idea of census taking becomes the occasion for a theological flight of fancy unlike anything that has come before in the biblical life story of David. Indeed, the biblical author was so put off by the census that he characterized it as a divine punishment for the sins of the Israelites.

"And again the anger of the Lord was kindled against Israel, and he moved David against them, saying: 'Go, number Israel and Judah.'" (2 Sam. 24:1)

So diabolical was the notion of a royal census that the author of the Book of Chronicles, whose work was intended to be a corrective to the Book of Samuel, insisted that the Devil made David do it: "And *Satan* stood up against Israel, and moved David to number Israel." (1 Chron. 21:1) Even Joab, who was always quick to support the power and prerogatives of the king, is shown to challenge David when it came to taking a census: "Why does my lord delight in this thing?" (2 Sam. 24:3) But the king insisted, and it fell to Joab, his captains, and the soldiers under their command to actually count heads under threat of arms. For the record, the Bible puts the population of Judah during the reign of King David at five hundred thousand men of fighting age with another eight hundred thousand men in the rest of Israel. (2 Sam. 24:9)[10]

Even though David was acting on divine authority, the king was guilt-stricken when the census was complete: "I have sinned greatly in what I have done." (2 Sam. 24:10) And God, perversely enough, agreed. So the prophet Gad showed up to report that God intended to punish Israel with one of three afflictions: seven years of famine, three days of pestilence, or three months during which David would "flee before thy foes while they pursue thee." (2 Sam. 24:13) Aghast at all three options, David refused to choose, although he asked Gad to let God know that he preferred not to "fall into the hand of man." (2 Sam. 24:14)

"So the Lord sent a pestilence upon Israel," the Bible reports, "and there died of the people from Dan even to Beersheba seventy thousand men." (2 Sam. 24:15) As the plague approached Jerusalem, God relented. "It is enough," he told the angel of death. "Now stay thy hand." (2 Sam. 24:16)

But the angel of death now showed itself to David as a ghostly specter hovering above the threshing-floor of a Jebusite named Araunah, and David was moved to beg God for mercy.

"Lo, I have sinned, but these sheep, what have they done?" David prayed, referring to the people of Israel. "Let thy hand, I pray thee, be against me, and against my father's house." (2 Sam. 24:17)

The sudden and spooky appearance of angels and devils is something wholly new in the experience of King David. Indeed, the very strangeness of the scene prompts some Bible scholars to look for hidden and forbidden meanings in the text. Perhaps the threshing-floor was a sacred site of the Jebusites, and the angel of death sent by the God of Israel was made to stand in for a non-Israelite plague god who was worshipped there.[11] But the Israelites, too, regarded threshing-floors as places of special sanctity, and the God of Israel had been known to manifest in such places.[12] Thus the angel at the threshing-floor can be seen as yet another fingerprint of a biblical source with a theological agenda—the angel's sudden appearance was a message from God, according to the prophet Gad, who explained to David that Yahweh wanted him to "rear an altar unto the Lord in the threshing-floor of Araunah the Jebusite." (2 Sam. 24:18)

When Araunah learned of the king's plan, he insisted on providing David with all of the necessaries for a ritual sacrifice: "Behold the oxen for the burnt-offering, and the threshing-instruments and the furniture of the oxen for the wood." (2 Sam. 24:22) David was apparently untroubled by the fact that a threshing-floor belonging to a Jebusite might have been used as the site of idol-worship and other pagan rituals. After all, he was accustomed to handling the teraphim and other idols, and some of his best friends were Gittites and Philistines, Pelethites and Cherethites, all of them idol-worshippers. But David insisted on paying for what Araunah had offered as gift.

"I will verily buy it at a price," declared David, "neither will I offer burnt-offerings unto the Lord my God which cost me nothing." (2 Sam. 24:24)

The two men settled on fifty shekels of silver as a fair price for the purchase of the threshing-floor and the cattle, too, and David proceeded to build an altar and offer up the cattle to Yahweh.

"So the Lord was entreated for the land, and the plague was stayed from Israel." (2 Sam. 24:25)

THE TEMPLE THAT DAVID DID NOT BUILD

So reads the very last line of the Book of Samuel. The formal biography of David continues briefly and then concludes in the opening passages of the Book of Kings, where the old king is shown to choose his successor among the willful sons who seek the throne. But the strange encounter between David and the angel of death at the threshing-floor will turn out to play a fundamental role in the history and destiny of the house of David and the people of ancient Israel.

Solomon will prevail among the sons of David, of course, and it is Solomon who will build the temple that the God of Israel requires of his Chosen People. Ultimately, the Bible fixes on the Temple of Solomon in Jerusalem as the single most crucial feature in both the credo and the practice of religion in ancient Israel.

The distant descendants of the desert nomads who followed a tent-shrine through the wilderness will be confined to worshipping Yahweh at a single magnificent temple.

But a crucial and potentially embarrassing question remains unanswered. If God desired and required a temple in Jerusalem, why didn't God's anointed build it? Perhaps the flesh-and-blood David did not build a temple because he was faithful to the oldest traditions of his people, which required only a tent-shrine, or perhaps because, as the Bible explains, God did not want a "man of blood" to build his sacred temple. In either case, the biblical author now seeks to link David to the temple that Solomon will go on to build, and the linkage begins with the appearance of the angel at the threshing-floor of Araunah.

The link between David and the Temple is only suggested in the Book of Samuel, but it is spoken out loud in the Book of Chronicles, where the tale of the threshing-floor is retold with a few significant variations. The Jebusite who owned the sacred site is called Ornan rather than Araunah in Chronicles, and the price paid by David is given as six hundred shekels of gold rather than fifty shekels of silver. But the most significant contrast between the two versions of the tale is the purpose for which David acquired the threshing-floor in the first place. According to the Book of Samuel, the threshing-floor was the site of a crude altar of sacrifice to Yahweh, but the Book of Chronicles makes it clear that the Temple will rise on the same site during the reign of David's son and successor, King Solomon.

"This is the house of the Lord God," David is made to declare in the Book of Chronicles, "and this is the altar of burnt-offering for Israel." (1 Chron. 22:1)

So eager was David, according to the Chronicler, that he began to assemble a corps of masons and a supply of gold and silver, cedar and stone, iron and brass, all of it to be used for "the house that is to be builded for the Lord," a structure that "must be exceeding magnificent, of fame and glory throughout all countries." (1 Chron. 22:5) But one critical detail remains the same in both Samuel and Chronicles: David is *not* permitted to actually build the temple. Rather the task falls to his son, and the Chronicler allows David himself to explain why.

"My son, as for me, it was in my heart to build a house unto the name of the Lord my God," David tells Solomon in the Book of Chronicles. "But the word of the Lord came to me, saying: 'Thou hast shed blood abundantly, and hast made great wars; thou shalt not build a house unto my name, because thou hast shed much blood upon the earth in my sight.'" (1 Chron. 22:7–8)

The Chronicler insists that Solomon, "a man of rest," rather than David, "a man of blood," was chosen by God to build the Temple at Jerusalem. Even so, another sharp point of irony remains hidden in the biblical text. Solomon, as we shall now see, was no less of an intriguer than his father, no less ruthless in his lust for power, no less willing to shed the blood of even his closest kin. David's final legacy to his son—and his specific deathbed instructions—will leave the throne of Israel awash in blood.

Chapter Fifteen

HEAT

*Abishag my angel has risen from her chair and approaches
without noise, wearing only a vivid scarf. Her eyes are as dark
as the tents of Kedar. I want my God back; and they send
me a girl.*

— KING DAVID IN *GOD KNOWS,* BY JOSEPH HELLER

A t the age of seventy, the king of Israel, once so fresh and full
of promise, once so strong and virile, lay alone in the bed
that had accommodated so many warm bodies. The courtiers who
hovered around the royal bedchamber in the palace at Jerusalem
fretted over his flagging spirits and failing health.

> Now king David was old and stricken in years; and they
> covered him with clothes, but he could get no heat.
>
> (1 Kings 1:1)

David is fully human again in the opening passages of the First
Book of Kings, and heartbreakingly so. The biblical source who
closed out the Book of Samuel with lofty theological musings and
ornate psalm-singing may have lost interest in the flesh-and-blood
David, but here we find an author, possibly the Court Historian,
who felt obliged to describe how David's life really ended. In fact,
the final scene in the life of David originally appeared in the Book

of Samuel, scholars suspect, but some later biblical editor cut it out and pasted it in the Book of Kings, perhaps in an effort to emphasize the legitimacy of the king who followed him to the throne.[1]

The final moments of David's life are played out against a backdrop of unspoken memories. As a shepherd boy, David bested Goliath in single combat, according to the biblical life story, and he managed to dodge King Saul's well-thrown spear. He spent years as a fugitive, a bandit, and a mercenary, all without suffering an injury or a defeat. He survived Saul's maniacal efforts to track him down and kill him, and he ultimately prevailed over Saul and his sons in the struggle for the kingship of all Israel. He fought uncounted battles against the traditional enemies of Israel, and he reigned for forty years over a court and a country that pulsed with assassination and betrayal and conspiracy. No one—not political rivals, rebellious sons, or cuckolded husbands—had been able to touch David. And yet, precisely because he was a mortal man and nothing more, he was eventually overtaken and brought down by the quiet but relentless passing of the years.

To symbolize the ravages of age and time, the biblical author focuses on the very quality that had always animated the figure of David in the Bible—his love for women—and here David suffers the unkindest cut of all.

HEAT

One of the courtiers who had attended David for many years—one who remembered his old appetites and recalled the days when his harem was a lively place—suggested a way to cheer his king.

> Let there be sought for my lord the king a young virgin, and let her stand before the king, and be a companion unto him, and let her lie in thy bosom, that my lord the king may get heat.
>
> (1 Kings 1:2)

So a kind of Bible-era beauty contest was conducted throughout the land of Israel until a suitable woman was found—a "fair damsel" called Abishag, a woman from the town of Shunam in the hill-country outside Jerusalem. She was recruited for duty in the harem, conveyed to the palace, and prepared for her introduction to the king. Surely the sight of Abishag the Shunamite, the warm touch of her young flesh against the king's chest, would revive his flagging spirits.

But even as the alluring Abishag was ushered into David's bedchamber, the king continued to shiver helplessly beneath his bedclothes. Abishag, as it turned out, served as a nurse rather than a lover to the old man in her care: "She was a very beautiful girl, and she took care of the king and waited on him, but he had no intercourse with her." (1 Kings 1:4) (NEB)

All that was left to David, as far as the Bible is concerned, was to select a successor from among his many ambitious and contentious sons, and then die.

DEATHBED POLITICS

David had buried many sons, Amnon and Absalom and the nameless first child of Bathsheba among them, but two of his remaining male offspring managed to put the royal succession into question and even crisis. Would the next king of Israel be Adonijah, David's eldest surviving son, or Solomon, the late-born son of David and Bathsheba?

These two contested with each other for the throne, and the wishes of the dying king would be crucial in determining which one of them would occupy it when their father died. The very idea of dynastic succession was something wholly new in ancient Israel, and no law or custom was available to resolve the conflicting claims of Adonijah and Solomon. Indeed, if a son of David succeeded him to the throne, it would be the first peaceful succession in the short history of the Israelite monarchy.

Adonijah, as the eldest son, seemed to take it for granted that he would inherit the crown one day. Like Absalom, the Bible reports, Adonijah was "a very handsome man." (1 Kings 1:6) (NEB) Unlike Absalom, he had never offended David with his conduct—at least until now. For as David's health began to fail, Adonijah began to ape his deceased brother by acting like a king without wearing a crown. Everywhere he went in Jerusalem, Adonijah traveled with "chariots and horsemen, and fifty men to run before him" (1 Kings 1:5), and he presided over showy ritual sacrifices, slaughtering "sheep and oxen and fatlings" at a ceremony from which Solomon, his brother and rival, was pointedly excluded. (1 Kings 1:9)

As the old king rested in the royal bedchamber, Adonijah hurried through the corridors of the palace, lobbying the king's cabinet and lining up allies in what promised to be a battle for the throne. Joab, David's ever-ruthless but ever-faithful general, sided with Adonijah, and so did Abiathar, the high priest who had survived Saul's slaughter of the priests of Nob and remained loyal to David ever since.

Solomon was more subtle in his politicking but no less effective. Zadok, the *other* high priest, and Nathan, the prophet, and Benaiah, commander of the palace guard, assured him of their support in the contest for the crown. And Solomon claimed the loyalty of one person who counted for more than all the rest in terms of influence on King David—Solomon's mother, Bathsheba, the love of David's life.

"Have you not heard that Adonijah has become king, all unknown to our lord David?" Nathan said to Bathsheba. "Now, come, let me advise you what to do for your own safety and for the safety of your son, Solomon." (1 Kings 1:11–12)[2]

Nathan urged Bathsheba to present herself to King David and remind him that he had once vowed to her that he would make Solomon his successor as king of Israel. Until now, the Bible has reported no such promise by David, and Bible scholar Robert Alter proposes the provocative idea that Nathan may simply have invented it. If so, Alter writes, the briefing of Bathsheba by Nathan may reflect his effort to enlist her assistance in "persuading the doddering David that he actually made this commitment."[3]

The final encounter between David and Bathsheba is charged with both political and sexual tension, a fitting note on which to end the life story of David. As Bathsheba entered the royal bedchamber, she spotted the comely young Abishag in the midst of her ministrations, but the old queen betrayed no lack of confidence in her own influence over David. Bathsheba simply ignored Abishag as she presented herself to David, bowing to the ground before her old lover in an ostentatious display of royal protocol.

"What troubles you?" David asked Bathsheba, the woman for whom he had once been willing to commit murder. (1 Kings 1:16)

"My lord, you swore to me, by the Lord your God, that my son Solomon should succeed you as king, and that he should sit on your throne," Bathsheba declared. "And now, behold, Adonijah reigns as king, and you, my lord the king, know it not." (1 Kings 1:17–18)[4]

Bathsheba's words—bold, assured, and guileful—must have struck David's ears like a scolding. Before this moment, we have heard only one sentence from the lips of Bathsheba, an utterance that changed David's life and the history of Israel forever: "I'm pregnant." But now, more than twenty years later, Bathsheba showed herself to be one of those articulate and compelling women—like the old woman of Tekoa and the wise woman of Abel—who are able to capture the hearts and minds of powerful men with nothing but their own commanding words. She proceeded to press her case, telling David about the lavish feast to which Adonijah had invited all of the king's sons except Solomon and describing in detail how Adonijah had put on a spectacular display of ritual sacrifice, offering up oxen, buffalo, and sheep in abundance. And she named names, listing each of the courtiers who were siding with Adonijah.

"And now, my lord the king, all Israel is looking to you to announce who is to succeed you on the throne," Bathsheba said. "Otherwise, when you sleep with your forefathers, my son Solomon and I shall be treated as criminals." (1 Kings 1:20–21)[5]

Nathan, who had slipped into the king's bedchamber during Bathsheba's address, confirmed that everything Bathsheba had told him was true and then added a few incriminating details of his own. The sons of King David—all of them except Solomon— were feasting even now with Adonijah, and so were Joab, the commander of the king's army, and even Abiathar, the high priest. All of them ate and drank with Adonijah, boldly toasting him as if he already wore David's crown: "Long live king Adonijah!" (1 Kings 1:25)

At length, the king bestirred himself and called upon Bathsheba to draw closer to his bed. The old woman whom David had loved so long ago had now succeeded where Abishag's youthful charms had failed—the king was hot with anger, and he gave Bathsheba the promise that she sought.

"As the Lord lives, who has delivered me from all my troubles," croaked the old king, "I swore by Yahweh, the God of Israel, that Solomon your son should succeed me, and that he should sit on my throne, and so will I do this day." (1 Kings 1:29–30)[6]

Bathsheba bowed again, her face to the floor, and offered one last poignant wish: "Let my lord king David live forever." (1 Kings 1:31) Her words were nothing more than a prayer, and David knew that some prayers went unanswered.

"LONG LIVE KING SOLOMON!"

Just as he had promised Bathsheba, David promptly set in motion the plan that would make Solomon the next king of Israel. First he summoned Benaiah and ordered him to assemble the elite corps of foreign mercenaries, the Cherethites and the Pelethites. The soldiers were to convey Solomon to the sacred spring of Gihon—and lest anyone fail to understand whom David had chosen as his successor, Solomon was to ride the king's own mule all the way to Gihon and back. (1 Kings 1:34)[7]

"Then he shall come and sit upon my throne," declared

David, "for he shall be king in my stead, and I have appointed him to be prince over Israel and over Judah." (1 Kings 1:35)

To which Benaiah, guarantor of Solomon's physical security, answered: "Amen." (1 Kings 1:36)

Solomon's anointment was vastly grander than his father's. David, of course, had been a shepherd boy when he was called from the fields and secretly anointed by Samuel with only his father and brothers as witnesses. Solomon, by contrast, was attended by an honor guard of soldiers, he was anointed with holy oil from the tent-shrine of Yahweh by both the prophet Nathan and the high priest Zadok, and he was surrounded by a vast crowd that had followed him to the sacred spring of Gihon and broke into wild celebration at the sight of the oil glistening in his hair.

> And they blew the ram's horn, and all the people said: "Long live king Solomon!" And all the people came up after him, and the people piped with pipes, and rejoiced with great joy, so that the earth rent with the sound of them.
>
> (1 Kings 1:39–40)

David's last promise to Bathsheba had been fulfilled, and the only surviving child of their passionate but illicit love affair was now king of Israel.

THE HORNS OF THE ALTAR

At the very moment of Solomon's anointment, as the Bible reveals, Adonijah and his own band of intimates—Joab and Abiathar and all the sons of David *except* Solomon—were celebrating what turned out to be Adonijah's premature claim on the kingship. Their revelries were disturbed by the distant shriek of the shofar, the sound of drums and horns, the swelling roar of a crowd.

"What is all this uproar in the city?" asked Joab, whose instinct and experience must have prompted him to wonder whether some fresh rebellion had broken out in Jerusalem. "What has happened?" (1 Kings 1:41) (NEB)

Jonathan, son of the high priest Abiathar, approached the house of Adonijah. He was flushed and out of breath.

"Come in," Adonijah said hopefully. "You are an honorable man and bring good tidings." (1 Kings 1:42)[8]

"Alas, our lord King David has made Solomon king!" Jonathan cried. He proceeded to describe all the particulars, including the soldiers who guarded Solomon, the priest and the prophet who anointed him with holy oil, and the frenzy of celebration that Solomon's anointment had inspired. And then he reported that David himself had confirmed Solomon as his chosen successor: " 'Blessed be the Lord, the God of Israel, who has set a successor on my throne this day,' " Jonathan reported, quoting the words of David, " 'while I am still alive to see it.' " (1 Kings 1:48)[9]

"The city is in an uproar," concluded Jonathan, abject and miserable. "That was the noise that you heard." (1 Kings 1:45)[10]

Then, as each man at Adonijah's table realized that he had staked his fortune on the wrong son of David, all of them began to scatter in panic. Soon Adonijah found himself abandoned, and panic seized him, too. He hastened to the altar of Yahweh, a squat column of stone with a hornlike protuberance on each corner, and he "caught hold on the horns of the altar," thus invoking an ancient tradition by which a man could claim the protection of Yahweh against his pursuers. (1 Kings 1:50)

"Behold, Adonijah fears king Solomon," it was reported to Solomon, "for he has laid hold on the horns of the altar, saying: 'Let king Solomon swear to me first of all that he will not slay his servant with the sword.' " (1 Kings 1:51)

Here was the very first test of Solomon's kingship. His father, as we have seen, was quick to forgive those who challenged his authority—but Solomon was equally quick to threaten his brother with death.

"If he shall show himself a worthy man, there shall not a hair of him fall to the earth," said Solomon of Adonijah, "but if wickedness be found in him, he shall die." (1 Kings 1:52)

When Adonijah heard of Solomon's words, he released his grip on the horned altar, made his way to the palace, and prostrated himself before his brother in abject surrender. Solomon was satisfied, at least for the moment, and he spared his brother's life. "Go to thy house," Solomon ordered Adonijah. But Solomon vowed to keep a closer watch on Adonijah than David had kept on Absalom, and he would not be so lenient if Adonijah betrayed any sign that he still coveted the throne. (1 Kings 1:53)

THE LAST WILL AND TESTAMENT OF DAVID

Now that his successor was safely seated on the throne, David fell into his last decline. The old king lived on even as the new king reigned, but not for much longer. "Now the days of David drew nigh that he should die," the Bible reports, "and he charged Solomon his son, saying: 'I go the way of all the earth.'" (1 Kings 2:2)

David now delivered a deathbed speech to Solomon. We might imagine that David, old and frail, struggled to utter his last words. But, unlike the valedictory speech that is reported in the closing pages of the Book of Samuel—"Now these are the last words of David" (2 Sam. 21:1)—his final instructions to Solomon as reported in the Book of Kings were blunt and bloody.

David charged Solomon to be resolute and ruthless in claiming and keeping the crown of Israel. Just as Moses *and* God once charged Joshua, conqueror of Canaan, to "be strong and of good courage" (Deut. 31:23, Josh. 1:6), David urged Solomon: "Be thou strong, and show thyself a man." (1 Kings 1:2)[11]

Next, David gave orders for what would be his final act of revenge. Indeed, he gave Solomon a hit list—"a last will and testament worthy of a dying Mafia capo" is how Robert Alter describes David's final words to his son and successor,[12] and indeed the scene was artfully copied by Francis Ford Coppola in *The Godfather*.

"You know how Joab treated me and what he did to two commanders-in-chief in Israel," said David, referring to Joab's assassination of Abner, general of Saul's army, and Amasa, general of Absalom's army. "He killed them both, breaking the peace by bloody acts of war, and with that blood he stained the belt about my waist and the sandals on my feet." (1 Kings 2:5) (NEB)

David's sudden insistence on settling old scores is something new and shocking, if only because we are accustomed to seeing David carefully distance himself from acts of revenge and political violence. Throughout his reign, David refused to acknowledge responsibility for the deaths of his enemies even when he benefited from them, and he constantly tried to hold back his brutal henchmen, Joab and his brothers, from acting on their bloodthirsty impulses. Now and then, of course, he failed—Joab had killed David's beloved son, Absalom, in defiance of the king's specific order. At the very end of his life, David was ready to take his own vengeance on Joab—and yet, even now, his instructions to Solomon were oblique, more like a poem than a death sentence.

"Do as your wisdom prompts you," said David to Solomon, "and let not his gray hairs go down to the grave in peace." (1 Kings 2:6) (NEB)[13]

David urged Solomon to show "constant friendship" to a man from Gilead named Barzillai, one of the allies who rallied to David's cause during the war with Absalom. But he revealed that he was still nursing a grudge against old Shimei, the man who had once cursed him as a "bloodstained fiend of hell." Twice before, David had spared Shimei from death at the hand of Abishai, first when Shimei dared to curse him and again when David issued a general amnesty after the defeat of Absalom. Now, however, David instructed Solomon to punish Shimei for the old insult, and he admitted that by doing so he was carefully sidestepping his own vow to God.

"True, I swore by the Lord that I would not put him to death with the sword, but you do not need to let him go unpunished now," reasoned the old king, sly and cagey to the end. "You are a wise man and will know how to deal with him—bring his gray hairs in blood to the grave." (1 Kings 2:8–9)[14]

Joab and Shimei, like David, were old men now. Their hair was gray, as David emphasized, and the old soldiers were surely toothless. But the very last thoughts that flashed through David's mind as he approached the day he had long anticipated—the day when he would go to join the dead baby whom he had refused to mourn—were thoughts of vengeance and bloodletting. To the very end, then, David was a "man of war" and a "man of blood."

SPIN DOCTOR

Some late biblical editor, who probably came along a few hundred years after these lines were first written down, found himself appalled at the brutality, cynicism, ruthlessness, and sheer impiety of David's final charge to Solomon. So he decided to give the dying king a few theologically correct lines to speak, and he boldly wrote these new lines into the old text.

> Keep the charge of the Lord thy God, to walk in his ways, to keep his statutes, and his commandments, and his ordinances, and his testimonies, according to that which is written in the law of Moses, that thou mayest prosper in all that thou doest.
>
> (1 Kings 2:3)

The words attributed to David in this passage bear the fingerprints of a biblical source known as the Deuteronomistic Historian, a title used by scholars to identify a school of priestly authors and editors whose theology was first defined in the Book of Deuteronomy. According to Deuteronomy, the fate of ancient Israel was *not* predetermined by God; rather, the Israelites enjoyed the gift of free will, and their fate depended on how they used it. So the promise of God to the house of David came with a big "if": "*If* thy children take heed to walk before me in truth with all their heart and with all their soul," David is made to quote God in a way that echoes the familiar phrases of Deuteronomy, "there shall not fail thee, said He, a man on the throne of Israel." (1 Kings 2:4)[15]

The biblical spin doctor at work here chose to ignore the

promise that God had once made to David through the prophet Nathan. "When thou shalt sleep with thy fathers, I will set up thy seed after thee," God had promised, "and I will establish the throne of his king *forever*." (2 Sam. 7:12)[16] The later biblical sources were not quite as confident and optimistic as the earlier ones, and they began to wonder out loud if the reign of the house of David was not conditioned on good behavior after all.

From somewhere far beneath the layers of theological spin, however, the thoroughly mortal voice of David can still be heard. He was not at all concerned about the pious conduct of his son or the goodwill of God. Rather, he uttered a few plainspoken words that summed up his own credo and his own theology: "Be strong and show yourself to be a *man*." (1 Kings 2:2) (NEB)

THE WAY OF ALL FLESH

At the moment of his birth, according to a tale preserved in the Midrash, David was destined to survive only three hours. "He would have died immediately," imagines the rabbinical storyteller, "had not Adam made him a present of 70 years."[17] But the biblical authors did not engage in such theological speculation in reporting the death of David, perhaps because they were mindful that his real life story was poignant enough and impressive enough. Indeed, even though more biblical text is devoted to David than to any other figure in the Hebrew Bible, relatively few tales are told about him in the vast accumulation of legend and lore that we find in the Talmud and the Midrash. The flesh-and-blood David is rendered in the Bible with such brilliance that mere mythmaking seems hardly worth the effort.

"I go the way of all the earth," said David to Solomon, and his biblical death notice is equally lyrical but also equally direct: "And David slept with his fathers and was buried in the City of David." (1 Kings 2:2, 10)

Indeed, the very last words of the biblical life story of David read like an obituary.

And the days that David reigned over Israel were forty years: seven years reigned he in Hebron, and thirty and three years reigned he in Jerusalem. And Solomon sat upon the throne of David his father; and his kingdom was firmly established."

(1 Kings 2:11–12)

Thus passed the living figure of David from the world of ordinary men and women into the realm of history and memory, theological speculation and messianic yearning. He will continue to be celebrated and even exalted in the pages of the Bible, and he will be slowly and subtly transformed into something rich and strange. But at this moment, the flesh-and-blood David, both a "man of blood" and "a man after God's own heart," slips into that good night toward which every human travels.

Chapter Sixteen

THE QUALITY OF LIGHT
AT TEL DAN

And I will make an everlasting covenant with you,
Even the sure mercies of David.

—ISAIAH 55:3

And as concerning that he raised him up from the dead, now
no more to return to corruption, he said on this wise, I will give
you the sure mercies of David.

—ACTS 13:34

Solomon mourned the passing of King David with a hit list in his hand. And, no less ambitious or ruthless than his dead father, Solomon set about carrying out David's final instructions with genuine enthusiasm. So it was that Solomon, whose name means "peaceful," ascended the throne on a flood tide of blood.[1]

Solomon's first victim, however, was one whose name did not appear on the death list—his brother Adonijah, the man he had forgiven for trying to take the throne away from him. If we take the biblical author at his word, Adonijah refused to give up his royal ambitions, and he now approached Bathsheba with a strange and shocking request.

THE CRIME OF STUPIDITY

"Do you come peaceably?" Bathsheba asked Adonijah as he presented himself at her quarters in the royal palace.

"Peaceably," affirmed Adonijah, who promptly began to kvetch about his own sad fate to the woman least likely to sympathize with him. "You know that the kingdom was mine, and all Israel was looking to me to be king, but I was passed over and the throne has gone to my brother." And then he added, piously but also a bit lamely: "It was his by the Lord's will."

Then Adonijah revealed the real purpose of his visit to Bathsheba.

"And now I make one small request of you," he said. "Do not refuse me."

"Say on," said Bathsheba, perhaps fascinated by Adonijah's naïveté and eager to know how far the fool would go in his foolishness.

"Speak to King Solomon—for he will not refuse you!—and ask that he give me Abishag the Shunamite in marriage." (1 Kings 2:12–18)[2]

The audacity of Adonijah's request must have stunned a savvy political insider like Bathsheba. To claim a king's concubine, as we have seen many times before, was to claim the crown. Solomon had once forgiven Adonijah for his royal ambitions, but surely he would not do so a second time! Indeed, Adonijah's demand was so plainly suicidal that scholars cannot take it seriously—perhaps, they suggest, Bathsheba falsely accused Adonijah of making a demand for Abishag in an effort to persuade her son to eliminate him as a potential rival, or maybe some later biblical author made up the whole encounter in order to provide a plausible excuse for Solomon's assassination of his own brother.

"We doubt if even the most fervid supporter of Solomon could have related this tale without tongue-in-cheek," writes Frank Moore Cross. "If Adonijah did in fact behave as claimed, he deserved to be executed—for stupidity."[3]

"Very well," promised Bathsheba, perhaps hiding a sly smile. "I will speak for you to the king." (1 Kings 2:18)[4]

Bathsheba hastened to Solomon and relayed Adonijah's remarkable demand for the hand of the king's concubine in marriage. As everyone in the royal household *except* Adonijah seemed to recognize, the request was a plain act of treason, and Solomon recognized it as such.

"You might as well ask for the throne!" cried Solomon. "So help me God, Adonijah shall pay for this with his life!" (1 Kings 2: 22, 23) (NEB)

HIT LIST

The task of putting Adonijah to death was assigned to Benaiah, captain of the praetorian guard, "a sinister thug who out-Joabs his predecessor."[5] Once Adonijah had been slain, Benaiah went to work on the other men whose names appeared on the hit list that David had bequeathed to his son.

First on the list was Joab himself, the old cohort and henchman who had served David so faithfully throughout his life. When Joab learned that he was under a death sentence, he fled to the tent-shrine of Yahweh and clung to the horned altar, just as Adonijah had once done.

"Come forth!" demanded Benaiah, unwilling to violate the sanctity of the shrine and the ancient tradition of sanctuary.

"Nay," replied Joab, "but I will die here." (1 Kings 2:30)

Benaiah returned to King Solomon and reported his dilemma, but the king did not share his henchman's pious concerns about entering the shrine of Yahweh with a sword and slaying a man who claimed sanctuary at the horned altar, which is what Joab had challenged him to do.

"Do as he said," ordered Solomon, "and fall upon him, and bury him." (1 Kings 2:31)

Solomon's excuse for violating the old tradition was that Joab deserved to die "because he fell upon two men more righteous and better than he"—Abner, commander of Saul's army, and Amasa, commander of Absalom's army—"and slew them with the sword." Solomon preferred to overlook the fact that Joab had also taken the life of his own half brother, Absalom. Perhaps because Solomon had just ordered the murder of another one of his half brothers, Adonijah, he was willing to overlook Joab's role in the death of Absalom.

"So delicate a brush stroke of irony shades a majestic and imposing royal amnesia," observes Joel Rosenberg. "The cornerstone of an eternal dynasty has been laid, and the bodies of its enemies and victims cemented in."[6]

Shimei, the next man whose death David had ordered, survived another three years. Solomon placed him under a kind of house arrest, sternly warning that he would forfeit his life if he ever dared to leave Jerusalem. One day, the Bible reports, two servants of Shimei ran away from his house and sought refuge in the Philistine city-state of Gath—and Shimei, no sharper than Adonijah, promptly saddled up his mule and rode off in pursuit. Somehow we are expected to believe that the conditions of Solomon's amnesty had slipped Shimei's mind. But, needless to say, Solomon had not forgotten. When Solomon learned of Shimei's escapade, he dispatched the faithful Benaiah to carry out the long-delayed death sentence.

To Abiathar, the high priest who had sided with Absalom in the struggle for the throne, Solomon showed a measure of mercy. "You deserve to die," Solomon warned the old priest, "but I shall not put you to death because you carried the Ark of the Lord God before my father David, and you shared in all the hardships that he endured." But Abiathar was condemned to spend the rest of his life under house arrest on his estate, and Zadok alone, who had possessed the sound political instinct to side with Solomon, was designated to preside as high priest of Israel.

King Solomon's extraordinary ruthlessness in ridding himself of enemies and rivals has convinced some scholars that David is wrongly blamed in the Bible for the crimes of his son. Perhaps, they speculate, the life story of David—or at least the so-called Succession Document that describes how Solomon came to be his successor—was first composed in the court of King Solomon to explain (and excuse) his willingness to kill for the crown. If, as the Bible records, Solomon was the fourth son of David and the offspring of a marriage that began in adultery, the royal chroniclers in Solomon's court might have felt it necessary to explain how and why he ended up on the throne ahead of his three older brothers. And, significantly, they may have decided that a frank account of *David's* life as a "man of blood" would make Solomon look somewhat less bloodthirsty, if only by comparison to his father.

"The palace intrigue which placed Solomon upon the throne," observes the pioneering Bible scholar Julius Wellhausen, "is narrated with a naïveté which is almost malicious. . . ."[7]

At last, when the purges and assassinations were complete and all of the potential rivals for power in ancient Israel had been eliminated, Solomon was ready to fulfill the promise of his name: he would reign in peace over the empire that his father had bequeathed to him, and his era would come to be known among scholars as the Solomonic Enlightenment. The Bible pronounces a similar judgment: "And Solomon sat upon the throne of David his father, and his kingdom was firmly established." (1 Kings 2:12)

THE BLINDED KING

The united monarchy over which David had reigned, however, did not survive Solomon's death. Indeed, the kingdom shattered along the same stress lines of tribal politics that can readily be seen in the life story of David. Only the tribe of Judah recognized Solomon's son as his successor. Ten of the other tribes now seceded from the tribal union and established their own monarchy. A king named Jereboam reigned over the breakaway northern kingdom, which is called "Israel" or sometimes "Ephraim" in the Bible, and a king named Rehoboam reigned over the southern kingdom of Judah from the City of David.*

The Book of Kings records the unhappy fate of these two rival

---

* Of the twelve tribes, only the tribe of Simeon rallied to King Rehoboam.

kingdoms. The northern kingdom was conquered by the Assyrians in 722 B.C.E. and its people were dispersed and destroyed—a catastrophe so complete that they have come to be known as the Lost Ten Tribes of Israel. The southern kingdom lasted a century and a half longer, and the house of David, among the longest-reigning dynasties in the ancient world, continued to provide kings for the land of Judah for a total of five centuries. But Judah, too, eventually fell to a foreign power when the Babylonians invaded and conquered the southern kingdom in 597 B.C.E. and began to send the aristocracy, intelligentsia, and priesthood into exile.

So the biblical authors who chronicled the long history of Israel and Judah were confronted with an awkward and unavoidable problem. God may have promised eternal kingship to David and his descendants—"And thy house and thy kingdom shall be made sure forever"—but history proved God to be wrong. The Babylonians occupied the land of Judah in 597 B.C.E. and swiftly deposed the reigning king and put a more compliant one on the throne. But the kingdom of Judah survived only until 586 B.C.E., when the Babylonians completed their conquest of Judah by destroying the Temple of Solomon, razing the city of Jerusalem, and dethroning the last Davidic king.

By now, of course, we have passed out of the realm of biblical myth and crossed into the terrain of historical fact. The king of Judah who reigned in Jerusalem at the time of the Babylonian invasion—Jehoiachin, a young man who claimed direct descent from King David—was among the first unfortunates to be deported to Babylon. Remarkably, both the fact and the circumstances of Jehoiachin's exile as reported in the Bible (2 Kings 24:12 ff., 25:27 ff.) are confirmed by fragmentary clay tablets that have been uncovered by archaeologists at the site of ancient Babylon. The tablets preserve an official record of the precise amount of the ration of oil issued to Jehoiachin and his family by their captors. Indeed, the fact that Jehoiachin is referred to as "the king of Judah" in the imperial archives suggests that the Babylonians still regarded him as the rightful monarch of the kingdom they had conquered.[8]

The very last reigning king of Judah was a man called Zedekiah.

He was a relative of Jehoiachin but had been chosen by the Baby-lonians to replace him on the throne, presumably because they expected Zedekiah to be a more obedient vassal. They were wrong. Zedekiah went into rebellion with the encouragement and assistance of the Egyptian pharaoh and other allies. But the Baby-lonians crushed the rebellion, laid waste to Jerusalem and the Temple, captured the fleeing king, and carried him off to a far cru-eler exile than Jehoiachin had known—all of which is reported in the Bible. (2 Kings 25:1 ff.)

The reign of King Zedekiah ended in humiliation and horror. The deposed king was forced to witness the murder of his sons—and the Babylonians made certain that it would be the very last sight he saw. "And they slew the sons of Zedekiah before his eyes, and put out the eyes of Zedekiah, and bound him in fetters, and carried him to Babylon." (2 Kings 25:7) Once in exile, according to the prophet Jeremiah, he was imprisoned and put to work as a slave in a mill house "till the day of his death." (Jer. 52:11)[9]

The men and women who had been exiled to Babylon began to return to the land of Judah in the late sixth century B.C.E., but they were now a people without a king or a country of their own. We might begin to call them "Jews," a term that derives from the name of the tribe of Judah but signifies a people and a faith rather than a sovereign nation. Indeed, the land of Judah became the province of Judea, a backwater of the Persian empire. Although the Jewish peo-ple would achieve a brief period of national independence under the Maccabees in the second century B.C.E., the long reign of the Davidic kings was over. Never again would a man in whose veins ran the blood of King David sit on the earthly throne of Judah. God's promise to David had been broken, or so it seemed, and the kingship of the house of David was not eternal after all.

MESSIAH

Confronted with the hard facts of history, the men and women who returned from Babylon to a ruined and kingless Jerusalem struggled to understand God's broken promise of eternal kingship. Maybe God had not been speaking literally of a dynasty of Davidic kings who would reign without interruption into eternity. Perhaps what he really meant (but failed to mention) was that the kingship of the house of David might be interrupted from time to time by some historical calamity, but a Davidic king would be restored to the throne one day in the distant future.

Slowly and subtly, the notion of eternal kingship began to be reworked and reinterpreted, and a new theological spin was put on God's vow to King David as reported in the Book of Samuel. David, of course, had been a man of flesh and blood who fought his way to the throne, but—according to the prophetic writings of the Bible and the commentaries of the Talmud—the *next* king from the house of David would be a spiritual emissary from God, both a king and a messiah, and he would reign not in the here and now but in the end times. And yet, even then, the Messiah-King would be a direct descendant of David. Indeed, he might be David himself, raised from the dead and elevated to the right hand of God. Thus was David transformed from an earthly king into a celestial one.

Here is exactly the point in history where "messiah" began to take on the profoundly mystical and history-changing meaning that is now attached to the word in both Jewish and Christian tradition. As used in the Book of Samuel, the phrase "anointed one" (*mashiach* in biblical Hebrew, "messiah" in English translation) refers to anyone who was anointed with oil in a ritual of coronation. Saul and David and most (but not all) of the Davidic kings were "anointed ones" in that sense. Later, the term was used in the Bible to identify anyone who merited the special favor of God; for example, the Persian emperor Cyrus II, who defeated the Babylonians and allowed the exiled people of Judah to return to their homeland and rebuild their Temple, is identified as an "anointed one" by the prophet Isaiah. (Isa. 45:1) But now "the anointed one" began to take on more exalted meanings, and the Messiah became the spiritual focus for the yearnings of an oppressed, heartbroken people. "Messiah," as the term came to be understood, now identified the redeemer whom God would send one day to establish the kingdom of heaven on earth.

"I saw in the night visions," goes the apocalyptic prophesy of Daniel, perhaps the most elaborate expression of the messianic idea in the Hebrew Bible, and one that deeply influenced Christian theology. "And, behold, there came with the clouds of heaven one like unto a son of man."

> And he came even to the Ancient of days,
> And he was brought near before Him,
> And there was given him dominion,
> And glory, and a kingdom,
> That all the peoples, nations, and languages
> Should serve him;
> His dominion is an everlasting dominion, which shall
>   not pass away,
> And his kingdom that which shall not be destroyed.
>   (Dan. 7:13–14)

The yearning for the Messiah only grew sharper as the subsequent generations in the land of Judah tasted for themselves the bitter experience of foreign occupation and oppression, first under the Persians, then the Greeks, and finally—after a brief period of independence that followed the uprising of the Maccabees—the Romans. Now and then, the emperor of Rome might put a quisling on a throne somewhere in the land called Palestine as a matter of political convenience, but these "ethnarchs" and "tetrarchs" ruled only miniature fiefdoms. The last man to bear the title "King of the Jews" was Herod the Great, a Roman puppet-king from the neighboring Arab land of Idumea, a man whose family had only recently converted to Judaism as a matter of opportunism and who was generally loathed by the Jewish people.[10]

By 70 C.E., when the Romans destroyed the Second Temple and razed Jerusalem to the ground, the messianic idea was the focus of both Judaism and Christianity, although Jews and Christians had reached very different conclusions about the identity of the Messiah. Christians, of course, believed that Jesus of Nazareth was the promised Messiah, and Jews were (and are) still awaiting him. On one thing, however, Christians and Jews agreed: the Messiah would be a direct descendant of King David, "a shoot out of the stock of Jesse." (Isa. 11:1)

Thus was the mortal David, the man whom we have come to know so well, eclipsed by the spectral David. "If the Messiah-King comes from among the living, David will be his name," goes the credo of the Talmudic sages. "If he comes from among the dead, it will be David himself."[11] And Paul affirms the very same credo from the Christian perspective, affirming that Jesus of Nazareth "was made of the seed of David according to the flesh, and declared to be the Son of God." (Rom. 1:3, 4) Indeed, the genealogies of Jesus in the Gospels of both Matthew and Luke trace his human lineage all the way back to King David (Matt. 1:17, Luke 3:31), even though, strictly speaking, Christian theology does not regard Jesus as the son of a mortal father.[12]

On one article of faith, then, Christians and Jews were in agreement: the ancient promise of eternal kingship that God conveyed to David through the prophecy of Nathan would be fulfilled one day, and on that day, the blood of David would flow in the veins of a savior, a redeemer, a liberator—the Messiah.

KING OF THE JEWS

The sacralization of David reaches its most exalted, if also its most poignant, expression in a passage of the Christian Bible where the royal bloodlines of King David are invoked to authenticate Jesus of Nazareth as the long-promised and long-delayed Messiah.

When the Gospel depicts the brutal legionnaires of Rome "bow[ing] the knee" to the scourged Jesus and hailing him as a king, it indicates that they meant only to mock him, and when they set a sign over his head as he hung on the cross—"This is Jesus the King of the Jews"—they meant only to accuse him of the political crime of insurrection for which he had been condemned to death. (Matt.27:29, 37) (KJV)[13] But the phrase that the Romans used to describe Jesus conveys a profound and powerful irony for any reader who knows that, according to the sacred traditions of both Judaism and Christianity, the blood of David will flow in the veins of the Messiah. That is why the genealogy of Jesus reaches all the way back to David, and Paul attests that Jesus was "made of the seed of David, according to his flesh." (Rom. 1:3) (KJV)

History confirms the political power of what is essentially a matter of true belief. The Roman army of occupation in Judea understood the persistent idea that the Messiah would be the descendant of David—and took it as seriously as the Christians and the Jews did. During the first century C.E., the Tenth Legion in Palestine remained under standing orders from four successive Roman emperors "to hunt out and execute any Jew who claimed to be a descendant of King David."[14] The order was given precisely because "political revolutionaries inevitably traced their right of governance back to King David."[15] And that statement remains true today. David, as we shall see, plays a crucial and perhaps decisive role in the current debate between Arabs and Israelis over the sovereignty of Jerusalem.

Thus, some three millennia after his death in Jerusalem, King David is still very much alive in the hearts and minds of mortal men and women in our own world, sometimes for good and sometimes for ill. "David, King of Israel," goes a passage of the Talmud that is still sung aloud as a song in the modern state of Israel and in Jewish communities throughout the world, "lives and endures."

THE USE AND MISUSE OF KING DAVID

David is still invoked more often and more vividly than any other figure in the Hebrew Bible. Of course, aside from David and Goliath, Noah and the Ark, and Moses on Mount Sinai, the Bible is not mentioned much in the arts and letters, the mass media and pop culture of postmodern America. But "David and Goliath," as we have already seen, survives as a convenient shorthand phrase in the vocabulary of newspaper headline writers and advertising copywriters, a glyph for the underdog who prevails against a much stronger adversary. Even as I was writing this book, I saw several different billboards and television commercials that depicted a young David in battle with Goliath in order to hawk computer chips, Internet services, frozen pizza, and fast-food restaurants.

Elsewhere in the world, however, David is conjured up with far greater passion and for matters of far greater consequence.

"Eshkol, you have the best army since King David," said Ezer Weizman, a founder of the Israeli Air Force and future president of Israel, to the prime minister of Israel on the eve of the Six-Day War in 1967. "If you don't attack, you will never be forgiven. If you do attack, you will be the conquering hero."[16]

After the victory in 1967, which restored the Old City of Jerusalem to Israeli sovereignty, a government minister was asked to comment on the conflicting claims of Arabs and Jews to the site where the City of David once stood and the Dome of the Rock and the al-Aqsa mosque, two of the most sacred sites in Islam, now stand. The minister asserted that the modern state of Israel enjoyed the legal right to clear the Temple Mount, as the site is known in Jewish tradition, because King David had purchased it from Araunah the Jebusite for fifty pieces of silver![17]

More recently, Yael Dayan, member of parliament and daughter of the Israeli war hero Moshe Dayan, cited the intimate relationship between David and Jonathan in support of a proposed law to extend civil rights to gay men and lesbians. She was beaten and cursed by some of her fellow members of the Knesset, who were outraged at her audacity in suggesting that King David might have been a bisexual.

As recently as 1997, a celebration of the "three thousandth anniversary" of Jerusalem was conducted in the modern state of Israel and in Jewish communities throughout the world. The significance of the anniversary, however, was downplayed in the publicity and the public festivities for the celebration. What actually happened three thousand years ago in Jerusalem? According to the Bible, it was the conquest of the Jebusite hill-town by the newly crowned king of Israel and his private army of foreign mercenaries, perhaps by means of a commando attack on the waterworks and the slaughter of "the blind and the lame." And the modern celebration of a military operation reported only in the Bible rang with shrill political symbolism—the Israelis, of course, were asserting their right to rule over an "undivided" Jerusalem in the face of Palestinian Arab demands for shared sovereignty over the city known in Islamic tradition as al-Quds, "the Holy."

Thus does the biblical King David come to figure in the current conflict between Arabs and Jews on that bloodstained patch of earth that we call the Holy Land. The most militant Israelis claim property rights over Jerusalem on the strength of David's purchase of a threshing-floor from an obscure Jebusite—yet another event mentioned only in the Bible—and the most militant Arabs deny that David ever existed. And, significantly, both factions look on archaeology not as a scholarly discipline but as a tool of politics and diplomacy, a way to corroborate their claims on the basis of hard evidence scratched out of the soil of the place the Bible calls the Promised Land.

Archaeology has always been an urgent interest for the founders and defenders of the modern Jewish state of Israel—it is no accident that Yigael Yadin, one of the preeminent archaeologists at work in Israel, was also a general of the Israeli Defense Forces, or that Moshe Dayan, hero of the Six-Day War, was a collector of antiquities. Not to be outdone, Palestinian Arab archaeologists are putting *their* scholarship to use for political purposes, too. A recent excavation of ancient Canaanite houses near the town of Nablus was offered as a validation of modern Arab aspirations for statehood in Palestine.

"These are our ancestors, these are our roots," insisted one Palestinian archaeologist, and a colleague added: "We hope in the future to make more discoveries to disprove Israeli claims that they have a right to this land."[18]

THE SEARCH FOR THE HISTORICAL DAVID

Of course, David has been hailed as a historical figure by a gallery of commentators ranging from an amateur Bible critic like Sigmund Freud—"It is real history," he writes of the Book of Samuel, "five hundred years before Herodotus, the 'Father of History' "[19]— to a fully credentialed Bible scholar like Donald Harman Akenson. "He is the first full-formed figure to be found in the Bible, and, indeed, is probably the first human being for whom we have a biography," Akenson writes. "I think that King David is the one figure whom the editor-writer *believes* is 100 percent historically real and also completely compelling from a storyteller's viewpoint."[20]

And yet a certain hedge can be discerned in the telltale phrase "from a storyteller's viewpoint." Even a scholar as convinced of David's historicity as Robert Alter—"There really was a David who fought a civil war against the house of Saul, achieved undisputed sovereignty over the twelve tribes, conquered Jerusalem, founded a dynasty, created a small empire, and was succeeded by his son Solomon"—subtly backs off from his own assertion. Although Alter writes that it is "possible" that the soap opera of David's intimate family life "may have been reported on good authority," he is intellectually honest enough to concede that the biblical stories "are not, strictly speaking, historiography, but rather the imaginative reenactment of history by a gifted writer." About all we can say with complete conviction, Alter seems to concede, is that the biblical life story of David "is surely one of the most stunning imaginative achievements of ancient literature."[21]

So we are left with an unanswered question: Is the biography of David a work of history, a work of literature, or an uncertain blend of both? And, ironically, the question is rendered all the more troubling by the obvious literary gifts of the man or woman who was the original author of the biblical life story of David. After all, a gifted author might readily produce a work of fiction that *seems* real without *being* so.

"David's biographer was a man of genius," declares Robert H.

Pfeiffer, who goes so far as to nominate an obscure biblical figure called Ahimaaz (2 Sam. 15:27) as the author of the earliest material found in Samuel. "Without any previous models as guide, he wrote a masterpiece, unsurpassed in historicity, psychological insight, literary style, and dramatic power."[22]

But there is a difference between a "stunning imaginative achievement" and "unsurpassed . . . historicity." Perhaps David seems so substantial for the same reason that a fictional character like Hamlet or Huck Finn or Holden Caulfield is memorable and compelling. When some scholars ponder the salacious details in the biblical story of David, they wonder out loud whether these passages could have been written by near contemporaries of David who were seeking to praise him.[23] Perhaps the biblical King David is best compared to the medieval King Arthur as we find him in Thomas Malory's *La Morte d'Arthur*, a fifteenth-century romantic saga that tells the story of a king who may or may not have lived and reigned a thousand years earlier. Like Arthur, David may have been a rude aboriginal chieftain whose obscure life was glorified beyond recognition by later mythmakers. And, as with Arthur, the historical evidence for King David has been hard to find.

WHO IS BURIED IN DAVID'S TOMB?

Over the centuries, the figure of David has been dressed up in a colorful mantle of myth and legend, all of it phony. A fifth-century Christian king established a monastery at the site of a tower that he believed to be the "Tower of David." The Crusaders who conquered Jerusalem in the twelfth century convinced themselves that they had discovered David's tomb, and they built a basilica to mark the site; when Saladin took Jerusalem back from the Crusaders, he added a mosque. But the so-called Tower of David was actually erected by Herod, and "David's Tomb," still marked on tourist maps of Jerusalem, is empty—or if anyone is actually buried there, it is not David.

Even the so-called Star of David, the symbol that has come to signify Judaism in general and the modern state of Israel in particular, has no real connection with King David, whether we regard him as a biblical or a historical figure. Indeed, the distinctive six-pointed star first came to be associated with David among alchemists and magic-users in medieval Christian and Islamic circles, and early Jewish sources linked the star sometimes to David, sometimes to Solomon, and sometimes to neither of them. The earliest written reference to the "Shield of David" (*magen David*), as the six-pointed star is known in Jewish usage, dates only to the fourteenth century. And it was not until the nineteenth century that the Star of David came to be adopted by the Jewish community as "a striking and simple sign which would 'symbolize' Judaism in the same way as the cross symbolizes Christianity," according to Gershom Scholem, a leading scholar of Jewish mysticism.[24]

So a close scrutiny of the historical evidence, such as it is, can be an unsettling experience. The very existence of David's mighty empire, so richly described in the pages of the Bible, is defended by some scholars only by arguing from a negative. The imperial powers that had contested with one another for dominance in Palestine at various times in history—the Egyptians, the Hittites, the Assyrians—were "quiescent," according to Bible historian Norman K. Gottwald, for a brief period around the beginning of the first millennium B.C.E. "Only in the tenth century had Israel been the dominant power in the region between the Nile and the Tigris-Euphrates valleys," argues Gottwald.[25] For one brief moment in history, then, the audacious ruler of a tiny tribal kingdom succeeded in creating a glorious empire in the cracks between the superpowers of the ancient world.

Still, as mighty as David and his little empire may have been, they wholly escaped the attention of the scribes and chroniclers of every other nation of the ancient world, and the story of his conquests is told *only* in the pages of the Bible. Scholars have searched in vain for any mention of David in other ancient texts, and the earliest archaeological evidence of King David is dated a century or two after his supposed reign. About the best case that can be made for the "historicity" of David is that his exploits as described in the Bible "fit reasonably well" with extra-biblical evidence, even if "there is no external corroboration" for the biblical account.[26]

The most radical of revisionist Bible scholars are willing to argue that the biblical David was originally (and, perhaps, only) understood as a cherished religious symbol and not a flesh-and-blood human being. Thus, for example, Thomas L. Thompson points out that we have "no evidence of a United Monarchy, no evidence of a capital in Jerusalem . . . , let alone an empire of the size the legends describe."[27] And he insists that we fundamentally misunderstand the very nature of the Bible when we seek to validate the biblical life story of David by digging in the soil in search of archaeological relics.

"It is a fundamental error of method to ask first after a historical David or Solomon, as biblical archaeologists often have done," Thompson argues. "The Bible does not hesitate to tell these stories as tall tales."[28]

Even the most temperate scholars, who continue to regard David as a historical figure and not merely a mythic one, feel compelled to concede that, whether or not the biblical authors understood David as the hero of a "tall tale," his life story cannot be corroborated with the archaeological evidence so far available to us.

"There is not a single contemporary reference to David or Solomon in the many neighbouring countries which certainly were keeping written records during the tenth century," writes archaeologist Magnus Magnusson. "Without the Biblical accounts, history would be totally unaware of the very existence of the twin founders of the tenth-century expansion of Israel/Judah into a major power, and archaeology would have been able to do little to indicate that it had ever taken place. As far as archaeology is concerned it was a paper (or papyrus) empire only."[29]

Archaeologists suggest, for example, that the City of David described in the Bible covered eleven or twelve acres of inten-

sively excavated ground.[30] "Jerusalem is probably the most excavated city in the world," observe the editors of *Biblical Archaeology
Review*[31]—and yet archaeologist Margaret Steiner confronts us
with an uncomfortable fact: "No remains of a town, let alone a
city, have ever been found: not a trace of an encircling wall, no
gate, no houses. Not a single piece of architecture. Simply nothing!"[32] A crumbling citadel at the site of ancient Gibeah was
identified by William F. Albright, the Bible scholar who first excavated the site in the 1920s, as the place where Saul reigned as the
first king of Israel—but no such evidence of the City of David has
ever been discovered.[33]

Indeed, precisely because no one else in the ancient world
seems to have noticed David or his kingdom, the restless search
for "facts on the ground"—or, more accurately, facts *in* the
ground—has taken on ever more energy and urgency. Only very
recently has the heroic effort to find a trace of the historical
David been rewarded with the first tantalizing glimmer of success.

THE QUALITY OF LIGHT AT TEL DAN

On July 23, 1993, a team of archaeologists was at work on a dig at
a place in northern Israel called Tel Dan. The site under excavation was an elaborate system of ramparts, walls, and gates, which
dated back to the mid-ninth century B.C.E. and were believed to
be the outer-works of the town that the Bible calls Dan, the
northernmost point in the land of Israel: "From Dan even unto
Beersheba" is the classic biblical phrase to describe the full reach
of the Promised Land (Judges 21:1).

Excavations at Tel Dan had begun in 1966 as an "emergency
project" of Israel's Department of Antiquities, but archaeologists
were still at work nearly thirty years later. On that day in 1993,
they were dismantling a portion of the wall that bordered a plaza
at the entrance to the outer gate of Dan. Like other ancient con-
structions, the wall included scraps of stonework that had been
broken up and reused as building materials at some point in the

distant past. But one stone in particular caught the eye of Gila Cook, the official surveyor of the archaeological expedition at Tel Dan, and she bent over to take a closer look.

What attracted her attention was a fragment of basalt, cracked and worn but somehow different from the other detritus that had been built into the wall by a Bronze Age laborer some three thousand years before. She had seen *something* on the stone, and now she was able to make out the letters, words, phrases that were incised on the polished surface.

"Taking a closer look at the stone while still *in situ* and helped by the direction of the early afternoon rays of the sun which illuminated the engraved lines on the stone, we could see the contours of the letters quite clearly," recall Avraham Biran and Joseph Naveh, members of the archaeological team. "The stone was easily removed as only a small part of it was embedded in the ground. Turning the stone to face the sun, the letters became even more legible. The words, separated by dots, sprung to life."[34]

To the astonishment of the archaeologists who now peered at the stone under the summer sun of the Galilee, the inscription on that battered fragment of basalt appeared to include the three consonants that spell out a name that was deeply familiar but, until then, had been found only in the pages of the Bible—the name of David.

The hunk of stone was a portion of a stela—an upright stone slab bearing a written inscription—that had been fashioned out of native basalt, polished to take the inscription, and then incised with an iron stylus at some moment in distant antiquity, perhaps as long ago as the early eighth century B.C.E. The inscription memorialized an event that had once been regarded as worthy of celebration, but the stela had been broken up and put to use as building material not long after it was made. And, for the next three thousand years, it remained buried inside a forgotten town wall somewhere in the Galilee.

As the archaeologists pored over the fragment, they were able to make out a portion of the original inscription. The language was early Aramaic, a sister language of biblical Hebrew, and the lettering style was dated to the ninth century B.C.E. Later, two more chunks of the same stela were found at the site, and more of the inscription was recovered. Archaeologists and biblical scholars were thrilled to discover that the inscription included a reference to David—or, more precisely, the *house* of David (*bet David*), a phrase that is interpreted to mean the royal dynasty founded by David.

Scholars cannot be entirely sure about any of the particulars of the stela from Tel Dan—when it was created, by whom, or for what reason. Even the reference to David is still obscure.[35] But according to the archaeologists who found it at Tel Dan, the stela was a monument raised by a Bible-era Aramean king to commemorate his victory in battle over two kings, one from the northern kingdom of Israel and the other from the southern kingdom of Judah, where the house of David reigned. These kings have been identified as Jehoram and Ahaziahu, both of whom are mentioned in the Book of Kings (2 Kings 8:25–26), and the key lines of the inscription have been reconstructed to read as follows:

> I [killed Jeho]ram son of [Ahab]
> king of Israel, and [I] killed [Ahaz]iahu son of [Jehoram kin-]
> g of the *House of David*. And I set [their towns into ruin and turned]
> their land into [desolation][36]

Strictly speaking, as we have noted, the inscription refers not to David himself but to the *house* of David. The phrase itself harks back to that famous promise of God to David in the "theological highlight" of the Book of Samuel: "And thy house and thy kingdom shall be made sure for ever before thee." (2 Sam. 7:16) Now, for the very first time, the existence of the house of David seemed to be confirmed by an archaeological relic that one could read with one's own eyes and hold in one's own hands. And the relic could be plausibly dated all the way back to the early eighth century B.C.E., a period only a century or so after the supposed lifetime of King David himself. Even though the stela recorded the *defeat* of a king from the house of David—and that's why it was broken up by the Israelites and used as building material—the antiquity of the Tel Dan inscription has been greeted with enthusiasm and even exultation.

"We have an ancient reference to King David," assert Bible scholars David Noel Freedman and Jeffrey C. Geoghegan. "The Tel Dan inscription also underscores the general historicity of the Biblical narratives. . . ."[37]

Not every Bible scholar is quite so convinced. Thomas L. Thompson, a revisionist who has challenged all the high hopes and conventional wisdom of "biblical archaeology," declares himself unconvinced by the discoveries at Tel Dan. He complains of "problems" with "the reading of the text, its dating and interpretation." His arguments, as always, are highly provocative. The dating of the stela is "optimistically early" and ought to be moved forward by a century or more. The missing words and letters make it impossible to prove that the stela makes a direct reference to King David. Indeed, he points out, the word that has been interpreted as "David" also appears on an important archaeological find from Jordan, the Mesha Stele of the ninth century B.C.E., where it is used as the divine title for an ancient god called Yahweh, who may or may not be the same deity who is identified as the God of Israel in the Bible. Although Thompson allows that David himself may or may not have been the founder of a "patronate"—a primitive tribal chieftainship—he insists that the Tel Dan stela "tells us nothing, as such, of a person David as the founder of that patronate in an earlier period."[38]

But the consensus of modern Bible scholarship holds that the Tel Dan inscription is important new evidence of the historicity of King David and the exploits described in the Bible. Indeed, the fragments of polished basalt and the intriguing inscription on them have taken on an almost religious significance in our irreligious era. At a talk I gave about my previous book, *Moses, A Life*, I was approached by a woman who was agitated and distressed to hear me report that no extra-biblical evidence of any kind confirms the historical existence of Moses. But she told me that she was comforted by her own sure knowledge that the *other* hero of the Hebrew Bible had been a man of flesh and blood.

"At least we still have David," she witnessed to me, "thanks to Tel Dan."

A MAN AFTER GOD'S OWN HEART

Thus strengthened in our conviction that a king called David once lived, however, we are left with a troubling question that cannot be answered by the Tel Dan inscription or any other archaeological relic. Exactly what are we meant to learn from King David as he is depicted in the Bible? Once we have read his biblical life story with open eyes—and once we have witnessed the shocking excesses of which he was capable—some of us may be left with the idea that he does not really belong in a book that holds itself out as a source of moral instruction for humankind!

David, as depicted in the Bible, is essentially "value-neutral," according to a chilling phrase now used as a term of praise. That is, David did not promulgate a code of moral conduct, nor did he exemplify one in his own tumultuous life and times. The biblical David was a warrior and a poet, but he was never a lawgiver or a teacher. Aside from a few passages where some later biblical author has put pious and ornate words into his mouth, David seemed to embrace only the thoroughly modern notion that nothing succeeds like success—or, when it came to satisfying his sexual appetite, the equally modern notion that nothing succeeds like excess.

"The one indisputable point about King David is that he is one hard case," writes Donald Harman Akenson. "He does what he has to do to preserve his power at all costs: just ask his seven brothers whom he jumped in the quest for the family's patrimony; King Saul whom he undercut as a monarch; Ahimelech, the priest whom he gulled out of Goliath's sword; Uriah, whom David arranged to have killed so that he could sleep with Uriah's wife, Bathsheba; and the tens of thousands of dead he left strewn about Palestine as he conquered his various neighbours, aggressive and pacific alike." And if we overlook these "hard" facts, as preachers and teachers have tended to do, we miss the whole point of the biblical life story of David. "That is exactly how a monarch should act," Akenson concludes. "He preserves his honour and his power; everything else is secondary."[39]

The Talmudic rabbis were so troubled by the plain facts of David's life—the cunning, cynicism, and carnality that he displays unapologetically in the pages of the Bible—that they simply dreamed up a new and improved David. "Whatever leisure time his royal duties afforded him, he spent in study and prayer," they imagined. "David's thinking and planning were wholly given to what is good and noble." Indeed, they were even capable of asserting, against all evidence in the Bible, that "he is one of the few pious men over whom the evil inclination had no power."[40] The kinder and gentler David of rabbinic fantasy, however, is plausible only to someone who has never opened the Bible or who ignores what the Bible actually says of David.

Other Bible readers may prefer the vision of David that we encounter in the prophetic writings of the Bible—a wholly celestial messiah-king who is no longer a "man of war," no longer a "man of blood," no longer a man at all. "A son is given unto us," exults the prophet Isaiah, and he offers a vision of heaven on earth that only grows more sublime as our experience of the real world grows more horrific. "And of peace there be no end," writes Isaiah, "upon the throne of David." (Isa. 9:5–6) Here he becomes the child-king who reigns in a utopia that resembles nothing in the life experience of the fleshly David.

> And the wolf shall dwell with the lamb,
> And the leopard shall lie down with the kid;
> And the calf and the young lion and the fatling together;
> And a little child shall lead them.
>
> (Isa. 11:6–9)

Such images still exert a powerful tug on the hearts and minds of men and women who are aghast at the world in which we find ourselves nowadays, a world that tolerates and even encourages "ethnic cleansing," child pornography, biological warfare, "squash" videos, and the miscellaneous horrors of modernity. Indeed, some corners of the Bible still offer a comfortable refuge for those who find themselves battered and bruised by what confronts us in newspapers and motion pictures, and on television and the Internet.

But more often the Bible is *not* a comforting book. If we are courageous enough to read it with open eyes and with an open mind, we discover that the Bible is provocative and challenging, unsettling and off-putting, sometimes even shocking and scandalous. And nowhere in the Bible are we confronted more forcefully with what it means to be a human being than in the biblical life story of David. The deepest of all the mysteries that confront us in the Hebrew Bible is the mystery of how a man as flawed as David can be a man after God's own heart.

One clue to the mystery is the very word that the Bible uses to describe David: he is, first and always, a *man*—or, if you prefer a gender-neutral translation of the Hebrew text, a human being. Even though the Bible insists on praising God above all, the deeply humanistic notion that man is the measure of all things is spoken out loud by David himself in Psalm 8, where he asks God a crucial question—"What is man, that thou art mindful of him?"—and then answers it in a way that affirms the primacy of humankind on earth.

> Yet thou hast made him but little lower than angels,*
> And hast crowned him with glory and honour.
> Thou hast made him to have dominion over the works
>   of thy hands,
> Thou hast put all things under his feet."
>
> (Ps. 8:5–7)

---

*"Little less than a *god*" is a more straightforward translation of the Hebrew text. (Ps. 8:5) (NEB) By now, we should not be surprised to find a slightly paganistic notion falling from the lips of David, even if later and fussier translators insisted on invoking angels rather than gods.

Indeed, the theology of the Hebrew Bible can be—and must be!—reduced to a human scale, if only to allow us to understand the moral instruction that it embodies. The venerable Bible scholar Gerhard von Rad, for example, discerns the undercurrents of "Solomonic humanism" in the story of David—and, crucially, he defines it as nothing less than "a wholly new departure in spirituality, a kind of 'enlightenment,' an awakening of spiritual self-consciousness."[41] Similarly, when the prophet Micah wonders out loud what God demands of us, his answer is a simple moral credo that can be understood and acted upon in the here and now: "Only to do justly and to love mercy, and to walk humbly with thy God." (Mic. 6:8) Even the prophet Isaiah, whose messianic visions are so sublime and yet so impossibly grand, wakes up to a much more urgent reality when he answers Micah's provocative question: What does God want of us?

> It is to share your bread with the hungry,
> And to take the wretched poor into your home;
> When you see the naked, cloth him,
> And not to ignore your own kin.
>
> (Isa. 58:7)[42]

David, of course, cannot readily be credited with the profound compassion or the fierce sense of social justice that inspired the prophets. But if we look beyond the brutal deathbed instructions that he issued to Solomon, his last charge to his beloved son seems to strike something of the same note. "Be thou strong," said David to Solomon, "and show thyself a man." (1 Kings 2:2) If we render the same phrase with a bit of Yiddish, we may come closer to understanding what God expected of David, what God expects of all of us—or, at least, what we ought to expect of ourselves. "Be a *mensch!*"

THE BIBLICAL BIOGRAPHERS OF DAVID

By almost any measure, David is the most commanding figure in the Hebrew Bible. His name is mentioned more than a thousand times, and more space is devoted to him than to any other biblical figure. Although the Patriarchs (Abraham, Isaac, and Jacob) and Moses are crucial to both biblical narrative and biblical theology, it is David who may have inspired the writing of the Bible in the first place. Indeed, David is present in the Bible even in passages where his name is never mentioned.

The life story of David sprawls across several books of the Hebrew Bible, and a great many different biblical sources can be identified in those books, or so modern Bible scholarship proposes.* The fundamental questions of authorship—the time, place, purpose, and identity of the biblical sources—are still hotly

---

*A "source," as the term is used in Bible scholarship, generally refers to a single individual or a group of individuals who authored or edited a biblical text.

debated. For that reason, the discussion that follows is only an overview of a complex, controversial, and ever-changing body of scholarship.

THE BOOK OF SAMUEL

The biography of David is reported at the greatest length and in the greatest detail in the Book of Samuel. Since biblical Hebrew is a language written in consonants only, the Hebrew text of the Book of Samuel was compact enough to be contained on a single scroll. But when the Bible was first translated into Greek, a language of both consonants and vowels, two separate scrolls were required, and so the single work was divided into the First Book of Samuel and the Second Book of Samuel.

By tradition, the authorship of the Book of Samuel is attributed principally to the prophet Samuel, who figures importantly in its opening chapters. The portion of Samuel that depicts events after the death of Samuel himself is traditionally attributed to the prophet Gad. Modern scholarship, however, detects a great many sources within the text of Samuel, although neither Samuel nor Gad is among them.

The core of the Book of Samuel, which consists of the formal biography of David, is sometimes described by scholars as "the history of David's rise to power" or, more elegantly, the Court History of David. For that reason, its author has been dubbed the Court Historian, although he is sometimes identified rather less evocatively by the letter code "S," a fanciful reference to Samuel. Because his account is so intimate, some scholars speculate that he may have been a member of the court of King David and perhaps even an eyewitness to some of the events he describes. Other scholars place him in the reign of King Solomon, David's son, or at an even later point in the history of ancient Israel. In any case, the Court Historian probably enjoyed access to the archives, battle reports, and chronicles of the royal house of David, and he cites a book, now lost to

us, where David's famous elegy of Saul and Jonathan was preserved: "Behold, it is written in the book of Jashar." (2 Sam.
1:18)

The work of the Court Historian has inspired enthusiastic
praise from Bible scholars and literary critics alike. "David's biographer was a man of genius," writes Robert H. Pfeiffer. "Without
any previous models as guide, he wrote a masterpiece, unsurpassed
in historicity, psychological insight, literary style, and dramatic
power."[1] Richard Elliot Friedman, in *The Hidden Book in the Bible*,
argues that the same literary genius created both the Court History and the portions of biblical narrative attributed to the source
known as "J,"* while Harold Bloom imagines in *The Book of J* that
"J is a *Gevurah* ('great lady') of post-Solomonic court circles, herself of Davidic blood, who began writing her great work in the
later years of Solomon, in close rapport and exchanging influences with her good friend the Court Historian, who wrote most
of what we now call 2 Samuel."[2]

But the Book of Samuel includes passages and whole chapters
that are thought to be the work of sources other than the Court
Historian. The portion of the text that is devoted to the Ark of
the Covenant, for example, is considered the work of a different
biblical source and is sometimes labeled "the Ark Narrative" to
distinguish it from the rest of Samuel. The account of how
Solomon bested his brothers in the struggle to succeed David on
the throne of Israel is regarded as a separate work by some scholars, who identify it as "the Succession Document." Other sections
of Samuel, including the passages where Samuel condemns the
very idea of kingship and fearlessly scolds the king of Israel, are

*The biblical author who generally calls God by his personal name ("Yahweh," or, as it
is spelled in German, "Jahweh") is known to scholars as the Yahwist, or "J." Another
biblical author, who uses the term "Elohim" ("God," or perhaps more accurately,
"gods") to identify the God of Israel, is known as the Elohist, or "E." A third biblical
source, whose work reveals a strong interest in sacred law and other priestly matters, is
identified as the Priestly Writer, or "P." A late biblical source who collected, combined,
and revised the biblical text is known as the Redactor, or "R." The author of the Book
of Deuteronomy is known as the Deuteronomist, or "D." See *The Harlot by the Side of
the Road*, appendix, "Who *Really* Wrote the Bible?"

thought to have originated among the same circles that produced and preserved the prophetic writings of the Bible.

The task of identifying and describing the sources of the Book of Samuel is rendered all the more challenging because, like many other books of the Bible, Samuel was extensively edited and "overwritten" by later biblical sources. The most important of these later sources is the school of priests and scribes known collectively as the Deuteronomistic Historian. Embracing the distinctive theology and rhetorical style that were first presented in the Book of Deuteronomy by a biblical author known as the Deuteronomist (or "D"), the Deuteronomistic Historian is credited with at least one and possibly several editorial revisions of Joshua, Judges, Samuel, and Kings—a process that brought the history of ancient Israel into conformity with the Deuteronomist's worldview. The Deuteronomistic Historian, at work no earlier than the seventh century B.C.E. and perhaps later, is probably responsible for the theological spin that we find in the Book of Samuel and, notably, the pious speeches attributed to David.

Precisely because the Book of Samuel is so frequently overwritten by multiple sources—and because the text has been edited and revised so extensively over the centuries—the attribution of any given passage may spark debate among Bible scholars. Then, too, various passages of the Book of Samuel come down to us in what scholars describe as a "difficult" or "troubled" or even "corrupted" form. For that reason, significant differences can be identified in various passages of Samuel as they are preserved in the Masoretic Text, the ancient Greek translation of the Bible known as the Septuagint, other ancient translations, and the Dead Sea Scrolls.

THE BOOK OF KINGS

The life story of David continues into the First Book of Kings and concludes in its opening chapters. The rest of Kings is devoted to the history of the northern kingdom of Israel and the southern kingdom of Judah, starting with the reign of Solomon and continuing through the conquest of Israel by the Assyrians in 722 B.C.E. and the conquest of Judah by the Babylonians in 586 B.C.E. Some scholars suspect that the opening passages of Kings, where the last days of David's life are described, originally appeared as part of the Book of Samuel and were moved into the Book of Kings by the Deuteronomistic Historian or some other biblical editor.

Like Samuel, the Book of Kings was originally contained on a single scroll and was divided into two books by the translators of the Septuagint. And as in Samuel, the authors of the Book of Kings report that they have relied on several archival sources now lost to us, including the Book of the Annals of Israel and the Book of the Annals of Judah. But Kings is wholly lacking in the moments of literary grace, political acumen, and high drama that make Samuel such a compelling work of literature. Rather, the Book of Kings is mostly a theological exercise—the Deuteronomistic Historian judges every king according to whether or not he adhered closely enough to the strict legal code that we find in the Book of Deuteronomy.

THE BOOK OF CHRONICLES

The life story of David is reprised in the First and Second Book of Chronicles, but it is a very different David who is presented here. Composed sometime in the late sixth century B.C.E. or later, perhaps by the same priestly source who composed the Book of Nehemiah and the Book of Ezra, Chronicles retells the history of Israel strictly from a theological point of view. The Chronicler, as the source of Chronicles is sometimes called, felt obliged to censor out all the lurid details of David's life as we find them in Samuel, including the love affair with Bathsheba, the murder of Uriah, the rape of Tamar, and the rebellion of Absalom. And he felt free to rewrite the history of David, rendering him as an unfailingly pious king and crediting him with an active role in preparations for the building of the Temple at Jerusalem. Appropriately enough, the original title of Chronicles in the Septuagint was *Paraleipomena*, which means "things omitted."

THE BOOK OF PSALMS

Pious tradition assigns the authorship of the entire Book of Psalms to King David himself, but modern scholarship allows that only a few of the psalms date back to the supposed lifetime of David—and none can be proven to be his own work. The oldest of the psalms may have originated in the coronation rituals of the Davidic kings, and Psalm 45 in particular, apparently composed for the wedding of an Israelite king and a foreign-born woman, may refer to King Solomon, David's son. Other psalms, however, are dated no earlier than the Babylonian Conquest and the destruction of the Temple of Solomon in 586 B.C.E. Still, various of the psalms are associated with specific events in the life of David. Psalm 51, for example, is linked to David's remorse over his sexual liaison with Bathsheba: "Hide thy face from my sins, and blot out all mine iniquities," pleads the man whom the Bible calls the "sweet singer" of Israel. "Create me a clean heart, O God." (Ps. 51:11–12) Notably, no such self-abasing prayers are uttered by King David as we come to know him in the work of the Court Historian, and we are left to wonder which depiction of David—the worldly-wise king or the pious penitent—is more faithful to the flesh-and-blood David who can be glimpsed beneath the surface of the ancient text.

DAVID AND THE AUTHORSHIP
OF THE HEBREW BIBLE

David figures importantly in portions of the Hebrew Bible even where he is not mentioned at all. Indeed, according to one fundamental theory of biblical authorship, the biography of David as embodied in the Court History may have been the seed out of which the rest of the Bible grew.

Scholars propose that the composition of the Court History began during the reign of David and continued during the reign of his son Solomon—a period of prosperity and cultural flowering known as the Solomonic Enlightenment. Other books of the Bible, including portions of the sweeping "primal history" in Genesis and the saga of Moses in Exodus and Numbers, may have been composed at roughly the same time by the author called J, perhaps in order to provide the "backstory" leading up to the glorious reign of David.

Thus, for example, Joel Rosenberg characterizes Genesis as "a 'midrash,' if you will, upon the Davidic history," that is, a theological commentary in the form of imaginative storytelling.[3] Walter Brueggemann characterizes portions of Genesis as "an extremely sophisticated statement by one of Israel's earliest, most profound theologians."[4] And, as we have already noted, Richard Elliot Friedman argues that J and the Court Historian are one and the same.

If David is only anticipated in the early books of the Bible, he is openly celebrated in the books that follow Samuel and Kings, including the Psalms and the prophetic writings. Even the Christian Bible recalls and honors David, describing Jesus of Nazareth as "made of the seed of David according to the flesh, and declared to be the Son of God." (Rom. 1:3, 4) The flesh-and-blood David was transformed by these later biblical authors from an earthly king into a celestial one and then into a messianic icon. That is why he remains the touchstone of theology throughout the Bible.

The dating of events and texts in early biblical history is much debated among scholars, and thus the dating used in this book is approximate and in many instances speculative, notably for events earlier than 722 B.C.E. Following Jewish and scholarly practice, I have adopted the designation B.C.E. (Before the Common Era) in place of the more familiar B.C. (Before Christ) and C.E. (Common Era) in place of A.D. (Anno Domini, "In the year of Our Lord").

Among the biblical sources were a few authors, probably the priestly scribes known collectively as the Priestly Writer, or "P," who were fairly obsessed with numbers; they insisted on measuring and counting and dating, and the results of their calculations are recorded with complete assurance throughout the Bible. Thus, the traditional starting point for fixing the dates of biblical lives and events is a passage in the Book of Kings where the biblical author reports that construction of the Temple at Jerusalem commenced "in the fourth year of Solomon's reign over Israel, the second month of that year," which was exactly 480 years "after the Israelites had come out of Egypt." (1 Kings 6:1) (NEB) Elsewhere the Bible is much less assured; the age of Saul when he became king of Israel, for example, is simply left blank, and his reign is given as only two years in the Masoretic Text. (1 Sam. 13:1) Indeed, the text was so obviously wrong that the Septuagint left the passage out altogether.

Nowadays scholars no longer rely on the self-dating passages of the Bible. Rather, they attempt to correlate the key dates in the biblical narrative with archaeological finds and ancient texts preserved by other peoples, at least where such evidence exists. The chronology offered here is intended to show the relationship in time between the events as set forth in the Bible and the composition, editing, and later discovery of the texts in which those events are recorded.

BEFORE THE COMMON ERA (B.C.E.)

Biblical Events	Biblical Sources and Texts
1800–1700 Wanderings of the Patriarchs (Abraham, Isaac, and Jacob) and the Matriarchs (Sarah, Rebekah, Leah, and Rachel)	
1700–1600 Joseph in Egypt; the settlement and enslavement of the Israelites	
1280 Exodus of the Israelites from Egypt under Moses	
1240–1200 Conquest of the land of Canaan by the Israelites under Joshua	
1200–1025 Israel under the rule of the Judges	*Earliest fragments of Hebrew poetry later preserved in the Bible*
1025–1005 Reign of King Saul	

1005	Reign of King David in Judah begins	
1000	Conquest of Jerusalem by King David	*Earliest portions of the Court History of David*
		Archives and chronicles consulted by later biblical authors
		Book of Jashar and other lost books mentioned in the Bible
965	Death of King David and commencement of the reign of King Solomon	*Court Historian at work*
964	Construction of the Temple of Solomon at Jerusalem begins	*Yahwist at work*
925	Death of King Solomon and division of the united monarchy into northern kingdom (Israel) and southern kingdom (Judah)	
880	Erection of the stela at Tel Dan, bearing the earliest extra-biblical reference to the House of David	*Elohist at work*
722	Conquest of the northern kingdom of Israel by the Assyrians and destruction of the "Lost Ten Tribes"	

700–600		*Deuteronomist and Deuteronomistic Historian at work*
622	King Josiah on the throne of Judah	*Discovery of the Book of Deuteronomy*
597	Babylonians occupy land of Judah	
596	Zedekiah, last descendant of King David to reign in Judah, ascends the throne	
587–586	Destruction of Solomon's Temple at Jerusalem, fall of the southern kingdom of Judah, and commencement of the Babylonian Exile Death of King Zedekiah	
538	End of the Babylonian Exile and return of the Jews to Jerusalem	
520	Dedication of the Second Temple at Jerusalem	
500		*Priestly Source at work*
400		*Chronicler at work* *Redactor at work; text of the Five Books of Moses fixed in final form*
250–100		*Translation of the Hebrew Bible into Greek (Septuagint)*

100	*Earliest surviving Hebrew texts of the Bible preserved at Qumran (Dead Sea Scrolls)*

COMMON ERA (C.E.)

70	Destruction of the Second Temple at Jerusalem by the Romans and dispersion of the Jewish people
90	*Final canonization of the Hebrew Bible*
50–150	*The Gospels and various other books of the New Testament composed and compiled*
405	*First translation of the Christian Bible from Greek into Latin (St. Jerome's Vulgate)*
500–1000	*Standardization of the Hebrew text of the Bible by the Masoretes (Masoretic Text)*
1526	*First translation of the Bible into English (William Tyndale's Pentateuch)*
1611	*King James (Authorized) Version of the Bible*

1947   *Discovery of the Dead
                                         Sea Scrolls*

1993   *Discovery of the stela at
                                         Tel Dan*

Endnotes

CHAPTER ONE
CHARISMA

1. Robert Polzin, *Samuel and the Deuteronomist*, pt. 2, *1 Samuel* (Bloomington: Indiana University Press, 1993), 156.

2. Raymond-Jean Frontain and Jan Wojcik, eds., *The David Myth in Western Literature* (West Lafayette, Ind.: Purdue University Press, 1980), 5.

3. Abram Leon Sachar, *A History of the Jews*, rev. ed. (New York: Alfred A. Knopf, 1967), 34.

4. G. Johannes Botterweck and Helmer Ringgren, eds., *Theological Dictionary of the Old Testament*, trans. John T. Willis, Geoffrey W. Bromley, and David E. Green (Grand Rapids, Mich.: William B. Eerdmans, 1978), vol. 3, 158.

5. Peter R. Ackroyd, "The Succession Narrative (So-called)," *Interpretation* 35, no. 4 (October 1981): 385.

6. Cited in Ralph Klein, "Chronicles, Book of, 1–2," in *The Anchor Bible Dictionary*, ed. David Noel Freedman (Garden City, N.Y.: Doubleday, 1992), vol. 1, 725.

7. Jan Wojcik, "Discriminations against David's Tragedy in Ancient Jewish and Christian Literature," in Frontain and Wojcik, *David Myth*, 27, citing Rabbi Samuel ben Nahmani in Talmud Shabbath.

8. Harold Bloom and David Rosenberg, *The Book of J* (Grove Weidenfeld, 1990), 40–41, referring to the work of Bible scholar Gerhard von Rad.

9. Martin Noth, *The Old Testament World*, trans. Victor I. Gruhn (Philadelphia: Fortress Press: 1966), 376–381.

10. Cited in Donald Harman Akenson, *Surpassing Wonder* (New York: Harcourt Brace, 1998), 363–364.

11. 1 Sam. 13:14. The Hebrew text includes a pronoun rather than a direct reference. "[T]he Lord hath sought a man after His own heart," Saul tells Samuel, "and the Lord hath appointed him to be prince over His people, because thou hast not kept that which the Lord commanded thee." The reference is to David.

12. 2 Sam. 16:7. According to most English translations of the text, including the JPS, David is condemned by a man called Shimei as a "man of blood, and base fellow." P. Kyle McCarter, Jr., however, renders the same phrase as "bloodstained fiend of hell" in his translation of 2 Samuel in the Anchor Bible series.

13. Albrecht Alt, *Essays on Old Testament History and Religion*, trans. R. A. Wilson (Oxford: Basil Blackwell, 1966), 178.

14. Quoted in Evan Thomas and Matthew Cooper, "Extracting a Confession," *Newsweek*, August 31, 1998, p. 34.

15. Bloom and Rosenberg, *Book of J* (New York: Grove Weidenfeld, 1990), 242.

16. Some scholars, most recently Richard Elliott Friedman in *The Hidden Book in the Bible* (San Francisco: HarperSanFrancisco, 1998), suggest that "J" was the source for much of the text that we find in the Book of Samuel.

17. Walter Brueggemann, "David and His Theologian," *Catholic Biblical Quarterly* 30, no. 2 (April 1968): 156, crediting Gerhard von Rad for the argument that chapters 2–11 of Genesis "are intended to be and indeed are an extremely sophisticated statement by one of Israel's earliest, most profound theologians."

18. David Rosenberg, *The Book of David* (New York: Harmony Books, 1997), 2.

CHAPTER TWO
THE WRONG KING

1. P. Kyle McCarter, Jr., trans., intro., and commentary, *I Samuel*, Anchor Bible (Garden City, N.Y.: Doubleday, 1980), 62.

2. Samuel was obliged by his mother's promise to Yahweh to take the so-called Nazirite vow, which required him to abstain from wine, "strong drink," and any other products made from the grape (including vinegar) and to leave his hair unshorn. (Num. 6:1–21) Another famous Nazirite was Samson, whose long hair was a sign of the sacred vow that was the real source of his strength: "For I have been a Nazirite unto God from my mother's womb," as Samson explained to the treacherous Delilah. (Judges 13:3–5, 7; 16:17)

3. Strictly speaking, God is here referring to the destruction of the priestly dynasty of Eli in Shiloh and its replacement by the house of Zadok at Jerusalem during the reign of David. (1 Sam. 3:14, 25) But the divine oracle can be understood to prefigure a revolution in the political and spiritual life of ancient Israel that reaches its highest expression in the accession of David to the throne.

4. McCarter, *I Samuel*, 18 ff. ("The middle stage in the growth of the First Book of Samuel . . . is prophetic in perspective and suspicious of the institution of monarchy.")

5. According to the Bible, the Philistines were the archetypal enemy of the Israelites. Scholarship suggests that they originated in the Aegean, and they were among

the waves of so-called Sea Peoples who began to migrate to the ancient Near East in the twelfth century B.C.E. The Egyptian pharaoh Ramses III defeated the Philistines in battle in 1190 B.C.E. and settled them as mercenaries in Canaan, where they later established themselves in five independent cities, including Ashkelon, Ashdod, Ekron, Gaza, and Gath. The geographical place name Palestine is derived from the Philistines.

6. Adapted from JPS. (The phrase "Adapted from . . ." is used in *King David* to indicate that I have taken the liberty of changing the punctuation, capitalization, and spelling as they appear in the cited source and omitting some words and phrases that do not change the meaning of the quoted material. See "A Note on Bibles and Biblical Usage" on page 347.)

7. *Goyim* is an Akkadian loan-word that means "nations" and is generally used in the Bible as a collective term of reference for non-Israelites. The KJV sometimes translates the word as "heathen," and it has come to be used as a lighthearted, but also slightly offensive, term for non-Jews.

8. Adapted from JPS. The complete text of Samuel's oration is found at 1 Sam. 8:10–22.

9. Paul Johnson, *A History of the Jews* (New York: Harper & Row, 1987), 49.

10. Jan Wojcik, "Discriminations against David's Tragedy in Ancient Jewish and Christian Literature," in Frontain and Wojcik, *David Myth*, 1980, 14.

11. Polzin, *Samuel and the Deuteronomist*, pt. 2; *1 Samuel*, 224, referring specifically to "the particular manner in which Saul dies" and attributing the passage to the biblical source known as the Deuteronomist.

12. Adapted from JPS and AB.

13. Adapted from KJV, NEB, and AB.

14. McCarter, *I Samuel*, 180.

15. According to a tale preserved in the Talmud (Horayot 11b and 12a), Moses himself prepared a supply of the stuff that lasted until the reformer-king Josiah ended the practice of anointing kings and high priests in the seventh century B.C.E.

16. The Masoretic Text omits the second and third sentences of Samuel's speech, which appear in translations based on the Septuagint. According to the JPS, Saul says: "Is it not that the Lord hath anointed thee to be prince over His inheritance?" (1 Sam. 10:1)

17. R. E. Clements, *Abraham and David* (London: S.C.M. Press, 1967), 49.

18. Adapted from JPS.

19. "Though the word 'lot' (*goral*) is not used here, the technical terminology of lot casting may be discerned. . . . The outcome of the lottery was believed to be divinely determined." McCarter, *I Samuel*, 192.

20. Strictly speaking, Saul was not raised to kingship when Samuel first anointed him. In the passages that describe the secret anointment (1 Sam. 10:1), Saul is described as a *nagid*—"prince," "leader," or "commander"—rather than as a *melek*—"king." The term may refer to a "king-designate" or, as we might put it, a crown prince (McCarter, *I Samuel*, 178–179). Elsewhere in the biblical account, however, Saul is presented as a king by Samuel and acclaimed as a king by the general populace.

21. The Ammonites were a Semitic people of the ancient Near East whose language was related to Hebrew and whose homeland was the eastern bank of the Jordan River. The site of its royal capital, Rabbah Ammon (or Rabbath-ammon), is identified with Ammon in what is now the modern state of Jordan. According to the Bible, Israel

and Ammon long disputed with each other for sovereignty over the east bank of the Jordan.

22. The Hebrew word translated in the Anchor Bible as "holocaust" (*olah*) is usually rendered in English-language Bibles as "burnt-offering" or "whole-offering" and identifies an offering that is burnt whole on the altar. Precisely because the word "holocaust" refers to a sacrificial offering to the God of Israel, some historians and critics prefer the Hebrew word *shoah* ("catastrophe") over "Holocaust" to describe the mass murder of six million Jewish men, women, and children by Nazi Germany and its allies.

23. Moab was located on a sixty-mile-long plateau along the eastern and northeastern shore of the Dead Sea, bordering on Ammon to the north, Edom to the south, and the land of Israel to the west. The Moabites, like the Ammonites, are described in the Bible as the descendants of Lot, nephew of the patriarch Abraham, and it is suggested that the Edomites are the descendants of Esau, brother of the patriarch Jacob. Thus, ironically, all three of these nations are regarded in the Bible as both the bitter enemies *and* the distant relations of the Israelites. (Gen. 19:37–38, 25:30) See my *The Harlot by the Side of the Road* (New York, Ballantine Books, 1997), chapter 3, "Life Against Death."

24. McCarter, *I Samuel*, 265.

25. A close reading of the Bible reveals that the in-laws of Moses are sometimes described as Midianites (Exod. 3:1) and sometimes as Kenites (Judg. 1:16, 4:11), and the two tribes may have been related. According to the so-called Kenite hypothesis, the Kenites may have been the first worshippers of Yahweh, and "Moses is supposed to have learned from his Kenite relatives both the name of God and the location of his holy mountain." Moshe Greenberg, *Understanding Exodus* (New York: Behrman House for Melton Research Center of the Jewish Theological Seminary of America, 1969), 48–49. Also see my *Moses, A Life* (New York: Ballantine Books, 1998), chapter 8, "The Sorcerer and the Sorcerer's Apprentice."

26. Adapted from NEB and New JPS.

27. See McCarter, *I Samuel*, 222, and text of the Revised English Bible in *The Complete Parallel Bible* (New York: Oxford University Press, 1993), 592.

28. The New Jerusalem Bible in *Complete Parallel Bible*, 593.

29. John Bright, *A History of Israel*, 2d ed. (Philadelphia: Westminster Press, 1972), 186.

30. "Such was Saul's unselfish devotion to the national interests that he retained not only the respect but also the affection of his subjects to the day of his death. He was never confronted, like David, with serious rebellions against his rule." Robert H. Pfeiffer, *Introduction to the Old Testament* (New York: Harper & Brothers, 1941), 347.

31. William Cowper, "Light Shining Out of Darkness," in *Treasury of Religious Quotations*, ed. Gerald Tomlinson (Englewood Cliffs, N.J.: Prentice Hall, 1991), 165.

32. Adapted from JPS and New JPS.

CHAPTER THREE
"HE IS THE ONE"

1. Adapted from JPS and NEB.
2. Adapted from JPS, NEB, and AB.
3. Adapted from JPS, NEB, and AB.

4. Adapted from JPS and AB.
5. Ginzberg, *Legends of the Jews*, vol. 6, 247, citing the Septuagint.
6. Tom Horner, *Jonathan Loved David* (Philadelphia: Westminster Press, 1978), 26.
7. Robert Alter, *The Art of Biblical Narrative* (New York: Basic Books, 1981), 35.
8. McCarter, *I Samuel*, 277.
9. Pfeiffer, *Introduction to the Old Testament*, 345, 363.
10. Oliver Taplin, "Homer," in *The Oxford History of the Classical World*, eds. John Boardman, Jasper Griffin, and Oswyn Murray (Oxford: Oxford University Press, 1986), 50.
11. Flavius Josephus, *Jewish Antiquities, Books V-VIII*, trans. H. St. J. Thackeray and Ralph Marcus (London: William Heinemann; Cambridge, Massachusetts: Harvard University Press, 1934), vol. 5, 249.
12. "Fits of acute mental depression alternating with violent explosions of anger" is how Robert Pfeiffer describes Saul's experience of spirit possession, and other modern commentators have speculated that Saul suffered from paranoid schizophrenia or bipolar syndrome. See Pfeiffer, *Introduction to the Old Testament*, 347.
13. "Saul's suffering is described theologically, not psychopathetically or psychologically," according to Bible scholar Hans Wilhelm Hertzberg, as quoted in McCarter, *I Samuel*, 281.
14. McCarter, *I Samuel*, 281.
15. The instrument that David played (*kinnor*) is generally called a harp in English translation, but scholars suggest that it more closely resembled a lyre, that is, a portable stringed instrument consisting of a soundbox with two projecting arms to which strings were attached.
16. Adapted from JPS and NEB.
17. Adapted from JPS and AB.
18. McCarter, *I Samuel*, 282.
19. The cubit, so familiar to Bible readers, is an ancient unit of measurement traditionally defined as the distance from elbow to the tip of the middle finger, about eighteen inches, and a span was the distance from the tip of the thumb to the tip of the middle finger of an open hand, about nine inches. Josephus, the Dead Sea Scrolls, and some versions of the Septuagint put Goliath's height at four cubits and a span, that is, a more realistic but still impressive height of six feet nine inches.
20. According to Israeli archaeologist Yigael Yadin, who was also a military officer with combat experience, a spear or javelin could be likened to a weaver's loom not because of its weight and thickness but because it was equipped with "a cord with a loop on the end . . . , giving the weapon the appearance of a weaver's leash rod." The cord and loop allowed the warrior to throw the weapon with greater force and accuracy. Yigael Yadin, *The Art of Warfare in Biblical Lands* (New York: McGraw-Hill, 1963), vol. 1, 10.
21. McCarter, *I Samuel*, 304, n. 28. "This is the only hint we get that tradition told of a strain in David's relationship with his brothers similar to that in the story of Joseph."
22. John Keegan, *A History of Warfare* (New York: Vintage Books, 1994), 91. See also P. Kyle McCarter, Jr., tr., notes, and comm., *II Samuel*, Anchor Bible (Garden City, N.Y.: Doubleday, 1984), 95.
23. McCarter, *I Samuel*, 292, n. 5, citing K. Galling, E. Sapir, and Y. Yadin.
24. Free, that is, from taxation and other obligations to the king.

25. Adapted from JPS and AB.

26. Adapted from JPS.

27. Adapted from JPS and AB.

28. Adapted from JPS and AB.

29. Moshe Greenberg, *Understanding Exodus*, 67–68; p. 68, n. 1.

30. Philo of Alexandria, *The Essential Philo*, ed. Nahum N. Glatzer (New York: Schocken Books, 1971), 204.

31. Julius Wellhausen, the founder of modern Bible scholarship, as quoted in McCarter, *I Samuel*, 295.

32. Scholarship suggests that a later biblical source tried to explain away the apparent contradiction between the two scenes by adding a single clumsy line to the text: "David went to and fro from Saul to feed his father's sheep at Bethlehem." (1 Sam. 17:16) In other words, we are meant to understand that David served as court musician to King Saul *and* shepherd of his father's flocks at the same time. But the effort at "harmonizing" the two versions of Saul and David's first meeting is unsuccessful—Saul does not recognize David when the two encounter each other on the battlefield.

33. Louis Ginzberg, *Legends of the Jews* (Philadelphia: Jewish Publication Society, 1909–1938), vol. 6, 260, n. 78, citing, inter alia, Mo'ed Katan.

34. "David" was once thought to be a military rank or title, like "general," rather than a personal name, at least for a brief period when a similar word (*davidum*) was first detected in a collection of ancient Near Eastern texts known as the Mari archives. Thus, it was suggested, "David" might be understood as the title of the warrior whose personal name was Elhanan. But the whole notion evaporated when it was later confirmed that *davidum* is derived from an Akkadian word that is best translated as "defeat" or "downfall," a title that no general or king (and King David least of all) would ever embrace! See D. R. Ap-Thomas, "Saul's 'Uncle,' " *Vetus Testamentum* 11, no. 3, July 1961, 244.

35. Bright, *History of Israel*, 188.

36. Alter, *Art of Biblical Narrative*, 118.

37. Botterweck and Ringgren, *Theological Dictionary of the Old Testament*, vol. 3, 158.

38. D. H. Lawrence, *David*, in *The Complete Plays of D. H. Lawrence* (London: William Heinemann, 1965), 91.

39. Israel H. Weisfeld, *David the King* (New York: Bloch Publishing Company, 1983), 5.

40. Julian Morgenstern, "David and Jonathan," *Journal of Biblical Literature* 78, pt. 4 (December 1959): 322.

41. Horner, *Jonathan Loved David*, 28.

42. Adapted from JPS.

CHAPTER FOUR
INNOCENT BLOOD

1. Joseph Heller, *God Knows* (New York: Alfred A. Knopf, 1984), 7–8.

2. Adapted from JPS.

3. Morgenstern, "David and Jonathan," 324.

4. Some versions of the Septuagint report that David brought back only one hun-

dred foreskins, but the Masoretic Text insists that David doubled the quota set by King Saul. McCarter, *I Samuel*, 316.

5. Adapted from NEB and AB.

6. Adapted from JPS and NEB.

7. *Teraphim*, a term that is generally translated as "household gods," refers to the idols believed to embody the spirits of pagan gods and goddesses who protected hearth and home and were used for ritual purposes in the ancient Near East, including the land of Israel.

8. Adapted from JPS and NEB.

9. The original Hebrew text of 1 Sam. 19:17 uses an idiomatic expression in the form of a question. "He said unto me: 'Let me go; why should I kill thee?' " is how the same passage is rendered in the JPS and the AB. Both translations, however, imply that Michal is falsely reporting that David threatened her with death.

10. The fact that the biblical author is comfortable in making use of menstruation as a plot point—and using it to show a woman getting the better of a man—has been cited as evidence that the biblical sources included both men and women and, in particular, that the source identified as J may have been a woman.

11. "Asherim" are thought to be living trees or carved wooden poles by which the Canaanite goddess called Asherah was depicted and worshipped.

12. The place where David and Samuel seek refuge, "Naioth," is regarded as a place name in the Masoretic Text and in many English translations, but more recent translations treat the word as a common noun and translate it as "the sheds" (NAB), "the huts" (NJB), or "the camps" (AB). McCarter (*I Samuel*, 380) understands "Naioth" as a reference to "a shepherd's camp pitched outside a city." Similarly, what the JPS translates as "the cistern that is in Secu" is rendered in the AB as "the cistern of the threshing floor that was upon the bare height." (1 Sam. 19:18, 22)

13. Earlier, when Samuel was shown to execute the Amalekite king whom Saul had spared in defiance of the death sentence imposed by God, the Bible insists that "Samuel never beheld Saul again to the day of his death." (1 Sam. 15:34) The fact that Saul and Samuel encounter each other here may indicate that the passage was added to the biblical text by a later source "who even surpassed the earlier writer in his contempt for Saul." McCarter, *I Samuel*, 331.

14. The text harks back to an earlier incident in which Saul, newly anointed by Samuel, encountered a band of prophets and fell into ecstatic prophesy along with them. (1 Sam. 10:10–11)

15. Adapted from JPS.

16. Adapted from JPS.

17. Adapted from JPS and NEB.

18. The first day of each month in the lunar calendar of ancient Israel was celebrated as a day of rest and an occasion for feasting (Num. 29:11–15; Amos 8:5) and remains a holy day in Jewish tradition.

19. Adapted from JPS and NEB.

20. Adapted from NEB.

21. The seating arrangements are described in detail in McCarter's lucid and plainspoken translation of the Hebrew text as it appears in the AB. (I Sam. 20:25)

22. Ejaculation, menstruation, contact with the carcass of a dead animal, or an unsightly skin condition, among many other things, rendered a man or woman temporarily "unclean" and thus unfit to participate in ritual observances, including the Feast of the

New Moon. "One who suffers from a malignant skin-disease shall wear his clothes torn, leave his hair dishevelled, conceal his upper lip, and cry, 'Unclean, unclean' " goes one of the biblical rules of ritual impurity. "He shall live apart and must stay outside the settlement." (Lev. 13:45–46) (NEB)

23. Adapted from JPS and NEB.

24. Adapted from JPS and NEB. Literally, Saul called Jonathan "You son of a rebellious servant girl," and then condemned him for "the disgrace of your mother's nakedness," that is, "disgrac[ing] his mother's genitals, whence he came forth." McCarter, *I Samuel*, 343.

25. Adapted from JPS and NEB.

CHAPTER FIVE
DESPERADO

1. Nob is believed to have been a "priestly city" of ancient Israel, located north of Jerusalem in the tribal land of Benjamin, near Saul's hometown of Gibeah.

2. Adapted from JPS and NEB.

3. Like much else in the lives of Moses and David as recorded in the Hebrew Bible, the incident is echoed in the life of Jesus as recorded in the Gospels. Jesus cited the example of Ahimelech and David to defend his disciples against the charge that they had violated the law by plucking and eating ears of corn on the Sabbath. "Have you not read what David did when he and his men were hungry?" (Matt. 12:3–4) (NEB)

4. Adapted from NEB.

5. Scholarship suggests the nature and use of the ephod was already a mystery to the final editors of the Bible, and they may have unwittingly preserved the references to the ephod as an idol or an idol-case. More commonly, the term is used in the Bible to refer to a priestly garment—David himself will wear an ephod while performing a ritual dance on the road to Jerusalem, an incident that will produce a scandal in the royal household and seal the fate of Saul's daughter Michal. See Julian Morgenstern, "The Ark, the Ephod, and the 'Tent of the Meeting' " (continued), *Hebrew Union College Annual* 18 (1943–1944): 3, 8–9, 11. See also John Lindblom, "Lot-casting in the Old Testament," *Vetus Testamentum* 12, no. 2 (April 1962): 171–172. "The ephod together with its idol is meant."

6. Adapted from JPS and NEB.

7. See E. A. Speiser, trans., intro., and notes, *Genesis*, Anchor Bible (Garden City, N.Y.: Doubleday, 1987), 44. JPS: "Sons of God." NEB: "Sons of the gods." (Gen. 6:1)

8. Like the teraphim in David's house and the ephod in the shrine of Yahweh, the semidivine origins of Goliath fit nowhere in the official theology of the Hebrew Bible, which insists that Yahweh is the *only* god and an asexual god at that. The notion that God had sons who mated with mortal women and sired a race of giants has been described by the revered Bible scholar Ephraim A. Speiser as "not only atypical of the Bible as a whole but also puzzling and controversial in the extreme." (Speiser, *Genesis*, 45). The best explanation, of course, is that the passage was borrowed from one of the pagan cultures amid which the ancient Israelites (including the biblical authors) lived and worked.

9. The Book of Samuel first describes David's hideout at Adullam as a cave, then

as a stronghold. (1 Sam. 22:1,4) (JPS) McCarter suggests that the text probably describes "a well-fortified hilltop" near the "Judahite fortress city" of Adullam. McCarter, *I Samuel*, 357.

10. A fortified city approximately sixteen miles southwest of Jerusalem in an area of wooded foothills known as the Shephelah.

11. Bright, *History of Israel*, 188–189.

12. Adapted from JPS.

13. All dialogue between God and human beings in the Book of Samuel is apparently derived from either the dreams and visions of prophets like Samuel or, more often, the simple yes-or-no answers that were solicited by kings and priests through various tools of divination, including the Ark of the Covenant, the ephod, and the mysterious objects known as the Urim and Thummim.

14. Adapted from JPS.

15. Adapted from JPS and AB. Ahimelech's reference to David as "commander of [Saul's] bodyguard" appears in the AB but not the JPS, which renders the Hebrew text as a reference to one who "giveth heed unto thy bidding."

16. Adapted from JPS.

17. Adapted from JPS.

18. Adapted from JPS and AB.

19. Here, of course, the ephod in question is a garment that identifies its wearer as a priest.

20. Adapted from JPS.

21. Emphasis added.

22. Adapted from JPS.

23. Adapted from JPS.

24. By tradition, the Calebites were the descendants of Caleb, the most valiant of the spies sent into Canaan by Moses in advance of the conquering army of Israel. Caleb is first introduced in the Bible as a prince of the tribe of Judah (Num. 13:6), but the Calebites are later described as non-Israelites who were only later incorporated into the tribe of Judah. (Josh. 15:13) Carmel was a village located eight miles southeast of Hebron, an ancient and sacred city in the tribal homeland of Judah that was given to the Calebites by Joshua. (Josh. 14:14)

25. McCarter (*I Samuel*, 396) defines *nabal* as "foolish, senseless . . . with the collat[eral] idea of *ignoble, disgraceful*." *The New English Bible* renders the word as "churlish." "He is just what his name Nabal means: 'Churl' is his name, and churlish his behaviour." (1 Sam. 25: 25) (NEB)

26. Adapted from JPS, NEB, and AB.

27. Adapted from JPS, NEB and AB. David's coarse if colorful way of referring to a man as "one who pisses against the wall" is translated literally in the King James Version of 1611, which memorably reads "pisseth" rather than "pisses." More recent (and more polite) translations of the Bible render the vivid phrase as "a male" (JPS) or "a mother's son" (NEB).

28. Adapted from JPS and NEB.

29. Adapted from JPS and NEB.

30. Adapted from JPS.

31. Adapted from NEB and AB.

32. Ahinoam's hometown of Jezreel was a village located near Carmel in the tribal

homeland of Judah, rather than the better-known city of the same name in northern Israel.

33. The locations of Hachilah and Jeshimon are unknown to modern Bible scholarship.

34. Adapted from JPS.

35. Maon, a few miles south of Hebron, was yet another hilltop site in the rugged wilderness of the tribal land of Judah.

36 "Cover his feet" is the euphemism for defecation that appears in the Hebrew text to describe what Saul is doing in the cave. Some fussy translators favor a literal rendering of the idiomatic expression in order to conceal what is actually going on.

37. Adapted from NEB.

38. Adapted from NEB.

39. Adapted from JPS.

40. Here is yet another example of a dreamy association between two passages in the Bible. The very same words were uttered by Judah, founder of the tribe that bears his name, when he learned that his daughter-in-law, Tamar, had tricked him into impregnating her by disguising herself as a harlot and seducing him. (Gen. 38) David is the distant descendant of one of the twin sons who were conceived in that act of seduction and incest, and the biblical author is subtly reminding readers of David's lineage.

41. Adapted from JPS.

42. Adapted from NEB.

43. Adapted from JPS and NEB.

44. Ziklag is believed to have been a town located to the southeast of modern Gaza, originally within the tribal lands of Simeon and later assigned to Judah. (Josh. 14:31)

45. Adapted from JPS and NEB.

46. Adapted from JPS and NEB. "Negev" means "dry southern country" and here refers to the southerly districts of each of the named tribes. The "Negev of Judah," for example, is apparently the district around the town of Beersheba in the tribal homeland of Judah. The Jerahmeelites and Kenites were non-Israelites who later came to be regarded as clans of the tribe of Judah. (1 Chron. 2:9, Josh. 14:14)

47. McCarter, *I Samuel*, 415.

48. Adapted from NEB and AB.

49. McCarter, *I Samuel*, 358–359, citing Budde and Smith.

50. Bright, *History of Israel*, 189.

51. Adapted from JPS and AB.

52. McCarter, *I Samuel*, 408.

53. Adapted from JPS.

54. Adapted from JPS.

CHAPTER SIX
GHOSTWIFE

1. Adapted from JPS.

2. The staging areas for the two armies were located in the northern stretches of Israel, near Mount Gilboa in the Jezreel Valley. The town of En-dor was located in the same vicinity, and a modern village still bears the old name.

3. Adapted from JPS and AB.

4. Pfeiffer, *Introduction to the Old Testament*, 342; Lindblom, "Lot-casting in the Old Testament," *Vetus Testamentum* 12, no. 2 (April 1962): 171–172.

5. Nowhere else in the Bible are we given such a clear example of how the Urim and Thummim were actually used to obtain an oracle from God. Curiously, these details appear in the Septuagint but not in the Masoretic Text, which preserves only an abbreviated version of the episode and makes no mention of the Urim and Thummim.

6. Lindblom, "Lot-casting in the Old Testament," 171–172.

7. Adapted from JPS and AB.

8. Adapted from JPS and KJV.

9. P. Kyle McCarter, Jr., an expert and imaginative translator of the biblical text, renders "witch" as "ghostwife" in the Anchor Bible. He points out that the Masoretic Text "conflates two terms referring to a (female) necromancer," that is, "ghostwife" and "ghostmistress." McCarter, *I Samuel*, 418.

10. Adapted from JPS and AB.

11. Adapted from JPS, NEB, and AB.

12. Adapted from JPS and AB.

13. Gerhard von Rad, *Moses* (London: United Society for Christian Literature, Lutterworth Press, 1960), 31.

14. Martin Buber, *Moses* (New York: Harper & Row, 1958), 7, n.1.

15. So unsettling is the incident at En-dor that some scholars believe it was once removed from the biblical text by a redactor "who was offended by its content" and then restored much later by another redactor who put it in the wrong place, which explains why the chronology and geography of the account are somewhat fractured. McCarter, *I Samuel*, 422.

16. Adapted from JPS and AB.

17. Adapted from JPS and AB.

18. Adapted from JPS and AB.

19. Adapted from JPS and AB.

20. Adapted from JPS and AB.

21. Adapted from JPS and AB.

22. "Israel," which means "he who striveth with God," is the name given to Jacob after he wrestled with and defeated a mysterious stranger who may have been an angel of God or God himself. "Thy name shall be called no more Jacob, but Israel, for thou has striven with God and with men, and has prevailed." (Gen. 32:29)

23. In J. Maxwell Miller and John H. Hayes, *A History of Ancient Israel and Judah* (Philadelphia: Westminster Press, 1986), 66.

24. Niels Peter Lemche, "Habiru, Hapiru," in Freedman, *Anchor Bible Dictionary*, vol. 3, 6–10.

25. See Roland de Vaux, *The Early History of Israel*, trans. David Smith (Philadelphia: Westminster Press, 1978), 215. "The band of outlaws whom David gathered around him "bear a strange resemblance to the movements of the warlike and looting Habiru who figure in the texts of Mari and Amarna. What is more, David's positions in the service of the Philistines and that of his men, whom the Philistines regarded as mercenaries and called 'the Hebrews,' are almost exactly parallel to that of the companies of Habiru who served the . . . various rulers in Palestine during the Amarna period."

26. Paul Johnson, *The Birth of the Modern* (New York: HarperCollins, 1991), 677–678.

27. Johnson, *Birth of the Modern*, 679.
28. Adapted from JPS.
29. Adapted from JPS and NEB.
30. Adapted from JPS and NEB.
31. Hebron, located some nineteen miles southwest of Jerusalem in the Judean highlands, was the home and, later, the burial place of Abraham and Sarah, the first patriarch and matriarch of the Israelites.
32. The Septuagint depicts Saul with an arrow in his belly, but the Masoretic Text says only that he was "in great anguish by reason of the archers," a phrase that the Anchor Bible renders as "writhed in fear of the archers."
33. Beth-shan was a Canaanite town, apparently under occupation by the Philistines, in the Jezreel Valley of northern Israel.
34. Adapted from JPS, NEB, and AB.
35. See McCarter, *II Samuel*, 65.
36. Quoted in Mitchell Dahood, trans., intro., and notes, *Psalms I, 1–50*, Anchor Bible (Garden City, N.Y.: Doubleday, 1966), xxx–xxxi.
37. Dahood, *Psalms I, 1–50*, xxx.
38. Pfeiffer, *Introduction to the Old Testament*, 351.
39. Weisfeld, *David the King*, 5
40. Pfeiffer, *Introduction to the Old Testament*, 351.
41. J. A. Thompson, "The Significance of the Verb *Love* in the David-Jonathan Narratives in 1 Samuel," *Vetus Testamentum* 24, no. 3 (July 1974): 334, 335, 337.
42. Adapted from NEB.
43. Raphael Patai, *Sex and Family in the Bible and the Middle East* (Garden City, N.Y.: Doubleday, 1959), 169, 170.
44. Horner, *Jonathan Loved David*, 20.
45. Horner, *Jonathan Loved David*, 20, 24.
46. Horner, *Jonathan Loved David*, citing S. R. Driver (emphasis added).
47. Quoted in Frontain and Wojcik, *David Myth*, 8.
48. Richard Howard, "The Giant on Giant Killing," quoted in Frontain and Wojcik, *David Myth*, 9.
49. Ted-Larry Pebworth, "Cowley's *Davideis* and the Exaltation of Friendship," in Frontain and Wojcik, *David Myth*, 101.
50. The Bible is uncertain about the number or names of Saul's sons, sometimes identifying three sons (Jonathan, Ishvi, and Malchishua) (1 Sam. 14–49) and sometimes four (Jonathan, Malchishua, Abinadab, and Ishbaal). (1 Chron. 8:33, 9:39) Ishbaal ("man of Baal") is called Ish-bosheth ("man of shame" in the Masoretic Text (2 Sam. 2:8), perhaps a way for ancient scribes to avoid any reference to the pagan god of ancient Canaan known as Baal. Some scholars propose that Ishvi, Ishbaal, and Ishbosheth are alternate names for one and the same person.
51. Gilead was a region on the east bank of the Jordan River, and Geshur was located in the vicinity of the Golan Heights. The Jezreel Valley lies near Mount Gilboa between the hill-country of Samaria and the Galilee. Benjamin was the smallest of the twelve tribes of Israel, and the one to which King Saul and his sons belonged. Ephraim was another Israelite tribe whose homeland was centered in the hill-country around the city of Shechem.

CHAPTER SEVEN
"SHALL THE SWORD DEVOUR FOREVER?"

1. Jabesh-Gilead was the frontier town on the far side of the Jordan River that Saul saved from the Ammonites at the very outset of his kingship, and now the townsfolk were repaying a debt of honor to their dead savior. See chapter 2.

2. Adapted from JPS.

3. Gibeon was located a few miles northwest of Jerusalem, and the pool mentioned in the Bible is identified with a deep pit cut into the native rock, eighty-two feet deep and thirty-seven feet wide, which was excavated in modern times.

4. Joab, Abishai, and Asahel were the sons of Zeruiah (2 Sam. 2:18), a woman who is identified as David's sister. (1 Chron. 2:16) Abner was the son of Ner (2 Sam. 2:12), a man who is identified as Saul's uncle. (1 Sam. 14:50).

5. Adapted from JPS and AB.

6. Josephus, *Jewish Antiquities, Books V-VIII*, vol. 5, 365.

7. Yigael Yadin, *The Art of Warfare in Biblical Lands* (New York: McGraw-Hill, 1963), vol. 2, 266, 267. "The 'game' they played was no game but a group of serious duels in the full technical sense of the term. . . . it shows that this form of military engagement, possibly under the Philistine influence, had been taken over as an accepted practice by the professional soldiers, the picked men of valor of both royal households."

8. New JPS, 472, n. f.

9. Adapted from JPS and New JPS.

10. Clinton Bailey, "How Desert Culture Helps Us Understand the Bible," *Bible Review* 7, no. 4 (August 1991): 20.

11. Abishai, like his brothers, is depicted as a man with a rash nature and a taste for rough justice. For example, when David and Abishai came upon the slumbering Saul, it was Abishai who proposed to assassinate him in his sleep. "Let me strike him and pin him to the ground with one thrust of the spear," Abishai implored David. "I will not have to strike twice." (1 Sam. 26:8) (NEB) David refused to allow the assassination of King Saul, but he would be forced to contend with the impulsive "sons of Zeruiah"— Joab and Abishai—yet again.

12. Adapted from JPS and New JPS.

13. Adapted from JPS and New JPS.

14. Anson Rainey, "Concubine," in *Encyclopedia Judaica*, corrected ed. (Jerusalem: Keter Publishing House, n.d.), vol. 5, 862.

15. Adapted from JPS and New JPS.

16. The fact that David would be forbidden to remarry his wife under biblical law (Deut. 24:1–4) apparently does not occur to him or the biblical author, perhaps because, as some scholars propose, the Book of Deuteronomy was not yet in existence.

17. Adapted from JPS.

18. J. Cheryl Exum, *Fragmented Women*, Journal for the Study of the Old Testament, supplement series 163 (Sheffield, England: JSOT Press, 1993): 22.

19. Adapted from JPS.

20. Adapted from New JPS and NEB.

21. Adapted from JPS and AB.

22. Joel Rosenberg, *King and Kin* (Bloomington: Indiana University Press, 1986), 166–167; Alter, *Art of Biblical Narrative*, 102.

23. Bright, *History of Israel*, 192; McCarter, *II Samuel*, 122.

CHAPTER EIGHT
CITY OF DAVID

1. Ginzberg, *Legends of the Jews*, vol. 1, 285, citing, inter alia, Targum Yerushalmi, MHG I, and Tehillim 76.

2. Weisfeld, *David the King,* 167, citing Pirke Rabbi Eliezer 36.

3. A very different tale is told in the Book of Judges, where it is reported that, shortly after the death of Joshua, "the children of Judah fought against Jerusalem, and took it, and smote it with the edge of the sword, and set the city on fire." (Judges 1:8) Amihai Mazar, one of the leading excavators of Jerusalem, shrugs off the inconsistent report in Judges as either "fictional" or perhaps a distorted memory of an assault by non-Israelites. Amihai Mazar, *Archaeology of the Land of the Bible: 10,000–586 B.C.E.* (New York: Doubleday, 1990), 333.

4. Bright, *History of Israel*, 195.

5. McCarter, *II Samuel*, 134–135.

6. McCarter, *II Samuel*, 140. David was expressing a distaste for the disabled that pervades the Bible, whose authors regarded a person with certain physical imperfections as ritually impure and unfit to participate in ceremonies of worship and sacrifice. (Lev. 21:16–23, Deut. 23:1–2) Thus, the Bible links David's hatred for "the lame and the blind" to the laws of ritual purity. "That is why they say: 'No one who is blind or lame shall come into the Lord's house.' " (2 Sam. 5:8) (NEB)

7. The excavation of a vertical shaft beneath the walls of Jerusalem in the nineteenth century by the British army engineer Charles Warren prompted a flurry of enthusiasm among Bible scholars, who identified the so-called Warren Shaft with the watercourse that is apparently mentioned in the biblical account of David's assault on the city. More recent and more temperate archaeologists are no longer convinced that the Warren Shaft dates as far back as the events described in the Bible.

8. The eyesight of the patriarch Isaac was impaired in his old age (Gen. 27:1), and the patriarch Jacob suffered an injury to his thigh during his wrestling match with God. (Gen. 32:26)

9. McCarter, *II Samuel*, 138–139, citing, inter alia, A. Finklestein, Pirke Rabbi Eliezer 36, Josephus, and J. Heller.

10. Karen Armstrong, *Jerusalem: One City, Three Faiths* (New York: Alfred A. Knopf, 1996), 37.

11. Adapted from JPS and NEB.

12. Joel Rosenberg, *King and Kin*, 165.

13. Joel Rosenberg, *King and Kin*, 166–167, citing Hannelis Schulte (biblical citations omitted).

14. Gerhard von Rad, *Old Testament Theology*, vol. 1, *The Theology of Israel's Historical Traditions*, trans. D.M.G. Stalker (New York: Harper & Row, 1962), 39.

15. Frank Moore Cross, *Canaanite Myth and Hebrew Epic* (Cambridge: Harvard University Press, 1973), 230.

16. Adapted from New JPS.

17. The Millo is believed to have been an earthwork, perhaps a ravine filled and packed with soil and debris, which was used to create building sites on the slope of the peak where the original Jebusite citadel and the City of David were located. The Chronicler, by the way, adds an intriguing detail that is missing from the Book of Samuel: "Joab restored the remainder of the city." (1 Chron. 11:8) (AB)

18. Tyre was the capital of ancient Phoenicia, which was located on the northern frontier of Israel in what is now Lebanon. According to the Bible, King Hiram was still on the throne several decades later and provided cedar and craftsmen to King Solomon to build the Temple at Jerusalem. (1 Kings 5:15–26) The cedars of lebanon were valued as building materials in the ancient world and were used in the construction of temples and palaces as far away as Egypt in the fourth millennium B.C.E. and Mesopotamia in the third millennium B.C.E.

19. A concubine, as the term is used in the Bible, was *not* merely a mistress or a sex slave. Rather, she was a "secondary wife" who enjoyed some, if not all, of the legal protection afforded to a wife whose marriage had been ritually consecrated. Crucially, the offspring of a man's concubine were recognized as his children for purposes of inheritance and succession. The fussy author of Chronicles, apparently sensitive to the unsavory associations of concubinage, refers only to David's *wives*. (1 Chron. 14:3)

The head count of David's children varies from eleven to seventeen in the ancient versions of the Hebrew Bible.

20. Adapted from AB. Other translations of the "troubled" text of 2 Sam. 5:24 are far less lucid. What the Anchor Bible renders as "the sound of the wind in the asherahs" is translated in the JPS as "the sound of marching in the tops of the mulberry-trees" and in the NEB as "a rustling sound in the tree-tops."

21. Adapted from JPS and AB. McCarter points out that "Geba" appears in place of "Gibeon" in the Masoretic Text, but he favors "Gibeon," which appears in the Septuagint. "Gibeon" also appears in 1 Chronicles 14:16 in the Masoretic Text.

22. The site of Kiriath-jearim, sometimes also called Baalah and Kiriat-baal in the Bible, is believed to be located fourteen miles northwest of Jerusalem. (Josh 15:9, 1 Chron 13:5)

23. *Yahweh Sabaoth* is conventionally translated as "Lord of Hosts," a phrase that does not convey the martial splendor that the biblical author intended.

24. The mice are mentioned in the Septuagint but not in the Masoretic Text, which refers only to the tumors. Some Bible commentators, including Martin Luther, have suggested that the Bible preserves the memory of an outbreak of bubonic plague that originated with diseased rodents from ships calling at the ports of the seafaring Philistines. Others propose that the tumors were symptoms of hemorrhoids or dysentery.

25. R. A. Carlson, *David, the Chosen King* (Stockholm: Almqvist & Wiksell, 1964), 59, citing but criticizing W. R. Arnold and W. Caspari.

26. The Hebrew word customarily rendered as "thousand" (*elep*) in various translations of the Bible may refer to a military unit rather than an actual head count. Thus, rather than a vast army of thirty thousand soldiers, David may have been accompanied by thirty units of infantry, each one consisting of only a dozen or so men.

27. Adapted from JPS and New JPS.

Obed-edom is described in the Bible as a Gittite (2 Sam. 6:10), that is, a man from the Philistine territory of Gath, whose king David had once served as a mercenary. Israel under King David, as we shall see, was multiculturally diverse, and even Philistines were admitted to the inner circles of his court. Remarkably, the Philistine from Gath was able to safely cohabit with the Ark even though a native-born Israelite died when he merely touched it.

28. The words attributed to David ("I'll bring the blessing back to my own house!") appear in the so-called Lucianic recension of the Septuagint but not in the Masoretic Text. "In view of the light it casts on David's motives," observes P. Kyle McCarter, Jr., "it

might have been deleted in MT by a scribe who wanted to protect David." McCarter, *II Samuel*, 165–166.

29. Adapted from New JPS and AB.

30. Adapted from JPS.

31. Adapted from JPS and New JPS.

32. Adapted from AB and New JPS.

33. Adapted from AB and New JPS.

34. Adapted from AB and New JPS.

35. David M. Howard Jr., "David (Person)," in *Anchor Bible Dictionary*, vol. 2, 44.

36. Carlson, *David, the Chosen King*, 61, citing but criticizing W. R. Arnold. "The ideology and composition of 2 Sam. could hardly be more profoundly misjudged."

37. Matitiahu Tsevat, "Studies in the Book of Samuel, III," *Hebrew Union College Annual* 34 (1963): 73.

38. Cross, *Canaanite Myth and Hebrew Epic*, 251.

39. See Cross, *Canaanite Myth and Hebrew Epic*, 73.

40. Elias Auerbach, *Moses*, trans. J. S. Bowden (Philadelphia: Westminster Press, 1968), 155.

Also see my *Moses*, chapter 9, "God of the Mountain, God of the Way."

41. Deuteronomy may have been the "book of the Law" that was mysteriously discovered in the Temple at Jerusalem during the reign of King Josiah in the late seventh century B.C.E. (2 Kings 22:8) Josiah was an ardent religious reformer who insisted on the centralization of worship in Jerusalem, and the newly discovered laws of Deuteronomy validated his reforms—a fact that leads some Bible scholars to suspect that the Book of Deuteronomy is a "pious fraud" that was composed at Josiah's direction!

42. Cross, *Canaanite Myth and Hebrew Epic*, 73.

CHAPTER NINE
AT THE TIME WHEN KINGS GO FORTH TO BATTLE

1. Adapted from JPS.

2. The revenge of the Gibeonites on the house of Saul is reported in chapter 21 of Second Samuel, but Bible scholars suspect that the incident must have taken place *before* David offered to shelter Saul's last surviving son, Mephibosheth, as reported in chapter 9 of Second Samuel.

3. Adapted from JPS.

4. According to Numbers 25:4, God ordered Moses to "hang up [the chiefs of the people] unto Yahweh in the face of the sun" as punishment for the idolatry and "harlotry" committed by the Israelites with "the daughters of Moab," and Deuteronomy 21:22–23 prescribes that the corpse of a man who has been executed for "a sin worthy of death" shall be hung from a tree. Both passages have been identified with crucifixion by some modern scholars, although the Masoretic Text and the Talmudic sages describe both forms of punishment as "hanging."

5. The Bible knows Jonathan's lame son both as "Meribaal" (1 Chron. 8:34) and as "Mephibosheth" (2 Sam. 4:4), probably because the scribes who preserved the Masoretic Text sought to avoid any reference to the Canaanite deity Baal.

6. Pfeiffer, *Introduction to the Old Testament*, 353.

7. Clements, *Abraham and David*, 49, n. 10, citing Gerhard von Rad. Some schol-

ars have speculated that the high priest Zadok may have been a native Jebusite rather than an Israelite, and the very notion that God might require a temple rather than a tent-shrine may be another borrowing from Canaanite religious practice. The Jebusite hypothesis and Zadok's bloodlines are hotly debated and sharply criticized by some Bible scholars. Chronicles, a relatively late book of the Bible, concocts a conventional lineage for Zadok, tracing him all the way back to Aaron, the brother of Moses and the first high priest of Israel. (1 Chron 5:27–41)

8. See Carlson, *David, the Chosen King*, 87; 89, f.n. 3; 91; 94–95, n. 2; citing, inter alia, J. R. Porter and Hos. 3:1.

9. Joel Rosenberg, *King and Kin*, 118.

Intriguingly, the Bible reveals that David himself was not a purebred Israelite. His ancestors included Tamar, a Canaanite woman who seduced her father-in-law, Judah (see chapter 11), and an equally beguiling Moabite woman, Ruth. (Ruth 4:18–22, 1 Chron. 2:3–15) When David fled from Saul and sought refuge in the wilderness, he prevailed upon the king of Moab to shelter his parents throughout his fugitive years. (1 Sam. 22:4) "Presumably, then," explains P. Kyle McCarter, Jr., "Jesse and his wife could claim some kind of a right of protection in Moab on the grounds of kinship." McCarter, *I Samuel*, 359. And David courted and married a woman named Maacah, daughter of the king of Geshur, an Aramean kingdom located to the east of Galilee. (2 Sam. 3:3) Thus, some scholars suggest that David was an outsider—a *habiru*—who insinuated himself into the politics of ancient Israel. "The most important means of royal legitimation in the ancient Near East (and in most dynastic monarchies) is genealogical connection," argues revisionist Bible scholar John van Seters. "But this is not used in the case of David. Isaiah can go back no further than Jesse when he speaks about a new dynastic beginning for the Judean monarchy." John van Seters, *Abraham in History and Tradition* (New Haven: Yale University Press, 1975), 152.

10. Joel Rosenberg, *King and Kin*, 127.

11. McCarter, *II Samuel*, 255, 256, citing O. Eissfeldt.

12. R. N. Whybray, *The Succession Narrative* (Naperville, Ill.: A. R. Allenson, 1968), 3.

13. McCarter, *II Samuel*, 496–497, citing (and criticizing) the work of K. Ellinger.

14. Norman K. Gottwald, *The Tribes of Yahweh* (Maryknoll, N.Y.: Orbis Books, 1979), 362, 363, 371. "[The Israelites] had never thought of themselves as necessarily twelve in number. The twelve-tribe scheme was originated by David for administrative purposes in order to recruit the citizen army or militia, and possibly also to raise taxes and to impose the corvée." Gottwald carefully qualifies his observations as only a "hypothesis."

15. Bright, 200, 202.

16. Joel Rosenberg, *King and Kin*, 137.

17. McCarter, *II Samuel*, 270.

18. Adapted from NEB.

CHAPTER TEN
THE DAUGHTER OF THE SEVEN GODS

1. The Hittites, a people that originated in the region that is now modern Turkey, once ruled an empire that contested with Egypt for dominance in the ancient Near East.

By the time of David, the Hittite empire was gone, although a few Hittites may have remained in the vicinity of Israel. The Bible, however, uses "Hittite" to identify several different peoples of the ancient world, including the Hivites and the Arameans, and so we cannot be sure of Uriah's origins.

2. Jan Wojcik, "Discriminations against David's Tragedy in Ancient Jewish and Christian Literature," in Frontain and Wojcik, *David Myth*, 34.

3. Armstrong, *Jerusalem*, 40.

4. Ginzberg, *Legends of the Jews*, vol. 4, 103, citing, inter alia, Sanhendrin 107a.

5. Wojcik, "Discriminations against David's Tragedy," in Frontain and Wojcik, *David Myth*, 29, citing, inter alia, Sanhendrin 107a.

6. Adapted from JPS, NEB, and AB.

7. Adapted from JPS.

8. Adapted from JPS and NEB.

9. Pfeiffer, *Introduction to the Old Testament*, 355.

10. Adapted from JPS and NEB.

11. Adapted from JPS and NEB.

12. William Foxwell Albright, *From the Stone Age to Christianity*, 2d ed. (Johns Hopkins Press, 1957), 305–306.

13. William Foxwell Albright, "Samuel and the Beginnings of the Prophetic Movement," in intro. Harry M. Orlinsky, *Interpreting the Prophetic Tradition: The Goldenson Lectures, 1955–1966* (Cincinnati: Hebrew Union College Press, New York: Ktav Publishing House, 1969), 161.

14. McCarter, *I Samuel*, 182.

15. McCarter, *I Samuel*, 182.

16. David is depicted as worshipping at "the house of Yahweh" (2 Sam. 12:20) (AB), but the Bible makes it clear that only a tent-shrine and not a temple was then in existence in Jerusalem. McCarter suggests that the "house of Yahweh" is either an anachronistic reference to the Temple of Solomon or else a Jebusite shrine that had been converted to the worship of Yahweh during the reign of King David. McCarter, *II Samuel*, 302.

17. Adapted from NEB, JPS, and AB.

18. J.P.E. Pedersen, *Israel*, vol. 4 (London: Oxford University Press: 1940), 455–457.

19. Walter Brueggemann, "The Trusted Creature," *Catholic Biblical Quarterly* 31, (1969): 489–490.

20. Some Bible critics have wondered out loud whether, in fact, Solomon was the one and only offspring of the adulterous affair, and the tale of an earlier child merely a cover story intended to conceal the illegitimate birth of the future king of Israel and builder of the Temple. Solomon's name may actually derive from the Hebrew word for "replacement," and the argument has been made that Solomon was regarded by his mother as a replacement for the dead Uriah rather than for the fictional firstborn son who supposedly died.

21. Jan Wojcik, "Discriminations against David's Tragedy," 26–27, citing Midrash Samuel.

22. Ginzberg, *Legends of the Jews*, vol. 4, 103, citing, inter alia, Shabbat 56a, Abodah Zarah 4b-5a. See also Wojcik, "Discriminations against David's Tragedy," 29.

23. Ginzberg, *Legends of the Jews*, vol. 4, 104, citing, inter alia, Sanhedrin 107a.

24. Exum, *Fragmented Women*, 173, 174.

25. Exum, *Fragmented Women*, 174, 175.
26. Frontain and Wojcik, *David Myth*, 3, describing the depiction of David and Bathsheba in Renaissance art and literature.
27. J. Blenkinsopp, "Theme and Motif in the Succession History (2 Sam. XI 2 ff) and the Yahwist Corpus," in *Supplements to Vetus Testamentum* (Leiden: E. J. Brill, 1966), 52.
28. Heller, *God Knows*, 10.
29. Adapted from JPS and AB (emphasis added).

CHAPTER ELEVEN
THE RAPE OF TAMAR

1. Adapted from JPS and NEB.
2. Adapted from JPS and NEB.
3. Adapted from JPS and NEB.
4. Adapted from JPS and NEB.
5. Adapted from JPS and NEB.
6. Adapted from JPS and NEB.
7. McCarter, *II Samuel*, 324, citing Sanhedrin 21a.
8. Gerald A. Larue, *Sex and the Bible* (Buffalo, N.Y.: Prometheus Books, 1983), 91–92.
9. Larue, *Sex and the Bible*, 91–92.
10. Joel Rosenberg, *King and Kin*, 144.
11. Adapted from JPS.
12. Speiser, *Genesis*, 91–93. "Tradition had apparently set much store by these incidents, but the key to them had been lost somewhere in the intervening distances of time and space."
13. James Plastaras, *The God of Exodus* (Milwaukee: Bruce Publishing Company, 1966), 208.
14. Adapted from JPS and NEB.
15. George Ridout, "The Rape of Tamar," in *Rhetorical Criticism*, eds. Jared J. Jackson and Martin Kessler (Pittsburgh: Pickwick Press, 1974), 77.
16. Speiser, *Genesis*, 289–290.
17. G. E. Mendenhall, *The Tenth Generation* (Baltimore: Johns Hopkins University Press, 1973), 54–55.
18. Phyllis Trible, *Texts of Terror* (Philadelphia: Fortress Press, 1984), 58, n. 16. For a fuller discussion of this topic, see *The Harlot by the Side of the Road*, chapter 15, "The Rape of Tamar."
19. Fokkelien van Dijk-Hemmes, "Tamar and the Limits of Patriarchy," in *Anti-Covenant*, ed. Mieke Bal (Sheffield, England: Almond Press, 1989), 140, citing a translation by Joennek Bekkenkamp.
20. McCarter, *II Samuel*, 322.
21. Dijk-Hemmes, "Tamar," 140–141.
22. Jared J. Jackson, "David's Throne," *Canadian Journal of Theology* 11, no. 3 (1965): 189.
23. Joel Rosenberg, *King and Kin*, 127, 137.
24. Curiously, the Septuagint reports that David did nothing to punish Amnon

and explains why, but the second phrase ("he would not hurt Amnon because he was his eldest son") is missing from the Masoretic Text. Some scholars suspect that the phrase was censored out of the Masoretic Text to downplay the fact that David allowed his daughter's rapist to go unpunished. Others insist that it is merely an example of a scribal error known as "haplography," that is, a phrase that was lost when some ancient scribe accidentally skipped a line while making a copy of the sacred text.

CHAPTER TWELVE
"BLOODSTAINED FIEND OF HELL!"

1. Adapted from JPS.
2. Adapted from JPS.
3. McCarter, *II Samuel*, 353.
4. Adapted from JPS and NEB.
5. Adapted from AB.
6. Adapted from JPS and NEB.
7. Adapted from JPS and NEB.
8. Adapted from JPS, NEB, and AB.
9. Adapted from JPS and NEB.
10. Absalom was actually the third-born son of David. The second-born, Chileab, disappears from the Bible after the report of his birth (2 Sam. 3:3), and he played no reported role in the struggle among David's sons to succeed their father on the throne of Israel. So inconsequential was the second son of David that the biblical authors were even confused about his name—he is sometimes called Chileab (2 Sam. 3:3), sometimes Daniel. (1 Chron. 3:1)
11. Joel Rosenberg, *King and Kin*, 141, 143.
12. O. Eissfeldt, *The Old Testament*, trans. P. R. Ackroyd (New York: Harper & Row, 1965), 12.
13. Adapted from JPS and NEB.
14. Adapted from JPS and NEB.
15. Adapted from JPS.
16. Alter, *Art of Biblical Narrative*, 102.
17. Adapted from JPS and NEB.
18. Adapted from JPS and AB.
19. Adapted from JPS.
20. Adapted from JPS and NEB.
21. McCarter, *II Samuel*, 372.
22. Adapted from JPS and NEB.
23. Adapted from JPS and AB.
24. Adapted from JPS and NEB.
25. Adapted from JPS and NEB.
26. Adapted from JPS and NEB.
27. Adapted from AB.
28. Bright, *History of Israel*, 207.

CHAPTER THIRTEEN
"O ABSALOM, MY SON, MY SON!"

1. Adapted from JPS, NEB, and AB.
2. Adapted from NEB and JPS.
3. Adapted from JPS and NEB.
4. Adapted from JPS and NEB.
5. Adapted from JPS and NEB.
6. Thanks to the free-associative narrative style of the Bible, the incident is meant to remind readers of earlier passages that faintly prefigure various events in the life story of David. Two spies from the conquering army of Israel were similarly sheltered from a king's patrol by a heroic Canaanite woman named Rahab, according to a passage in the Book of Joshua. As a reward for her heroism, Rahab was spared during the invasion of Canaan, and she identified herself to the Israelites by hanging a red thread from her window. (Josh. 2:1–19) Still earlier in the biblical narrative, a red thread figures in the tale of Tamar, who was impregnated with twin sons by her father-in-law and used a red thread to identify which of the two babies was born first. (Gen. 38:28) And the heroism of Rahab in lowering the Israelite spies to safety is reprised in Michal's rescue of David from assassins sent by King Saul! All of these dreamy linkages were meant to suggest the operation of divine will at every moment in the events of history.
7. Adapted from JPS and AB.
8. Adapted from JPS and AB.
9. McCarter, *II Samuel*, 406, citing Josephus (Ant. 7.239) and the Talmud (Sotah 9b).
10. Adapted from JPS and NEB.
11. Adapted from JPS and NEB.
12. The word conventionally translated as "darts" may, in fact, refer to sharpened sticks of wood that Joab used to strike Absalom.
13. Adapted from JPS and NEB.
14. Adapted from JPS and NEB.
15. Adapted from JPS and NEB.
16. Adapted from NEB.
17. Adapted from JPS and NEB.
18. D. M. Gunn, "Narrative Patterns and Oral Tradition in Judges and Samuel," *Vetus Testamentum* 24, no. 3 (July 1974), 296.

CHAPTER FOURTEEN
AN ANGEL AT THE THRESHING-FLOOR

1. Adapted from JPS, NEB, and AB.
2. The biblical text suggests that Joab tipped the scabbard that he wore at his hip and caused the sword to fall to the ground as if by accident. Then he bent down, picked up the sword, but neglected to replace it in the scabbard. Thus did Joab "conceal his treachery," as the New English Bible renders the difficult text, and the sword remained in his hand when he embraced Amasa. (2 Sam. 20:9)
3. McCarter, *II Samuel*, 1984, 430.
4. Chapter 21 of the Second Book of Samuel records several incidents that

apparently occurred much earlier in David's reign, including the slaughter of seven sons of King Saul by the Gibeonites and a series of skirmishes with the Philistines. Here, for example, the Bible reports that it was a man named Elhanan, rather than young David, who "slew Goliath the Gittite, the staff of whose spear was like a weaver's beam." (2 Sam. 21:19) Scholarship suggests that these passages were among "a miscellany of unrelated items" collected by one of the biblical editors and deposited in this chapter. "Attempts to determine the reason for its present position," observes P. Kyle McCarter, Jr., "will probably not succeed." McCarter, *II Samuel*, 451.

5. Dahood, *Psalms I, 1–50*, 104. McCarter concedes the "high antiquity" of the passage, portions of which may date back to the supposed lifetime of David in the tenth century B.C.E., but he cautions against claims of "Davidic authorship" of the psalm itself. McCarter, *II Samuel*, 473, 475.

6. Bloom and Rosenberg, *Book of J*, 38.

7. Artur Weiser, *The Psalms: A Commentary*, trans. H. Hartwell (Philadelphia: Westminster Press, 1962), 187.

8. Robert Alter, *The David Story* (New York: W. W. Norton, 1999), 336.

9. David M. Howard, Jr., "David (Person)," in *Anchor Bible Dictionary*, vol. 2, 44.

10. Bible scholarship no longer takes these or any other biblical head counts very seriously. If the Hebrew word conventionally translated as "thousands" is understood to be a military unit numbering 5 to 14 men, as one scholar has proposed, the number of draft-age men would be no greater than 18,220 men and as few as 6,500.

11. McCarter, *II Samuel*, 511, citing (and criticizing) W. Fuss, H. Schmid, and K. Rupprecht.

12. See, for example, Judges 6:37 and 2 Samuel 6:6.

CHAPTER FIFTEEN
HEAT

1. Alter, *David Story*, 363.

2. Adapted from NEB.

3. Alter, *David Story*, 366.

4. Adapted from JPS and NEB.

5. Adapted from JPS and NEB.

6. Adapted from JPS and NEB.

7. A mule, rather than an ass or a horse, was apparently the preferred mount for royalty in ancient Israel, even though the Bible prohibits the crossbreeding of horse and ass that produces a mule. (Lev. 19:19) The conflict between holy law and day-to-day practice is another bit of evidence that the law codes of the Bible may have been compiled *after* the supposed lifetime of David and the authorship of his biblical life story.

8. Adapted from JPS and NEB.

9. Adapted from JPS and NEB.

10. Adapted from JPS and NEB.

11. Adapted from JPS.

12. Alter, *David Story*, 374.

13. "Let not his hoar head go down to the grave in peace" is how the same phrase is rendered in the King James Version. The Hebrew word generally translated as "grave" is

sheol, a term that is used in the Bible to refer to the place where one goes when he or she dies. In that sense, *sheol* seems to refer to the "underworld" or the "abode of the dead" rather than the grave where a corpse is buried. The word *sheol* is translated as "Hades" in the Septuagint, but *sheol* in the Hebrew Bible is not equivalent to the Christian notion of hell as the realm of the Devil or the place where sinners are punished.

14. Adapted from JPS and NEB.
15. Adapted from JPS.
16. Adapted from JPS (emphasis added).
17. Angelo S. Rappoport, *Ancient Israel* (London: Senate, 1995), vol. 3, 11.

CHAPTER SIXTEEN
THE QUALITY OF LIGHT AT TEL DAN

1. JPS, 1084, f.n. e.
2. Adapted from JPS and NEB.
3. Cross, *Canaanite Myth and Hebrew Epic*, 237.
4. Adapted from JPS and NEB.
5. Joel Rosenberg, *King and Kin*, 187.
6. Joel Rosenberg, *King and Kin*, 188.
7. Quoted in Joel Rosenberg, *King and Kin*, 100.
8. See John M. Berridge, "Jehoiachin (Person)," in *Anchor Bible Dictionary*, vol. 3, 662.
9. Most versions of the Bible refer only to Zedekiah's imprisonment, but the Septuagint reports his confinement in "the house of the mill" (Jer. 52:11), where, according to Robert Althann, "he would have had to perform the degrading task of grinding with a hand-mill." Robert Althann, "Zedekiah (Person)," in *Anchor Bible Dictionary*, vol. 6, 1070.
10. Herod the Great was followed to the throne by his grandson and great-grandson, Agrippa I and Agrippa II, each of whom might have plausibly claimed to be king *over* the Jews. The title bestowed upon them by the Roman emperor was "Great King, Friend of Caesar, Pious and Friend of the Romans."
11. See Akenson, *Surpassing Wonder*, 363–364.
12. Intriguingly, Matthew traces the lineage of Jesus through Solomon, while Luke identifies a different son of David as the forebear of Jesus, presumably to avoid linking Jesus with a king who is shown in the Bible to dabble with pagan gods and goddesses under the influence of his many foreign wives!
13. "INRI," an acronym that appears on the placard over the head of Jesus in depictions of the crucifixion, stands for the Latin phrase that is rendered as "Jesus of Nazareth, King of the Jews."
14. Armstrong, *Jerusalem*, 153.
15. Akenson, *Surpassing Wonder*, 193.
16. Weizman recalled his colorful remark during a filmed interview that appears in a 1999 documentary, *The 50 Years War: Israel and the Arabs*, produced by WGBH Boston and Brian Lapping Associates and distributed by PBS Home Video. But Weizman does not mention King David in his published memoir, *On Eagles' Wings*, where he quotes himself as telling Prime Minister Levi Eshkol: "The armed forces are ready and prepared

for war. If you give the order, Jewish history will remember you as a great leader. If you don't, it will never forgive you!" Ezer Weizman, *On Eagles' Wings* (New York: Berkeley Publishing, 1976), 209.

17. Armstrong, *Jerusalem*, 408. "The minister, however, did not actually recommend this course of action, since Jewish law stated that only the messiah would be permitted to build the Third Temple." The purchase (2 Sam. 24:24) is described in chapter 14 of the present book.

18. "Palestinian Archaeologists Uncover Canaanite Dwellings," *Biblical Archaeology Review*, (November/December 1998), p. 25.

19. Sigmund Freud, *Moses and Monotheism* (New York: Vintage Books, 1967), 51.

20. Akenson, *Surpassing Wonder*, 40; 424, n. 45.

21. Alter, *Art of Biblical Narrative*, 35.

22. Pfeiffer, *Introduction to the Old Testament*, 357.

23. "To regard this scandalization of the monarchy as originating in the Solomonic period," writes John Van Seters, another leading revisionist in Bible scholarship, "is to my mind entirely incredible." Van Seters, *Abraham in History and Tradition*, 151.

24. Gershom Scholem, "Magen David," in *Encyclopedia Judaica*, vol. 11, 695.

25. Gottwald, *Tribes of Yahweh*, 380–381.

26. Akenson, *Surpassing Wonder*, 521. The quoted phrases appear in the title of a chart; capitalization has been omitted.

27. Thomas L. Thompson, *The Mythic Past* (Basic Books, 1999), 164.

28. Thompson, *Mythic Past*, 45.

29. Magnus Magnusson, *Archaeology of the Bible* (New York: Simon & Schuster, 1977), 155–156.

30. Magnusson, *Archaeology of the Bible*, 134.

31. "David's Jerusalem, Fiction or Reality?" in *Biblical Archaeology Review* (July/August 1998): 25.

32. Margaret Steiner, "It's Not There," in *Biblical Archaeology Review* (July/August 1998): 26.

33. Albright, *From the Stone Age to Christianity*, 292.

34. Avraham Biran and Joseph Naveh, "An Aramaic Stele Fragment from Tel Dan," *Israel Exploration Journal* 43, nos. 2–3 (1993): 84.

35. Biran and Naveh, "Aramaic Stele," 87. "Since the preserved letters in each line comprise only a small part of the text, any reconstruction is very tentative."

36. Biran and Naveh, "The Tel Dan Inscription," *Israel Exploration Journal* 45, no. 1 (1995): 13 (emphasis added).

37. David Noel Freedman and Jeffrey C. Geoghegan, " 'House of David' Is There?", *Biblical Archaeology Review* 21, no. 2 (March/April 1995), 79.

38. Thomas L. Thompson, *Mythic Past*, 203–204.

39. Akenson, *Surpassing Wonder*, 45–46.

40. Ginzberg, *Legends of the Jews*, vol. 4, 101, 103, citing, inter alia, Sukkah 26b, Baba Batra 17a.

41. Cited in Brueggemann, "David and His Theologian," 156, n. 1.

42. As rendered into English in *The New Mahzor for Rosh Hashanah and Yom Kippur (Mahzor Haddash)*, eds. Sidney Greenberg and Jonathan D. Levine (Bridgeport, Conn.: Prayer Book Press, 1978), 557.

APPENDIX
THE BIBLICAL BIOGRAPHERS OF DAVID

1. Pfeiffer, *Introduction to the Old Testament*, 357.

2. Bloom and Rosenberg, *Book of J*, 19.

3. Joel Rosenberg, *King and Kin*, xiii.

4. Brueggemann, "David and His Theologian," *Catholic Biblical Quarterly* 30, no. 2 (April 1968): 156.

A NOTE ON BIBLES AND BIBLICAL USAGE

When quoting from various English translations of the Bible, I have used abbreviations in the text to identify the sources. These abbreviations are given in the list below, along with the full title and bibliographical information for the various Bibles. Following the abbreviations list is a list of the other versions of the Bible that I have consulted. Where no specific source is given in the text or an endnote, the quotation is taken from the 1961 edition of the Jewish Publication Society's *The Holy Scriptures According to the Masoretic Text*.

Among the many translations I consulted, the most ambitious and illuminating is P. Kyle McCarter, Jr.'s superb translation of the First and Second Books of Samuel in the Anchor Bible series. McCarter brings to bear in his translation both a poet's grasp of language and a scholar's mastery of Bible scholarship—he offers a fresh and sometimes surprising rendering of the familiar biblical text along with extensive notes and commentary, and his scholarship is unprecedented and unparalleled. Thus, for example, McCarter offers a translation that gives much richer and more provocative meanings to even the most familiar passages, and he is able to provide alternate readings of the sometimes obscure passages by expertly comparing the Masoretic Text, the Septuagint and other ancient translations, the "rewritten Bible" of Josephus, and the Dead Sea Scrolls, and then summing up the differences in a line or two of deft commentary.

Now and then I have taken the liberty of modifying some aspects of the quoted biblical text without using brackets or ellipses to indicate the changes. As a general rule, I have not indicated minor and inconsequential changes in capitalization or punctuation or the deletion of words and phrases from a quoted passage when the deleted material does not alter the meaning of the text. In many passages I have modernized the archaic language of the King James Version—changing "thou" to "you," for example—but in other passages I have retained the archaisms in order to suggest the solemnity or formality of the occasion reported in the Bible. Wherever I have changed the biblical text more extensively—or where I have combined words and phrases from more than one Bible translation—I use the phrase "adapted from" and I identify the sources in an endnote.

God is given a great many names, titles, and honorifics in the biblical text, including "Elohim," which means, literally, "gods" and is conventionally translated as "God," and the Hebrew consonants corresponding to YHWH, generally understood to be the personal name of God and rendered as "Yahweh" in scholarly translations. By a long and sacred tradition in Judaism, the personal name of God is not to be written outside the scrolls of the Torah and is never to be spoken out loud. For that reason, YHWH is replaced with the euphemism "the Lord" in all Jewish translations and many Christian translations intended for religious rather than scholarly use.

Scholars, however, prefer the more straightforward practice of transliterating the personal name of God as "YHWH" or "Yahweh." Thus, the Anchor Bible *always* renders the name of God as

"Yahweh" rather than using the traditional substitute, and, by contrast, the Bible translations published by the Jewish Publication Society *never* use the word "Yahweh." I have generally adopted the usage of the Bible that I am quoting, although I have taken the liberty of using "Yahweh" when the context suggests that the God of Israel is being contrasted to or distinguished from the other gods and goddesses known to the ancient world.

BIBLES CITED IN THE TEXT OR ENDNOTES, WITH ABBREVIATIONS

AB Cogan, Mordechai, and Hayim Tadmor, trans., intro., and commentary. *II Kings*. Anchor Bible, vol. 11. New York: Doubleday, 1988.

Dahood, Mitchell, trans., intro., and notes. *Psalms I, 1–50*. Anchor Bible, vol 16. Garden City, N.Y.: Doubleday, 1966.

Ford, J. Massyngberde, trans., intro., and commentary. *Revelation*. Anchor Bible, vol. 38. Garden City, N.Y.: Doubleday, 1975.

McCarter, P. Kyle, Jr., trans., intro., and commentary. *I Samuel*. Anchor Bible, vol. 8. Garden City, N.Y.: Doubleday, 1980.

McCarter, P. Kyle, Jr., trans., intro., and commentary. *II Samuel*. Anchor Bible, vol. 9. Garden City, N.Y.: Doubleday, 1984.

Myers, Jacob M., trans., intro., and commentary. *I Chronicles*. Anchor Bible, vol. 12. New York: Doubleday, 1965.

Speiser, E. A., trans., intro., and notes. *Genesis*. Anchor Bible, vol. 1 (orig. pub. 1962). Garden City, N.Y.: Doubleday, 1987.

JPS *The Holy Scriptures According to the Masoretic Text*. Philadelphia: Jewish Publication Society, 1917; 1961.

KJV Scofield, C. I., ed. *The Scofield Reference Bible* (Authorized King James Version). New York: Oxford University Press, 1917; 1945.

NEB *The New English Bible with the Apocrypha*. 2d ed. New York: Oxford University Press, 1970.

New JPS *Tanakh, The Holy Scriptures: The New JPS Translation According to the Traditional Hebrew Text*. Philadelphia: Jewish Publication Society, 1985.

Other Bibles

The Complete Parallel Bible: Containing the Old and New Testaments with the Apocryphal/Deuterocanonical Books. New York: Oxford University Press, 1993.

Hertz, J. H., ed. *The Pentateuch and Haftorahs*. 2d ed. London: Soncino Press, 1981.

The Holy Bible Containing the Old and New Testaments in the King James Version. Nashville: Thomas Nelson, 1985.

May, Herbert G., and Bruce M. Metzger, eds. *The New Oxford Annotated Bible with the Apocrypha: Revised Standard Version*. New York: Oxford University Press, 1993.

Metzger, Bruce M., and Roland E. Murphy, eds. *The New Oxford Annotated Bible with the Apocrypha*. New York: Oxford University Press, 1994.

The New American Bible. Catholic Bible Association of America. Chicago: Catholic Press, 1971.

Reference Works

Botterweck, G. Johannes, and Helmer Ringgren, eds. *Theological Dictionary of the Old Testament*. vol. 3. Translated by John T. Willis, Geoffrey W. Bromley, and David E. Green. Grand Rapids, Mich.: William B. Eerdmans, 1978.

Browning, W.R.F., ed. *A Dictionary of the Bible*. Oxford and New York: Oxford University Press, 1996.

Encyclopedia Judaica, 17 vols. corrected ed. Jerusalem: Keter Publishing House, n.d.

Freedman, David Noel, gen. ed. *The Anchor Bible Dictionary*. 6 vols. New York: Doubleday, 1992.

Other Books

Akenson, Donald Harman. *Surpassing Wonder: The Invention of the Bible and the Talmuds*. New York: Harcourt Brace, 1998.

Albright, William Foxwell. *From the Stone Age to Christianity: Monotheism and the Historical Process*. 2d ed. Baltimore: Johns Hopkins Press, 1957; 1967.

———. "Samuel and the Beginnings of the Prophetic Movement," In intro. by Harry M. Orlinsky, 149–176. *Interpreting the Prophetic Tradition: The Goldenson Lectures, 1955–1966*, Cincinnati: Hebrew Union College Press, New York: Ktav Publishing House, 1969.

Alt, Albrecht. *Essays on Old Testament History and Religion*. Translated by R. A. Wilson. Oxford: Basil Blackwell, 1966.

Alter, Robert. *The Art of Biblical Narrative*. New York: Basic Books, 1981.

———. *The David Story: A Translation with Commentary of 1 and 2 Samuel*. New York: W. W. Norton, 1999.

Armstrong, Karen. *A History of God: The 4000-Year Quest of Judaism, Christianity, and Islam*. New York: Alfred A. Knopf, 1993.

———. *Jerusalem: One City, Three Faiths*. New York: Alfred A. Knopf, 1996.

Auerbach, Elias. *Moses*. Translated by J. S. Bowden. Old Testament Library. Philadelphia: Westminster Press, 1968.

Bal, Mieke, ed. *Anti-Covenant: Counter-Reading Women's Lives in the Hebrew Bible*. Sheffield, England: Almond Press, 1989.

Biale, David. *Power and Powerlessness in Jewish History*. New York: Schocken Books, 1986.

Blenkinsopp, J. "Theme and Motif in the Succession History (2 Sam. XI 2 ff.) and the Yahwist Corpus." In *Supplements to Vetus Testamentum* (volume du Congres, Geneve, 1965), 44–57. Leiden: E. J. Brill, 1966.

Bloom, Harold. *Shakespeare: The Invention of the Human*. New York: Riverhead Books, 1998.

———. *The Western Canon: The Books and Schools of the Ages*. New York: Harcourt Brace, 1994.

Bloom, Harold, and David Rosenberg. *The Book of J*. New York: Grove Weidenfeld, 1990.

Boardman, John, Jasper Griffin, and Oswyn Murray, eds. *The Oxford History of the Classical World*. Oxford: Oxford University Press, 1986.

Bright, John. *A History of Israel*. 2d ed. Philadelphia: Westminster Press, 1972.

Buber, Martin. *Moses: The Revelation and the Covenant*. New York: Harper & Row, 1958.

Carlson, R. A. *David, the Chosen King: A Traditio-historical Approach to the Second Book of Samuel*. Translated by Eric J. Sharpe and Stanley Rudman. Stockholm: Almqvist & Wiksell, 1964.

Clements, R. E. *Abraham and David: Genesis XV and Its Meaning for Israelite Tradition*. Studies in Biblical Theology, 2d series, 5. London: S.C.M. Press, 1967.

Cross, Frank Moore. *Canaanite Myth and Hebrew Epic: Essays in the History of the Religion of Israel*. Cambridge: Harvard University Press, 1973.

Davis, John J. *The Birth of a Kingdom: Studies in I–II Samuel and I Kings 1–11*. Grand Rapids, Mich.: Baker Book House, 1970.

Day, Peggy L., ed. *Gender and Difference in Ancient Israel*. Minneapolis, Minn.: Fortress Press, 1989.

Dryden, John. "Absalom and Achitophel." In *The Norton Anthology of English Literature*, 5th ed., edited by M. H. Abrams, vol. 1. New York: W. W. Norton, 1986.

Eissfeldt, O. *The Old Testament: An Introduction*. Translated by P. R. Ackroyd. New York: Harper & Row, 1965.

Exum, J. Cheryl. *Fragmented Women: Feminist (Sub)versions of Biblical Narratives*. Journal for the Study of the Old Testament, supplement series 163. Sheffield, England: JSOT Press, 1993.

Freud, Sigmund. *Moses and Monotheism*. Translated by Katherine Jones. Orig. pub.1939. New York: Vintage Books, 1967.

Friedman, Richard Elliott. *The Hidden Book in the Bible*. San Francisco: HarperSanFrancisco, 1998.

————. *Who Wrote the Bible?* Englewood Cliffs, N.J.: Prentice Hall, 1987.

Frontain, Raymond-Jean, and Jan Wojcik, eds. *The David Myth in Western Literature*. West Lafayette, Ind.: Purdue University Press, 1980.

Frye, Northrop. *The Great Code: The Bible and Literature*. New York: Harcourt Brace Jovanovich, 1982.

Gaebelein, Frank E., gen. ed. *The Expositor's Bible Commentary*. vol. 1. Grand Rapids: Zondervan Publishing House, 1979.

Gide, André. *Saul*. In *My Theater: Five Plays and an Essay*, translated by Jackson Matthews. New York: Alfred A. Knopf, 1952.

Gilbert, Martin. *Atlas of Jewish History*. 3d ed. New York: Dorset Press, 1984.

Ginzberg, Louis. *The Legends of the Jews*. Translated by Henrietta Szold. 7 vols. Philadelphia: Jewish Publication Society, 1909–1938.

Gottwald, Norman K. *All the Kingdoms of the Earth: Israelite Prophecy and International Relations in the Ancient Near East*. New York: Harper & Row, 1964.

————. *The Tribes of Yahweh: A Sociology of the Religion of Liberated Israel, 1250–1050 B.C.E.* Maryknoll, N.Y.: Orbis Books, 1979

Greenberg, Moshe. *Understanding Exodus*. Heritage of Biblical Israel, vol. 2, pt. 1. New York: Behrman House for Melton Research Center of the Jewish Theological Seminary of America, 1969.

Greenberg, Sidney, and Jonathan D. Levine, eds. *The New Mahzor for Rosh Hashanah and Yom Kippur (Mahzor Haddash)*. Bridgeport, Conn.: Prayer Book Press, 1978.

Harrington, Daniel J. "Pseudo-Philo, *Liber Antiquitatum Biblicarum*." In *Outside the Old*

Testament, edited by M. De Jonge, 6–25, Cambridge: Cambridge University Press, 1985.

Harris, Roberta L. *The World of the Bible*. New York and London: Thames & Hudson, 1995.

Harris, Stephen L. *Understanding the Bible: A Reader's Introduction*. 2d ed. Palo Alto, Calif., and London: Mayfield Publishing Company, 1985.

Heller, Joseph. *God Knows*. New York: Alfred A. Knopf, 1984.

Heym, Stefan. *The King David Report*. New York: G. P. Putnam's Sons, 1973.

Horner, Tom. *Jonathan Loved David: Homosexuality in Biblical Times*. Philadelphia: Westminster Press, 1978.

Howard, Richard. *Fellow Feelings: Poems*. New York: Atheneum, 1976.

Jackson, Jared J., and Martin Kessler, eds. *Rhetorical Criticism: Essays in Honor of James Muilenburg*. Pittsburgh: Pickwick Press, 1974.

Johnson, Paul. *The Birth of the Modern: World Society 1815–1830*. New York: HarperCollins, 1991.

————. *A History of the Jews*. New York: Harper & Row, 1987.

Josephus, Flavius. *Jewish Antiquities, Books V–VIII*. Vol. 5. Translated by H. St. J. Thackeray and Ralph Marcus. London: William Heinemann; Cambridge, Massachusetts: Harvard University Press, 1934.

Keegan, John. *A History of Warfare*. New York: Vintage Books, 1994.

Keller, Werner. *The Bible as History*. 2d rev. ed. New York: William Morrow, 1981.

Kirsch, Jonathan. *The Harlot by the Side of the Road: Forbidden Tales of the Bible*. New York: Ballantine Books, 1997.

————. *Moses, A Life*. New York: Ballantine Books, 1998.

Larue, Gerald A. *Sex and the Bible*. Buffalo, N.Y.: Prometheus Books, 1983.

Lawrence, D. H. *The Complete Plays of D. H. Lawrence*. London: William Heinemann, 1965.

Leach, Edmund. "Why Did Moses Have a Sister?" In *Structuralist Interpretations of Biblical Myth*, edited by Edmund Leach and D. Alan Aycock, 33–66. Cambridge and New York: Cambridge University Press, 1983.

Magnusson, Magnus. *Archaeology of the Bible*. New York: Simon & Schuster, 1977.

Mazar, Amihai. *Archaeology of the Land of the Bible: 10,000–586 B.C.E.* New York: Doubleday, 1990.

Mendenhall, G. E. *The Tenth Generation: The Origins of the Biblical Tradition*. Baltimore: Johns Hopkins University Press, 1973.

Miles, Jack. *God: A Biography*. New York: Alfred A. Knopf, 1995.

Miller, J. Maxwell, and John H. Hayes. *A History of Ancient Israel and Judah*. Philadelphia: Westminster Press, 1986.

Newman, Louis I. *The Hasidic Anthology: Tales and Teachings of the Hasidim*. New York: Charles Scribner's Sons, 1934.

Noth, Martin. "David and Israel in II Samuel VII." In *The Laws in the Pentateuch, and Other Studies*, translated by D. R. Ap-Thomas, 250–259. Philadelphia: Fortress Press, 1967.

————. *The Old Testament World*. Translated by Victor I. Gruhn. Philadelphia: Fortress Press, 1966.

Patai, Raphael. *The Arab Mind*. New York: Charles Scribner's Sons, 1976.

————. *The Jewish Mind*. New York: Charles Scribner's Sons, 1977.

————. *Sex and Family in the Bible and the Middle East*. Garden City, N.Y.: Doubleday, 1959.

Pedersen, J.P.E. *Israel*. vol. 4. London: Oxford University Press, 1940.

Penchansky, David. "Staying the Night: Intertextuality in Genesis and Judges." In *Reading between Texts: Intertextuality and the Hebrew Bible*, edited by Danna Nolan Fewell, 77–97. Louisville, Ky.: Westminster–John Knox Press, 1992.

Pfeiffer, Robert H. *Introduction to the Old Testament*. New York: Harper & Brothers, 1941.

Philo of Alexandria. *The Essential Philo*. Edited by Nahum N. Glatzer. New York: Schocken Books, 1971.

Plastaras, James. *The God of Exodus: The Theology of the Exodus Narratives*. Milwaukee: Bruce Publishing Company, 1966.

Polzin, Robert. *Samuel and the Deuteronomist: A Literary Study of the Deuteronomic History*, pt. 2, *1 Samuel*. Bloomington: Indiana University Press, 1993.

Rappoport, Angelo S. *Ancient Israel*. Vol. 3. London: Senate, 1995.

Rosenberg, David. *The Book of David*. New York: Harmony Books, 1997.

Rosenberg, Joel. *King and Kin: Political Allegory in the Hebrew Bible*. Bloomington: Indiana University Press, 1986.

Sachar, Abram Leon. *A History of the Jews*. Rev. ed. New York: Alfred A. Knopf, 1967.

Sellin, Ernst. *Introduction to the Old Testament*. Translated by David E. Green. Revised and rewritten by Georg Fohrer. Nashville: Abingdon Press, 1968.

Speiser, E. A. "Of Shoes and Shekels." In *Oriental and Biblical Studies: Collected Writings of E. A. Speiser*, edited by J. J. Finkelstein and M. Greenberg, 151–159. Philadelphia: University of Pennyslvania Press, 1967.

Thompson, Thomas L. *The Historicity of the Patriarchal Narrative: The Quest for the Historical Abraham*. Berlin and New York: Walter de Gruyter, 1974.

———. *The Mythic Past: Biblical Archaeology and the Myth of Israel*. New York: Basic Books, 1999.

Tomlinson, Gerald, comp. and ed. *Treasury of Religious Quotations*. Englewood Cliffs, N.J.: Prentice Hall, 1991.

Trible, Phyllis. *Texts of Terror: Literary-Feminist Readings of Biblical Narratives*. Philadelphia: Fortress Press: 1984.

Van Seters, John. *Abraham in History and Tradition*. New Haven: Yale University Press, 1975.

Vaux, Roland de. *The Early History of Israel*. Translated by David Smith. Philadelphia: Westminster Press, 1978.

Von Rad, Gerhard. *Moses*. World Christian Books, 2d series, no. 32. London: United Society for Christian Literature, Lutterworth Press, 1960.

———. *Old Testament Theology*, vol. 1, *The Theology of Israel's Historical Traditions*. Translated by D.M.G. Stalker. New York: Harper & Row, 1962.

Weiser, Artur. *The Psalms, A Commentary*. Translated by H. Hartwell. Old Testament Library. Philadelphia: Westminster Press, 1962.

Weisfeld, Israel H. *David the King*. New York: Bloch Publishing Company, 1983.

Weizman, Ezer. *On Eagles' Wings*. New York: Berkley Publishing, 1976.

Whybray, R. N. *The Succession Narrative: A Study of II Sam 9–20 and I Kings 1 and 2*. Studies in Biblical Theology, 2d series, 9. Naperville, Ill.: A. R. Allenson. 1968.

Yadin, Yigael. *The Art of Warfare in Biblical Lands in the Light of Archaeological Study*. Translated by M. Pearlman. 2 vols. New York: McGraw-Hill, 1963.

BIBLIOGRAPHY

Scholarly Journals and Other Periodicals

Ackroyd, Peter R. "The Succession Narrative (So-called)." *Interpretation* 35, no. 4 (October 1981): 383–396.

Allen, E. L. "Jesus and Moses in the New Testament." *Expository Times* (Edinburgh) 67 (October 1955–September 1956): 104–106.

Ap-Thomas, D. R. "Saul's 'Uncle.' " *Vetus Testamentum* 11, no. 3 (July 1961): 241–245.

Bailey, Clinton. "How Desert Culture Helps Us Understand the Bible." *Bible Review* 7, no. 4 (August 1991): 14–38.

Biran, Avraham, and Joseph Naveh. "An Aramaic Stele Fragment from Tel Dan," *Israel Exploration Journal* 43, nos. 2–3 (1993): 81–98.

———. "The Tel Dan Inscription: A New Fragment." *Israel Exploration Journal* 45, no. 1 (1995): 1–18.

Brueggemann, Walter. "David and His Theologian." *Catholic Biblical Quarterly* 30, no. 2 (April 1968): 156–181.

———. "Kingship and Chaos (A Study in Tenth Century Theology)." *Catholic Biblical Quarterly* 33, no. 3 (July 1971): 317–332.

———. "The Trusted Creature." *Catholic Biblical Quarterly* 31 (1969): 484–498.

Coats, G. W. "Parable, Fable, and Anecdote: Storytelling in the Succession Narrative." *Interpretation* 35, no. 4 (October 1981): 368–382.

" 'David' Found at Dan." *Biblical Archaeology Review* 20, no. 2 (March/April 1994): 26–39.

"David's Jerusalem, Fiction or Reality?" *Biblical Archaeology Review* 24, no. 4 (July/August 1998): 25.

"Face to Face: Biblical Minimalists Meet Their Challengers," *Biblical Archaeology Review* 23, no. 4 (July/August 1997): 26–42.

Freedman, David Noel, and Jeffrey C. Geoghegan. " 'House of David' Is There?" *Biblical Archaeology Review* 21, no. 2 (March/April 1995): 78–79.

Gunn, D. M. "Narrative Patterns and Oral Tradition in Judges and Samuel." *Vetus Testamentum* 24, no. 3 (July 1974): 286–317.

Haran, Menahem. "Shiloh and Jerusalem: The Origin of the Priestly Tradition in the Pentateuch." *Journal of Biblical Literature* 81, pt. 1 (March 1962): 14–24.

Jackson, Jared L. "David's Throne: Patterns in the Succession Story." *Canadian Journal of Theology* 11, no. 3 (1965): 183–195.

Levy, Abraham. "The Only Relic from Herod's Temple?" *Biblical Archaeology Review* 24, no. 4 (July/August 1998): 20.

Lindblom, John. "Lot-casting in the Old Testament." *Vetus Testamentum* 12, no. 2 (April 1962): 164–178.

McCarter, P. Kyle, Jr. " 'Plots, True or False': The Succession Narrative as Court Apologetic." *Intepretation* 35, no. 4 (October 1981): 355–367.

McCarthy, Dennis J. "II Samuel 7 and the Structure of the Deuteronomic History." *Journal of Biblical Literature* 84, pt. 2 (June 1965): 131–138.

Morgenstern, Julian. "The Ark, the Ephod, and the 'Tent of the Meeting' " (continued). *Hebrew Union College Annual* 18 (1943–1944): 1–52.

———. "David and Jonathan." *Journal of Biblical Literature* 78, pt. 4 (December 1959): 322–325.

Muraoka, Takamitsu. "Linguistic Notes on the Aramaic Inscription from Tel Dan." *Israel Exploration Journal* 45, no. 1 (1995): 19–21.

Niditch, Susan. "The Wronged Woman Righted." *Harvard Theological Review* 72, nos. 1–2 (January-April 1979): 149.

"Palestinian Archaeologists Uncover Canaanite Dwellings," *Biblical Archaeology Review* (November/December 1998): 25.

Rainey, Anson. "The 'House of David' and the House of Deconstructionists." *Biblical Archaeology Review* 20, no. 6 (November/December 1994): 47.

Rendsburg, Gary A. "On the Writing [Bet-David] in the Aramaic Inscription from Tel Dan," *Israel Exploration Journal* 45, no. 1 (1995): 22–25.

Steiner, Margaret. "It's Not There: Archaeology Proves a Negative." *Biblical Archaeology Review* (July/August 1998): 26–33.

Thomas, Evan, and Matthew Cooper. "Extracting a Confession." *Newsweek*, August 31, 1998: 34.

Thompson, J. A. " The Significance of the Verb *Love* in the David-Jonathan Narratives in 1 Samuel." *Vetus Testamentum* 24, no. 3 (July 1974): 334–338.

Thornton, T.C.G. "Charismatic Kingship in Israel and Judah." *Journal of Theological Studies* 14, pt. 1 (April 1963): 1–11.

———. "Studies in Samuel: I. Davidic Propaganda in the Books of Samuel." *Church Quarterly Review* 168 (October–December 1967): 413–423.

Tsevat, Matitiahu. "Studies in the Book of Samuel, III: The Steadfast House: What Was David Promised in II Sam. 7:11b–16?" *Hebrew Union College Annual* 34 (1963): 71–82.

Van Seters, John. "Problems in the Literary Analysis of the Court History of David." *Journal for the Study of the Old Testament*, issue 1 (December 1976): 22–29.

Ventura, Michael. "Letters at 3 A.M.: The Book of Wildness." *LA Village View*, December 24–30, 1993: 5.

Weinfeld, M. "The Covenant of Grant in the Old Testament and in the Ancient Near East," *Journal of the American Oriental Society* 90 (1970): 184–203.

Woo, Elaine. "Joseph Heller, Author of 'Catch-22,' Dies." *Los Angeles Times*, December 14, 1999.

King *David* could not have been written without the love, companionship, wisdom, high spirits, and good humor of my wife, Ann Benjamin Kirsch, and our children, Adam Benjamin Kirsch and Jennifer Rachel Kirsch. Each is a passionate reader and a gifted writer, and each knows exactly how to encourage a fellow writer at his work.

Dennis Mitchell, my law partner and dear friend, created and guarded the space within our practice where I have been able to write books and book reviews since the first day we hung out a shingle together.

Vera Tobin and Andrew Solomon ably assisted in the research for *King David*, thus extending my reach into the library stacks at the University of California at Berkeley and Columbia University. And I made good use of the research completed by my son, Adam, for my earlier books, *The Harlot by the Side of the Road* and *Moses, A Life*.

At the offices of Kirsch & Mitchell in Los Angeles, each work day is brightened—and my work load is lightened—by Judy Woo and Angie Yoon, my valued colleagues and cherished friends.

Laurie Fox at the Linda Chester Literary Agency is not only my agent but also a dear friend and a fellow writer of distinction, a muse and a guardian angel.

The incomparable Linda Chester and all of her colleagues at the Linda Chester Literary Agency have long sustained me and my work with the kind of attention, energy, and ambition that every author seeks (but does not always find) in a literary agent.

Gina Centrello and Joanne Wyckoff at The Ballantine Publishing Group in New York have generously shared their expertise and vision in the writing and publishing of *King David*.

Virginia Faber and Janet Fletcher contributed their generous and discerning editorial attentions to all three of my books about the Bible, including *King David*.

Whether we find ourselves together at some far-flung book fair or at home at the holidays, lighting candles and singing songs, I have cherished the experience of knowing and working with Marie Coolman, Heather Smith, and Robin Benway at the West Coast publicity office of Ballantine.

Among the many booksellers across the United States who have welcomed me to their stores and encouraged me in my work, I owe a special debt of gratitude to Doug Dutton, Diane Leslie, Lise Friedman, and Ed Conklin at Dutton's in Brentwood; Stan Hynds and Linda Urban at Vroman's in Pasadena; Stan Madson and Jeanne D'Arcy at the Bodhi Tree in West Hollywood; Peggy Jackson at Borders in Montclair; and Michael Graziano at Borders in Pasadena.

Rabbi Michael Gotlieb at Kehillat Maarav in Los Angeles has opened his heart and shared his wisdom with my whole family.

Bernadette Shih is a gifted writer whose friendship and colleagueship are a source of inspiration and delight.

Finally, I warmly and gratefully acknowledge the following generous people, each of whom has supported and encouraged me in my work in many different ways:

At the *Los Angeles Times*, M. J. Smith and Elena Nelson Howe in the Southern California Living section, and Steve Wasserman, Tom Curwen, Nick Owchar, Cara Mia di Massa, Susan Salter Reynolds, and Ethel Alexander in the Book Review.

Also at the *Los Angeles Times*, Larry Stammer and Mary Rourke.

At KPCC-FM in Pasadena, Larry Mantle, Ilsa Setziol, Jackie Oclaray, Linda Othenin-Girard, Kitty Felde, Christal Smith, and Aimee Machado.

At the Publishers Marketing Association, Jan Nathan and Terry Nathan.

At the *Jewish Journal*, Gene Lichtenstein and Rob Eshman.

Tony Cohan at Acrobat Books, publisher of my books on publishing law.

At PEN Center USA West, Sherrill Britton, Larry Siems, and Eric Lax.

My mother and stepfather, Dvora and Elmer Heller.

Clare Ferraro, Liz Williams, and Rachel Tarlow Gul, who have long nurtured and inspired me in my writing.

Connie Martinson, whose broadcasts have shed light on so many books and authors.

Carolyn See, Jack Miles, Karen Armstrong, Harlan Ellison, Judith Orloff, and Janet Baker.

The Rev. Peter Gomes, Rabbi Harold Schulweis, Rabbi Isaiah Zeldin, Rabbi Allen Freehling, Rabbi Will Kramer, and Pastor Mitch Henson.

Raye Birk and Candace Barrett Birk, Len and Pat Solomon, Chuck Taylor and Suzye Ogawa, Sheldon Kadish and Mary Ann Rosenfeld, Scott Baker, Ellen Newman, Jacob Gabay, Inge-Lise DeWolfe, Fred Huffman, Jill Johnson Keeney, and Rae Lewis.

KING DAVID
The Real Life of the Man Who Ruled Israel

JONATHAN KIRSCH

A Reader's Guide

A Conversation with the Readers

Wherever I go to talk about King David—*bookstores and book clubs, colleges and libraries, synagogues and churches—I am gratified (but not really surprised) to find a lively interest in a man who lived three thousand years ago yet seems as fully alive today as he does in the pages of the Bible itself.*

Here are some of the questions I have been asked by readers of King David, *and the answers that I have given. I have also suggested a few topics for discussion with your fellow readers of the book. I hope they will prompt you to ask other questions—and to come up with answers—of your own.*

—Jonathan Kirsch

Q: **From among all the men and women in the Bible, why did you choose to write about David?**

JK: The best way to explain my decision to write a book about King David is that I snuck up on him—or, perhaps more accurately, he snuck up on me! My first book about the Bible, *The Harlot by the Side of the Road*, focuses on seven "forbidden" tales of the Bible. Only one of the stories—the rape of Tamar, David's daughter— features David himself. But, as I explored the origins and meanings of these seven "forbidden" tales, I began to see David beneath the surface of the biblical text. As Gerhard Von Rad (a modern Bible scholar) puts it, an "undersong" about David can be detected throughout the Bible. And so I found myself drawn to David himself, and I decided to explore and try to explain the crucial role that David plays, both in the Bible and in our lives.

Q: **You've also written a biography of Moses [*Moses, A Life*]. Who do you feel is more important, Moses or David?**

JK: Of all the figures in the Hebrew Bible, Moses is the most commanding, but David is the most intriguing. Moses has been favored over David among deeply religious people in Judaism, Christianity, and Islam because he is presented as a pious man, a prophet, and a lawgiver. His story is full of shocks and surprises— as I pointed out in *Moses, A Life*—but it is somewhat easier to overlook the more unsettling aspects of his life and character and focus only on the sacred law that he offered to humankind, starting with the Ten Commandments but also the bulk of biblical law.

David, by contrast, is a far more troubling and even tantalizing figure. He is presented in the Bible, with perfect candor and in sizzling detail, as a man of both truly heroic achievement and scandalous conduct. His ambitions and appetites—as a warrior, as a lover, as a king—are gargantuan and irresistible. Of course, if we read only the biblical passages that are favored in sermons and Bible study, David comes across as a heroic figure—the man who literally invented biblical Israel, turned it from a band of rival tribes into a strong nation, and made himself both a king and an emperor. But if we read the *whole* story of David, if we read the Bible with open eyes and an open mind, we see that he is also portrayed, at moments, as a voyeur, an exhibitionist, an adulterer, a trickster, an extortionist, even a murderer.

The fact, however, is that David was just as fascinating to the original authors of the Bible as he is to modern readers. His biblical biographer was compelled to record all the dirty little secrets of David's private life as well as the mighty achievements of his public life, and every biblical author who came along later seemed to have David in mind as he—or she—added new passages or whole new books to the Bible. That's what explains the "undersong" of David—he can be detected in passages of the Bible where he is not even mentioned.

Q: If David's life is so scandalous, why is he described in the Bible as "a man after [God's] own heart"?

JK: The single most tantalizing theological puzzle in the Bible is the contrast between David's real life, which is full of human flaws and failings, and David's high standing as God's favorite. God enters into covenants with Abraham and Moses, for example, but they are strictly conditional—if the Israelites obey God's law, then God will bless them; if not, God will curse them. But God's promise to David is unconditional: David and his heirs will *always* reign as kings of Israel. Nothing that David does, as shown in the Bible, prompts God to revoke his blessing.

One way to work out the puzzle is to credit God with the insight that a human being is not capable of being, or expected to be, a plaster saint. A single human life may have moments of moral grandeur and moments of moral failing, and one does not necessarily cancel out the other. That's certainly true in the life of David as it is reported in the Bible—he is described as both "a bloody fiend from hell" and "a man after God's own heart."

Another way to understand the attitude of the Bible toward David is that, as one scholar puts it, David is "the quintessential winner." And, then as now, nothing succeeds like success. So the biblical author is willing to praise David for his earthly accomplishments and overlook his earthly failings, and he reports that God feels the same way toward David.

The same is true of our attitude toward many political and military leaders—Franklin Roosevelt and Dwight Eisenhower, for example, both conducted extramarital affairs during World War II, but very few of us condemn them for their moral failings when we consider their role in defeating Nazi Germany and its allies.

Q: **If God's promise of kingship to David was eternal, what explains the fact that the dynasty of King David eventually came to an end?**

JK: The contradiction between God's promise and the historical record is undeniable, and it caused plenty of consternation among the biblical authors. Eventually, the apparent contradiction was resolved by focusing on the doctrine of the Messiah—God will one day send a Messiah to reign over us, and he will be a descendant of King David. Thus, in both Jewish and Christian tradition, the eternal kingship of David is understood to mean that, one day, a descendant of David will return as the Messiah.

According to Christian tradition, of course, the Messiah is Jesus of Nazareth, and that is why the Gospels trace the genealogy of Jesus all the way back to David. According to Jewish tradition, the Messiah has yet to come, but when the Messiah does finally come, he will be a descendant of David or, according to a mystical tradition in Judaism, the resurrected David himself.

The idea that the Messiah is a descendant of King David, therefore, is one of the very few points of theology upon which Christians and Jews agree!

A Reader's Guide

Q: **Was David gay?**

JK: The Bible plainly reports that men as well as women fell in love with David, and David describes his love for Jonathan, son of King Saul, in tender and even passionate terms: "Wonderful was thy love to me, passing the love of women." (2 Sam. 1:26) According to pious tradition, David is speaking of a pure and platonic love. More recently, however, some Bible scholars have been willing to wonder out loud whether the two men were more than just friends. Certainly some of their encounters with each other suggest an intimacy that may have gone beyond friendship, and sexual relations between men were hardly unusual in the ancient world. Of course, David was just as passionate about the women in his life, and he clearly engaged in a great many sexual relationships with women. Still, if we read with an open mind what the Bible actually says, we have to entertain the idea that David may have been bisexual.

Q: **Was David abusive or exploitive toward women?**

JK: David's relationships with the women in his life were highly passionate but also deeply troubled. He was capable of falling deeply in love with a woman, but he was also capable of acting imperiously and even abusively toward women.

The marriage between David and Michal, for example, is an example of a relationship that begins in the thrall of spontaneous affection and ends up in bitterness and estrangement. The courtship between David and Abigail, if we can call it a courtship, shows David as a coarse and even threatening figure. That's why some feminist Bible scholars regard the Bible as a whole and the life story of David in particular as the work of authors who were hostile toward women.

Still, the bond between David and Bathsheba, which begins in adultery, bastardy, and murder, was clearly a heartfelt and lifelong commitment between the two of them. At the end of his life, David is unable to summon up any carnal desire for the beautiful young Abishag, for example, but he readily gives Bathsheba everything she demands, including a crown for their son, Solomon.

King David

Q: Do you believe that David really existed?

JK: When I wrote about Moses, I was compelled to report the scholarly consensus, and my own conviction, that Moses is a legendary or even a purely mythic figure. But David, by contrast, is almost certainly a flesh-and-blood human being. The Tel-Dan inscriptions that I describe in chapter sixteen of *King David* are compelling evidence that David really lived and reigned, but the evidence is not merely archaeological. David comes across as a real human being precisely because the Bible gives us such rich and convincing details about his life, his deeds, his emotions, and his relationships. Unlike most other biblical figures—including, for example, Moses—David is fully three-dimensional. I agree with Freud when he insists that the Book of Samuel is "real history."

Q: What is the connection between King David and the Star of David?

JK: As it turns out, this is the single most frequently asked question that I encounter when I talk about *King David*! The question is answered in detail in chapter sixteen of the book, but the short answer is that the Star of David has *no* historical connection with David. The six-sided star, which has come to symbolize Judaism in general and the State of Israel in particular, was first linked to David by medieval alchemists and magic-users in Christian and Islamic circles in the Middle Ages. Not until the fourteenth century was it first used in Jewish settings, and not until the late nineteenth century was it adopted as a symbol of Judaism. In fact, virtually all the sites in Jerusalem that are traditionally associated with David have no real historical connection with him.

Reading Group Questions and Topics for Discussion

1. In *King David*, I have compared David to John F. Kennedy as examples of leaders with "charisma." Do you find David to be a charismatic figure even though, like JFK, he was capable of both heroic and scandalous conduct?

2. The Bible shows that both men and women fall in love with David, and some scholars believe that David's relationship to Jonathan was more than purely platonic. Do you find any homoerotic overtones in the encounters between David and Jonathan and the words that David speaks about Jonathan?

3. One theory of biblical authorship proposes that the Bible began with the life story of David, and everything else was built up around David's story. Do you find this theory to be convincing? When you read the Book of Samuel, do you hear the voices of several different authors or just one?

4. Two different versions of David's life story are given in the Bible. The Book of Samuel gives us the adults-only, R-rated version, and the Book of Chronicles gives a child-safe, G-rated version. If the Book of Samuel had been lost, and only the Book of Chronicles had survived, do you think the Bible itself and the Bible-based religions would have turned out differently?

5. Some Bible scholars suggest that David knew, or should have known, that his son, Amnon, intended to rape his daughter, Tamar, and they blame David for sending Tamar to Amnon's bedchamber. Do you agree that David bears some responsibility for what happened to his daughter?

6. David has been criticized for being a sentimental and indulgent father. For example, he fails to punish Amnon for raping Tamar, and he gives orders that none of his soldiers should harm Absalom when they go into battle against him. Do you see David's attitude toward his sons as a praiseworthy quality or a sign of weakness?

7. Some feminist Bible critics suggest that the women in David's life are sexually abused and exploited. One scholar, for example, says that Bathsheba is "raped by the pen" because the Bible allows us to watch her at various intimate moments. Do you think women are treated inappropriately in the biblical life story of David?

8. Although God vows to "raise up evil against thee out of thine

own house" as retribution for David's sin with Bathsheba (2 Sam. 12:11), David himself is never directly punished. The illegitimate baby dies, Tamar is the victim of rape, Amnon is assassinated, and Absalom is killed in battle—but David dies in his bed. Do you think he is suitably punished for his affair with Bathsheba and his role in the murder of Uriah?

9. In *King David*, I argue that "[s]omething crucial in human history begins with the biblical figure of King David," and I suggest that he is "the original alpha male," "the first superstar," an "authentic sex symbol," and "the quintessential winner." Do you agree that David can be credited (or blamed) for shaping, as I put it, "what we expect of ourselves and, even more so, of the men and women who lead us"?

10. Sometimes it seems that powerful people are held to a different standard than ordinary people when it comes to their private moral conduct. In *King David*, I suggest that these ideas about leadership begin with the biblical figure of David. Do you agree? Do you think David sets a good example or a bad example for what we have come to expect of our leaders?

11. Shakespeare borrowed many of his plots from other sources but never from the Bible. Still, some readers see similarities between King Lear and King Saul, for example, or between Hamlet and David. Do you see any influences on Shakespeare and his work that can be traced back to the Bible in general and King David in particular?

12. David is more often invoked in modern Israel, where he is admired as a military leader, than in pious Jewish tradition. Do you think the history of the Jewish people would have turned out differently if David had been given a more prominent role in Jewish tradition?

13. As discussed earlier, Bible scholar Gerhard Von Rad describes an "undersong" of David's story running throughout the Bible. Do you see or feel such an undersong in your reading of the Bible? Where?

© Marilyn Sanders

Jonathan Kirsch, a book columnist for the
Los Angeles Times and author of the bestselling
and critically acclaimed *Moses: A Life* and
The Harlot by the Side of the Road, writes and lectures
widely on biblical, literary, and legal topics.
A member of the National Book Critics Circle,
President of PEN Center USA West, and a former
correspondent for *Newsweek*, he lives in Los Angeles.

Printed in the United States
by Baker & Taylor Publisher Services